# DRESSED
## FOR THE
# KINGDOM
## OF GOD

GARMENTS OF A CHRISTIAN WOMAN:
A 21ST CENTURY PERSPECTIVE AND
WOMEN OF THE NEW TESTAMENT:
BOOK TWO

CARLOTTA MARIA SHINN-RUSSELL

# TABLE OF CONTENTS

# DRESSED
## FOR THE
# KINGDOM
## *of* GOD

GARMENTS OF A CHRISTIAN WOMAN:
A 21ST CENTURY PERSPECTIVE AND WOMEN
OF THE NEW TESTAMENT: BOOK TWO

CARLOTTA MARIA SHINN-RUSSELL

SHINN
RUSSELL
BOOKS & PUBLICATIONS

# SCRIPTURE SOURCES

In Book Two of *Dressed for the Kingdom of God: The Garments of a Christian Woman: A 21ˢᵗ-Century Perspective and Women of the New Testament,* I used Scripture from different publications of the Bible: which includes The King James Version, The New King James Version, and The Life Application Study (NIV) being my main sources for Scripture. Using different publications of Bibles, the reader can compare and contrast the different copies in the books; all copies of the Bibles used stays true to the Scriptures, [The Word of God].

# DEDICATION

*The 21st-Century Perspective* continues with Book Two. I dedicated both books to my brother Johnnie Lee Shinn. He is a loving, kind, and resolute Christian man.

When I was a babe in Christ, he helped me with encouraging words, Scriptures, and lessons about life I probably would not have been successful getting through to this point in my maturity as a Christian Woman had he not studied with me.

I consider it a blessing from God to have a sweet and kind brother like John, a faithful man of God. He encouraged me to author this two-book analogy, from a 21st-Century Perspective and include examples of women of the Old and New Testaments for writing, *"Dressed for the Kingdom of God: The Garments of a Christian Woman: A 21st-Century Perspective and Women of the New Testament"*, is Book Two, of the Analogy: from a 21st-Century Perspective.

Hence, the dedication goes to all who read and find the words between these pages beneficial and encouraging as each reader who Honor and Glorify God in their lives.

# QUOTATIONS

*"The real security in Christianity is to be found in its benevolent morality, in its exquisite adaptations to human heart, in the facility with which its scheme accommodates itself to the capacity of every human intellect, in the consolation which it has to the house of mourning, in light with which it brightens the great mystery of the grave."*

**Thomas Macaulay**

*"I do not feel obliged to believe that the same God who has endowed us with senses, reason, and intellect has intended us to forego their use."*

**Galileo Galilei**

*"If a man's eye is on the Eternal, his intellect will grow."*

**Ralph Waldo Emerson**

*"The human intellect is the great truth-organ; realities, as they exist, are the subjects of its study; and knowledge is the result of its acquaintance with the things which it investigates."*

**Moses Harvey**

*"For understanding in spiritual matters, the golden rule is not intellect but obedience."*

**Oswald Chambers**

*"Those who cannot learn from history are doomed to repeat it."*

**George Santayana**

*"Only the dead has seen the end of the war!"*

**George Santayana**

*"It is revenge the devil sometimes takes upon the virtuous that he entraps them by the force of the very passion they have suppressed and themselves superior to."*

**George Santayana**

*"Happiness is a choice, not a side effect."*

*"Fortunately, I have my positive shield up today your negativity will not be able to penetrate it."*

*"It is not about if you have chaos in your life, it's about how well you manage it."*

*"A comfort zone is your personalized way of setting limitations for yourself."*

*"Don't overthink it."*

*"Life is not complicated your perception is."*

*"Happiness can be just as contagious as misery."*

**Favorites Quotes**

*Man has to change God does not change, deviate, or backup."*

**Dr. Loyd C. Harris, Minister**

*"Everything important to you spiritually comes from God our source of power on the way to something else."*

**David Myers, Minister**

# The creator and creation

The beauty of God's world stands as a bride adorned for her forever spouse.
The branches of the trees sway and dance to the music of creation as a wife to
sweet and alluring words of her mate's voice like the musical notes of a song.
As a ballerina does to the captivating notes of the mastery of Beethoven's Ninth
The sun brings warmth to the day as do the gentle smile of an innocent child.
The Moon sends coolness to the night while the clouds hide the warmness of the light.
Creation stands as a signature of ownership as the name on the line of a contract
signifies its Pac.
Universal creation, filial peace, and reverence bows before the Almighty
Perfect mates of creation obedient and loving stands as a symbol of respect
Man follows the pattern of obedience drawn by the hand of the Maker of all things.
The music of heaven plays for man to dance as the tree's sways before the wind,
Bending to its authority so should the creature bend before the Creator.
Eternal God of the Universe, the purchaser of Salvation, and giver of the
Holy Spirit, Teacher and Guide.

*Carlotta Maria Shinn Russell*
*[March 2023]*

# DAVID'S ADORATION AND HONOR TO GOD: THE GLORIOUS MAJESTY, EXCELLENT AND MOST HIGH GOD, YAHWEH, CREATOR, SAVIOR, AND PROVIDER OF ALL THINGS.

### *To the Chief Musician upon Gittith: A Psalm of David.*
### *[Psalms 8:1-9]*

*O Lord our Lord, how excellent is thy name in all the earth!*
*Who has set thy glory above the heavens?*
*Out of the mouth of babes and suckling's hast thou ordained strength because of*
*thine enemies, that thou mightiest still the enemy and the avenger.*
*When I consider Thy heavens, the work of Thy fingers, the moon, and the stars,*
*which Thou hast ordained: what is man, that Thou art mindful of him? And the son*
*of man, that Thou visited him?*

*For Thou hast made Him a little lower than the angels, and hast crowned Him*
*with glory and honor. Thou made Him to have dominion over the works of Thy hands;*
*Thou hast put all things under His feet:*

*All sheep and oxen; yea, and the beasts of the field, the fowl of the air, and the fish*
*of the sea; and whatsoever pass through the paths of the seas. O Lord our Lord, how*
*excellent is Thy Name in all the earth!*

PROLOGUE

# THE RULE OF THE SOVEREIGN GOD

*"Remind the people to be subject to rulers and authorities, to be obedient, to be ready to do whatever is good, to slander no one, to be peaceable and considerate, and always to be gentle toward everyone. At one time, we too were foolish, disobedient, deceived, and enslaved by all kinds of passions and pleasures. We lived in malice and envy; being hated and hating one another; but; when the kindness and love of God our Savior appeared; He saved us, not because of righteous things we had done, but because of His mercy. He saved us through the washing of rebirth and renewal by the Holy Spirit, whom He poured out on us generously through Jesus Christ our Savior that being justified by His grace, we should be made heirs according to the hope of eternal life," [Titus 3:1-7].*

As the centuries pass, man uses different styles of communication; and the different types of cultures that come and go are like revolving doors. Besides, all this, peoples' attitudes change as their lives change, with what is relevant at that time, even human taste in foods change, as do the fashions we wear with the coming and going of seasons. In this world, candidates change that people votes in and out of power. Traditions in families are subject to change; as well as, in societies. However, the ruler of the universe and the One who holds our life in His hands never changes – God does not change the pattern for our lives. God is not seasonal nor is His Commands for us to live by. He does not change because man changes with what is popular now. He says of Himself, *"I am the Lord, I change not," [Malachi 3:6].*

We are ruled by a Sovereign God…when we look at the meaning of Sovereign whether it is in Scripture or a secular sense, it is possessing supreme or ultimate power. In this world, the power of a ruler can only go so far even with them thinking or believing they have supreme or ultimate power. Human rights are still at play in the secular sense of having supreme rule or power.

However, when we come to the authority and rule of God our Father and Creator we look at His power in the most supreme sense. Webster Dictionary (1823) defines Supreme as final or last. Therefore, the God we serve has the final and last word in the universe. He has the power to decide and do whatever He deems necessary for us and in our lives. He can do it without fault or criticism because He is the creator of the universe and all that exists.

We cannot question His decisions, we are not knowledgeable enough, we cannot advise Him, where were we when He created the universe? We cannot assist Him with anything that needs doing, and only He has the absolute right to decide what is best in the lives of His people. God set the standards for our life wrote the rulebook and is Judge, as well as is our Savior.

The Scripture reminds us that from of old, Christ has not changed and the Pattern He put in place stands. As centuries come and go, humans are born and die, and the seasons change each year; however, His ultimate power never changes; nor does the pattern for our lives, "*But you, Bethlehem Ephrathah, though you are small among the clans of Judah, out of you will come for Me One who will be ruler over Israel, whose origins are from of old, from ancient times,*" *[Micah 5:2]*.

Consider the adjectives in the next paragraph when you are thinking of the power of God and His Supreme Authority. He alone is the creator and has supreme power for all times. The Scriptures reminds us that He said, "*I am the Vine, ye are the branches: He that abide in Me, and I in him, the same bring forth much fruit: for without Me, ye can do nothing,*" *[John 15:5]*.

The adjectives describing the Sovereignty of God are supreme, absolute, unrestricted, unrestrained, unbounded, boundless, infinite, ultimate, total, unconditional, full, utter, paramount, principal, chief, dominant, predominant, ruling, royal, regal, kingly, and monarchical. God does not need to explain His actions to us. He is merciful because it is a defining point of our God's character; as well, He understands we humans are imperfect beings.

Christ came to earth to live among us to know how we feel, and the things we experience in life. He knows when we pray the experiences and emotions that beset us, "*For we have not a High Priest who cannot be touched with the feeling of our infirmities; but, was in all points, tempted like as we are, yet without sin,*" *[Hebrews 4:15]*.

Continuing from Book one, in serving God, obedience to our Lord and Savior Jesus Christ, cannot be done, in an ad hoc manner (when necessary or on an as-need basis). Jesus Christ did not leave us ad hoc guidelines, but a defined pattern of how we can be pleasing to God.

In today's society, we use when making an analogy, what is known as, the Five W's (who, what, when, where, and why).

Today's society hosts an almost adhocracy culture; one modeling those that exist in organizations that welcomes change on trending innovations fostering an adaptive mindset. God's people cannot adopt an ad hoc mentality, "God in my life when necessary or on an as-need basis."

Jesus said, *"I and My Father are One," [John 10:30];* and *"I do all things to please My*

*Father," [John 8:29b].*

God did not give each of us a different Plan of Salvation, nor did He say, "You can conduct yourself in a manner in which [you] see fit."Peter questioned Jesus on the Mount of Configuration, whether to build a tabernacle to Moses, Elijah, and Him; God's response to Peter, *"While he was still speaking, behold, a bright cloud overshadowed them: and behold a voice out of the cloud, which said, This is My beloved Son, in whom I am well pleased; hear ye Him," [Matthew 17:5].*

This very statement quickly puts what the expectations of God are into a clear and explicit perspective, *"Hear ye Him."* Whom are we hearing? The focus we are to have is to look to Jesus our Savior: God's only Begotten Son, the Lamb of God who took away the sins of the world.

Jesus died only once for humanity for all times. His Blood runs backward and forwards to meet that blood requirement to be the perfect sacrifice pleasing to God.

There is no more sacrifice for sin as it was in the Old Testament. Each year the Priest went into the Holy of Holies and offered the blood sacrifice of bulls and goats for the people's sins rolling them forward for one more year; yet, never taking them away.

Once we obey the Gospel of Christ (through baptism), we come, in contact, with the Blood of Christ, the Lamb of God, and our sins are taken away by His sacrifice. However, there is a condition to our sins being taken away we must be obedient to God's Word and live for Jesus is what we do in signing that blood covenant, which says, we are a child of the King and will live by those Commands Christ left for us.

We know that we are not perfect; Christ's Blood is a continuous propitiation for our sins because by nature we are sinful people. God presented Christ's Blood as an acceptable atonement and sacrifice and it continually compensates for our sins, "*God presented Christ as a Sacrifice of Atonement, through the shedding of His blood—to be received by faith. He did this to demonstrate His righteousness because in His forbearance He had left the sins committed beforehand unpunished,*" [Romans 3:25].

Once we come to God and obey the Gospel of Jesus Christ, we have an Advocate with the Father, Jesus Christ, if we are living faithful, growing in the knowledge of our Savior, seeking first the Kingdom of Heaven and all its righteousness, and humbly asking for forgiveness of sin. There is the condition – (if) …

The Scripture tells us that un-repented sin is unforgiven sin, "*If you say we have no sin then we are liars, and the truth is not you,*" [I John 1:8].

There are no paragons (epitomes of perfection) on earth in and of ourselves: we can only be shining examples through Jesus Christ.

A Christian should not set out to knowingly sin; but we sin sometimes, even doing all we can to avoid it; yet we still knowingly sin, if we do we repent, and a change is necessary. This is the time to hit our reset buttons and not ignore that we are guilty but confess our sins and learn from that experience. We can identify this as growing … along with seeking the Word of God to help us, with faith in the promise, if we sin, we have a conditional guarantee from Jesus, "*If we confess our sins, He is faithful, and just to forgive us our sins and to cleanse us from all unrighteousness [I John 1:9].*

As Paul commended the Corinthians believers that they excelled in everything, we in this 21st-Century can follow their example and are models as they were, at that time. The expectation Christ has for His people have not changed; Christ does not change only we change; as people change sometimes, we conduct our lives in faithfulness and obedience as if it is a Kaleidoscope Wheel.

Cambridge Dictionary defines Kaleidoscope as a changing and enjoyable mixture or pattern. Sometimes we live our lives, as it is a wheel of changing colors, smells, and sounds. Manufactured patterns change, they are not designed to be consistent but change with seasons, events, times, and individuals.

We tend to color our world to fit our moods with what we desire at that time. This has not changed either, the patterns are enjoyable we design, as is with the definition of Kaleidoscope; it is human nature to want to do as they coin the phrase, "Mix it up." We can do as the Corinthians, excel in all things, "*But since you excel in everything, in faith, in speech, in knowledge, in complete earnestness, and in the love you have kindled in you…see that you also excel in the grace of giving," [2 Corinthians 8:7].*

*"Therefore, show these men the proof of your love and one reason for our pride in you so that the Church can see it," [2 Corinthians 8:24].*

When we give proof of our love, it also includes dedicating our entire life to God. We cannot come to God then go cold or dark, as is used in today's terminology. We continue to excel and not fall into the example Demas did of choosing his former way of life over the life as a Child of God. In his second letter to Timothy Paul wrote, *"For Demas hath forsaken me, having loved this present world, and is departed unto Thessalonica," [2 Timothy 4:10a].*

Christians cannot allow themselves to fall into what "can be" labeled as a faithfulness recession. Recession, as seen in this world, like the economy, when it lacks a sufficient level of activity, is dangerous. This concept can be applied to, inactivity and the consistent neglect of working in the Kingdom of God beginning with Worship and the five steps each Lord's Day. It is necessary to remain aware and exhibit consistent sobriety in our lives as is possible.

We are God's Watchmen, in our day and time, as were Ezekiel the Prophet and other Prophets noted in the Scripture. God sent him to warn and admonish His people of their sins. The righteous were turning to sin, and the sinners he warned to turn from their evil ways. God gives us this responsibility if you see a brother at fault and you turn him from his sinful way, you have saved your brother, first considering yourself – you could fall into this same temptation, *"Brothers and sisters, if someone is caught in a sin you who live by the Spirit should restore that person gently. But watch yourselves, or you also may be tempted," [Galatians 6:1].*

We can think of ourselves as an Ezekiel of the 21st-Century having garments of being "Watchmen". However, we like Ezekiel must recognize that we cannot accomplish anything without God. We are helpless before God. We, from time to time do not recognize this, the "I" or "Me" of ourselves blinds us to that helplessness and we do not humble ourselves because of our [I] or [me] "getting in the way." The physical cannot trump the Spiritual in our lives; it is a dangerous cliff to traverse. Until we recognize, as Ezekiel did, and fall before God in helplessness that He cannot accomplish those things in our lives until we admit to ourselves, He is the only power that exists and all other things in Heaven and on earth exists only by and through Him, including Satan.

We are to seek advice from God rather than asking Google by reading articles of interest on subjects we glean information from to understand. Humans often tend to look to the physical or secular side of life rather than seeking God and His Wisdom, which is the Spiritual side of life. We need to be aware of the physical side of life and the things we learn there as well, yet here also we are to put God ahead of all things about our lives.

Nothing in the secular side of life can offer us a definite answer to the tribulations of the Spiritual life; nor can they give us peace…peace is only in God. In our physical life, the results are the same; God is the only answer to that side of our lives as well. He brings balance to life; He does not deal in only Spirituality but is involved totally, in all things concerning humanity.

The uncertainties of this life keep humans in constant bewilderment or a vacuum. Humans seek this world over for something that does not exist in any long-term way. We think we have peace then sudden destruction. At best, our days are hairy and full of confusion. We are wise to declutter our lives – or life will overwhelm you to the point where all your focus is gone.

We cannot be nomads in life any more than we can be Christian Nomads wandering from congregation to congregation but identify or place our allegiance with one congregation and worship under that Eldership; as with our physical life, we need focus. We are readily aware that, even with congregations, we need to identify with the one where you are comfortable serving and where you can grow spiritually. There is no perfect situation anywhere because we are imperfect beings. Nor can we wander from idol god to idol god and be pleasing to the one true God of heaven who's our allegiance belongs to for His grace and mercy toward man. However, we cannot serve God with our physical life and be pleasing to Him, because the carnal side of us is the main driving force.

Rather, we serve God in Spirit and Truth, using the Bible as our source for life and those things pleasing to God where you see loving-kindness, as well as, joy displaying all the Fruit of the Spirit, and are people trying with all their hearts to serve God is what we all desire. …Once God's people were like nomads; but now, are one body, one faith, and one baptism; we believe the same things, speak the same thing, live our life according to the example left by our Savior, and continue in faithfulness guided by the Holy Spirit.

Peter reminds us that, *"Knowing this first, that no prophecy of the scripture is of any private interpretation,"* [2 Peter 1:20].

In essence, man applying their meanings to what the Scripture says is not acceptable to God nor will it benefit us spiritually. God did not leave room for a man to interpret what the Scripture means; rather, the Apostles, through the Holy Spirit gave the true meaning of that (the) Scripture. We can understand what God wants us to do through our study of the Word to be pleasing to Him.

Also, we have the gift of the Holy Spirit to help guide us into all righteousness. All who obey the requirements for being in Christ Jesus receive the gift of the Holy Spirit without respect of person. God does not give the gift to one and not to others who have obeyed the same Gospel of Christ.

God is a jealous God. He told Ezekiel to tell His people Israel they were like two sisters who involved themselves in going after idol gods. They chased, after all, committing adultery with any from their youth up. The Sovereign God said, *"They were lewd and promiscuous, and He would punish them according to their sins,"* the word of the Lord came to me (Ezekiel): *"Son of man, there were two women, daughters of the same mother. They became prostitutes in Egypt, engaging in prostitution from their youth. In that land, their breasts were fondled, and their virgin bosoms caressed. The older was named Oholah, and her sister was Oholibah. They were mine and gave birth to sons and daughters. Oholah is Samaria, and Oholibah is Jerusalem. "Oholah engaged in prostitution while she was still mine; and she lusted after her lovers, the Assyrians-warriors clothed in blue, governors and commanders, all of them handsome young men, and mounted horsemen. She gave herself as a prostitute to all the elite of the Assyrians and defiled herself with all the idols of everyone she lusted after. She did not give up the prostitution she began in Egypt, when during her youth men slept with her, caressed her virgin bosom, and poured out their lust on her. "Therefore, I delivered her into the hands of her lovers, the Assyrians, for whom she lusted. They stripped her naked, took away her sons and daughters, and killed her with the sword. She became a byword among women, and punishment was inflicted on her,"* [Ezekiel 23:1-10].

God compared the actions and lives of His people to the ways of these two sisters. They were unfaithful and ran after all the things of this world and its gods. They ignored His commands and defied His Commandments; their ways worsened over the years resulting in being put in exile time after time because of their disobedience.

God is still the Sovereign God who spoke to Ezekiel in this manner, *"Open your mouth and speak to the people,"* *"Whosoever will listen let them listen, and whosoever refuse let them refuse, for they are rebellious people, [Ezekiel 3:27].*

Ezekiel described the garments the people wore; we cannot wear these types of garments. The people did not keep God's law, nor did they keep the laws of the pagans around them, Ezekiel noted their garments of disobedience in this manner, "*Therefore this is what the Sovereign Lord says: You have been more unruly than the nations around you and have not followed my decrees or kept my laws. You have not even conformed to the standards of the nations around you,*" [Ezekiel 5:7].

The people of God refusing to keep God's Law or even the laws of the land at that time sends us a loud message and warning of the wrath of God that is poured out on defiant people in any century.

The wrath of God is not anything we can survive, "*See, the day! See, it comes! Doom has burst forth, the rod has budded, and arrogance has blossomed!*" [Ezekiel 7:10].

There is no intermission in our service to God. The urgency of Salvation and our service to God does not allow an interlude. There is only one act/scene. We do not get a second act of Salvation. In the secular world, in a screenplay or musical production, this is an actuality but is of human creation.

Christianity does not afford us an *Entr'acte,* it a continuous and ongoing until God's purpose for man is accomplished; for all who desires to take advantage of the Salvation Christ purchased and must become obedient followers of our Savior and wear proudly and humbly the Name of Jesus.

Paul reminds us, "*For I am not ashamed of the Gospel of Christ: for it is the power of God unto salvation to everyone that believeth; to the Jew first, and also to the Greek. For therein is the righteousness of God revealed from faith to faith: as it is written, the just shall live by faith,*" [Romans 1:16-17].

The Scriptures are hermetically sealed. They are airtight. There can be no changes or additions made to God's Word. God does not change the written Word guiding our lives; it is without change for all times and every generation without exception. We have the Old Testament and the Prophets to teach and give us hope, and we serve God in the New Testament dispensation through His mercy and grace purchased by Jesus Christ and guided by the same Holy Spirit.

What God speaks tells man what will happen, has happened, will continue to happen. All we need do is study Scripture and see what is happening around us as the Lord told Isaiah to write in His judgment against the nations. We cannot ignore what the Scripture warns us will happen and who the God of Heaven is we serve. Look is the command! His promises are mated with the Scripture we read. Isaiah wrote, *"Look in the Scroll of the Lord and read: None of these will be missing, not one will lack her mate. For it is His mouth that has given the order, and His Spirit will gather them together," [Isaiah 34:16].*

When we think of the word [mate] regarding Scripture, is identical in meaning. Something or someone identical is a replica without the ability evident there to know the difference. The repetition we see happened when there is defiance, Scripture records the warnings given the people, by the Creator of the Universe. When we think of mates when it comes to husband and wife, they become one body, one heart, and one mind; yet the two are individuals.

God sent Israel messages in various ways by Prophets, Spiritual leaders, and Judges of Israel, but the Word of God did not change with any of the messengers sent nor does His will for His people. I heard a comment that I equated to this statement, "The package is not more important than the content."

Sometimes we dismiss the message because of the messenger. If that messenger does not/did not fit the criterion (image of the messenger) we have/they had affixed in our/their minds we consider the message as not being true/valid. It reminds me of the saying, 'You can't see the forest for looking at the trees.'

This was true with the coming of the King of Israel. Christ came in a humble manner, born of a woman whose husband was of the Tribe of Judah and from the House of David, the King. As foretold by the Scriptures, Jesus was raised in the poor humble village of Nazareth, rejected during His earthly Ministry, and finally scourged accused by the Chief Priest and Pharisees, and then crucified by the people.

The Package (Our Savior) did not look like people imagined. He did not have the appearance of a King but of a humble shepherd. The King came and the people did not recognize, nor accept Him. The message and the Prophecy foretold was what the people should have heard not looks at the way the messenger was dressed and that He was born, into the house of Joseph a Carpenter, especially when they knew the Prophecy of the Messiah and the message given by John the Baptist.

When we follow Jesus Christ, it is necessary to be ready to change our lives and live for Him. Listen to what He said discipleship cost, *"And when Jesus saw the great multitudes about Him, He gave a command to depart to the other side. Then a certain* scribe came and said to Him, *"Teacher, I will follow you wherever you go."* And Jesus said to him, *"Foxes have holes and birds of the air*havenests, but the Son of Man has nowhere to lay*His*head."Then another of His disciples said to Him, *"Lord, let me first go and bury my father."* And Jesus said to him, *"Follow Me and let the dead bury their dead,"* *[Matthew 8:18-22].*

Our desire is (should be) to draw closer to God. James gives us the way in the fourth chapter how we can be closer or draw near to God, *"Submit yourselves then, to God. Resist the devil, and he will flee from you, come near to God and He will come near to you. Wash your hands you sinners, and purify your hearts, you double-minded. Grieve, mourn, and wail. Change your laughter to mourning and your joy to gloom. Humble yourself before the Lord, and He will lift you up,"* *[James 4:7-10].*

When we draw near and humble ourselves to God, Master of the universe, this should remind us that He is God the Father and our Lord and Savior Jesus Christ. Paul encourages us also in that he wrote, *"For sin shall no longer be your master because you are not under the law but under grace,"* *[Romans 6:14].*

The Holy Spirit helps us to be strong and move forward in our spirituality to become a pleasing and humble servant before Jesus Christ our Lord. God gives us our worth, not man. Pride and arrogance are destructive – humility and obedience are pleasing to God and bodes well for us in this life and the life to come. The Word of God, according to Scripture, will either:

- **Convict our hearts and lives**, as John reminds us, *"When He comes, He will prove the world to be in the wrong about sin and righteousness and judgment,"* *[John 16:8].*

And *"For the word of God*isquick, and powerful, and sharper than any two-*edged sword, piercing even to the dividing asunder of soul and spirit, and of the joints and marrow, and*isa discerner of the thoughts and intents of the heart,"* *[Hebrews 4:12].*

- **Convince our hearts**, of the necessity of taking advantage of the Salvation Christ purchased and obey His will for our lives, *"Then Peter and the Other Disciples said, "We ought to obey God rather than man,"* *[Acts 5:29].* Further, Paul reminds us to *"Since, then, we* *know what it is to fear the Lord, we try to persuade others. What we are is plain to God and I hope it is also plain to your conscience," [2 Corinthians 5:11].*

- **Convert our hearts,** (prick our conscience) because we realize there is only one way to partake of the Salvation Christ purchased, *"For the sorrow that is according to the will of God produces a repentance without regret, leading to salvation, but the sorrow of the world produces death," [2 Corinthians 7:10].*

We have to give up [us] for Him – our life is no more what we desire but what His desire is for our life.

The Messianic Prophecy was fulfilled by Jesus Christ our Lord and Savior, *"But thou, Bethlehem Ephratah, though thou be little among the thousands of Judah, yet out of thee shall He come forth unto me that is to be ruler in Israel; whose goings forth have been from of old, from everlasting," [Ibid].*

Man cannot capture the essence of God in a book. The Living Word speaks of the essence of God, yet not giving knowledge of the entirety of the Creator. Man has the ability and opportunity to learn the Principles God desires that His people follow. He gave us the pattern to create the garments we are to wear and the principles we are as servants to obey that is pleasing to Him. The universe cannot capture the essence of God and He created it – the awesomeness of it gives us an idea of how powerful and magnificent God is.

God is The Creator of both heaven and earth is a statement that we should pause and consider!

Sisters, we must come to God in a state of wanting and needing, without sight, walking blind, and trusting the promises of the unseen God. This is a living faith that the Creator can provide for our every need. We have nothing to give God rather we come to Him for the blessing. The false gods of this earth that man put faith in are like broken cisterns that cannot hold water. Holes in jars will not hold the liquid poured into it, as fast as you pour the liquid in it leaks out. Humans trust in the gods they create and the ones they can see more than the God of Heaven giver of all things. When we forsake God for the treasures of this world, we are cutting off our true lifeline. God described the actions of His people at that time in this way, *"For My people have committed two evils; they have forsaken Me the fountain of living waters and hewed them out cisterns, brokencisterns, that can hold no water," [Jeremiah 1:13].*

There is no help in any other god that man manufactures for himself. It/ they have not ears to hear, or mouths to speaks, nor the ability to give life, nor those things needed in this life. There is no wisdom in forsaking God.

Serving God is the substance and soul of our existence. We cannot redact the Scripture (take it out of context to the point it fits the scenario we are creating or eliminate the all parts) until we are comfortable with what it says. When we read the Word of God and instructions given by God it does make one uncomfortable as well, it convicts us of our human weakness and allows us to see the need for God in our lives. [...].The intent of the Scripture (God's message to man) is for instruction and correction. We are receiving what is necessary to life and eternity from our Father in Heaven. [...].

Once we understand these two facts, we can grow in grace, knowledge, and understanding of the Word of God and the plan He has for the life of each individual from the beginning of time. [...].Coloring the Scripture to please ourselves will not change the Word of God; it works against us, not for us. Humility is submitting our lives totally to God and His, not our will, for our lives. Obedience is using wisdom; defiance is a tool of the devil and is destructive.

- *Can the creature say to the creator, this does not meet my desires and the way I want to live my life?*
- *What do you think God's response will be?*
- *Look at the list of things you want to do and desires that you wish to fulfill in your life and ask yourself, how does that (my) garments of the desire of the things in this world match up with the Word of God?*

Our garments of desires have to be cut from the pattern God designed not Satan. Things of the world are patterns designed by Satan.

Our very existence belongs to God. We come with faith to the Creator for the gifts that only He can give. Hear Paul in his letter to the Ephesians, *"That in the ages to come He might shew the exceeding riches of His grace in His kindness toward us through Christ Jesus. For by grace are ye saved through faith; and that not of yourselves: it is the gift of God: not of works, lest any man should boast. For we are His workmanship, created in Christ Jesus unto good works, which God hath before ordained that we should walk in them," [Ephesians 2:7-10].*

God gave man the greatest treasure that will ever be throughout eternity, *"Now Jesus Himself was about thirty years old when He began His ministry. He was the Son, so it was thought, of Joseph, the son of Heli, the son of Matthat, the son of Levi, the son of Melki, the son of Jannai, the son of Joseph," [Luke 3:23-38].*

*"The son of Amminadab, the son of Ram, the son of Hezron, the son of Perez, the son of Judah," [Luke 3:33].*

Luke records Jesus' genealogy back through generations and ends in this manner, *"Which was the son of Enos, which was the son of Seth, which was the son of Adam, which was the son of God," [Luke 3:38].*

Being a Child of God is an honor …. It is not a right; we have done nothing to earn it!

CHAPTER ONE

# WHO WE ARE AS CHRISTIANS A PLACE AND TITLE OF HONOR

The Scripture defines a Christian as People of Christ. The People of Christ follow His teachings; we are constantly reminded that Jesus said, "*If you love Me keep My Commandments,*" *[John 14:15].*

If we are followers of Christ, we follow His example. The word [follow] indicates He is the leader. He set the tone for what is righteous, holy, and acceptable in God's sight, not humans.

Luke the Physician recaps for us the dispute among the Apostles of Christ who sat at the table as to who was the greatest in the Kingdom. The Scripture reminds us that just as the Apostles were faithful to Christ when we are faithful we will have a place at the table with our Savior when we obey the Gospel of Salvation, "*You are those who have stood by Me in my trials. And I confer on you a kingdom, just as My Father conferred one on Me, so that you may eat and drink at My Table in My Kingdom,*" *[Luke 22:28-29a].*

According to Vine (2005), Christian is a word formed after the Roman style, signifying an adherent of Jesus, was first applied, as such by the Gentiles, "*And when he found him, he brought him to Antioch. So, for a whole year Barnabas and Saul met with the Church and taught great numbers of people. The Disciples were called Christians first at Antioch,*" *[Acts 11:26; Acts 26:28],* [Page 54].

Peter writes that living for God we will suffer, in that suffering; there is an honor because we suffer for our Lord and Savior. He suffered for us to purchase our Salvation, following Christ demands that we who follow His path of obedience to God will encounter trials, tribulations, and grief in this world, "*However, if you suffer as a Christians, do not be ashamed, but praise God that you bear that name,*" *[I Peter 4:16].*

The word Christian, as in societies in Biblical times, was thought, of in a scornful or distasteful manner. The association with Christians put one in danger, it made other factions of the Pharisee (Sanhedrin) who feared losing their power; or that the powers to be (Rome) would take their power away from them. They

1

desired separation from any association with the people following the preaching of Jesus at that time denying He was the promised Messiah and was not truthful with the people. This defines straddling the fence; they were keepers of the Law but did not keep the Law. Christ described them as whitewashed tombs full of dead men bones, "*Woe to you, teachers of the law and Pharisees, you hypocrites! You are like whitewashed tombs, which look beautiful on the outside, but the inside is full of the bones of the dead and everything unclean,*" [Matthew 23:27].

They had the appearance of righteousness, laid the heavy burden of keeping the Law on the people, but did not keep the Law themselves. They did not accept Jesus as the Messiah foretold by the Law that they knew very well. Neither did they accept Jesus as their Savior and Lord. The Sanhedrin paid Judas Iscariot thirty (30) pieces of silver to betray Jesus. They tried Jesus before the Sanhedrin Council before they sent Him before Pilot and other Roman authorities. It is evident or should have been after they tried and crucified the Savior of the world. His words were (is) a fact. Jesus did not need to defend Himself. The Sanhedrin was trying to preserve a kingdom that did not exist here on this earth. Jesus made it plain His sacrifice and the kingdom that exists is not worldly, but Spiritual. He came to offer His life as a sacrifice so that we might live in that eternal kingdom; without His death, we would not have that opportunity. Jesus said, "*My Kingdom is not of this world. If it were, My servants would fight to prevent My arrest by the Jewish leaders. But now My Kingdom is from another place,*" [John 18:36].

Christianity was a foreign concept. Followers of Christ were also known as being in "The Way." Paul, a Roman citizen, persecuted the Christians that were in "The Way." He was a Pharisee of Pharisees, taught at the feet of Gamaliel. In the actions, he took against the people of Christ at that time, thought he was serving God, did not get the concept of Christianity until he met Christ on The Road to Damascus.

We cannot squander tomorrow by reaching back for yesterday desiring a life that was and not living the life that is – choices made wisely brings life, as well, choices made unwisely, can be deadly – eternally.

When we look at a Christian and who the people of Christ are, which describes who Christ is and those attributes that a Christian display is framed in this manner, included are fourteen attributes the Bible gives which describes followers of Jesus the Savior of the World:

2

**We cannot live on both sides of the law and grace.** Christ fulfilled the law, nailed it to the Cross. In contrast, neither can we be of the world and the Kingdom of Christ, *"No man can serve two masters: for either he will hate the one and love the other; or else he will hold to the one, and despise the other,"* [Matthew 6:24].

**We are members of the Body of Christ:** Christ is the Head of His Kingdom, *"Which He wrought in Christ when He raised Him from the dead and set Him at His right hand in the heavenly places; Far above all principality, and power, and might, and dominion and every name that is named, not only in this world but also in that which is to come. And hath put all things under His feet and gave Him to be the head over all things to the Church, which is His Body, the fullness of Him that fills all in all,"* [Ephesians 1:21-23].

**Christ purchased the Church with His Blood,** *"Upon this rock, I will build My Church and the gates of Hell shall not prevail against It,"* and I say also unto thee, That thou art Peter, and upon this rock, I will build My church; and the gates of hell shall not prevail against It. And I will give unto thee the keys of the Kingdom of Heaven: and whatsoever thou shalt bind on earth shall be bound in heaven: and whatsoever thou shalt loose on earth shall be loosed in heaven. Then charged He His disciples that they should tell no man that He was Jesus the Christ,"* [Matthew 16:18-20].

Peter recognized Christ as the Son of God and Savior of the world. Christians have the keys to the Kingdom of Heaven, the Gospel, the death, burial, and resurrection of Jesus Christ.

**We are members of the Body of Christ** as Paul expressed, *"For as we have many members in one body and all members have not the same office: So, we, being many, are one Body in Christ, and every one member's one of another. Having then gifts differing according to the grace that is given to us, whether prophecy, let us prophesy according to the proportion of faith; Or ministry, let us wait on our ministering: or he that teaches, on teaching; Or he that exhorts, on exhortation: he that giveth, let him do it with simplicity; he that rule, with diligence; he that shows mercy, with cheerfulness,"* [Romans 12:4-8].

**Each member of the Body has an important function,** *"Just as a body, though one has many parts, but all its many parts forms one body, so it is with Christ,"* [I Corinthians 12:12-31].

**We Wear the Name Christian; a name worthy of Honor,** *"And when he found him, he brought him to Antioch. So, for a whole year Barnabas and Saul met with the Church and taught great numbers of people. The Disciples were called Christians first at Antioch," [Acts 11:26].* King Agrippa recognized the honor of the name Christian in his statement to Paul when he came before him and spoke of the Salvation that Jesus purchased, *"Then Agrippa said unto Paul, Almost thou persuade me to be a Christian," [Acts 26:28].*

Peter warns us that wearing the name of Christian comes with a price, people of God suffer for wearing the name and that suffering glorifies God, *"Yet if any man suffers as a Christian, let him not be ashamed; but let him glorify God on this behalf," [I Peter 4:16].*

Peter and John were arrested for teaching in the name of Jesus Christ; yet they taught, listen to their response to the possibility of suffering for being faithful servants of our Lord and Savior. The Sadducees did not believe in Angels, death, and Resurrection, *"And as they spake unto the people, the priests, and the captain of the temple, and the Sadducees, came upon them, being grieved that they taught the people, and preached through Jesus the resurrection from the dead. And they laid hands on them and put them in hold unto the next day: for it was now eventide. Howbeit many of them which heard the word believed; and the number of the men was about five thousand," [Acts 4:1-4].*

**We are to have the same attitude that Peter and John who knew they might suffer for speaking but they spoke,** *"But that it spread no further among the people, let us straightly threaten them that they speak henceforth to no man in this name. And they called them and commanded them not to speak at all nor teach in the Name of Jesus. But Peter and John answered and said unto them, whether it be right in the sight of God to hearken unto you more than unto God, judge ye. For we cannot but speak the things which we have seen and heard," [Acts 4:17-20].*

**We put on a new man.** The first step into Christ is belief before we can put on the new garments of faith, *"How, then, can they call on the one they have not believed in? And how can they believe in the one of whom they have not heard? And how can they hear without someone preaching to them? And how can anyone preach unless they are sent? As it is written: "How beautiful are the feet of those who bring Good News!" [Romans 10:14-15].*

When we pray to Jesus, for strength to speak, in the face of danger or opposition, He will give us the boldness we need. We see in the example above of John and Peter and their prayer; they prayed for boldness, *"Now, Lord, look on their threats, and grant to Your servantsthat with all boldness they may speak Your Word," [Acts 4:29].*

Sisters our garments should be like those of Jesus. We are to be as our Savior is in actions, in speech, in prayer, in faith, and in belief in the promises of God given from the beginning time.

**Being Spiritually clothed is being fully dressed in the Gospel of Christ**. When we prepare to travel, for work, or just for the day ahead, we dress in our physical clothing to cover our bodies. Why not be clothed with Jesus ready for spreading His Word and telling our fellowman about the Salvation Christ purchased for all humanity, *"Do not lie to each other, since you have taken off your old self with its practice and have put on the new self, which, is being renewed in knowledge in the image of its Creator. Where there is no Gentile or Jew, circumcised or uncircumcised, barbarian, Scythian, slave or free, but Christ is all and is in all. Therefore, as God's chosen people, holy and dearly loved, clothe yourselves with compassion, kindness, humility, gentleness, and patience," [Colossians 3:9-12].*

Paul tells us to also in a letter he wrote to the Romans that, *"And that, knowing the time, that now it is high time to awake out of sleep: for now, is our salvation nearer than when we believed. The night is far spent; the day is at hand, let us, therefore, cast off the works of darkness, and let us put on the armor of light. Let us walk honestly, as in the day: not in rioting and drunkenness not in chambering and wantonness, not in strife and envying; but put on ye the Lord Jesus Christ, and make no provision for the flesh, to fulfill the lusts thereof," [Romans 13:11-14].*

Job reminds us in a parable about being clothed in Jesus this way, *"I put on righteousness, and it clothed me: my judgment was as a robe and a diadem. I was eyes to the blind, and feet was I to the lame," [Job 29:14-15].*

A robe, sisters, is a proper dress of a state of dignity. The garments of the Gospel of Christ are robes of dignity and diadem, headdresses of righteousness. Sisters we can wear these garments as lights to all those around us by sharing the light (eyes to the blind) and going into all the world (feet to the lame) as Job reminds us.

David expresses being clothed in God this way, *"Let the priest be clothed with righteousness: and let they saints shout for joy,"* [Psalms 132:9].

- *Our garments should reflect Christ, how do our garments look to the onlookers, like Christ or like Satan?*
- *Are we living in integrity, honesty with all our moral fiber we can muster, or do they see lip service; say but do not?*

We are baptized into Christ and raised to walk in the newness of life wearing different garments than before our new birth: we put on a new man, *"For all of you who are baptized in Christ have clothed yourself with Christ,"* [Galatians 3:27; Mark 16:16].

Our garments, like baptism, we need to be clothed in Jesus Christ, both is a submersion under – we are under the water and our physical bodies are beneath the clothing with which we cover our bodies. Our garments spiritual and physical should reflect that you are a child of God. We cannot allow our choices to disenfranchise us from Christ.

When we are baptized (born again) Jesus breathes the breath of life in our Spirit. This new birth can juxtapose with the creation of the first man Adam. God fashioned him in His image and breathed life into Adam and he became a living being.

Once we put on Christ, we cannot live any longer as we once did allow the flesh to guide our actions. A new light has dawned in our life and the darkness has lifted. We cannot wear the old garments of sinful lust as Paul warns us, *"But put ye on the Lord Jesus Christ, and make not provision for the flesh, to fulfill the lusts thereof,"* [Romans 13:14].

**We are wearing the armor of light**. Living in spiritual lethargy equals being drunk and not aware, walking in the mists of this world will blind our minds to the truth. We are children of light must, *"Put to death, therefore, whatever belongs to your earthly nature: sexual immorality, impurity, lust, evil desires and greed, which is idolatry,"* [Colossians 3:15].

**When constantly being exposed to unbelievers your actions and what they see in you, should reflect the Light of Christ**. As a child of God, we must allow wisdom to guide our actions and words not speak recklessly when interacting with them. When speaking our speech is always seasoned with salt and spoken in grace, *"Be wise in the way you act toward outsiders; make the most of every opportunity. Let your conversation be always full of grace, seasoned with salt, so that you may know how to answer everyone,"* [Colossians 4:5-6].

When speaking the mystery of Christ, we are to have the same mindset of Paul in our request to our fellow brethren, *"Withal praying also for us, that God would open unto us a door of utterance, to speak the mystery of Christ, for which I am also in bonds,"* [Colossians 4:3].

We as Christians aspire to speak our words in due season when it is appropriate and not rattle off as an unwise person would. Just to have something to say is not a justifiable reason to talk too much. Jesus said about speaking, *"But let your communication be, Yea, yea; Nay, nay: for whatsoever is more than this cometh of evil,"* [Matthew 5:37].

Our words can lift in due season [at] the right time; our words can tear down [if] spoken without forethought or does not help the situation; our words can anger if we fail to give the appropriate response to what is being addressed at that time. The Scriptures point out Job's friends and the way they answered was not suitable. Essentially Job's friends were not of any help or comfort to him, *"I have heard many things like these; you are miserable comforters, all of you!"* [Job 16:2].

Job was suffering, in great distress, in pain, in every aspect of his life. Their words only exacerbated the situation and were condemned by God because they did not speak the truth, *"After the Lord had said these things to Job, He said to Eliphaz, the Temanite, "I am angry with you and your two friends because you have not spoken the truth about Me, as my servant Job has. So now, take seven bulls and seven rams, and go to My servant Job and sacrifice a burnt offering for yourselves. My servant Job will pray for you, and I will accept his prayer and not deal with you according to your folly. You have not spoken the truth about Me, as My servant Job has. So Eliphaz, the Temanite, Bildad the Shuhite and Zophar the Naamathite did what the Lord told them; and the Lord accepted Job's prayer,"* [Job 42:7-9].

It is unwise to speak recklessly, God is in Heaven, and we are on earth; He is the potter, and we are the clay controlling our words is a priority; remember the warning of James about the tongue, *"The tongue the smallest member but most deadly,"* [Ibid].

Peter tells us we continue to spread the truth to everyone and teach them of *'what doth saith the Lord;'* further, Peter reminds us we are to Reverence Christ sanctifying Him in our hearts; making Him the center of your life.

As well, preparing ourselves, and are ready to tell everyone we come in contact with about Jesus and Salvation, even during the trials and tribulations that comes upon us, *"But sanctify the Lord God in your hearts: and be ready always to answer every man that asks you a reason of the hope that is in you with meekness and fear," [I Peter 3:15].*

**God's Word is not a foreign language**. We all speak the same thing. There is but one Spiritual Tongue we speak that is of the Word of God. The Word of God might seem strange to people, but we speak those words regardless. We cannot stop speaking as Peter and John told the people, *"But Peter and John replied, "Which is right in God's eyes: to listen to you, or to Him? You be the judges! As for us, we cannot help speaking about what we have seen and heard." After further threats, they let them go. They could not decide how to punish them, because all the people were praising God for what had happened," [Acts 4:19-21].*

**We are Christ's voice**. He left us this charge to, "Go *into all the world and preach the Gospel to all creation," [Mark 16:15].*

Paul reminds us we have a tool that is fail-safe, prayer. We devote ourselves to Prayer while working in the Kingdom of God on the way to eternity, *"Pray without ceasing," [I Thessalonians 5:17].*

**The Called of God:** [*Romans 1:6, I Corinthians 12:23-24] we are called to:*

Repent, [*Matthew 9:13*]
Fellowship with Christ, [*I Corinthians 1:9*].
To Peace, [*Ephesians 2:17, Philippians 4:17; Colossians 3:14-15' Romans 12:18;*]
Peace is a Practice the Fruit of the Spirit [*Galatians 5:22-26*].
Eternal Life, [*I Timothy 6:12, I Peter 3:9; I Peter 5:10;*]
Be a citizen of God's Kingdom, [*I Thessalonians 2:12; to Liberty, Galatians 5:13; John 8:32*].

**A Worker,** Labor in the Kingdom, *[2 Timothy 2:15, 2 Corinthians 6:1, Philippians 4:3].* We work in the vineyard, [*Titus 2:14*], many were full of good works as we must be. Dorcas is a good example, [*Acts 9:36*].

8

**A Disciple**: A Disciple is a follower; an adherent to the doctrines of another *[Acts 11:26]*, Luke tells us as he begins the Book of Acts – My former account O'Theophilus, *[Acts 1, 2, 7 & 9:1-10, 25]*.

**A Child of God**: *[I John 3:9-10]*, or child of the devil paints a portrait of those in direct opposition to God because Satan is their god, *[John 8:42-44]*. There are two descriptions here people of the Kingdom of God and people of the world. Children have relationships with their earthly parents as they will have or desire to have with the Heavenly Father if they are His Child. We are a child of God and He is our Father.

**A Believer**: *[Acts 2:44, 4:32; 5:14]*. To have confidence and trust in God and His promises. *[Acts 2:8-9, 10, 16' Acts 14:2]*. Peter spoke, *"And when there had been much disputing, Peter rose and said, men and brethren, you know how that a good while ago God made choice among us, that the Gentiles by my mouth should hear the word of the gospel and believe. And God which knoweth the hearts, bare them, witness, giving them the Holy Spirit, even as He did unto us," [Acts 15:7-8]* – Scripture of Belief, *[John 8:31-32]* – We believe in God, Jesus, and the Holy Spirit. What we call the Holy Trinity are three personifications but are one, we trust God.

**A Servant of God**: *[Romans 1:1, Philippians 1:1, Titus 1:1-2; 2 Timothy 2:24]*. We are obedient to our Master. We have only one Master; we trust our Master to guide us; we trust our Master to protect us; we trust our Master to provide for us.

**A Steward**: *[Luke 16:1-12]*, are servants, but in a higher sense, they are/ were trusted with the master's wealth, overseeing His properties. The Steward that comes to mind of course is one of our favorite Biblical accounts of Joseph as a Stewart to Potiphar, who was also a manager under Pharaoh. We are good Stewarts with our money, talents, time, and The Word of God. We are blessed with the responsibility, for the use of the things with which God gifts us. We can be faithful or unfaithful Stewards, *[Luke 16:1-15]*, another favorite account is of the covetous unwise rich man, who tore down his barns to build a bigger one, whose will his wealth be after he is gone? He was not rich toward God, *[Luke 12:13-21]*. The Parable of the Talents, *[Matthews 25:14-30]* – do we hide the gifts God blesses us with, or do we put them to usury to build God's Kingdom and serve Him?

**A Soldier**: a soldier who fight wars, win battles, marches forward to victory. We are fellow soldiers in the Kingdom of God, [*Philippians 2:25, Philemon 2, I Timothy 1:18, 2 Timothy 2:3, 4:7, I Timothy 6:12; Revelation 12:17, Revelation 19:19, Ephesians 6:12];* Paul said, "*We are not wrestling with flesh and blood, but with principalities, against powers, against rulers of the darkness of this world and spiritual wickedness in high places*", [*Ephesians 6:12].*

These are places we cannot discern with the naked eye. Satan is real…in the spiritual warfare we are in, he is not visible either, but the results of his war against God's people are very evident. Paul in [*Ephesians 6:10-20],* gives us our armor for this warfare without it we would not be prepared for the ensuing battle he makes ready to fight with the people of God.

**A Saint**, *[I Corinthians 1:2; I Corinthians 6:9-1],* as set apart people that are washed and sanctified… *[2 Thessalonians 2:13-14];* we focus on cleansing our lives of all worldly and fleshly sins that can drag us down. David's prayer to God, "*Search me, O God, and know my heart: try me, and know my thoughts: And see if there be any wicked way in me, and lead me in the way everlasting,*" *[Psalms 139:23-24].*

Then Jeremiah, tells us that, "*I God searches the mind and heart to give to each one according to his doings,*" *[Jeremiah 17:10].*

Jesus prayed for God to "*Sanctify them through Thy Truth, Thy Word is Truth,*" *[John 17:17].*

Christ is the Word that became flesh and dwelled among men. "*God in sundry times and divers' manners spoke to the people by the Prophets, but in the last day has spoken to us through His Son,*" *[John 1:1; Hebrews 1:1], [John 1:1; Hebrews 1:1]*And Paul wrote, "*The Word of God is used for correction, reproof, instructions in righteousness that the man of God may be thoroughly furnished,*" *[2 Timothy 3:16-17].*

**Pilgrims and Sojourners**…Abraham was a sojourner as was Lot his Nephew, foreigners, and stranger in other lands, [*Genesis 12:10, I Peter 2:1]1*; Luke wrote on the Day of Pentecost there were pilgrims and sojourners from all over the land, *"And when the day of Pentecost was fully come, they were all with one accord in one place. And suddenly there came a sound from heaven as of a rushing mighty wind, and it filled all the house where they were sitting. And there appeared unto them cloven tongues like as of fire, and it sat upon each of them. And they were all filled with the Holy Ghost and began to* *speak with other tongues, as the Spirit gave them utterance. And there were dwelling at Jerusalem Jews, devout men, out of every nation under heaven. Now when this was noised abroad, the multitude came together and was confounded, because that every man heard them speak in his own language. And they were all amazed and marveled, saying one to another, "Behold, are not all these which speak Galileans? And how hear we every man in our own tongue, wherein we were born? Parthians, and Medes, and Elamites, and the dwellers in Mesopotamia, and in Judaea, and Cappadocia, in Pontus, and Asia, Phrygia, and Pamphylia, in Egypt, and in the parts of Libya about Cyrene, and strangers of Rome, Jews, and proselytes, [Acts 2:10; Acts 17:21].*

Joel the Prophet spoke of the Day of the Lord (Day of Pentecost), and the outpouring of the Spirit of God. The vision of Joel was not only for the people on the Day of Pentecost but for every believer. We know once we are a child of God, the Spirit of God dwells with us and in us. *"And afterward, I will pour out My Spirit on all people. Your son and daughters will prophesy, your old men will dream dreams, your young men will see visions. Even on My servants both men and women, I will pour out My Spirit in those days. I will show wonders in the heavens and on the earth, blood, and billows of smoke. The sun will be turned into darkness and the moon to blood before the coming of the great and dreadful day of the Lord. And everyone who calls on the name of the Lord will be saved, for on Mount Zion and in Jerusalem, there will be deliverance as the Lord has said, even among the survivors whom the Lord calls", [Joel 2:28-32]. "We have citizenship in Heaven ", [Philippians 3:20a].* This earth is not our home. The Word of God is not a stationary concern but fluid in nature not at a standstill, but on the move. Likewise, His people are on the move as well. The Word of God is a treasure given to us to share and not hidden. The Word is a precious treasure revealed to us through the manifestation of God's Son and our Savior Jesus Christ. The people of God, living throughout the world share the Salvation Christ purchased through their teaching of the Word.

**A Priest**: [*Hebrews 5:1*]; Christ is a Priest after the order of Melchizedek Priest of Salem who had no beginning and no endings, [*Hebrew 3:1; 5:10, 7; Hebrews 7:24-28; 7:12-18*]. The people of God have the qualities of being a Priest of God's Kingdom.

**Adopted/Grafted into the Family of Jesus**: He is our Savior and our Brother. He laid down His life for each of us. We have the choice to follow His Commands and are willing for Jesus, through the Holy Spirit, to lead us so that our lives will be pleasing to our Father in Heaven, *"For He chose us in Him before the creation of*

11

*the world to be Holy and Blameless In His sight in love. He predestined us for adoption to sonship through Jesus Christ in accordance with His pleasure and will – to the praise of His glorious grace, which He has freely given us in the One He loves. In Him we have redemption through the blood, the forgiveness of Sin in accordance with the riches of God to the grace He has lavished on us," [Ephesians 1:4-8].*

**Pioneers of faith:** Sisters, pioneer women were part of the westward expansion. Using this, in a spiritual-sense sister we are part of the continued forward movement and soldiers in the army of God to spread the Word of God to all in our frontier of influence. Christian women of God establish homes, create an environment of peace and love in that home, plant, and harvest the fruit from the seeds of love and faithfulness that grew. We see the example of the Proverbial Woman in Scripture and those attributes she possessed, shared, used, embraced for the Glory of God, *[Proverbs 31:1-31]*.

One of the most important tasks Christian Women have is the role of mothers. As mothers, women train their children in every aspect of life. The Scripture tells us to, "*Train up a child in the way that he should go and when he is old will not depart from it,*" *[Proverbs 22:6]*.

Wallace (1865) first published a very compelling poem that resounds throughout the ages, for its truth. God gave women a special talent and beauty of the heart that is unmatched in this world. The poem, **"The Hand that Rocks the Cradle Is the Hand that Rules the World,"** paints a vivid picture:

*"Blessings onthe handof women!*
*Angels guard its strength and grace.*
*In the palace, cottage, hovel,*
*Oh, no matter where the place;*
*Would that never storms assailed it,*
*Rainbows ever gently curled,*
*Forthe hand, that rocks the cradle.*
*[Is]the hand*that rules the world."

This is true, women have a great influence on the direction of their children's lives and influence on society overall. We see this in the account of women in the Scripture, but especially with a focus on Lois and Eunice, mother, and grandmother of Timothy a faithful servant of Jesus, and a fellow brother and student of Paul the Apostle taught and trained him accurately in the Word of God who was faithful in this task. As well, influence the lives of others. Priscilla taught Apollos. Their lives were examples, he could follow, in faithfulness, living for Christ, and making Him the center of his world.

They were examples of strong women of faith. Timothy saw the faithful example of his parents and that faithfulness gave him the foundation for being a strong warrior for the cause of Christ. As Paul, an apostle of Jesus Christ by the will of God, according to the promise of life, which is in Christ Jesus, wrote *"To Timothy, my dearly beloved son: Grace, mercy, and peace, from God the Father and Christ Jesus our Lord. I thank God, whom I serve from my forefathers with pure conscience, that without ceasing. I have remembrance of thee in my prayers night and day; greatly desiring to see thee, being mindful of thy tears, that I may be filled with joy; When I call to remembrance the unfeigned faith that is in thee, which dwelt first in thy grandmother Lois, and thy mother Eunice; and I am persuaded that in thee also."*

*"Wherefore I put thee in remembrance that thou stir up the gift of God, which is in thee by the laying on of my hands. For God hath not given us the spirit of fear; but of power, and of love, and of a sound mind."*

*"Be not thou, therefore, ashamed of the testimony of our Lord nor of me, His prisoner: but be thou partaker of the afflictions of the gospel according to the power of God; Who hath saved us, and called us with a holy calling, not according to our works; but, according to His purpose and grace; which was given us in Christ Jesus before the world began."*

*"But is now made manifest by the appearing of our Savior Jesus Christ, who hath abolished death, and hath brought life and immortality to light through the gospel: Whereunto I am appointed a preacher, and an apostle, and a teacher of the Gentiles."*

*"For thee, which cause, I also suffer these things: nevertheless, I am not ashamed: for I know whom I have believed and am persuaded that He is able to keep that which I have committed unto Him against that day. Hold fast the form of sound words, which thou hast heard of me, in faith and love which is in Christ Jesus. That good thing which was committed unto thee kept by the Holy Ghost which dwelled in us,"* [2 Timothy 1:1-15].

In this 21st-Century, there is so much debate about women breaking through the glass ceiling in business and multiple other ways have not achieved that pinnacle. However, we as women in the sight of God have never faced a glass ceiling. The woman in God's sight has an elevated place. Looking at the women throughout the Scripture they had important roles: Queen of Sheba, Ruth, Esther, Abigail, Abishag, and Deborah: just to name a few. Only humans create walls, glass ceiling not God. *"There is no respect of person with our God,"* [Ibid].

Attitudes and actions, of the people (Disciples) of Christ, are seen, by the love they have for their fellow man and how generous (merciful) we are. Our actions are characteristics of love (how we behave ourselves) in the Body of Christ, *"But love your enemies, and do good, and lend, hoping for nothing again; and your reward shall be great, and ye shall be the children of the Highest: for He is kind unto the unthankful and to the evil. Be ye therefore merciful, as your Father also is merciful,"* *[Luke 6:35–36].*

Luke further writes, *"Give, and it shall be given unto you; good measure, pressed down, and shaken together, and running over, shall men give into your bosom. For with the same measure that ye mete withal; it shall be measured to you again,"* *[Luke 6:38].*

The Christian characteristics we are to see and not see in our lives James compares and contrasts of a Christian and those that we should avoid or correct if we become aware they are part of our lives. Those attributes we need, can only be discerned through study, and wisdom that comes from God is given freely; we are but to ask.

We are to have selfless love for our fellowman. Our reward will be great in Heaven. We receive part of that reward on earth, but the greater reward will be in eternity and peace with God for as long as He lives…He has no beginning and no end.

As Christians, we remind ourselves constantly, we are not our fellowman's judge. God is the judge. We are to follow His teaching and assist our brethren in this life. We all struggle with challenges in life some more than others. When we judge, we can see only what that person is doing at that particular time. God judges the heart and not only our actions. Usually, the actions of man are situational in nature or reactive in perception, *"And He spake a parable unto them, Can the blind lead the blind? Shall they not both fall into the ditch? The disciple is not above his master: but everyone who is perfect shall be as his master. And why behold thou the mote that is in thy brother's eye, but perceives not the beam that is in your eye? Either how canst thou say to thy brother, brother let me pull out the mote that is in your eye when thou thyself behold not the beam that is in thine own eye? Thou hypocrite, cast out first the beam out of thine own eye, and then shalt thou see clearly to pull out the mote that is in thy brother's eye,"* *[Luke 6:39–42].*

We are no one's master here on earth. The best we can do is police our perimeter and lives and not to see everyone else's shortcomings to the extent we forget to look at ourselves or refuse to admit any impediment on our part. Paul further warns, *"For all have sinned and fallen short of the glory of God,"* *[Romans 3:23].*

Jesus said to the crowd when they desired to stone the woman taken in adultery, "*He who is without sin among you, let him first cast a stone at her,*" [*John 8:7a*].

Those who were in that crowd of judges with the stones in hand dropped them and walked away.

- *While we stand in a crowd with the stones in hand (the words on our tongue) like those who condemned this woman, do we examine our hearts while we are judging to see if there is any way we can condemn?*
- *Are we perfect?*
- *What part of your life have you mastered apart from the aid of Christ and the teaching of the Holy Spirit?*

When we compare a mote and a beam: a mote in the sense at that time was a body of water of some kind, either large or small, which is fluid. Water flows as with the error one finds self in at times, it is short-lived usually. We go to that brother or sister to discuss with them or ask them what we can do to assist.

A beam is a solid hard plank of wood overtime become difficult to move, or it begins to rot if not maintained. It blurs our vision to our errors, but we can see everyone else's. A beam or perception of self-righteousness blinds us to reality and puts you in the same crowd with the Scribes and Pharisees who thought themselves to be righteous requiring everyone else to bow to the letter of the law but did not do right themselves.

Outside they had the appearances of righteousness but inside their hearts were dead. They had forgotten how to be human. Even a machine needs oil, or it will rust. We cannot conduct ourselves like a machine performing with participation without recognition. Our lives have to get to the point where we can get the mote out of other's eyes. We are to be careful judging lest we fall into the same error we are trying to correct in other lives.

- *Do others see the same things in your life needing correcting, while you are attempting to correct others?*

A question in the spiritual checklist the Great Physician has given to us, with which we can measure ourselves.

There will be Spiritual storms in our lives once we obey the Gospel. I have had them come in bunches at a time. It is how we manage those dark times that evaluate our faith, which attests to how strong we are and how strong our relationship is with Christ's teachings. Christ compared it to a tree and the type of fruit it produces … "*a tree is known by its fruit,*" *[Ibid]*.

Another symbolic example is given us to know that also a faithful Christian following Jesus' teaching produces Spiritual fruit pleasing to God.

In contrast, as it is with the tree that buds and produces fruit that never grows to maturity, never ripens, the grower has not taken time to fertilize the soil the fruit it produces is not beneficial if one consumes it. We cannot allow our garments to be like the tree whose fruit never matures, which is not pleasing to God.

Fruit trees bear healthy, delicious, and beneficial fruit when the gardener prunes, fertilizes, waters, and cares, for the trees according to instructions. In the same sense, if we do not follow Christ's instructions we will not bear mature fruit no more than a tree not cared for according to instructions, "*For a good tree bring not forth corrupt fruit; neither doth a corrupt tree bring forth good fruit. For every tree is known by its fruit: for of thorns, men do not gather figs, nor of a bramble bush gather, they grapes. A good man out of the good treasure of his heart brings forth that which is good, and an evil man out of the evil treasure of his heart brings forth that which is evil: for of the abundance of the heart his mouth speaks,*" *[Luke 6:43-45]*.

When we build our foundation on the Word of God and make His Word the center of our lives, no one can shake our faith if we are obeying Christ according to His Word. We are not so easily tempted with evil and the wiles of Satan if our foundation is solid and we are rooted and grounded in the Word of God.

A man's spiritual house is as strong as the man who built it.

- *Do we build our house [faith and hope] on Christ [our rock] and eternity so when a storm comes our house [faith] stands strong?*
- *In contrast, do we build our houses on the [pleasures of life and the world], and when storms come the foundation of sand buckles and the house falls?*

Our lives take a bad turn for the worse when we depend on the things of this world for our future and not Christ. The lack of a solid foundation destroyed the house, as did the first storm when it came! Wrong foundation:

it should be a spiritual one, not a material one, *"Why do you call me, 'Lord, Lord,' and do not do what I say? As for everyone who comes to Me, hears My Words, and puts them into practice, I will show you what they are like. They are like a man building a house that dug down deep and laid the foundation on the rock. When a flood came, the torrent struck that house but could not shake it, because it was well built," [Luke 6:46-48].*

The winds of trouble blow sometimes in life without end; there is no way to escape them in this life. I think of the Hurricanes on the Gulf Coast how fierce they are, and the outer bands of the wind reach the Gulf Coast days sometimes before the eye of the storm arrives. The rain pours as if someone is emptying a large bucket of water all at once. It falls in sheets, a blinding rain preventing clear vision. The swirling bands bring the water of the Atlantic Ocean into the Gulf, and then into Mobile Bay dumping it all on land.

The ground saturated with water causes flooding. If you are on the east wall of the storm, you are in trouble; there is where the most devastating danger lies. The eye reaches the land and hovers for long periods before it moves on. I compare the storms we face in life to a hurricane. These hurricanes are hard to get through and if you survive, the loss of property because of the devastation is hard to recover from successfully before another one hits, there are no guarantees in this life because it is temporary.

We see the example of Abraham leaving his home and going to a land not known living in tents, which indicates to us this is not our permanent dwelling and we have no continuing city here. We like Abraham, are called to leave our self-sufficient faith, and take the journey living by Faith in God's Promises, realizing that this is not our final home. It is a temporary assignment for a specific purpose in our service to God. The Chapter of Faith in the Book of Hebrews reminds us of what Abraham put faith in, *"For he looked for a city which hath foundations, whose builder and makerisGod," [Hebrews 11:10].*

- *What keeps us from building our eternal home on the foundation Christ laid?*

While we are here, if our foundation is Christ, we can withstand the spiritual and physical storms that come into our lives. Storms do not last forever they move on, but are in incremental succession, we never know when another one will hit, so you prepare.

We are all wise to do the same in our spiritual life, dig down deep cementing our lives in Christ so when the storm passes by we may be damaged, but not destroyed, and are still standing.

Christ gave us a code: hear and do.

- ***We can read the Scripture, but if never applied what good are they?***

We look at ourselves in the reflections of a mirror. We see an image of who we are in our physical form. The Word of God is a mirror into our soul. The Scripture describes the look of the soul that is pleasing to God. When we ignore what we see, (Scripture describes) and act just the opposite, equals a person who does not know the Scripture or know and ignore.

We know from studying, what is pleasing to God. But yet we conduct ourselves in a way not acceptable (ignore) to Christ acting in a worldly manner, "*For if any be a hearer of the word and not a doer, he is like unto a man beholding his natural face in a glass: For he beholds himself, and go his way, and straightway forget what manner of man he was,*" *[James 1:23-24].*

The wisdom of the world is demonic; it produces strife and not peace. There is no peace in Satan. He is the source of destruction and evil. We cannot be self-seeking and envious as a child of God these characteristics are earthly and of the devil. Listen to the wisdom of James, "*But if you harbor bitter envy and selfish ambition in your hearts, do not boast about it or deny the truth. Such "wisdom" does not come down from heaven but is earthly, unspiritual, and demonic. For where you have envy and selfish ambition, there you find disorder and every evil practice,*" *[James 3:14-16].*

The wisdom that comes from God described in Scripture is directly opposite from the wisdom of the world. The attributes of wisdom from Heaven that God's people are to have are a quiet nature, tender, thoughtful, obedient, forgiving, compassionate, and bearing acceptable fruit to God, doing good deeds to and for their fellowman, unprejudiced, and genuine, "*But the wisdom that comes from heaven is first of all pure; then peace-loving, considerate, submissive, full of mercy and good fruit, impartial and sincere. Peacemakers who sow in peace reap a harvest of righteousness,*" *[James 3:17-18].*

People of God sow peace and not division. When we sow the seeds of peace the fruit yielded is of uprightness, which is pleasing to God. James reminds us that, "*Peacemakers who sow in peace reaps a harvest of righteousness,*" *[Ibid].*

Sisters, our garments should resonate every day of the people we are to be according to the Word of God. He created humans to obey the pattern He created for our lives and not serve other gods, but serve the one and only Triune God, maker of Heaven and Earth.

Isaiah reminds us when God is pleased with our ways we have this promise, *"Before they call I will answer; while they are still speaking I will hear," [Isaiah 65:24].*

*"For I know the thoughts that I think toward you, saith theLord, thoughts of peace, and not of evil, to give you an expected end. Then shall ye call upon Me, and ye shall go and pray unto Me, and I will hearken unto you. And ye shall seek Me and find Me when ye shall search for Me with all your heart," [Jeremiah 29:11-13].*

Sisters,' leaning-in, to the Salvation purchased by Christ is wise, and continuing to lean forward never going back, looking back, slowing down, or any action of the like is beneficial to our life now and for eternity. A foot race, especially one of miles in length requires endurance, which demands a pace where we thereby achieve a balance. In a race, running too fast can deplete your energy and stamina, which adversely affects your endurance and at that point may suffer burnout. It requires us to wear garments of stability for the race for eternity is where (stamina) is required.

We try to create a point of equilibrium in our secular life so must we in our spiritual without neglecting the physical part of life or the spiritual. We have a responsibility to God in our physical and spiritual life: our families (physical and spiritual), jobs, friends, parents, children, spouses, et cetera are all under the umbrella of our life when serving God so that He might be pleased. Leaning in is not easy, but doable sisters. Christ did not promise easy; He said it is possible. He set the example of leaning-in...

- *Christ gave His life. Can we do any less than giving (living for God) our life?*

We, sisters, have a place of honor in the Kingdom of God as well as we know how we ought to conduct ourselves in the House of God. That appropriate conduct is not just limited to the congregational worship but is in an overarching manner in the sense of being appropriate in every area of life that our ways might be pleasing to God and our light holds high the righteous banner of the Lord.

Moses and Christ seeds of leadership...

CHAPTER TWO

# MOSES AND CHRIST SEEDS OF LEADERSHIP

As the years passed and people began to multiply on earth after the flood, God sent Prophets, Judges, and other leaders to guide His people and deliver His law and Commandments; the message of the importance, of His people being obedient to them.

The people stiff-necked and defiant continued to be disobedient which bought upon their selves' punishment. God put the people in exile, bondage, time after time, for disobedience and the worship of idol gods: because they were not willing to change and be obedient. Man cannot add his expectations to what steps God wants humans to do in worship to be pleasing to Him; nor in life; He set the pattern, no man can regardless of the era in which they live. He did not make us stick figures to just occupy space, but to serve Him; not stand as if we are statues.

Their service to God, at that point, was in an ad hoc manner only obeying when necessary because of the cruel bondage and slavery leveled upon them by leaders of the pagan world. However, the worse of the bondage, at one juncture, was by Pharaoh, who did not know Joseph and acted out of fear because of the number of people of the tribe of Israel at that time.

The one people (the House of God) also ran after the things of the world God warned them not to do. Each generation that was born, lived, and died continued in an ad hoc manner until the coming of Jesus Christ. Moses (one man of God) stood against the Egyptian Empire. Jesus Christ (one God-Man) stood against all the evil of the world. God is a God of Oneness from the beginning of time until now.

In the Old Testament, Pharaoh ordered that all boy children be destroyed looking for the (deliverer), "*Then the King of Egypt told the Hebrew midwives, whose names were Shiphrah and Puah, "When you help the Hebrew women in childbirth, look at the child when you deliver it. If it is a boy, kill it, but if it is a girl, let it live. However, the midwives feared God and did not obey the king of Egypt's orders. They let the boys live. So, the king of Egypt called for the midwives. He asked them, "Why have you done this? Why have you let the boys live?" The midwives answered Pharaoh, "Hebrew women are not like Egyptian women. They are so healthy that they have their babies before a midwife arrives." God was good to the midwives, "So the people increased in number and became very strong. Because the midwives feared God, He gave them families of their own." Then Pharaoh commanded all his people to throw into the Nile every Hebrew boy that was born, but to let every girl live," [Exodus 1:15-22].*

Moses was 40 years old at the time he first stood against the Egyptian Taskmaster and killed him because he beat a slave. He was God's deliver for His people who did not realize he was at that time, *"And Moses said unto God, Whoam I that, I should go unto Pharaoh, and that I should bring forth the children of Israel out of Egypt? [Exodus 3:11; Acts 7:30].*

Moses was that seed of God to deliver His people from the cruel lash of the Egyptian evil taskmaster. Christ is the seed of God to deliver man for all times from the cruel lash of sin's evil taskmaster. Our God's Word is consistent throughout Scripture.

Moses was 40 years old when he began his ministry.

The basket or the ark that saved Moses is indicative of God's plan of Salvation for His people as was the Ark that saved the household of Noah because his ways pleased God…God who knows and sees the heart of man, knew the heart of Moses as well.

There was none greater than Moses who knew God face-to-face until Jesus *"Since then, no prophet has risen in Israel like Moses, whom the Lord knew face to face; who did all those signs and wonders the Lord sent him to do in Egypt-to Pharaoh; and to all his officials and his whole land: For no one has ever shown the mighty power or performed the awesome deeds that Moses did, in the sight of all Israel," [Deuteronomy 34:10-12].*

Christ was 30 years old when he began his ministry.

In the New Testament, Herod ordered all boy children under the age of 2 years of age be killed looking for the Savior (the Messiah), *"When Herod saw that the wise men had tricked him, he was furious. So, he gave an order to kill all the baby boys in Bethlehem and in the surrounding area who were two years old or younger. This was in keeping with the time he learned from the wise men," [Matthew 2:16].*

The evil perpetrated by Satan cannot thwart God's plans. Satan is as active or even more so now as he was at the beginning of time. Christ stood against the empire of evil to purchase our salvation that we might live for an eternity with God. Moses stood against the evil of the Pharaoh's empire and led the people to God at the foot of Mt. Sinai.

Christ is that Mt. Sinai we come to for deliverance and salvation.

Here on earth, we are walking, as Israel did, in a Wilderness of Shur: difficulty, pain, and suffering beset our lives every day. In our daily walk, eternity drives us forward, ever forward. Christ is our life-giving stream of water as the people drank from the life-giving steam from the rock in the wilderness, "*Then Moses raised his hand and struck the rock twice with his staff so that a great amount of water gushed out, and the congregation and their livestock were able to drink,*" [Numbers 20:11].

*He split the rocks in the wilderness and gave them drink as abundant as the seas,*" [Psalms 78:15].

"*And all drank the same Spiritual Drink. For they drank of that Spiritual Rock that followed them, and that Rock was Christ,*" [I Corinthians 10:4].

Christ was their Spiritual Drink then as He is our Spiritual Drink now.

The first birth of freedom started with Moses as he led the children of Israel to freedom from slavery and the cruelty of the taskmaster's whip in Egypt. Moses chose to suffer with the people of God rather than live any longer in the Palace of Pharaoh who continually suppressed his people, "*By faith Moses, when he had grown up, refused to be known as the son of Pharaoh's daughter. He chose to be suffering along with the people of God rather than to enjoy the fleeting pleasures of sin. He regarded disgrace for the sake of Christ as of greater value than the treasures of Egypt because he was looking ahead to his reward. By faith he left Egypt, not fearing the king's anger; he persevered because he saw Him who is invisible,*" [Hebrews 11:24-27].

That seed of freedom started with the birth of a leader in the lowly hut of Amram and Jochebed, "*Now Amram took for himself Jochebed, his father's sister, as wife; and she bore him Aaron and Moses. And the years of the life of Amram were one hundred and thirty-seven,*" [Exodus 6:20].

As with Moses, the Lord, and Savior, God-man started from the seed of David, born in a lowly stable to Jewish parents Mary and Joseph. As Moses was, a chosen leader raised by a man not his biological father, so was Jesus our Lord and Savior.

Jesus also, raised by Joseph who was not his biological father but chosen by God, in the genealogy of the family of King David of Israel to raise His only begotten Son to become our leader and guide to Salvation. Then purchased that Salvation on the Cross of Calvary, *"Now the birth of Jesus Christ was on this wise: When as His mother Mary was espoused to Joseph before they came together, she was found with child of the Holy Ghost."*

*"Then Joseph her husband being a just man, and not willing to make her a public example was minded to put her away privily; but, while he thought on these things, behold, the angel of the Lord appeared unto him in a dream saying, "Joseph, thou son of David, fear not to take unto thee Mary thy wife: for that which is conceived in her is of the Holy Ghost. And she shall bring forth a son, and thou shalt call his name Jesus: for he shall save his people from their sins." "Now all this was done that it might be fulfilled which was spoken of the Lord by the prophet, saying, "Behold, a virgin shall be with child, and shall bring forth a son, and they shall call His name Emmanuel, which being interpreted is, God with us." Then Joseph being raised from sleep did as the angel of the Lord had bidden him and took unto him his wife: And knew her not till she had brought forth her firstborn son: and he called His name Jesus,"* [Matthew 1:18-25].

Moses gave his life for his people, Christ gave His life for His Bride, His Body, and The Church that bears His name that we might have a path back to God and be free from the taskmaster of sin and its whip of evilness. Christ defeated Satan when He hung on the Cross and took upon Himself the sins of all humankind.

Christ gave us a new command, *"A new commandment I give to you, that you love one another: just as I have loved you, you also are to love one another." If you are a follower of Jesus, a Christian, a child of God through faith in Christ, you are a person under authority. You are not your own,"* [John 13:34].

Law came through Moses, Grace and Truth came through Jesus Christ who purchased the right for all to be partakers of grace and truth who desires to obey, *"For the law was given by Moses, but grace and truth came by Jesus Christ,"* [John 1:17].

The people in Moses' time defied the commands of God and paid the price for disobedience. In the Book of Numbers, Moses gave instances of the people disobeying God and suffering the consequences and his prayer to God for mercy and grace toward the people for their disobedience, *"Whenever the ark set out, Moses said, "Rise up, Lord! May your enemies be scattered; may your foes flee before you. Whenever it came to rest, he said, "Return, Lord, to the countless thousands of Israel,"* *[Numbers 10:35-36]*.

We, in this 21ˢᵗ-Century, are no different from the people then; we can either follow Christ and the new commands He left or defy them and pay the eternal price of absence from the presence of God. *"If you love me keep My commandments,"* *[John 14:15]* is the same command given the people in Moses' time.

Christ is standing at the door knocking now, however; we know that refusing to hear His voice will harden our hearts, *"As has just been said: "Today if you hear His voice, do not harden your hearts as you did in the rebellion,"* *[Hebrews 3:15]*.

The disobedience fires stoked by (Satan) trailed the people of God right in the New Testament times. Stephen spoke of their stiff-necked ways in the New Testament times as Moses spoke of in Old Testament times. He warned them of their ways before they stoned him to death, *"Ye stiff-necked and uncircumcised in heart and ears, ye do always resist the Holy Ghost: as your fathers did, so do you. Which of the prophets have not your fathers persecuted? And they have slain them, which showed before of the coming of the Just One; of whom ye have been now the betrayers and murderers: Who have received the law by the disposition of angels and have not kept it. When they heard these things, they were cut to the heart, and they gnashed on him with their teeth. But he, being full of the Holy Ghost, looked up steadfastly into heaven, and saw the glory of God, and Jesus standing on the right hand of God, And said, Behold, I see the heavens opened, and the Son of man standing on the right hand of God. Then they cried out with a loud voice, and stopped their ears, and ran upon him with one accord, cast him out of the city, and stoned him: and the witnesses laid down their clothes at a young man's feet, whose name was Saul,"* *[Acts 7:51-58]*.

Stephen painted a vivid picture for them of their errors and sins; they were no different from their ancestors in their disobedience to God's commands and as their forefathers did, killed the prophets; they killed Our Lord and Savior Jesus Christ who took away the sins of the world. They could not face the truth about themselves, nor did they want him telling them they killed the Savior of the World with a message of life and salvation. They could not destroy the message, so they destroyed the messenger (Stephen).

Moses' seed was from a Levitical Priesthood. He was to intercede between the people of Israel and God to serve at the Alter, of God to bring the Law to the people. Moses was the Lawgiver and judged the people of Israel. At that time, Moses took upon himself the responsibility of the people of God to guide them, lead them, teach them, and admonish them of all things pleasing or displeasing to God.

Moses was that seed planted in the Kingdom of Egypt in the House of Pharaoh to be the deliverer spoken of to lead God's people out of bondage and the cruelty of the evil taskmaster the Egyptians levied upon them by the Pharaoh who knew not the ways of Joseph after his death.

Christ came from the seed of David planted in the House of David through Joseph who we can think of as a man after God's own heart as was David the King before him. There always has to be a seed…seeds are the start of life.

The Son of God is our pattern of leadership. God gave Christ all power, *"But unto the Son, He saith, Thy throne, O God, is forever and ever: a Scepter of righteousness is the Scepter of thy Kingdom. Thou hast loved righteousness, and hated iniquity; therefore God, even thy God, hath anointed Thee with the oil of gladness above thy fellows," [Hebrews 1:8-9].*

Jesus is the only begotten Son of God higher than humanity and Angels. Jesus is true knowledge and morally pure: the Eternal God and Savior.

The Scripture is clear on the position both of man and Angels in creation, Jesus is God – God the Son, *"Who being the brightness of his glory, and the express image of His person, and upholding all things by the word of His power, when He had by Himself purged our sins, sat down on the right hand of the Majesty on high: Being made so much better than the angels, as He hath by inheritance obtained a more excellent name than they. For unto which of the angels said He at any time, "Thou art my Son, this day have I begotten thee." And again, I will be to Him a Father, and He shall be to me a Son? And again, when He bringeth in the first begotten into the world, He saith, And let all the angels of God worship Him. And of the angels, He saith, Who maketh His angels' spirits, and His ministers a flame of fire. But unto the Son, He saith, Thy throne, O God, is forever and ever: a Scepter of Righteousness is the Scepter of thy Kingdom," [Hebrews 1:3-8].*

We have victory in Jesus Christ Our Lord and Savior. The life one lives in Jesus gives them success over their past and hope for their future found only in Jesus and no other. Any victories we have in our lives here on earth are temporal unless they are in Jesus Christ. We can overcome the world because He did; however, that triumph does not come without faith, obedience, and work; all through the grace and mercy that God gifted us, in Christ through the death, burial, and resurrection of His Son.

On Calvary's Hill, we see Repentance, Redemption, and Rejection. Christ redeemed man from sin. He paid the price with His life willing to upon Himself the yoke of sin and carried it, so it no longer separated man from God. We read of one example of repentance with one of the thieves asking that our redeemer remember him when He comes into His Kingdom. Christ replied, "*This day you will be with Me in Paradise,*" *[Ibid]*.

Then we read of one of the thieves rejecting the redemption, "*If you are a God come down off the cross and save yourself.*" *[Ibid]*. At that point, he joined the attitudes of the scoffers at the foot of the cross. Hence, even today the rejection of the redemption Christ purchased puts us at the foot of the cross with those who accept, scoff at, or accusers our Lord and Savior.

Leadership skills, even in modern society, are characteristics a person is born with, or in Moses and Jesus' cases were born for that purpose.

As this 21st-Century society teaches us in business, management skills are learned, but not leadership; that inherited quality can be developed but not taught. There is a certain charisma about that person readily identifiable setting them apart and that is noticeably far above those who are not blessed with this gift of charisma found in a leader.

History in the Old Testament and the New Testament identifies leaders who have those characteristics. God did not send Jesus in a Kingly manner as supposed but was humbly born as a child through fleshly parents to testify of His nature recognized by the people of Israel as one of them. There were those who followed the leadership of Jesus through uncertainty at times, believed by faith in His Words, and followed finally His examples.

Christ left the Twelve Apostles to continue that leadership He begins and finally imparting the Gospel of Salvation to Jews and Gentiles bringing them into the [Fold] Jesus came to earth to die for and open up a pathway for them back to a one-on-one relationship with God the Father, who is overall.

We all have gifts God blesses us with regardless of how small, large, or the number of talents we have, are to use them for His Glory. Moses, through training, at the feet of Pharaoh, became a warrior, a statistician, a builder, walked with Kings and Princesses, and moved without fear in defense of his people. We see others with gifts and talents. We look at their humble environments, admire them, and marvel at their talents. The Scriptures point out that Christ gives gifts and talent according to their several abilities.

He imparts to us those skills and abilities. He knows what we can handle or what we are good at; it is up to us to develop and use them because there will be an accounting before God for their use or lack of use. Christ spoke the Parable of the Man and his talent. He gave us these seeds of leadership we are to use them. Two leaders of His archetype in the New Testament are Peter and Paul.

Christ knew their capabilities and what people to send them to – to spread the Gospel, Initially, Peter was sent to the Jews and Paul was sent to the Gentiles, but their teaching and works included both Jews and Gentiles. Peter was a Fisherman. He used that skill to become fishers of men. Paul was a Roman scholar, he used his skills to connect with both Jews and Gentiles, as well as move about the Roman Empire.

God knows all and sees what seeds of leadership we have…we sister, have garments of leadership, use them so the accounting before God's Throne will be, *"Well done My good and faithful servant, take your rest," [Ibid].*

- ***Does this Scripture invoke your desire to be faithful or at best sound familiar sister?***

The message has not changed from the time of our ancestors, 'to be pleasing to God,' requires obedience.

God commands we love Him and obey His Word, *"The Word became flesh and dwelled among men," [John 1:1].*

*"He saith not, And to seeds as of many, but as one and to thy seed, which is Christ." And "I will put enmity between thee and the woman, and between thy seed and her seed; it shall bruise thy head, and thou shalt bruise his heel," [Genesis 3:15].*

*"I will establish my covenant as an everlasting covenant between me and you, and your descendants after you for the generations to come, to be your God and the God of your descendants after you. The whole land of Canaan, where you now reside as a foreigner, I will give as an everlasting possession to you and your descendants after you; and I will be their God," [Genesis 17:7-8].*

There is noticeable stress on the word "seed" as it refers to an individual there, Christ...in fulfillment of the promise to Abraham...this is a unique use of seed it is one not many, (Vine, P334); it is seed here as singular showing that seed was Christ.

His seed referred to in *[John 3:9]* is easy to understand this seed is many referring to the faithful servants of God (His seed) abiding in Him, we do not continue sinning. Our spiritual lives are in Christ given by God to those who abide in Him.

According to Vine, "Once we are added to the Body of Christ, there is no possibility of removal or extraction, the child of God remains eternally related to Christ, who lives in sin...have never become so related he has not the principle of life in him." [P304 P2, Vine (Seed)].

To serve God faithfully the seed of Christ has to abide in us not on our bases but according to the pattern given by Jesus Christ.

In the Book of Psalms, David's Psalms of *Prayers of Ascent* to God helps us to remember how to honor and worship Him. Then recognizing that we are ever under the protection, grace, and mercy of God – He is the head of our family (first in our life), life itself only exists through God. We can have confidence in Him in all things that come into our lives whether they are good or bad, will never leave us alone. He is a loving and forgiving God, worthy of trust and we can have contentment in these facts.

When we honor God, we are pleasing to Him and that is a blessing for us. We have joy in our relationship with our God and forgiveness when we sin and continue to walk with Him in that straight and narrow way. I think of these examples of the Psalms of Ascent:

*"I will lift mine eyes to the Lord which come my help? My help comes from the Lord the Maker of heaven and earth," [Psalms 121:1].*

*"I was glad when they said unto me, let us go into the house of the Lord,"* *[Psalms 122:1].*

*"I lift my eyes to you, to you who sit enthroned in heaven. As the eyes of slaves to the hand of their master, as the eyes of a female slave to the hand of her mistress, so our eyes look to the Lord our God, till he shows us His mercy,"* *[Psalms 123:1].*

*"If the Lord had not been on our side – let Israel say – if the Lord had not been on our side when people attacked us, they would have swallowed us alive when their anger flared against us, the flood would have engulfed us the torrent would have swept over us, the raging waters would have swept us away,"* *[Psalms 124:1-4].*

*"Unless the Lord builds the house, the builder labors in vain. Unless the Lord watches over the city, the guards stand watch in vain. In vain you rise early and stay up late, toiling for food to eat – for he grants sleep to those He loves,"* *[Psalms 127:1-2].*

*"Blessed are all who fear the Lord, who walk in obedience to Him. You will eat the fruit of your labor, blessings, and prosperity will be yours,"* *[Psalms 128:1-2].*

*"My heart is not proud, Lord, my eyes are not haughty; I do not concern myself with great matters or things too wonderful for me. But I have calmed and quieted myself, I am like a weaned child with its mother, like a weaned child I am content,"* *[Psalms 131:1-2].*

Sisters God is a protector and nourisher of His people. I could not include all the Psalms' Prayers of Ascent; nevertheless, the Psalms' Prayers of Ascents included supports the points made of our God, Lord, Savior, Teacher, and Guide. The Prayers of Ascent above expresses the love and appreciation we can show, how to honor Him through prayer and recognition that He, is the mighty God with all power, and might there is none mightier.

- *So why would we bondage away our privilege of worship to the evilest adversary man has in this world?*

Christ is the Seed of God who dwelled among men. King David, a man after God's own heart, recognized "Who" God [is] and that He [is]. Thank God, for the Seed – He left us a clear path to Salvation.

We are to follow the Aroma He left…our garments of change…

CHAPTER THREE

# GARMENTS OF CHANGE: AN AROMA

Our garments of works and actions must not be named amongst those who are rebellious and full of meaningless talk as some were who were rebuked for not being good. Paul wrote in his instructions to Titus, *"For there are many unruly and vain talkers and deceivers, especially they of the circumcision: Whose mouths must be stopped, who subvert whole houses, teaching things which they ought not, for filthy lucre's sake. One of themselves, even a prophet of their own, said," The Cretans are always liars, evil beasts, slow bellies."*

Paul continued his letter to Titus in this manner, *"This witness is true. Wherefore rebuke them sharply, that they may be sound in the faith; not giving heed to Jewish fables, and commandments of men, that turn from the truth. Unto the pure, all things are pure: but unto them that are defiled, and unbelieving is nothing pure; but even their mind and conscience is defiled. They profess that they know God; but in works they deny him, being abominable, and disobedient, and unto every good work reprobates," [Titus 1:10-16].*

Being good is a choice. In serving God, our garments should have an aroma of eagerness. According to Roget, "Eager is defined as an excitement, fervor, an ambitious, a thirst, a longing, and with zestfulness."

Paul reminds the older or mature women, they should be examples and bring their fellow sisters along in the Gospel, giving them a pattern of what aroma, their garments should have, *"The aged women likewise, that they be in behavior as become holiness, not false accusers, not given to much wine, teachers of good things. That they may teach the young women to be sober, to love their husbands, to love their children, To be discreet, chaste, keepers at home, good, obedient to their husbands, that the word of God be not blasphemed," [Titus 2:3-5].*

*"For the grace of God that brings salvation hath appeared to all men, teaching us that, denying ungodliness and worldly lusts, we should live soberly, righteously, and godly, in this present world. Looking for that blessed hope, and the glorious appearing of the great God and our Savior Jesus Christ, Who gave himself for us, that He might redeem us from all iniquity, and purify unto Himself a peculiar people, zealous of good works. These things speak, and exhort, and rebuke with all authority. Let no man despise thee." [Titus 2:11-15].*

Christ leads us. We as humans know the smells of physical aromas. The ability to smell is a function of one of the five of our God-given senses. With this sense of smell, we can discern whether the smell of an aroma is good or bad. The smell, when it is pleasant, inspires our taste buds and that can be our taste buds of appetite or beauty. In contrast, a bad aroma can and will have the opposite effect. It can destroy or discourage our desires for the food or product (such as Limburger Cheese or the unattractive smell of inexpensive cologne).

The Word of God has a pleasant aroma, taste, and smell, except it is in a spiritual sense.

The desire, for the beauty of the Word of God, the aroma and fragrance of Salvation and Eternity it gives off, should draw (pull) one in, giving them the desire, for that aroma to permeate through every aspect of their life. Paul wrote, *"But thanks be to God, who always leads us as captives in Christ's triumphal procession and uses us to spread the aroma of the knowledge of Him everywhere," [2 Corinthians 2:14].*

The Lord's Supper (Communion) each Lord's Day gives off a fragrance of Salvation. We can taste forgiveness, peace, the joy of eternity, and the taste of Christ's immeasurable sacrifice and love for us; that fragrance is not the taste of the emblems, but what they represent.

Our garments of faithfulness should have the pleasing aroma of Jesus Christ so that we might continue to carry that banner of faithfulness to God with it evident and seeable to all. We, the people of God, must serve our Lord in spirit and truth, so no negative aromas will proceed from or follow us. We are to walk circumspectly [monitoring] our walk, at all times, that we might not give off unpleasant scents or the scents of Satan be named amongst us as Paul reminds us, *"We are not unaware of the schemes of Satan," [2 Corinthians 2:11].*

He is consistently looking and desiring to outwit the people of God. He is diligently working to this end in a tenaciously unrelenting manner with wise evilness and cunning that we cannot, in-and-of our self-comprehend without the aid of the inspired Word of God and guidance, from the Holy Spirit.

In the minute domiciles of our minds, humans know right/wrong; life/death; good/evil; but sometimes, suppress these attributes especially the right and good, if it does not fit into the goals we are looking to accomplish. We are to take care of our garments, so they reflect only good and right, that the spiritual aroma is positive and not negative.

A lesser of two evils is not a valid statement. It is of human devising, a nonsense assertion. God gives us two choices life/death or good/evil.

Lesser of two evils … we have all used this euphemism in our lifetime. There is no such thing as the lesser of two evils. This is a desire of man to [weasel out] help us feel better within so our conscience will not condemn us of wrong, this assertion sends a distasteful aroma to God. God does not give us a lesser of two evils. God gives us two choices life/death or good/evil. He never contradicts Himself. This is what it would be like if he accepted man's watered-down versions of right/wrong according to their standards.

Satan's arsenal of wiles is deception without change. […]

Jude, the Apostle, warns of the dangers of listening to false teachers, scoffers are all of Satan their father and teacher. He describes those who follow false teachers and scoff at the authority and powers of God even the Spiritual world. They are of those who follow in the footsteps of Cain who killed his brother and Balaam who deceive people for money, and like Korah, they all perished in their rebellion, *(Jude 11)*.

He illustrates their rebellion and defiance in this way, "*They are like shameless shepherds who care only for themselves. They are like clouds blowing over the land without giving any rain. They are like trees in autumn that are doubly dead, for they bear no fruit and have been pulled up by the roots. They are like wild waves of the sea, churning up the foam of their shameful deeds. They are like wandering stars, doomed forever to blackest darkness,*" [Jude 12b–13].

Peter mirrors the description of Jude for false teachers or those who would scoff, "*These false teachers are like unthinking animals, creatures of instinct, born to be caught and destroyed. They scoff at things they do not understand, and like animals, they will be destroyed. Their destruction is their reward for the harm they have done. They love to indulge in evil pleasures in broad daylight. They are a disgrace and a stain among you. They delight in deception even as they eat with you in your fellowship meals. They commit adultery and their eyes, and their desire for sin is never satisfied. They live under God's curse. They have wandered off the right road and followed the steps of Balaam son of Beor who loved to earn money by doing wrong. But Balaam was stopped from his mad course when his donkey rebuked him with a human voice,"* [2 Peter 2:12-16].

Indulging in Sin is an enduring risk to take. It is persisting never giving up because our adversary never gives up. Satan preservers in his desire to have your soul for eternity and continue to use his wiles to trap us sisters ... being on our guard, at all times, are wise.

Sisters our garments should not have the aroma of a Balaam, a scoffer, false teacher, or Cain, but the scent should be of righteousness, obedience, love, humility, honesty, integrity, faithfulness, working out our Salvation in fear and trembling not in arrogance and pride.

As mentioned before, there are only two voices the voice of God and the voice of Satan, the question again whose voice are you listening to? The voices can be easily identified in Scripture.

Moses wrote this message to the people of God at that time concerning these subjects. Listen to the voice of the Scripture, *"See, I set before you today life and prosperity, death, and destruction. In that, I command you today to love the Lord your God, to walk in His ways, and to keep His commandments and His statutes, and His judgments, that thou mayest live and multiply: and the Lord thy God will bless thee in the land whither thou goest to possess it. But if thine heart turns away, so that thou wilt, not heart, but shall be drawn away, and worship other gods, and serve them. I denounce unto you this day, that ye shall surely perish, and that ye shall not prolong your days upon the land, whither thou passed over Jordan to go to possess it. I call heaven and earth to record this day against you that I have set before you; life and death, blessing and cursing; therefore, chose life that both thou and thy seed may live. And thou mayest love the Lord they God, and that thou mayest observe His voice, and that thou mayest cleave unto Him for He is thy life, and the length of thy days, that thou mayest dwell in the land when which the Lord swore unto they fathers to Abraham, to Isaac, and to Jacob to give them."* [Deuteronomy 30:15-20].

Paul gives us the same warning of how God's people are to conduct themselves choosing life and blessings; how the example of our living in faithfulness and obedience before men are pleasing to God, *"You yourselves are our letter written on our hearts known and read by men. You should show that you are a letter from Christ the results of our ministry, written not with ink, but with the spirit of the Living God, not on tablets of stone but on the tablets of human hearts,"* [2 Corinthians 3:2-3].

Being that example for Christ, like Christ, and of Christ; others believe more of what they see in this respect than what they read on pages written in black and white. We are ambassadors of Christ, our garment's aroma should give off pleasant fragrances because our confidence is not of man but God, *"Not that we are competent in ourselves to claim anything for ourselves, but our competence comes from God. He has made us competent as ministers of a new covenant not of the letter but of the Spirit; for the letter kills, but the Spirit gives life,"* *[2 Corinthians 3:5-6].*

The written letter of the Law was passing away as was a fact. When the people looked at Moses, they could not see the end of what was passing because of the veil over his face indicating over time the law was fleeting and not permanent. We do not serve God through the letter of the Law but through the Spirit, *"Therefore, since we have such hope, we are very bold. We are not like Moses, who would put a veil over his face to prevent the Israelites from seeing the end of what was passing away. However, their minds were made dull, for to this day, the same veil remains when the old covenant is read. It has not been removed because only in Christ is it taken away. Even to this day when Moses is read, a veil covers their hearts. But, whenever anyone turns to the Lord, the veil is taken away. Now the Lord is the Spirit, and where the Spirit of the Lord is, there is freedom. And we all, who with unveiled faces contemplate the Lord's glory, are being transformed into His image with ever-increasing glory, which comes from the Lord, who is the Spirit,"* *[2 Corinthians 3:12-18].*

While the law remained it caused difficulty in service and obedience to God; it could only be removed through Christ, *"Blotting out the handwriting of ordinances that was against us, which was contrary to us, and took it out of the way, nailing it to His cross,"* *[Colossians 2:14].*

Think of the aroma the Garden of Eden had at the beginning of time, as we know it. The garden was fresh, untouched, pure, without the spot, nor a blemish of sin, or disobedience. God planted the garden in the East of Eden with all its mystery and fascination at play that puzzles our minds even today. Eden is a mystery to man, but it existed, yet the purity that was there pre-man in this instance; I briefly focus on in a transitory manner.

Babies at birth have a distinct scent and aroma that is pleasing and inviting to a mother. The sweetness of their breath is so that a mother wants to love and endlessly kiss her baby. They are pure and innocent. God gives us them as a gift of innocence to show us what purity looks like, smells like, and sounds like, especially the sound of a baby's cooing. All of this is a sweet-smelling aroma that reaches the Spiritual Nostrils of God and is pleasing to Him in every way.

The Garden Adam and Eve were placed in had a sweet-smelling aroma of beauty and innocence. God desired that they send up the same aroma that existed before sin entered the garden of purity and in their innocent lives.

Once baptized into Christ, we are pure before God. All the world and what we did before we became part of the Bride of Christ, His Church, are spiritually gone; we start anew … a new birth, as Christ told Nicodemus.

Jesus replied, *"Very truly I tell you, no one can see the Kingdom of God unless they are born again." "How can someone be born when they are old?"* Nicodemus asked. *"Surely they cannot enter a second time into their mother's womb to be born!"*

Jesus answered, *"Very truly I tell you, no one can enter the Kingdom of God unless they are born of water and the Spirit. Flesh gives birth to flesh, but the Spirit gives birth to Spirit. You should not be surprised at my saying, 'You must be born again.' The wind blows wherever it pleases. You hear its sound, but you cannot tell where it comes from or where it is going. So, it is with everyone born of the Spirit,"* [John 3:3-8].

We cannot enter the womb and be born again; but through Christ, we have that opportunity to be born again. It is a choice. Our physical birth involves water…we lived in the womb immersed in water (fluid). Our Spiritual birth involves immersion in water. As a result of the immersion, we are newborn babes in both physical and spiritual births and through a process of time grow to maturity.

Our aroma, at our birth, with the aid of the Holy Spirit, is sweet and goes up to Heaven as a pleasing fragrance to God. After our initial babes in Christ [novice] experience, we grow and continue to send up a pleasing scent of faithfulness before God. There are always downsides to any actions we take. The [but] is when we willfully sin and defy God's Word; that, like Limburger Cheese's aroma, has a distasteful scent so is the aroma of sin unpleasant before God as with Adam and Eve, was not pleased with the smell of defiance before His Throne and the Holy Angels. In today's societal language, 'it does not pass the smell test.'When I was in Paris, especially there, Limburger Cheese was one of the food items on the Buffet Breakfast Bar one morning. The scent exuded from the buffet before I got near it and was very distinctively invading my nostrils, almost cutting off my breath. The distasteful smell of the cheese on the buffet awakened my taste buds in an objectionable way. We say in this society, "Maybe if I could get it past my nose it may not taste so bad." Our noses are the first line of defense, a vanguard for our taste buds located in our tongues.

My fellow tourist behind me saw my reaction and said, "It is very tasty once you get it past your nose." She smiled when I said, "If it does not pass my smell test, it is already a turnoff, and I will not try the taste test."

She replied, "I thought so as well, I held my nose and tasted it." I just smiled, nodded, and thought, "No way I will trust that I trust my nose and what it is telling me."

Sin is like that; trust your nose (Knows) the Gospel for the first whiff of wrong according to God's Word. Our taste buds can be on track using the Word of God as our guide. Our nose guides us about aromas physically. The Word of God will guide us about the aromas of sin in a Spiritual sense.

We have examples we can refer back to in our physical existence that are parallel to our Spiritual sense. We know how to check the aroma with physical scents first and if it does not pass our physical smell test then we can check the Spiritual scent (aroma) of sin by studying the Word of God.

Our children have an aroma to them when they are growing, they have a little sweaty scent, sometimes musty, and rank smell they have inherent to children because they run and play, we immediately give them or have them take a bath to rid them of the unpleasant smell.

The way we teach them about the cleanliness of their bodies, we also teach them right and wrong.

When they go against the teaching for their safety and healthy growth; their actions are distasteful and send off an unpleasant aroma to their parents; when children are obedient to their parents it is a pleasant aroma; translate this to what God wants for His children. When our ways please God, they have a pleasing aroma…acceptable to our Lord…

We cannot afford to have Halitosis of the mouth in a physical sense; it has an unpleasant scent to it causing others to distance themselves from that person. My husband kept Listerine at all times in his truck and gargled throughout the day so he would not be offensive to others when talking, 'especially, he did not want to offend me ever,' he said, which I appreciated. Not only did he practice this when away from home, but when he was at home as well…needless to say, that I freshen my mouth constantly as well, with mints, Listerine, cough drops, and whatever it took to freshen my breath so I would not offend my husband or others.

We have breath sprays, breath mints, and the process goes on and on…we take so much caution to ensure we do not offend our fellowmen, or they offend us. We, in a humble manner, never wanting to insult our brethren who have Halitosis, offer them a breath mint, or kindly tell them. That offer of a mint tells them without words that there is a problem with their breath. The cause of Physical Halitosis is our systems telling us there are malfunctions in our mouth, throat, for lack of care; or we are not attending to the preventive task necessary to keep the bacteria from forming.

In the Spiritual sense, we cannot afford to have Halitosis of the Spirit either; it has a distasteful aroma causing our actions and ways to be displeasing to God. Christ left us an example of how to avoid Spiritual Halitosis, "*I do all things to please My Father in Heaven," [Ibid].*

- *Do we take preventive measures using Spiritual breath mints, Spiritual breath sprays, the Listerine to gargle continuously to prevent the basis that Spiritual Halitosis begins with, sin?*

With the distasteful aroma sin gives, the preventive measures Christ gave us are fluid in a continuous way that will prevent the repugnant odor that surrounds and envelops it. As with us caring that our brethren has a problem with the physical, we are to tell them when they are off track Spirituality, "*Brethren if a man is overtaken in a fault, ye which is spiritual, restore such a one in the spirit of meekness; considering thyself, lest thou also be tempted," [Galatians 6:1].*

We do not want our brethren to be embarrassed by their Physical Halitosis, why is it so hard to translate this into their spiritual errors. Sin is a bacterium, which grows and permeates one's life, heart, mind, and actions. Webster defines Bacterium as a member of a large group of unicellular microorganisms, which have cell walls but lack organelles and an organized nucleus, including those that can cause disease.

This microorganism causes disease, infection, infirmity, malady, illness, and sickness. Sin is like a large unicellular microorganism it causes a multiplicity of problems in human lives, we never know how, when, or where it will manifest itself. Paul warns us to, "*Put on the whole armor of God that you might be able to fight against the wiles of the devil," [Ephesians 6:10].*

We can describe the wiles of Satan and their effects as mentioned above. That is why our garments should reflect a fragrance of care and concern; it is a sign of love in both cases our desire for our brethren to be the best both spiritually and physically. The Scripture tells us that, *"Love does no harm to a neighbor (brethren). Therefore, love is the fulfillment of the law," [Romans 13:10].*

Washing sins away are a change of garments that also dictates that the aroma changes. When we have a change of garments for our Lord and Savior there is [no] going back to what we once knew as normal. There are [no] normal forever after's; there is only life before we came to Christ and life after we come to Christ.

We cannot change our garments of morality as if they are changes of seasons. Our moral garments should shine brightly before others continuously so all can know and see a consistency in our garments of the standards of God. Our faithfulness to God cannot be situational nor give way to relevancy. There is a cultural pressure out there regardless of the century in which you live, that can lean, if allowed, heavily upon our perspective or outlook on life.

Our focus is to stay faithful to God and His will for our lives, not follow the changing cultures that come and go seasonally, as well. Satan will, as mentioned before, provide whatever you so desire and the pathway for you to walk to fulfill those desires.

James refers to those who practice faithfulness as the first fruits of Christ – as God gave us birth through the Word of Truth that we might be a kind of first fruits of all He created. The first-century Christians at that time were of the first fruits given birth through obedience and baptism into the Body of Christ purchased with His Blood. We in our century can continue to be part of those who were of the first fruits to be born into the Eternal Kingdom of God.

We can understand this through the Parables of a farmer and the first fruits to bear of his crop that year … as in the same reference to us (people of God) giving of our first fruits whether it is money, time, or service, etc. God first is the point I am making, regardless of what we do; our first fruits we dedicate to God, because of our Savior Jesus Christ – He gave His All for us. He is our creator and the creator of all things. We are a people set aside (Saints) for the purpose that God has for our life in service to Him.

Our garments of focus are the mission Christ left for us first to save ourselves from this untoward generation, and then save others because we know how to offer them the Salvation Christ purchased for the whole of humanity, we have to "go" into the whole world mandate (command). Our attitudes toward the Word of God are essential to obedience we cannot [say] and [do not do] as is expressed in *[James 1:19-25]*.

Our garment of self-control is important if we want to be pleasing to God. The tongue of man is at all times on trial. We check to see if what we say and know if the words are appropriate for the aroma of Christian conduct, which is attitude. We embrace attitudes of humility, subjection, praise, honor is all to our God, and not boastfulness. James reminds us, "*Brothers and sisters, do not slander one another. Anyone who speaks against a brother or sister or judges them speaks against the law and judges it. When you judge the law, you are not keeping it, but sitting in judgment on it. There is only one Lawgiver and judge, the one who is able to save and destroy. But you – who are you to judge your neighbor. Now listen, you who say, "Today or tomorrow we will go to this or that city, spend a year there, carry on business, and make money." Why you do not even know what will happen tomorrow? What is your life? You are a mist that appears for a little while and then vanishes. Instead, you ought to say, "If it is the Lord's will, we will live and do this or that," [James 4:11-15]*.

Consider these questions sisters.

- *Do I revere and respect the Word of God?*
- *Do I take life and tomorrow for granted?*
- *Do I treat my brethren as Christ commands?*
- *Do I watch my speech and words to others?*
- *Do I sit in judgment?*
- *What is my attitude in the face of persecution?*
- *What is my attitude toward serving God faithfully and allowing Him to assist me in my daily walk?*
- *When we face challenging times that test us, and we are tempted to retaliate verbally, what should our attitudes be?*
- *Do we say I serve God and then do the opposite?*

The example James gave of beholding your face in the mirror and then forgetting who you are is not found among the garments of change in our moral walk but the change that comes should be pleasing to God through growth in the Kingdom.

Looking at others in a judgmental way and forgetting we are subject to the same errors in our life as our brethren or fellowman. The song Moses recited to

Israel warns of acting as a nation (person) without sense and not with wisdom. Our garments should be of using the wisdom of God when we are dealing with our fellowman period sisters and not as the world does thinking that God does not have the last say in life for all humans. God told Moses concerning the actions of the nation of Israel at that time, "*They are a nation without sense there is no discernment in them. If only they were wise and would understand this and discern what their end will be.*" [Deuteronomy 32:29].

Each day, after we give our lives to Christ, our Spiritual garments change like the physical ones we grow out of them, they get too small, do not fit well anymore, by this, we know we are growing, as we should. In this respect, with our physical garments, we discard or give them away; with our spiritual garments, as well this is a sign of growth in the Kingdom Christ established.

There is one difference between our physical and spiritual garments, we do not discard the spiritual garments we have outgrown; we change them for more mature ones. We keep all spiritual garments even if it is just in memory so we can know or recognize if our growth has a pleasing scent to God.

Sisters, we cannot be of those whose garments reflect Halitosis of the Spirit, if it does; we need to correct it as quickly as possible. We cannot hold our Spiritual noses and forge forward when sin is present because that whiff tells us that it is in direct defiance to God's Word and His will for our lives.

There can be no former normal...the only normal we have is that Christ is in our lives. Satan ensures that there is no consistency in our normal after our obedience through baptism. We enter the war at that point and there is nothing normal about physical or spiritual warfare, battles change every day as does the strategy used to fight these battles.

I think sometimes of the word normal. I hear mothers say after their baby is born my life will get back to normal.

- **When has any woman's life been normal again the way it was (pre-baby)?**

It is like sitting through a movie trying to figure out what the plot is and what comes next. My life felt like a mystery after my children were born. We give away ourselves to that precious little one, with that change it is a major shift from old normal to a new normal.

***We can then ask ourselves, is it so hard to give away ourselves to our Precious Lord and Savior?***

Those garments require a major change as well to serve Christ. The change has to be in desire, attitude, willingness, eagerness, and necessity (DAWEN). It is (**THE WIN**) just as it sounds.

I think of a quote by Emerson, *"Truth is the property, of no individual; but is the treasure of all men."*

This should be a concept understood by all of humanity, Scripture continues to be the Truth, which does belong to no one person, but is for all to partake of and when we find that truth; it is a treasure, which has eternal benefits.

Jesus prayed to God for His Disciples, *"Sanctify them through Thy truth: Thy Word is Truth. As Thou has sent Me into the world, even so, have I also sent them into the world; and for their sakes, I sanctify Myself, that they also might be sanctified through the Truth," [John 17:17-23].*

When we accept the Salvation Christ purchased, which also makes us aware we are dealing with the Predator. He is alive and well…these two Truths we cannot escape, Satan (Predator) is an enemy of the people of God and Salvation for man came only through Christ, *"Forthe lawwas given byMoses,but grace and truth cameby Jesus Christ," [John 1:17].*

CHAPTER FOUR

# THE 21ST-CENTURY PREDATOR

Satan is a predator - seekers have predatory characteristics.

In the animal kingdom, they (predators) walk, slinking about not knowing what they might see but seeking, looking, and trying to see what victims of the animal kingdom may be weak so they can take advantage of that weakness. We, (people of God) Scripture warns us about (Satan's) predatory skills.

We cannot allow our weakness in Christ to be a target of Satan. On the National Geographic Channel, I watched the Water Buffalo sometimes when a member of their herd is weak; they surround him/her to protect them from the predator until they are stronger. We stand against our foe as members of Christ's Body when one is weak as Paul said, "*We then that are strong ought to bear the infirmities of the weak, and not to please ourselves,*" [Romans 15:1].

In Africa, there is an insect called the Fatted Bug, it is so tiny and weak by itself; they, by instinct, for survival, for protection, from predators whether it is plants, or other predators, band together for survival. To look at it…it resembles the Hyacinth Flower a small fragrant plant, which stands strong and beautiful. Their (Fatted bug) banding together against a predator ensures their survival.

The Fatted Bug's quest for survival should open our eyes to the fact that we cannot survive in this life alone either on our journey to our eternal home; alone we can compare our size (strength against Satan) without Jesus Christ to a Fatted Bug. It is necessary that we too surround ourselves with our fellow brethren for the same strength that the Fatted Bugs have when banned together.

We know the predator we face, which is much more dangerous than any predator's ability to destroy here on earth. There are different predators man fear, but none is deadly as the one whose wiles can cause our spiritual destruction and cost us our eternal home and peace with God.

Hyacinthus is a symbol of peace, commitment, beauty, also power, and pride. The Hyacinth Flowers often found in Christian Churches of this century are symbols of happiness and love.

Each member of the Lord's Body, in and of themselves, is ineffective against Satan's predatory wiles; however, like the Fatted Bug, the members of the Lord's Body as a whole (banded together) can stand against our common enemy Satan. In Heaven, this is a beautiful sight; this strength sends up a delightfully fragrant aroma that is pleasing to God.

Satan prowling around is dangerous. We try to avoid being unaware, though we know this about him, still let our guards down sometimes, without realizing it. Paul reminds us to, *"Put on the whole armor of God that you might be able to fight against the wiles of the devil," [Ephesians 6:10-20].*

We wear the whole armor because we do not know at what moment what part of our spiritual body he will attack. Cracks in our homes allow bugs, insects, or other undesirable elements in. We fill in all cracks with physical putty in our homes. We can fill in our spiritual crack with spiritual putty. Contrariwise, with the cracks filled with the physical putty lasts for a while; on the other hand, with the spiritual putty, it is a continuous effort daily to keep out or eliminate undesirable elements of sin Satan forces or will force if we do not remain well-suited for the battle, in our spiritual lives.

We have the instructions for looking for and filling cracks or weak areas of our faith with Spiritual Putty (Scripture) when serving God, *"Study to show thyself approved unto God, a workman need not be ashamed rightly dividing the Word of truth," [2 Timothy 2:15].*

I defined Satan's schemes with verbs (actions) or with adjectives (descriptive). I considered these four areas in the predatory actions of Satan against God's people: stalking (verb), patrolling (verb), prowling (verb), and roaming (verb) (SPPR):

- **Stalking** is to follow, creep upon, ambush, haunt, hunt, and shadow. This world is Satan's haunt; he tries to permeate his spirit of evilness in a pervasive way into your mind. The evilness he peddles as good can molest you spiritually if you are not aware of his schemes. Presenting evil as good is a scheme of Satan, which will inhabit your mind and soul if allowed.

- **Patrolling** is to guard, protect, watching, walking the beat, or range. In this sense, the word patrol is a verb. He protects his established territory continually expanding it geographically with his spirit of evilness.
- **Prowling** is to move stealthily, cruise, hunt, lurk, range, rove, scavenge, skulk, snake, or steal. Satan moves with precision. When we think of cruising…smooth comes to my mind hunting the next victim in a defined range at that time. A scavenger looks for dead or unwanted items as with a scavenger hunt humans participate in for fun: they look for certain items that might not be desirable, are forgotten, or are rejected by others.
- **Roaming** is to wander about, drift, meander, like a vagabond (adjective), gallivant, unsettled, nomadic, and transient. Satan knows his eternal home with God is lost to him. The Scripture mentioned another vagabond Cain because the aroma of his sacrifice was not pleasing to God because of jealousy, rose up, and slew his brother Abel referenced in Book One, Chapter Nine, [Eve's Choice: The Results].

Satan is hunting chasing for a kill, looking for that scent of disobedience and weakness. Disobedience and defiance have an aroma to them displeasing to God but pleasing to Satan.

- *Check your garments sister, check the scent, who does it please, the one and only God and Savior of the Universe, or the god of this world?*

Satan is on a mission. All souls are under his scrutiny.

Satan is a deceiver-in-chief of this world. His aim, the sole purpose is to destroy. There is no good in him.

We are almost in a steeplechase barely ahead of him. His schemes change when he must fulfill that quest. We can be sure he is an excellent investigator when he goes after a victim he has a list of "what" is lacking in your service to God that he can target working from the root of the weakness upward.

In this sense, the definition of the word scheme I used is as an adjective, it describes one that is deceitful and sly. Paul said, "*We are not unaware of his schemes,*" [Ibid].

His attacks are in a calculative, cunning, and crafty manner. His schemes are well defined, almost artful. He has – had centuries to perfect them. He, as the common phrase used, "knows every trick in the book," because he is the master of trickery and in an underhanded slippery scientific way, wily. We say this of a fox, consider his ways, and put Satan in that fill-in-the-blank paragraph of your life.

There are many predators on earth in the animal kingdom at all levels. Think of just one with moves that are plotting, stalking, crouching, and watching the target it intends to kill. Any weakness in the predator's target or their separation from the herd can be and is deadly. The predator searches (roams) to identify, locate, and plan to the minute, the time to take the target down.

The female Lionesses are expert hunters. They are the most precise hunters of the cat class, just watching them in a documentary is frightening just imagine coming in contact with one. I saw a female Lion at the Gulf Breeze Zoo, in Florida, years ago, when reflecting on this visit, just looking at her from an observation deck is scary. With that description in mind, translate this powerful female predator with the cunning and wiles she has to the spiritual predator we face. As dangerous as she is, we can multiply this exponentially when it comes to the adversary with which we have to deal. Satan is more dangerous than any other predator on earth one might encounter. The Scripture warns us of his wiles. We as Christians are wise to remember this fact and wear that warning as a frontlet before our eyes.

Satan, with his predatory skills, is a humbugger, he deals in deception, trickery, he will mislead, fool, hoodwink, hoax, dupe, and takes you in. Peter describes with these adjectives the character of his actions and warns us in this way, "*Be sober, be vigilant; because your adversary the devil, as a roaring lion, walked about, seeking whom he may devour,*" *[I Peter 5:8].*

The people of God cannot participate in any of the deceptions he pushes. John also reminds us, "*He that commits sin is of the devil; for the devil sinned from the beginning,*" *[I John 3:8].*

The Book of Jude tells us about the evilness of Satan. He has no scruples for who/whom he goes after. He argued for the body of Moses, but the Archangel Michael did not say anything to condemn Satan though he spoke evil of Moses, "*But even the Archangel Michael, when he was disputing with the devil about the body of Moses did not condemn him for slander but said, "The Lord rebuke thee,*" *[Luke 9].*

Yet when we follow the example of the Archangel Michael, we say the same, *"The Lord rebuke thee," [Ibid],* or as Jesus said to Peter proposing that He does not go to Jerusalem to fulfill the purpose for His being on earth, *"Get thee behind me Satan," [Ibid].*

If Michael the Archangel with his power and might recognized that only God's power exceeds Satan, we should also recognize this fact that we cannot deal with Satan; he is a roaring lion ready to devour.

Lions are deadly and frightening; they are the largest predator on earth in the cat family. He has no mercy on his victims; you cannot entreat his favor, beg off his attack until a later day, outrun him when he is attacking; nor will climbing a tree help, he is a cat. Cats are skillful. They are experts at climbing, scaling trees, and hunting.

Translate the deadly abilities of a Lion to Satan. Also, look at the male Lion: his mane is impressive, his power is impressive, and his speed is amazing, standing against a skyline, he is beautiful, this is a deceptive way to view him: he is deadly. I think of the movie the Lion King, it is fun for children to enjoy as a cartoon; however, a Lion is not a cartoon, the danger they pose is a reality as with the danger that surrounds Satan.

Satan comes to humans in different ways. He will provide temporarily any scenario you might desire to lure you into one of his traps. We are to take heed when God warns us of his wiles. Wiles are tricks or stratagems practiced for ensnaring or deception; he is a sly insidious predator using any artifice to destroy his victims. When one is insidious, they proceed in a gradual, subtle way, but with harmful effect. Satan's end game is always the same, it never changes, entrapment of your soul, which leads to destruction.

One who practices artifice uses clever, cunning, or expedients devices, especially used to trick or deceive others; using this stratagem: he is good at planning and scheming, especially one used to outwit an opponent or achieve an end. All of these describe Satan our adversary. He is, from the beginning, a practiced liar, deceiver, and instigator. Sometimes his devices appear to glitters like gold or can be as dark as a December night when the clouds hide the moon.

There is nothing bright about Satan and his strategy; it leads ultimately to spiritual and physical ruin. He ravishes your souls and heart leading you out on the same limb he led Eve; it had a dropping-off point with her using the wings he provided for her flight to error and disobedience.

Your soul is red meat to Satan. He is prowling like a Lion. Your weaknesses are a target for him. This fact is one we need to be constantly mindful of in our daily walk not just at certain times, but daily. As the Lion ravages its victim's body, there is nothing left after he devours the flesh except residue. Put Satan's name there instead of the Lion. He eats away at your heart and soul until there is the only residue of whom you once were leaving no way for you to bounce back.

The wiles of Satan are like the weeds I used as an example in Chapter 14 in Book 1: Declutter our Lives Pruning and Weeding our Gardens. Weeds will continue to pop up and eat up all the good nutrients the soil produces for the healthy plants; additionally, entwining themselves around the root of those plants if allowed. We wear garments of intent in this sense. We are on a pursuit of intent to continually prune and weed our spiritual gardens that there be no roots of evil (Satan wiles) siphoning off the healthy fertilizer, [The Word of God], from the healthy soils, of which our Salvation is planted.

The efficaciousness of Satan's playbook is capable of producing the results (effects) he so desires. The history of his long-standing success, recorded in the lives of the ones we read of in Scripture he trapped by his ability to use it to his advantage. Watch and pray should be part of our daily diet and service to God. We bring our bodies under submission daily. It is not a one-time effort, but we awaken each day with this in our Spiritual "To do" list. When the focus of our mind (heart) is on Jesus, our bodies follow the direction our heart gives it.

Our attitudes, sisters, are what get us to the next level with bringing our lives and bodies in subjection to Christ. The head controls our body and not vice versa. We are at a constant war in our minds fighting two battles: fighting against Satan and battling our way through this life and all its challenges to be deserving of that Mansion (Place) Christ went back to Heaven to prepare for us. He fought the battles life presents and that sisters should give us hope both spiritually and physically.

Our Savior suffered while on earth; therefore, he understands what we undergo in our daily walk. If we remind ourselves every day, of this fact; it makes the journey we undertake as people of Christ less stressful and hope brighter because we can stand strong in our Faith... *"Faith is the substance of things hoped for and the evidence of things not seen," [Hebrews 11:1].*

Heaven is waiting at the end of that tedious journey...

The Woman at the well blesses, became blessed with the healthy soil of the Word of God physically refreshed the Savior with water from Jacob's well, and become refreshed by the Savior with the eternal waters of Salvation.

CHAPTER FIVE

# GARMENTS OF THE WOMAN AT THE WELL REFRESHING THE SAVIOR

Opportunity is ever before us. Jesus took the opportunity afforded Him, as did the woman at the well, *"There cometh a woman of Samaria to draw water: Jesus said unto her, "Give me to drink." (For His disciples were gone away unto the city to buy meat.)* Then said the woman of Samaria unto him, *"How is it that thou, being a Jew, ask a drink of me, which am a woman of Samaria? For the Jews have no dealings with the Samaritans."* Jesus answered and said unto her, *"If thou knew the gift of God, and who it is that said to thee, Give me to drink; thou would have asked of Him, and He would have given thee Living Water."*

*"The woman said unto him, "Sir, thou hast nothing to draw with, and the well is deep: from whence then hast thou that living water? Art thou greater than our father Jacob, which gave us the well, and drank thereof himself, and his children, and his cattle"?* Jesus answered and said unto her, *"Whosoever drink of this water shall thirst again: But whosoever drink of the water that I shall give him shall never thirst; but the water that I shall give him shall be in him a well of water springing up into everlasting life."* The woman said unto him," *Sir, give me this water, that I thirst not, neither come hither to draw,"* [John 4:7-15].

An opportunity exists with every encounter we make; we must ask ourselves if we wear the garments as Jesus did of looking for every opportunity that presents itself. Alternatively, looking for opportunities starting with the person where they are as Christ did with the Samaritan Woman about thirst and the living water.

We all have areas of our lives that need improvements. Christ does not consider one sin above the other or one sin worse than any other sins. John the Apostle reminds us that, *"All unrighteousness is sin: and there is a sin not unto death,"* [I John 5:17].

We, by nature, know right and wrong. The woman at the well knew the sin she participated in was wrong. It was a hard life for a single woman to face at that time. We see individual examples of women whose survival depended on, or they thought it did their involvement with men, especially other women's husbands.

This is an age-old interaction between males and females as long as there are females men will flock to or take their invitation to come. Solomon wrote, "*But whoso commit adultery with a woman lack understanding: he that doeth it destroys his own soul*," *[Proverbs 6:32].*

Proverbs warn the man about the wiles of a woman of questionable character. She whispers, "*Stolen waters are sweet, and bread eaten in secret is pleasant*," *[Proverbs 9:17].*

The Preacher (Qoheleth), charges us not to be, "*Overly righteous or overly wicked.*" He comments further that, *"In this meaningless life of mine, I have seen both of these the righteous perishing in their righteousness and the wicked living long in their wickedness. Do not be overly righteous nor be overly wise, why destroy yourself. Do not be over wicked and do not be a fool–why die before your time. It is good to grasp the one and not let go of the other. Whosoever fears God will avoid all extremes,"* *[Ecclesiastes 7:15-17].*

Solomon warns us in this way about false righteousness using legality to push righteousness that is borne subjectively from our perception of what is right and using a legal stance to do so. Besides, immorality is just as much a sin as over righteousness. We are righteous in our eyes and care only about what we see or think of as right.

After we hear the Word of God from others, we at that point study and continue to learn and develop a relationship with God that He desires of all His Children. The woman at the well started her journey with belief. The evidence of Christ being a Prophet was her thoughts, which stood before her. A man telling her everything she had ever done. He knew of the five husbands she had been involved with and the one she is involved with now is not her husband.

Adultery is and has always been, distasteful in God's sight. A change of life and focus was on the horizon for (Chance) the Woman at the Well. Acceptance of the living waters Jesus offered her that she would never thirst again was a renewal of her life, thoughts, actions, desires, and daily activities. She would never need to draw from another well to quench her thirst. She had found one she could be married to for an eternity. As with anything in life, whether business or spirituality, opportunity costs.

We must choose our opportunities wisely; we can only take advantage of but one opportunity at a time. When two presents themselves as they did for Chance; she could have chosen to go back and continue to drink of the bitter waters of adultery and fornication or draw from the Well and drink of the eternal waters that offered her the opportunity to enjoy Salvation and the flowing living waters only Jesus can give, which changed her life.

She looked a little further down the road of life's choices and saw the eternal living waters Christ offered to accept the new life and obey His will for her by leaving a life of nakedness and shame and put on the new white garments of purity and Salvation He offered. The Waters of Life flow through our hearts and soul daily if that is the opportunity we chose. The opportunity would cost had she chosen to go back to her everyday activity of adultery and fornication; that cost would be an eternity of separation from God and Jesus Christ.

We cannot walk in life living in two worlds living day to day fulfilling our desires and the needs of the flesh and serve God in the same body. We cannot serve the mammon of fleshly desire and please Christ at the same time. The brushstrokes of Salvation paint a full canvas of our lives and not a small picture or portrait, which leaves no room for other outlying brush strokes on the canvas of our lives. Jesus said, "*I and my Father are One,*" *[John 10:30]*. God said, "*I am the Lord thy God, thou shall have no other God before Me,*" *[Exodus 20:3]*. "*Thou shall love the Lord thy God with all thy heart, with all thy mind, and all thy soul,*" *[Matthew 22:37]*.

The portrait of this life, as with the Samaritan Woman Chance, only allows one artist at a time, we choose who we want to paint our eternity. We can only wear the garment of one, either the God of Heaven when we drink the Waters of Salvation we never thirst again or the god of this world who only offers continuous thirst and an eternity with him away from God. The life Chance once lived she knew would not be fulfilling to her ever again. She counted all loss to the world as a gain for Jesus Christ. She knew Christ did not see her as a Samaritan Woman, but one of His creations who He offered the opportunity to live a Holy life before Him.

The Scripture tells us God (Christ) cares for all His creation, "*Then Peter openedhismouth, and said, of a truth, I perceive that God is no respecter of persons,*" *[Acts 10:34]: but accept all who desires to come to Him.*" Also, "*There is neither Jew nor Greek, neither bond nor free, male or female: for all is one in Jesus Christ,*" *[Galatians 3:28].*

The Woman at the Well accepted Jesus and spread the good news to all who would hear her. Her garment of chance was as her name in this chapter, "Chance," she took that opportunity to change her life and become an obedient servant to Jesus our Savior. That opportunity did cost her...the cost was one she was willing to pay. She wore or rather changed her garment to one of joy, peace, longsuffering, love, temperance, and bought the garment of Her body and its desires under subjection to Jesus Christ to love and serve Him in Spirit and Truth leaving the slavery of sins her life wrote for her until the point she met Her Lord and Savior.

The Samaritan Woman went to the well to get physical water to quench her thirst and received the water, which has an eternal benefit to it. She came with only a water pot and a thirst and left with the waters of eternal life flowing filling her heart never to thirst again. It takes determination for us, as it did for her, to choose to inherit Eternity.

The woman at the well was drinking from a broken cistern one that held only water for a short time. It would not be necessary for her to continue returning to Jacob's well for the Spiritual water. The eternal water offered by our Savior offers does not come from a broken cistern nor is it dipped from a physical well. The Eternal Water from Christ is through a Cistern that is not nor can be broken. Christ is the unending water eternally and eliminates thirst water that cures the thirst for the Soul.

Digging for the truth requires strength of determination using our muscle and a shovel of faith...

CHAPTER SIX

# STRENGTH OF DETERMINATION AND THE SHOVEL OF FAITH OUR GARMENTS OF DIGGING FOR THE TRUTH

*"The Lord is in His Holy Temple, the Lord's throne is in Heaven: His eyes behold, His eyelids try, the children of men," [Psalms 11:4].*

In Egypt, the People of God used mud and straw to make bricks and build a future for the people (Egyptians), who had enslaved them. Our mud and straw are the Word of God and our willingness to obey God's Word builds for us an eternal future. They also, over time, because of the decisions made by their taskmaster as additional punishment, had to glean stubbles of straw to make their quota of bricks. They gleaned stubbles of straw by night, made bricks, and built the cities of Pharaoh by day. They had little time to rest. This is the look of life in the clutches of Satan; he is good at adding more misery to your life. Life in-of-itself is unforgiving we do not need any added misery and difficulty.

I think of this in respect especially to gleaning in our service to God in the 21st- Century. We need to glean from the Word of God the Plan of Salvation that is necessary for us to take advantage of that Salvation purchased by Christ on the Cross. Shank (2012), in the book, *Muscle and a Shovel*, purposes that we must glean, dig for the truth with the muscles of our desires to be pleasing to God and obey His desires for our lives.

In an excerpt from Chapter 40, Shank wrote, **"Yes It Is about You!"** Satan appears as he has throughout time as something other than what he is. He has deceived countless men and women through his powers, through signs that seem heavenly in origin, and by remarkable wonders. Why have countless souls been and continue to be deceived? *"**Because they do not love nor will they receive (obey) the truth,**" [Ibid] (P5 P348).*

Satan has numerous powers of deception in his playbook of schemes.

It takes time and effort to glean from the Word of God. When we do come to that field where we know that a Pearl of Great Price is hidden, as the Scripture reminds us, in one of Jesus' Parables, the man bought the field that he could own that Pearl of Great price. Christ, through His Word is bidding us come is that field of Salvation. Until we understand and believe that life and Salvation are, only in Jesus Christ, we will not come out of the world because Satan deceives people into believing if they are good, they are spiritually safe, and God is pleased, which of course, is false.

Growth requires discernment of the Scripture; the only way we grow from infancy to maturity, *"For when for the time ye ought to be teachers, ye have need that one teach you again which be the first principles of the oracles of God; and are become such as have need of milk, and not of strong meat. For everyone that uses milk is unskillful in the word of righteousness: for he is a babe. But strong meat belongs to them that are of full age, even those who by reason of use have their senses exercised to discern both good and evil,"* [Hebrews 5:12-14].

As babies grow they need less milk, (babies cannot digest meat or solid food), but as their teeth grow in, can chew and digest solid foods, so it is with the Word of God. Our ability to digest the Word of God comes with growth, maturity, and understanding which requires study as Paul instructed Timothy, *"Study to show thyself approved unto God; a workman need not be ashamed rightly dividing the Word of truth,"* [2 Timothy 2:15].

To accomplish this takes practicing what we learn in our lives with understanding then growth comes. This is a picture of a maturing Christian. The responsibility of Christians is to teach the elementary principles of faith to all believers. It is essential Christians teach these principles and not move past the basics of faith and babes in Christ will then understand that Christ is the fulfillment of the Law. He is the High Priest, as was Melchizedek Priest of Salem, who has no beginning or end, according to Scripture, but a Priest forever, as is, our Lord and Savior. Christ is our focus; therefore, we should have no other belief except the one He left for us through His Body, which is the Church that bears His name. Christ fulfilled the Law on the Cross of Calvary.

We are to be baptized (purchase that field) so that we might have access to the truth (The Gospel of Salvation) hidden there waiting for us to take advantage of our purchase and live for Jesus, sending up a sweet-smelling aroma of obedience and humility submitting our lives to Christ. We are to bring our bodies and souls in subjection to His will. *"But I keep under my body and bring it into subjection: lest that by any means, when I have preached to others, I myself should be a castaway," [I Corinthians 9:27].*

We are encouraged to reach outside of the inner man, and we will come in contact with Rivers of Living Waters, *"I thank my God upon every remembrance of you, always in every prayer of mine for you all making request with joy, for your fellowship in the gospel from the first day until now. Being confident of this very thing, that He which hath begun a good work in you will perform it until the day of Jesus Christ," [Philippians 1:3-6].*

Truth is painful; pain brings about pearls of exceeding beauty. Growth is painful regardless of whether they are human, animal, or plant. Growth is a process and laborious. Inherent to growth is a struggle and with labor comes pain, but in the end, if we are faithful, the results are the healing waters of Heaven to partake of the Fruit of the Tree of Life. When we are refined in the fires of struggle and growth, the luster of the Pearl's (faithfulness and obedience) beauty shines through, for all to see.

Pearls can be individual or on a string, but they are always attached to something. Strings of pearls not only include our Spiritual family, but also our friends, physical family, co-workers, acquaintances, husbands, even enemies are on that string we cannot get through life without encountering an enemy. Satan (our enemy) is common to everyone.

We, like pearls, as did Joseph in *[Genesis 6:50]*, face this struggle and growth in search for the truth: irritants, hate, and attempted seduction by wiles of Satan. Potiphar's wife accused Joseph of making advances to her, which was an untruth; he was a prisoner of his faith and faced jail. He believed and trusted in the God of Heaven that whatever happened He would be with him. It is also a possibility that we as servants of God can be subject to some incarceration because of an untruth, we just never know what fate will befall us during our growth process, in our service to God, in the search for the truth, or the overall journey during our lifetime.

The Word of God covering us should be our motivation, as it was for Joseph. We constantly face the challenges of evil and good on our journey; all of this is in digging for the truth and then obeying it as Peter told the Sanhedrin when they told them not to teach in Jesus' name, *"The Apostles were brought in and made to appear before the Sanhedrin to be questioned by the high priest. "We gave you strict* orders not to teach in this name," he said. "Yet you have filled Jerusalem with your teaching and are determined to make us guilty of this man's blood." Peter and the other apostles replied, "We must obey God rather than human beings!" [Acts 5:27-29].

Scriptures give us a definition of Truth. Jesus said, "I am the Way, the Truth, and the Life", [John 14:6; and "In Him was Life, and the Life was the light of men," [John 1:4].

Sisters, we are standing on the backs of those who were successful in serving God and staying faithful without fail, until the end. Though they went through suffering at the measure we cannot understand yet, that enormous level of suffering has put a positive light and hope for all those who have stood for the truth and following faithfully facing all that the adversary (Satan) of man can cause in their lives.

We have hope. Christ said, "Live faithful until the end and I will never forsake you or leave you," [Ibid]. Christ suffered for humanity as a whole. All those whose backs we stand on suffered at some point in their lives because they stood firm for the truth and so can and must we stand firm for the truth. Jesus said, "I am the Way, the Truth, and the Life," [Ibid].

What we might face causes fear. We know it does, but that fear is cast out by perfect love. Our faith in Christ has His promise. We live day-by-day and do not borrow from tomorrow. The promise is only today. Matthew writes, "Sufficient unto today is the evil (trouble) thereof," [Matthew 6:34b].

Hence, we have enough to deal with today, not tomorrow – tomorrow has not arrived, so let us deal with today and have hope for tomorrow. The only thing we can do for tomorrow is make plans, whether we are living or not when it arrives. James notes, "Now listen to you who say today or tomorrow we will go to this or that city, spend a year there, carry on business, and make money. Listen to James, "Whereas ye know not what shall be on the morrow. For what is your life? It is even a vapor, that appeareth for a little time, and then vanishes away," [James 4:13-14].

The truth still stands tall whether we as humans want to admit it or not. God's Word does not fail when sent to perform the work of God. It (His Word) does not return to Him void, but accomplishes what He pleases not what we please, "So shall My word be that goeth forth out of My mouth: it shall not return unto Me void, but it shall accomplish that which I please, and it shall prosper in the thing whereto I sent it," [Isaiah 55:11].

We note the two words used. To prosper is to (accomplish) and void is (empty). Prosper is an action verb defined as being successful. To Void is a noun meaning an empty space, which we should note that God's Word does not leave empty spaces nor is there anything on earth that can void (negate or nullify) His commands.

Truth is that which is true or according to fact or reality. The Scriptural definition of Truth is the pattern the people of God use as their guide and not what man thinks is truth. Christ is our confirmation of Truth – Truth is not an affirmation (someone supporting our belief) of what we want it to be, but what is actuality (facts). Christ is the light of the world, we as people of God reflect that light as the moon reflects the light of the sun.

**Truth cannot be compromised, rather it glorifies God,** "*If any man speaks, let him speak as the oracles of God; if any man minister, let him do it as of the ability which God giveth: that God in all things may be glorified through Jesus Christ, to whom be praise and dominion forever and ever. Amen,*" *[I Peter 4:11]; [I Kings 3:23-27; Matthew 26: 3, 64; Galatians 1:8-9].*

**We must search, for the truth and then seek to please God.** After finding it, accept it as a whole and not in bits and pieces according to the situation at that time, "*By Myself, I can do nothing; I judge only as I hear, and My judgment is just, for I seek not to please Myself but Him who sent Me,*" *[John 5:30; 2 Timothy 3:16-17].*

**The Word of God is a Treasure, of knowledge and wisdom,** "*My goal is that they may be encouraged in heart and united in love; so that they may have the full riches of complete understanding, in order, that they may know the mystery of God, namely, Christ, in whom are hidden all the treasures of wisdom and knowledge,*" *[Colossians 2:2-3].*

Peter encourages new Christians (babes in Christ) as well this warning can apply to all servants of God: time is, of the essence, being diligent is prudent, and staying aware is wise. There are three ways to make your calling an election sure:

**Following the Guide,** "*After having escaped the corruption in the world caused by evil desires: For this very reason, make every effort to add to your faith goodness and to goodness, knowledge, and to knowledge, self-control, and to self-control, perseverance, and to perseverance, godliness, and to godliness, mutual affection, and to mutual affection love. For if you possess these qualities in increasing measure, they* *will keep you from being ineffective and unproductive in your knowledge of our Lord Jesus Christ," [2 Peter 1:4c-8].*

**Recognizing the Danger**, *"But there were also false prophets among the people, just as there will be false teachers among you: they will secretly introduce destructive heresies, even denying the sovereign Lord who bought them – bringing swift destruction on themselves. Many will follow their depraved conduct and will bring the way of truth into dispute. In their greed, these teachers will exploit you with fabricated stories," [2 Peter 2: 1-3a].*

**Believing in that Hope**, *"But do not forget this one thing, dear friends, with the Lord a day is like a thousand years, and a thousand years are like a day. The Lord is not slack in keeping His promise, as some understand slackness. Instead, He is patient with you, not wanting anyone to perish, but everyone to come to repentance. Therefore, dear friends, since you have been forewarned be on your guard, so that you may not be carried away by the error of the lawless and fall from your secure position. But grow in the grace and knowledge of our Lord and Savior Jesus Christ. To Him be glory now and forever, Amen," [2 Peter 3:8-9, 17-18].*

We as Christians are not in the consoling business, but the truth and righteousness business. We cannot placate (pacify) the feelings of others saying what they want to hear and not what the Truth of God is ... God does not accept our excuses, nor will He accept ones that are consoled into thinking they are right in what they are doing when we know very well it is not right. Obedience is according to God's plan for a man, not our or your plan. Jesus has the last word on where we spend eternity, why can we not allow Him to make those decisions in our life now!

Christ left specific instructions to life and righteousness unchangeable and fixed through eternity as long as God lives. There is a life of peace beyond the darkness of this world and its veil of tears. A place where there are no tears, heartache, pain, or death ... only life and peace with our Triune God who is worthy of the battles we face in this world that is attached to one's life, and the Spiritual battles Satan wages against the people of God.

When we neglect to allow truth to be the foundation of our lives then sin will fill that vacancy in our lives. At that point, we, like the nation of Israel, could/ cannot correct the sinful path they (we), were (are) on. Humans, regardless of the century they live in cannot overcome sin in-and-of themselves. The power to conquer sin belongs to God alone. Isaiah reminds us how important truth is to God in our life, "*Truth is nowhere to be found, and whoever shuns evil becomes a prey. The Lord looked and was displeased that there was no justice. He saw that there was no one; He was appalled that there was no one to intervene, so His own arm achieved salvation for Him and His own righteousness sustained Him,*" [Isaiah 59:15-16].

Eternity with God is the pearl of great price in the field of this world with the struggles we face so that we might inherit eternity. Our Father is worth any struggle we face. Our Lord and Savior Jesus Christ thought us worth the battle He won ending with His Crucifixion on the cruel Cross-of-Calvary…no matter how many times that I read the Crucifixion account in the Bible it is fresh each time I read it. Thank God for the constant reminder of the price Christ paid. Each Lord's Day sisters we are reminded, of this fact less we forget the cost of our Salvation, '*This do in remembrance of Me, for as often as you eat this bread and drink this cup you do shew the Lord's Death until He comes,*" [Ibid].

Truth is necessary. We in good conscience cannot speak any less. Saying what others want to hear will not bode well for them or us. By neglecting this fact puts us on a collision course with the Righteous God of Heaven where truth, not consolation will prevail. Serving God in obedience and righteousness according to the Scripture is essential for life here and life in eternity.

Biblical Truth is dogmatic, and compromise is not an option. Truth is unbending and fixed about the Word of God. We cannot live our lives in the rearview mirror; even life there is temporary.

Lot's Wife and the Rearview mirror …turning and the single glance back… the painful cost …

CHAPTER SEVEN

# LOT'S WIFE AND THE PROVERBIAL REARVIEW MIRROR EXPERIENCE HER GARMENTS OF FOCUS: WHICH ONES ARE YOU WEARING?

Ms. Lot had a proverbial rearview mirror experience. We cannot drive a car and fix our eyes on the rearview mirror of life when it comes to living and the choices we make. What is behind us is only important in the sense that it affords us a learning experience. Our focusshould beon the road ahead and what is on each side of it.

God created man with peripheral vision to use. We should ask these questions of ourselves!

- *What effect will the issues in front of me have on my life?*
- *What is in front of me is paramount: but what are the effects of the outliers around me?*
- *The impact these outliers have in my life, will thatmannerbe negative or positive?*

Had Ms. Lot been vigilant and took the [Word] of the Angels at face value, she could have most likely prevented the turpitude of sins of which her daughterswere involved. She could have guided her daughters in a godlymannerand Lot would have the strength a wife gives her husband as his helpmeet (by being an emotional, spiritual, and physical asset) and friend. A threefold cord has durability, God, Lot, and her, *"And if one prevail against him, two shall withstand him; and a threefold cord is not quickly broken,"* *[Ecclesiastics 4:12].*

Her actions (disobedience) also penned the example, for her daughters, who carried Sodom in a bag. They left Sodom and Gomorrah but took with them the deep-seated sinful ways of those twin-cities. Lot's wife, looking back, indicated the regret she had in leaving her home, the magnificent cities, their family, friends, and their way of life (peradventure even looking back for curiosity)! We know the rhyme about curiosity killing the cat.

Lot prospered in Sodom. All of this was in her rearview mirror. She took her eyes off the road to safety and suffered a spiritual collision with God's commands of obedience. He put their feet on a path of life that led them to safety, and she wanted to live a rearview mirror moment and it cost her – her life and her family. Not only did she pay; but also, her family paid through suffering as well, which the sins and defiance of God will for their lives seen in the following generations of Lot's descendants.

When we make decisions or take actions in direct defiance of God's command, it cost our families as well. The Physics of this is as Newton's Third Law defines, *"For every action, there is an equal and opposite reaction."* – "The statement means that in every interaction, there is a pair of forces acting on the two interacting objects. The size of the forces on the first object equals the size of the forces on the second object."

Our decisions, as with Ms. Lot, affected all her family's tomorrows, which God blessed them to see, as well will affect us in the same manner [principle]. Regret is an unrelenting taskmaster. Sisters, consider these thoughts were a possibility that went through her mind in her last moment of life as we evaluate the decisions we make at certain times in our lives:

- *What do you think that she said, at that moment, she knew that her disobedience was costing her – her life?*
- *What have I done?*
- *What will happen to my family?*
- *Who will guide my daughters?*
- *I have let my husband down; what have I done?*
- *I have defied the God of Heaven; what have I done?*

The Scripture speaks to what the direct effects are of the sins of disobedience and looking back will cost. We see what Ezekiel's warning is of the actions, of men at that time. The scene God showed he penned in Scripture, for a rearview mirror moment, from which we can benefit, *"And He brought me into the inner court of the Lord's house, and behold, at the door of the temple of the Lord, between the porch and the altar, were about five and twenty men, with their backs toward the temple of the Lord; and their faces toward the east; and they worshipped the [sun] toward the east."*

Ezekiel wrote, *"Then He said unto me, hast thou seen this, O son of man? Is it a light thing to the house of Judah that they commit the abominations, which they commit here? For they have filled the land with violence and have returned to provoke Me to anger: and, lo, they put the branch to their nose," [Ezekiel 8:16–17].*

What our harvest yields is from the seeds we plant.

- *We ask ourselves, is this the harvest I want? "Do not be deceived: God is not mocked, for whatever one sows, that will he also reap," [Galatians 6:7].*

This is a fact we cannot get around…

We see so much of the action/reaction, affect/effect in our world today. We see it especially with ineffective communication; we see it with the foods we eat; the medications we take, and the lives we choose to live.

Rearview mirror type living gives one a clouded view, taking away their focus from true life, in real-time. Once we make the decision or choice to come out of the world to Christ, we cannot continue to desire the life we once lived. We came to Christ because we realized through study and teaching that, *"All that is in the world is the lust of the flesh, the lust of the eye, and the pride of life, is not of the Father, but of the world," [1John 2:16].*

Ask yourself this question:

- *Why would I desire to go back to my old life after being spiritually and emotionally free and cleansed through Baptism receiving the Gift of the Holy Spirit?*

The very reason we desire to change our life and come out of living in the world is to be one of those who are in the world but not of the world any longer. We are speaking here in both the physical and the spiritual sense. We know physically we are living in the world but spiritually we have changed our residence to the Kingdom of God that Christ purchased with His Blood for our Salvation.

While physically driving vehicles, just a glance in the rearview mirror, even for a short period, can cost us, we can rear-end another vehicle that can cause a chain reaction injuring others, including ourselves. This equal looking down, looking away, texting, and driving, which are all under the umbrella of rearview mirror-type actions.

However, when we spiritually turn all the way around and look back, as Ms. Lot did, we suffer great losses spiritually and physically encompassing and influencing those around us and our and their entire life. It does not just affect our family but has an effect on those who are in our paradigm of influence as well as dimming the lights of our ability to inspire others for Christ. We are to let our lights shine positively, *"Let your light so shine before men, that they may see your good works, and glorify your Father which is in heaven," [Matthew 5:16].*

- *What light does your garment reflect for your family, friends, and onlookers who know you are a Christian and that you chose to leave the worldly residence (old life) and live in the Spiritual Kingdom Christ purchased, and serve God when you turn back?*

It could mean someone's Salvation, cause a sister or brother to stumble, or give someone when it comes to their spirituality, a false sense of security, Jesus said unto him, *"No man, having puthishandtothe plow, and looking back, is fit fortheKingdom of God," [Luke 9:62].*

We cannot in this day and time, wear the rearview mirror garments that Ms. Lot and others wore in defiance of God's command for our lives. God knows what is best for us and it is not always popular in our minds. Sisters, we can greatly shape our environments, as we know, from studying God's Word, using that garment of encouragement to be a bright shining light for Christ in others life and not a dimly lit candle that flickers out at the first light breezing of the winds of trials and tribulations. Our actions can put out a potential bright light for Christ.

Take a mental journey back thousands of years to the scene, of the destruction, of Sodom and Gomorrah.

- *If you could ask the wife of Lot what she would do differently what do, you think she would say?*
- *Would she look back? Alternatively, she could have joined her husband Lot in following his example of obedience to the commands, of God; or,*
- *Would she tell you to follow the messenger's instructions to the letter?*
- *Then ask yourself, if my looking back desiring even a morsel of my past life, would I risk the chance that – that one look or desire will pull me back?*
- *If I look back and desire that life in this 21st- Century, with all of the attractiveness it has to offer, am I strong enough at that point, to turn my back on the treasures of the world leave them behind and go forward toward Zion?*

Too often, our fellow sisters and brothers have faced these questions, as well as tests that come into their lives, about obedience. The Scripture gives us examples of those who desired what the world offers over the Gifts of God.

Remember the warning of our Savior, *"And Jesus said unto him, No man, having put his hand to the plow, and looking back, is fit for the Kingdom of God,"* [*Ibid*].

- *Would Lot's wife tell you it is deadly to defy God?*

Again, we see the Pillar of Salt, as a testament, resulting fromone-actof disobedience (hesitation). Also, the example of Eve and Adam; theywere expelledfrom the Garden of Eden. We can equate the Kingdom of Heaven in the same way. God does not accept any defiance of His commands or foot-dragging.

When He said do not look back, He was not just talking to hear Self-say something. He is God, Holy, Righteous, Worthy of Honor, Worthy of Praise, and Worthy of Obedience because He is the Creator of the Universe and our Lord and Savior. The idol gods (pleasures of this world) man are guilty of putting before Him has neither the power nor the ability to act, speak, bless, or punish, but rather worshiping them will cause one to lose their soul; gods that man makes are for man and not God. As well, there are many forms of false gods in this world and men make them to their perils. Humans, so many times, take God for granted. Statements of the like, 'God will understand.' He does understand human weaknesses and our propensity to sin. Henceforth, He also understands you (I) did not or does do what is commanded.

Paul tells us, *"For allhave sinned and fallen short of the glory of God,"* [*Romans 3:23*].

We cannot use this as an excuse to continue to sin; but use this to acquaint us with the knowledge that we can sin; then do all we can to avoid sinning. However, if we ask for forgiveness and repent of those sins, He is faithful and just to forgive us. When we know better and are told directly, as was the Wife of Lot, and we knowingly (willfully) sin regardless, we are in danger of the wrath of God, at all times, because we are consciously sinning. God does not accept excuses, reasons, or us putting it in an expectation mode of Him being the one who the burden is on, and none on the one who sinned, taking God for granted, in the end, is deadly.

Paul wrote God shows no favoritism to anyone, *"For there is no respecter of person with God," [Romans 2:11].*

God does not judge or apply His command by who is in power, has been successful, whether they are poor, or rich; nor does he judge by race. His Word is solid as the family of Lot found itto beso.

- *After we read the Biblical account of the escape from Sodom and Gomorrah, we cannot ask Ms. Lot if God meant what He said; nevertheless, we can ask ourselves if God changes His commandments or expectations for anyone?*
- *Contemplate this, the Biblical account of Ms. Lot then ask yourself if God meant what He said to Ms. Lot?*
- *What will your answers be after you sit and mull over the questions above?*

Consider, every aspect, before you look in the rearview mirror with thewishto go back into that life Christ's Blood washed you clean of, and you now wear those new garments of Christianity.

Rearview mirrors are also for safety. There is not always a negative aspect to it… it prevents accidents as well and helps uscheckwhat is happening around us; but we cannot dwell there for any period-of-time, wisdom dictates that we glance to take in the situation around us and then return our focus to the road ahead. Rearview mirror activity spiritually can help us avoid error and not be displeasing to our Lord and Savior, *"Thing written aforetime are written for our learning," [Romans 15:4-5].*

- *Why pay the price when we can quickly check by using that rearview mirror of the Word in The Old Testament, and New Testaments to know if the present path we are on is leading us to trouble or success?*

Eternity is a high price to pay to dwell on rearview mirror living. Biblical History record the price Ms. Lot paid she lost her physical life. When a man does not take God's warnings seriously: the pay rate, in the end, is costly. God does not change; He is just and righteous; His Word stands, and His promises are certain.

The Pillar of Salt that was once Ms. Lot stands as a reminder of the cost of defiance and disobedience, visually trying to walk on both sides of the fence. We will leavethe question ofwhere she spends Eternity with God because we cannot make that judgment.

Sisters, we cannot allow Satan to create in us a Negative Spiritual Attitude Attention Span. He wants humans to believe that we can live our lives in thewaywethinknecessary and still be pleasing to God.

Satan is masterful in taking Scripture out of context and assisting us in applying the Scripture to what we want to do. We must understand within the contextualism of the Scripture what God is saying to us and not allow Satan to pervert the Scripture and use it against us. Again, he will lead you into that **Negative Spiritual Attitude Attention Span**. He never uses the entire Scripture, but parts of it, putting verses together to say what you want it to say and mean what you want it to mean. He likes to push the snapshot view of the commands of God, another of his tricks. He is an opportunistic liar. Satan is recalcitrant opposing all authority. He has an obstinately uncooperative attitude toward authority or discipline and if we fall into his traps of pleasure will have the same attitude.

Comparatively so, a **Positive Spiritual Attitude Attention Span** comes with studying the Scripture to show our selves approved of God, as Paul wrote to Timothy in *[2 Timothy 2:15]*. Thenafter being aware of thecommands Scripture give us of what God wants for our lives and follow them. The Angels gave Ms. Lot the commands of God, she followed them only to a certain point and then allowed what was to become what is, and that became her destruction.

A guilty verdict is not what anyone wants in the present court systems we live under; certainly, we do not want a guilty verdict of disobedience from our Lord and Savior, the ramifications are far worse than a guilty verdict on earth. At least the one received in this physical life has a limit – the spiritual verdict is eternal, with no end, whether it is guilty or well done my good and faithful servant. We must rightly divide the Word of Truth. God will not accept our service under half-truths as pleasing to Him. The Scripture expresses consistently the fact that Satan is a genius of deception and disguise. We cannot ignore the basics of our faith and the commands that Jesus left for us.

- *Ask yourself often each day, 'whose voice am I hearing and listening (heeding) to?'*

Do not underestimate the powers of Satan in evilness, deceptions, divisiveness, or disdain for God and His people. Hate drives every action Satan takes. His every step is to create a false picture of God and His overall nature. Paul says, *"We are not unaware of his wiles," [Ibid]*.

He deceived Eve by quoting half-truths and Satan has not, nor will he ever change. He has, through the ages, fined-tuned his wiles and playbook of deception and isvery skillfulat it. He will create in your mind a Negative Spiritual Attitude Attention Span as he did in Ms. Lot. We cannot allow Satan to lead us into suffering in a pay-as-you-go life. Ms. Lot took her eyes off God and Hisdesirefor her to give her life to Him in service and obedience.

There are costs to everything we do and the decisions we make. This is not a sometimes, but every time, whether it is immediate or, in the future, it costs. Satan hates the fact his long-term decision of challenging God's power and authority cost him his soul and will spend an eternity in the Lake of Fire that burns with fire and brimstone, and where worms never die.

This is a picture of misery in his future and will be in ours (yours) if we fall prey to the Negative Spiritual Attitude Attention Span he pushes. He knew God created the universe and alltherein.

- *How would he a created being challenge the Creator?*
- *How would we (you) challenge the Creator?*
- *Do we allow our children to tell us what to do and defy our instructions to them in our efforts to guide them so they can growto beproductive spiritual servants in the Kingdom of God and responsible adults in this physical world?*

Ms. Lot's Positive Spiritual Attitude Attention Span was short-lived, and she looked back. Satan orchestrated herwishfor that old life after God's rescue. We can imagine he was busy reminding her: what sheleftand painted a dismal picture of the wilderness and what was ahead, and Ms. Lot fell prey to it. He will serve you and me from the same dish of deception as he did Ms. Lot.

Our focus is on what Scripture says to each of us individually," *So, as the Holy Spirit says, Today, if [you] hear His voice do not harden your hearts as you did in the rebellion during the time of testing in the wilderness, where [your] ancestors tested and tried me though for forty years they saw what I did. That is why I was angry with that generation, I said, "Their hearts are always going astray, and they have not known my ways. So, I declared on oath in my wrath, They shall never enter My rest."*

The Hebrew writers continued, *"See to it brothers and sisters, that none of [you] has a sinful, unbelieving heart that turns away from the living God. But encourage one another daily, as long as it is called, "Today," so that none of [you] may be hardened by sin's deceitfulness. We have come to share in Christ if indeed we hold our original conviction firmly to the very end. As it has been said, "Today, if [you] hear His voice do not harden your hearts as [you] did in the rebellion," [Hebrews 3:7-15].*

- *We serve God with both feet on one (same) side of the fence, not one foot in the world and the other foot in the Kingdom…straddling a fence is difficult: The choice will be the Church (Kingdom of Christ) or the world (kingdom of Satan)?*

It becomes a battle that we could easily lose sisters.

We do all we can day-to-day to serve God pleasingly, as well as learn from our predecessors. God gives us examples so that we might learn and have hope, *"For whatsoever things were written aforetime were written for our learning, that we through patience and comfort of the scriptures might have hope. Now the God of patience and consolation grant you to be like-minded one toward another according to Christ Jesus," [Ibid].*

Sisters, let us resolve with ourselves not to wear garments, of trying to imagine what may have been Ms. Lot's Eternal fate. Instead, focus our garments on the lessons of disobedience she left. Let us not test God in defiance of His commands; on the contrary; practice obedience and the preventive measures Christ left for us to follow; which, leads to Eternity and peace with God the Father, God the Son, and God the Holy Spirit.

The example of Ms. Lot's disobedience using the rearview mirror of what [was] in her life should give us a vision of hope if we are obedient and one of despair if we are disobedient.

Anna, a Prophetess, a faithful servant of God, and a woman of great age had: – A Vision of Hope. Her comfort was in the promises of redemption through the Messiah from God and not security in the world.

# A PROPHETESS OF GOD: AND HER VISION OF HOPE

Anna, a woman of great age possessed wisdom; led by the Spirit of God, she was one of the first to bear witness of Jesus the Savior. A Prophetess indicates her closeness to God. Anna gave her life to prayer and worshiping God from the time she was widowed seven years from her virginity, *"And there was one Anna, a prophetess, the daughter of Phanuel, of the tribe of Asher: she was of a great age and had lived with a husband seven years from her virginity,"* [Luke 2:36].

Anna was by count nearly or over 100 years of age. In her wisdom, she never lost hope in the promised Messiah. It was a hard choice to make first love her husband and then chose to live in a holy way before God, a price she was willing to pay that took enormous strength and determination. Anna physically came out of the world and lived and served in the Temple until God called her home, *"He will be a holy place; for both Israel and Judah he will be a stone that causes people to stumble and a rock that makes them fall. And for the people of Jerusalem, he will be a trap and a snare. Many of them will stumble; they will fall and be broken; and they will be snared and captured,"* [Isaiah 8:14-15].

God was Anna's Holy Place as He is our Holy Place if we choose to serve Him over the needs of the flesh or the desire not to be part of the world, *"But for you who revere My name, the sun of righteousness will rise with healing in its rays. And you will go out and frolic like well-fed calves,"* [Malachi 4:2].

I watched the calves on my husband and my farm after they ate from the feed troughs or either, the younger ones drank milk until their little tummies would look as if they would burst. When they were well fed would run, jump, and play for hours all over our pasture while their mothers and the Bull watched them, this is a good description of the look of inward joy displayed outwardly.

Those who love and serve God can look forward to the joy of being with God for an eternity we can celebrate with all of our brothers and sisters who were faithful to God. We have inward joy now serving God we can display outwardly with how brightly our lights are shining to the world. As well, thinking of the joy in heaven over one who repents now, what will it look like, or sound like in Heaven when God tells us *"Well done My good and faithful servants take your rest?"[Matthew 25:21].*

Anna was the Prophetess who recognized Christ as the Messiah. Anna spoke by divine inspiration; considered a spokeswoman, *"There was also a prophet, Anna, the daughter ofPenuel, of the tribe of Asher. She was very old; she had lived with her husband seven years after her marriage and then was a widow until she was eighty-four. She never left the temple but worshiped night and day fasting and praying. Coming up to them at that very moment, she gave thanks to God and spoke about the child to all who were looking forward tothe redemption ofJerusalem,"* [Luke 2:36–38].

Her faithfulness to God was her focus. Anna chose the better path of life after her husband was no longer with her. Daily she gave herself to prayer and service to God. Being close to God is what Jesus wants of all His people. We can have the same dedication to God serving Him in Spirit and Truth. Anna was in the temple physically praying to God each day. Paul tells us to, *"Pray without ceasing,"* [I Thessalonians 5:17].

Anna's mind was daily on prayer and service to God. She saidbyeto the life outside the Temple and served God in Spirit and Truth every day for the rest of her life, *"Thou wilt keep him in perfect peace, whose mindis stayedon thee: because he trusts in thee,"* [Isaiah 26:3].

We are the temple of God, as we can present our bodies as living sacrifices as Anna did in the temple in Jerusalem at that time, *"I beseech you therefore, brethren, by the mercies of God, that you present your bodies a living sacrifice, holy, acceptable to God, which is your reasonable service,"* [Romans 12:1].

Wecan beAnna's of the 21ˢᵗ Century. Her garment of faithfulness is an example. Anna's garment was good and not evil. The scripture says of her reputation that she was of God and did what was good as John told Gaius and Demetrius, *"Beloved, follow not that which is evil, but that which is good. He that doeth good is of God: but he that doeth evil hath not seen God,"* [3 John 11].

The Scripture records she had a good report.

- *What does your (my) garment of reputation say about us?*

Anna spoke througha revelation fromGodaboutthe Messiah and redemption of Israel. As Christ asked Peter, *"Who do you say that I am?"* *[Matthew 16:15].*

Peter answered, *"You are the Christ, the Son of the living God," [Matthew 15:16].*

Jesus answered and said unto him, *"Blessed art thou, Simon son of Jonah: for flesh and blood hath not revealeditunto thee, but my Fatherwhich isin heaven,"[Matthew 16:17].*

Anna loved God and had the mindset we should have spiritually today. She spoke of the promised Messiah…we must speak of the same Messiah who is our Savior and the fact that He redeemed the world, died for our sins, and gave His precious blood for our chance to livein eternity withGod. We cannot speak of Christ enough to others. Christ left us the same directive to, *"Go into all the world and preach the Gospel to every creature," [Mark 16:15].* And *"Go ye therefore, and teach all nations, baptizing them in the name of the Father, and of the Son, and of the Holy Spirit," [Matthew 28:16].*

According to Vine (2005), Sacrifice is living according to God's expectations. There are marid kinds of sacrifices in this life; however, the sacrifice that God requires of His children and faithful servants is our Love. Our total love, faithfulness, and obedience are quintessential to pleasing Him.

Anna counted all loss to the world as a gain for Christ…

CHAPTER NINE

# COUNTING ALL GAIN AS LOSS
# PART I

*"But Daniel resolved not to defile himself with the royal food and wine, and he asked the chief*
*official for permission not to defile himself this way."*

*"Now, God had caused the official to show favor and compassion to Daniel,"* but the official told Daniel, *"I am afraid of my lord the king, who has assigned your food and drink. Why should he see you looking worse than the other young men do your age? The king would then have my head because of you."*

Daniel said to the guard whom the Chief Official had appointed over Hananiah, Mishael, Azariah, and him, *"Please test your servants for ten days: Give us nothing but vegetables to eat and water to drink. Then compare our appearance with that of the young men who eat the royal food and treat your servants in accordance with what you see."* Therefore, he agreed to this and tested them for ten days.

*"At the end of the ten days, they looked healthier and better nourished than any of the young men who ate the royal food. So, the guard took away their choice food and the wine they were to drink and gave them vegetables instead."*

*"At the end of the time set by the king to bring them into his service, the chief official presented them to Nebuchadnezzar. The king talked with them, and he found none equal to Daniel, Hananiah, Mishael, and Azariah: so, they entered the king's service. In every matter of wisdom and understanding about which the king questioned them, he found them ten times better than all the magicians and enchanters in his whole kingdom,"* [Daniel 1:8-20].

In our secular life, we learn, in our spiritual life, we learn, by doing or trying. We are in ourfirstacceptance of Jesus our Savior, a novice, and have to grow in the Gospel of Jesus Christ. Sisters, time brings about the harsh reality, transformation into a mature and faithful Christian is not instantaneous but goes through a process with the fires of life; thosetrials and tribulationsburn away the chaff, so the good grains of our faithfulnessare seen. Daniel and his friends trusted God. They knew He was their Security, Teacher, Savior, and Friend.

We treat our physical bumps and bruises with antiseptic and then protect them with a band-aide to ward away germs, hence they are temporary and have to be replaced with each bath of antiseptic; we treat our spiritual bruises with the Word of God no band-aide is necessary. The Gospel of Christ is sufficient in all things. One must bewilling to go through the fires of the spiritual furnaces and allow God to forge our spiritual metal in the fires of righteousness. God is exact in what pleases Him. Studying the actions of our forefathers we can see, there were those who were willing to walk before God in righteousness that took them through the plagues of life andbondageof cruelty Daniel and his friends experienced, yet he/they did not lose their faith no matter the difficulty, of the test they faced.

They kept that glimmer of hope of redemption ever before them regardless of how dim it seemed and believed that God would deliver them if it were according to His Will and would send that promised deliverer at the appointed time. He did deliver them, as he delivered all humankind out of sin sending His only begotten son into the world. He forged that path for us leaving an example of success in serving God.

Christ did not consider Himself above fulfilling the inconvenient truth theplacein which man has put God's Word. Christ knew what He was to face pulling off His Robes of Glory and coming to earth, to redeem humanity.

- **What do you think Christ considered His actions on behalf of man's loss or gain? Of course, it is a definite gain sister!**

He did not say when it was the appointed time for Him to come to earth, "Not now Father, maybe another century. I am just not ready to face the fires of human sins, their attitudes of unbelief, their disobedience, carry that cross to Calvary's Hill, hang there, die with nails through my hands and feet, and with a crown of thrones pressed on my head, while the crowd below mocks me."

This paints a gruesome picture of what Christ went through as he faced those fires that forge one's life into an acceptablewayto live pleasingly to God. Neither did Jesus say, "I will go as soon as possible (ASAP)." This acronym and its meaning are of human devising and used from a person's perspective. It all ends with the same meaning if used when asked todoa task, if it is not something that is convenient at that time or is something you do not want to do, will elongate the time with ASAP, which can mean never, or at best put it off as long as you can. Christ did not think of dying for our Salvation in thisway but took upon Him the sins of the world willingly at God's appointed time and with no, "I will do it later."

When Christ walked the earth He was God and Man and the example of how to live righteous as godly men before His throne knowing that this earth is not all to life but presents the trails that one must go throughto beworthy of the death our Savior died. We count all things as a loss to the world to gain Christ and Eternity with God. We cannot wait to obey; it is to our disadvantage when we do. The words of the Hebrews writer, "*The day you hear His voice harden not your hearts,*" *[Ibid]*. About this command, '*the day you hear His voice*' bears no inference to ASAP (maybe later, or when it is convenient).

The inconvenient truth thatis rejected, pushed aside, added to, or taken away from through the eons of centuries that humans have seen come and go, will not change, "*ForIamtheLord,Ichangenot; therefore, ye sons of Jacob arenotconsumed,*" *[Malachi 3:6]*.

Isaiah reminds us, "*For My thoughts are not your thoughts, neither are yourwaysMyways,*" *declares the Lord.* And "*For as the heavens are higher than the earth, so are My ways higher than your ways, and My thoughts than your thoughts,*" *[Isaiah 55:9]*.

It is a given that we do not understand every expectation God places on humans so they will be worthy to inherit Heaven for an eternity, but wedothem through faith, as did Daniel, so we can live in those mansions He promised us, "*Let not your heart be troubled: ye believe in God, believe also in Me. In My Father's House are many Mansions: if it were not so, I would have told you. I go to prepare a place for you. And, if I go and prepare a place for you, I will come again, and receive you unto Myself; that where I am, there yemay bealso. And whither I go ye know, and the way ye know,*" *[John 10:1-4]*.

Man's expectations of God are unrealistic. We cannot fit Him into a mental mold we have developed to put Him and His Word (inconvenient truth) into until we need Him. When weare troubled, we will call on God, or our jobs are on the line, or any other issue in our lives that goes awry. He then becomes the center of our lives; however, when the emergency passes, we get back to what weconsideras "normal" and push Him aside again, until the next issue (s) comes up.

We should ask ourselves what is the archetype, of the garment I am wearing!

- *Do I consider it an inconvenient truth or count all things as a loss to the world that I might gain Jesus Christ and Eternal Salvation?*

Christ left for us what passion, fervency, and love for the truth, service, and faithfulness to God should look like, in our lives.

Paul reminds us of the archetype of our garmentsshould bethat *"We put no stumbling block in anyone's path so that our ministrywill not bediscredited.Rather, as servants of God, we commend ourselves in every way: in great endurance; in troubles, hardships and distresses;in beatings, imprisonments and riots; in hard work, sleepless nights and hunger;in purity, understanding, patience, and kindness; in the Holy Spirit and in sincere love;in truthful speech and in the power of God; with weapons of righteousness, in the right hand and in the left;through glory and dishonor, bad report and good report; genuine, yet regarded as impostors;known, yet regarded as unknown; dying, and yet we live on; beaten, and yet not killed;sorrowful, yet always rejoicing; poor, yet making many rich; having nothing, and yet possessing everything,"* [2 Corinthians 6:3-10].

When Paul and other warriors faced hardships, they leaned on Christ; but then again, when things were good or going well, they did not leave Christ. Our service to God is ongoing, in good times or bad times. He promised to be with us in good times and bad times, not just when times are good. I am [only] with you in good times are human characteristics. My mother titled it as being a fair-weather friend, with you as long as things are going well, but when trouble lifts its ugly head, it is too hard for them to stay and see trouble or difficulties through with you.

Counting all things as loss for Christ requires a change. We transform, exchange, or shift our lives for the privilege that is worthy of God adding us to the Kingdom. We are not ageless we are sitting on the banks of life sisters.Our garments of Spiritual maturity shouldshowin our lives to all onlookers who pass our bank.

Even if they (onlookers) do not at that pivotal moment join us, should continue to show our faithfulness in Christ and commitment to God's service. We cannot come to Christ with our baggage of pain and expect to live for Christ andcontinue to hang onto certain baggage as it was before we came to Him. All that we were, we count loss to the world to gain Christ… Christ nailed the baggage of sin thatwas countedagainst us to the Cross taking them upon His shoulders.

**Characteristics of our Goal**

- **We are diligently working – Is involved in getting to Heaven,** *"Peter replied, "Repent and be baptized, every one of you, in the name of Jesus Christ for the forgiveness of your sins. And you will receive the gift of the Holy Spirit," [Acts 2:38].*
- *"Our goal of Heaven is real,* "*When they see the purity and reverence of your lives," [I Peter 3:2].*
- **Working for Heaven can become a challenge,** *"And now what are you waiting for? Get up, be baptized, and wash your sins away, calling on His name," Acts 22:16; Luke 3:3, Acts 16:34].*
- **We set a goal and keep your eyes on the goal,** "*Rejoice always, pray continually, give thanks in all circumstances for this is God's will for you in Christ Jesus," [I Thessalonians 5:16]. "I press toward the mark for the prize of the high calling of God in Christ Jesus," Philippians 3:14].*
- **We do not dwell in or on the past,** "*And ye now, therefore, have sorrow: but I will see you again, and your heart shall rejoice, and your joy no man taketh from you," [John 16:22, Ephesians 4:4-6].*
- **We are enthusiastic about opportunities or challenges,** "*Therefore we were buried with Him through baptism into death, that just as Christ was raised from the dead by the glory of the Father, even so, we also should walk in newness of life," [Romans 6:4, Acts 8:3-4].*
- **We never leave God out of our plans,** "*And hath put all things under his feet, and gave Him to be the head over all things to the church, which is His body, the fullness of Him that fills all in all," [Ephesians 1:22-23].*
- **We keep our priorities in their proper place,** "*Praising God, and enjoying the favor of all the people. And the Lord added to their number daily those who were being saved," [Acts 2:47].*
- **We are positive thinkers,** "*Let your conversation be without covetousness; and be content with such things as ye have for He hath said, I will never leave thee, nor forsake thee," [Hebrews 13:5].*

*"And the peace of God, which transcends all understanding, will guard your hearts and your minds in Christ Jesus. Finally, brothers and sisters, whatever is true, whatever is noble, whatever is right, whatever is pure, whatever is lovely, whatever is admirable–if anything is excellent or praiseworthy–think about such things. Whatever you have learned or received or heard from Me or seen in Me put it into practice. And the God of peace will be with you," [Philippians 4:7-9].*

- **We allow Faith to be our root and foundation,** "*From six calamities He will rescue you; in seven no harm will touch you,*" [*Job 5:19*].

"*The Lord tries the righteous: but the wicked and him that love violence His soul hates,*" [*Psalms 11:5*].

We cannot go back after coming to Christ and pick up the baggage again usually adding more to it and be pleasing to Him, neither can we continue to start over, time after time; but, grow to maturity, not desiring the baggage again we once carried. This is a picture of someone straddling the fence. What side are you walking on Christ or Satan, we cannot do both, if we try we will encounter the opposition we cannot defeat or withstand. Christ said, "*Iknow thy works, that thou art neither cold norhot: I would thou were coldorhot,*" [*Revelation 3:15*].

This stance is so repulsive to Jesus that He will spew you out of His mouth. To the Church of Laodicea, the revelation given to John he writes, "*So because you are lukewarm, neither hot nor cold, I am about to spit you out of My mouth,*" [*Revelation 3:16*].

**Have you tasted half-cold (lukewarm) coffee after it has been hot, it is distasteful to the pallet, and taste buds?**

What we gain in the world is a loss for Christ; we cannot prefer things of the world to the things of Christ, which is Salvation and Eternity with God.

When we, as people, of God, cannot make a firm stand for Christ, wanting to be that Sunday Christian or when it is convenient there is a problem you are betwixt and between not completely giving up past taste (the world) and all its attractions, but wanting to be in the Kingdom at the same time. Christ said, "*We are neither hot nor cold;*" He desires that we make a choice and stand with it. Thinking of being distasteful or repugnant to Christ, describes that which makes Him sick. Consider the thing that reviles you in taste (Limburger Cheese) as I mentioned in Chapter 2, The Aroma. How much more so do we sicken our Savior with indecision; it equals throwing the Blood purchased Salvation He suffered on the Cross-to obtain for us as the perfect Sacrificial Lamb pleasing to God, back in His face.

Christ warns about being lukewarm not completely committing yourself to God leaving cracks and places where Satan can enter and take advantage of that weak area. We cannot halfway commit our life to Christ, by trying totally to live in the world and the Kingdom. When we love God and are obedient to him: we can purify our lives with the Word of God.

It is dangerous to be lukewarm; continually dabbling in the pleasures of the world, is a green light for Satan, *"When an impure spirit comes out of a person, it goes through arid places seeking rest and does not find it. Then says, 'I will return to the house I left.' When it arrives, it finds the house unoccupied, swept clean, and put in order. Then it goes and takes with it seven other spirits more wicked than itself, and they go in and live there. And the final condition of that person is worse than the first. This is how it will be with this wicked generation,"* [Matthew 12:43-45].

The Scripture tells us we cannot put our hand to the plow and look back, Jesus replied, «*No one who puts ahandtotheplowandlooksbackis fit for service in the Kingdom of God,"* [Luke 9:62].

In essence, if we are neither hot nor cold do not deserve to be presented to God the Father; there are no spots or blemishes on, in, or of the Bride of Christ, which in the last day He will present to His Father. The Church at Laodicea neglecting to serve Christ cared more for their wealth and believed they did not need anything, *"You say, 'I am rich; I have acquired wealth and do not need a thing.' But you do not realize that you are wretched, pitiful, poor, blind, and naked,"* [Revelation 3:17].

They were only destroying themselves and their neglect had blinded them and hardened their hearts to the point they did not know they were sick and needed healing. They were wretched, poor, pitiful, blind, and naked. When we see these conditions in the lives of people, it causes us to want to do something to alleviate their pain and condition. Christ did this for us spiritually; the description given by Jesus was of the dismal look of the spiritual life the members at the Church at Laodicea were living even though they had considerable earthly wealth.

Yet, they lack the most vital things they need. First, they needed healing from the misery they had bought upon themselves with their Bladen neglect of service and faithfulness to Christ.

We come before God naked without proper garments to cover our nakedness. Christ provides those garments through his death on the cross-the garment of Salvation, the necessary armor we need to be pleasing to Him. Christ changed our garment to one washed white in His blood, no stain or hint of sin is on these new garments. New indicates without fault, sin, or blemishes. Satan cannot make us sin only entice us to. We have to participate especially in the context of us choosing what we want to do or not do.

Christ gave them the solution and prescription for the disease that had beset them overtime, *"I counsel you to buy from Me gold refined in the fire, so you can become rich and have white clothes to wear, so you can cover your shameful nakedness, and salve to put on your eyes, so you can see," [Revelation 3:18].*

We live in a world filled with physical weakness and illness and we would like to be well, feel good, or avoid the illnesses that are inherent to the tent we inhabit. Yet, we know that the Spiritual condition is more important than the physical part of our lives.

The physical is temporal; the Spiritual is eternal. Paul's affliction in weakness should give us courage because of the weakness or the thorn in the flesh he experienced, but was strong spiritually, *"Three times I pleaded with the Lord to take it away from me"* But He said to me, *"My grace is sufficient for you, for My power is made perfect in weakness."* Our response should be like Paul, *"Therefore I will boast all the more gladly about my weaknesses, so that Christ's power may rest on me," [2 Corinthians 12:8-9].*

Paul continued to work in the Kingdom even though he had a thorn in the flesh. The Scripture is not specific where it was nor exactly what it was; we know he had a thorn. We all have thorns of some kind in our flesh or as a part of this tent we inhabit.

Weaknesses develop our character and teach us to depend on God. Our talents, skills, abilities, knowledge, energy level, or even physical efforts when we face obstacles in our lives we depend on God; it is then we realize all these blessings and gifts are from God. Humans depending on themselves without God are ineffective, but when we depend on God, we are completely effective.

The Scripture reminds us, *"I can do all things through Christ which strengthens me," [Philippians 4:13].* Further, Mark tells us Christ said, "And Jesus looking upon them saith, *"With men [it is] impossible, but not with God: for with God all things are possible,"* *[Mark 10:27]; A*lso, *"Jesus said unto him, If thou canst believe, all things [are] possible to him that believeth,"* *[Mark 9:23].*

We are to remember temptation is ever-present at all times, no matter the gifts we are blessed with from God, should not allow our skills and abilities to tempt us not to take the journey in life with God in whatever we do. We are wise when we are thankful for the privilege of being His child and seek God's guidance in every area of our life, because only He is all-sufficient, all-knowing, all-seeing, in all, through all, and overall.

Our Lord and Savior walked through the fires of sins and disobedience man had purchased for himself over the centuries and nailed them to the Cross. We become rich when we serve God in Spirit and in Truth, which purifies our garments of sin and make them acceptable to Christ and the purity of that garment covers the shameful nakedness of our sins. Man's sins are ever before God. We know what shamefulness is, disgrace and humiliation. In short, humanity had disgraced themselves in the sight of God; it disgusted Christ to view them in their sickened condition, which had made them blind to what their responsibility was in fulfilling their service to Him.

Baptism into Christ means a complete change takes place. We conduct ourselves in a manner that will not embarrass our Savior. We do not want parts of our body to show that will disgrace other parts that are being faithful to God and functioning in a manner pleasing to God. Man in-and-of-themselves has enough to deal with without letting mammon (money) or the like to be their stumbling stone. They need Spiritual Salve to heal their eyes so they could see their error and return to their only Lord and Savior Jesus Christ.

In essence, sisters Hananiah (Shadrach), Mishael (Meshach), Azariah (Abednego), and Daniel's faith anchor were in the promises of God and believe that He can do all things, if were according to His will, no matter what life held for them.

- *Do our garments have the same look of faith and belief?*

Baptism is a major heart event in our lives. It changes both hearts and minds our emotions, thoughts, our reasoning, our desires, our focuses (whom, what, why) the change is necessary that we focus on, not thinking and acting carnal, but slowly replacing our carnality with spirituality each day. This equal pulling off the man with his baggage and replacing that baggage with faith, which is, "*The substance of things hoped for, and the evidence of things not seen," [Hebrews 11:1].*

Thus, putting our trust in Jesus; wherefore not allowing Satan to lead us into a see-saw faithfulness to God dangerous in an up-down manner in our faithfulness equaling to straddling the fence, lukewarmness nor allowing any or negative pattern to slip into our lives and take up resident thereby becoming our norm. Therefore, it will, if we are not watchful, achieving at that point a deficit in our faithfulness.

As we serve God, we can see ourselves in those two points we are dependent on God's power and His patience, "*See ye first the Kingdom of Heaven and all its righteousness and all these things will be added unto you," [Matthew 6:33].*

Rebirth, Reborn, Regeneration...

CHAPTER TEN

# COMING TO JESUS BY NIGHT
## REBIRTH, TRANSFORMATION, AND REGENERATION

Now there was a Pharisee, a man named Nicodemus who was a member of the Jewish ruling council (Sanhedrin). He came to Jesus by night and said, *"Rabbi, we know that you are a teacher who has come from God. For one could perform the signs you are doing if God were not with him," [John 3:1-2].*

Jesus replied, *"Very truly I tell you, no one can see the Kingdom of God unless they are born again," [John 3:3].*

*"How can someone be born when they are old?"* Nicodemus asked, *"Surely they cannot enter a second time into their mother's womb and be born?" [John 3:4].*

Jesus answered, *"Very truly I tee you, no can enter the Kingdom of God unless they are born of water and the Spirit. Flesh gives birth to flesh, but the Spirit gives birth to spirit. You should not be surprised at My saying, "you must be born again. The wind blows wherever it pleases. You hear its sound, but you cannot tell where it comes from or where it is going. So, it is with everyone born of the Spirit," [John 3:5-8].*

*"How can this be?"* Nicodemus asked, *[John 3:9].*

*"If it is sown a natural body, it is raised a spiritual body. If there is a natural body, there is also a spiritual body," [I Corinthians 15:44].*

*"You are Israel's teacher,"* Jesus said, *"and do you not understand these things"* *Very truly I tell you, we speak of what we know, and we testify to what we have seen, but still, you people do not accept our testimony. I have spoken to you of earthly things, and you do not believe, how then will you believe if I speak of heavenly things? No one has ever gone into heaven except the One who came from heaven – the Son of Man. Just as Moses lifted up the snake in the wilderness, so the Son of Man must be lifted up, that everyone who believes may have eternal life in Him," [John 3:9-15].*

The caveat cannot swallow the premise based on whether you continue in the commands of Jesus. We cannot just be baptized, and it ends there rather it begins there and goes forward. That is where the real battle begins for eternity. Christ purchased our Salvation. The action required of us is taking advantage of that Salvation and continue on that spiritual journey Christ set in motion. The analogy that rolling stones gather no moss is a reality. Moss only grows and consumes a tree when it is stationary we are not trees but living, breathing, and thinking human beings with the ability to be logical and use our reasoning and understand what is written for us is penned indelibly in time; God does not change.

He sent Christ to purchase our salvation and to die for our sins. Anyone using rationality would know we cannot set our standards and be acceptable to God. The Scripture is our standard, *"Let the one who does wrong continue to do wrong; let the vile person continue to be vile; let the one who does right continue to do right; and let the holy person continue to be holy," [Revelation 22:11]*.

It goes back to the caveat swallowing up the premise. We have a caveat of time in our lives to obey and accept Salvation. The longer we reject God and minimize what Christ did, the further we go down that road of no return.

The gospel is not veiled, *"Therefore seeing we have this ministry, as we have received mercy, we faint not; But have renounced the hidden things of dishonesty, not walking in craftiness, nor handling the word of God deceitfully; but by the manifestation of the truth commending ourselves to every man's conscience in the sight of God. But, if our gospel be hid, it is hidden to them that are lost: In whom the god of this world hath blinded the minds of them, which believe not, lest the light of the glorious Gospel of Christ, who is the image of God, should shine unto them. For we preach not ourselves, but Christ Jesus the Lord; and ourselves your servants for Jesus' sake. For God, who commanded the light to shine out of darkness, hath shined in our hearts, to give the light of the knowledge of the glory of God in the face of Jesus Christ," [2 Corinthians 4:1-6]*.

Christ came to reveal the truth of the Gospel and fulfill the Prophecy in place since the beginning of time, *"And I will put enmity between you and the woman, and between your seed and her Seed; he shall bruise your head, and you shall bruise his heel," [Genesis 3:15]*.

The Gospel is open for all to take advantage of; if you do not believe or listen to the voice of Satan you will continue to be blinded, by his wiles of deceit so that you will not believe; he does not want you to know the truth. He will use the truth against you if you listen that is why studying is so important.

In our day and time, it is known as taking the Word of God out of context...
not explaining the full meaning or making that Scripture apply to what we
want it to mean is the same thing the false prophets do. We cannot cherry-pick
Scripture, this is also a tool of Satan ... only applying Scripture that makes us
comfortable and does not require that we be fully obedient to the Word of God.

We should not be surprised at anything that Satan does, Paul reminds us he
masqueraded as an angel of light; and *"For such are false apostles, deceitful workers,
transforming themselves into apostles of Christ. And no wonder! For Satan, himself,
transforms his self, into an angel of light. Therefore, it is no great thing if his ministers
also transform themselves into ministers of righteousness, whose end will be according
to their works,"* [2 Corinthians 11:13-15 & 11:1-12].

The premise Satan feeds man is that we have all our lives to come to God,
but realistically we do not. The chance is one will be so caught up in the events
of this life, time passes almost unnoticed; we can let time get away from us. This
is an unintended consequence. When we come to that reality, sometimes it is
a matter of being too late, *"So as the Holy Spirit says, the day you hear His voice
harden not your heart as in the wilderness, when you tested Me and saw my anger for
forty years,"* [Hebrews 3:7:15].

The premise of time and the chance we weigh against the actual time and
opportunity in place, not one that we create for ourselves, which is not acceptable
to God.

Nicodemus and Joseph of Arimathea initially came to Jesus by night.
Looking at this in a different way than the account in [Book 1] to think and
consider what they might have thought them being so compelled by what they
knew about the prophecy of the coming Messiah since the beginning of time.
The danger of them being in direct conflict with the Sanhedrin Council and
their authority, which they feared the Roman Government would take away,
was a reality.

The Roman Government hated and feared what Christianity meant; with
this in mind, considering their fellow Councilmen of the Sanhedrin, Joseph of
Arimathea and Nicodemus came to Jesus by night. They had that burning desire
to know, to understand what Christianity meant as opposed to Judaism the faith
of Israel as a people of God, and understand the teaching of Christ, which was
a new concept to them.

The Law, which is what they were living under at that time, does not help in achieving Righteousness. We are reminded in Scripture Nicodemus was of the Sanhedrin Council who knew the Law well. Christ came to fulfill the Law and all righteousness that we might obtain Salvation, not through our righteousness, but righteousness through the Savior of the world. It is not within man to be righteous, *"Even so ye also outwardly appear righteous unto men, but within ye are full of hypocrisy and iniquity,"* [Matthew 23:28].

God is a God of oneness; we cannot conduct ourselves like "chickens with their heads off" (carried about with every wind of doctrine we hear that is pleasing to our hearing palate) about the truth. Matthews reminds us of this fact, *"Ye hypocrites, well did Esaias prophesy of you, saying, This people draw nigh unto me with their mouth, and honor me with their lips, but their heart is far from me. But in vain, they do worship me, teaching for doctrines the commandments of men. And He called the multitude, and said unto them, hear, and understand,"* [Matthew 15:7-10].

*"Not that which go into the mouth defile a man; but that which cometh out of the mouth, this defiles a man. Then came His disciples, and said unto Him, Knows thou that the Pharisees were offended after they heard this saying? But He answered and said, 'Every plant, which My Heavenly Father hath not planted, shall be rooted up,"* [Matthew 15:11-13].

Christ's death would have been for nothing if the Law is what Nicodemus understood would have fulfilled righteousness then our Savior suffered in vain. The Law existed but did not offer life only death. Christ came to offer us something better than death but life through Salvation, grace, and mercy. We must take the stand that says, *"For through the Law I died to the Law so that I might live for God,"* [Galatians 2:19].

My point is sisters, whether they came initially to Jesus by night, they came. This is a peep show of how love replaced fear. John reminds us, *"There is no fear in love; but perfect love cast out fear: because fear hath torment. He that fear is not made perfect in love,"* [I John 1:4:18].

It is dangerous for humans to treat truth like a foreign language; it is common for children when they are in their formative years to treat truth in this manner; however, we are not children. They do not, in their young years, quite get the concept of the necessity of being truthful but will say whatever they think will get them out of trouble or allow them to go where they want to go or fulfill their desires.

Over time, children and adults alike will learn there is but one truth. Jesus said, *"I am the Way, the Truth, and the Life," [John 14:6].*

From the beginning of time, Scripture has informed us of the *"I Am"* of time and eternity. Jesus is there from the beginning, and He will be there in the end, *"I Am the Alpha and the Omega, the First and the Last, the Beginning and the End," [Revelation 12:13].*

In human imagination, truth is whatever they want it to be. Our garments fit as God commands not what we imagine. The pattern man uses is not of God but is manmade. We do not learn the [lack] of ability to be mindful of what is the truth from God but humans and their insatiable desires. We cannot allow truth to be a foreign language. Even with other languages, we study to understand the meaning.

The truth of the Scripture seemed like a foreign language to Nicodemus and Joseph of Arimathea in the beginning. However, as time went on, the more exposure they have the more their understanding opened up as will ours if we search, study, and dig for the truth using our muscle and shovel of intellect and ability to acquire knowledge as they did.

This takes desire and love for, first your Salvation and wanting to know Jesus and be pleasing to Him; then coming to Him so that we can receive remission of sin through His blood sacrificed on the Cross of Calvary more than two thousand years ago.

Our Savior bought Reformation, Transformation, and Regeneration comes with a change of mind or attitude.

Paul gave us the pattern to follow achieving in achieving our rebirth:

- *Let love be without dissimulation. Abhor that which is evil; cleave to that which is good.*
- *Be kindly affectionate one to another with brotherly love; in honor preferring one another.*
- *Not slothful in business; fervent in spirit; serving the Lord.*
- *Rejoicing in hope; patient in tribulation; continuing instant in prayer.*
- *Distributing to the necessity of saints given to hospitality.*
- *Bless them, which persecute you: bless, and curse not.*
- *Rejoice with them that do rejoice, and weep with them that weep.*

- *Be of the same mind one toward another. Mind not high things but condescend to men of low estate. Be not wise in your own conceits.*
- *Recompense to no man evil for evil. Provide things honest in the sight of all men.*
- *If it is possible, as much as lieth in you, live peaceably with all men.*
- *Dearly beloved, avenge not yourselves, but rather give place unto wrath: for it is written, Vengeance is mine; I will repay, saith the Lord.*
- *Therefore, if thine enemy hunger, feed him, if he thirsts, give him drink for in so doing thou shalt heap coals of fire on his head.*
- *Be not overcome of evil, but overcome evil with good,"* [Romans 12:9-21].

We cannot divorce reformation from transformation both are essential to rebirth and regeneration. The world at the time our Savior walked on earth and now is like a Mosaic. It was not just for one people, but the plan of God slowly and systematically built that Mosaic, starting with the giving of the Law and finally Christ ushered in mercy, grace, and Salvation.

God adds to the Church such as should be saved; the Mosaic grows in size every day, "*Praising God, and enjoying the favor of all the people. And the Lord added to their number daily those who were being saved,"* [Acts 2:47].

We are all part of the unified Body of Christ. Spiritual Israel consists of, Jews, Gentiles, bond, slave, and free. All who desire to be saved are to take-up their cross and follow our Lord and Savior Jesus Christ.

The Scripture admonishes us to, "*Examine yourselves, whether ye be in the faith; prove yourselves. Know ye not that that Jesus Christ is in you, except ye be reprobates? However, I trust that ye shall know that we are not reprobates. Now I pray to God that ye do no evil; not that we should appear approved, but that ye should do that which is honest, though we are as reprobates,"* [2 Corinthians 13:5-7].

Those baptized under the Cloud, in the sea, were also according to the will of God, "*They were all baptized into Moses in the cloud and in the sea,"* [I Corinthians 10:2].

We are also a part of them through Christ and not separated from them or them from us. God's standards do not change they are the same for everyone irrespective of the century or geographical location.

The Pharisees and Scribes watched Jesus' every move, to build the evidence against Him. They were furious Jesus outwitted them and they plotted to destroy him. Their anger and fear of the Salvation Jesus bought into the world fulfilling the Law, lead them in their being responsible for His death, *"But the Pharisees went out and plotted how they might kill Jesus," [Matthew 12:14, Mark 3:6].*

Jesus taught the importance of treating our fellowman with love and kindness, including our enemies through we are to hate the sin but love the sinner. Enemies are part of our life. They are a reality and not a myth. Jesus tells us how to handle that enemy, *"But I say unto you which hear, Love your enemies, do good to them which hate you, Bless them that curse you, and pray for them which despitefully use you. And unto him that smites thee on the one cheek offer also the other; and him that taketh away thy cloak forbid not to take thy coat also," [Luke 6:27-29].*

When dealing with our enemy, we need help and not attempt it on our own. A prayer of David the King, *"Fret not thyself because of evildoers, neither be thou envious against the workers of iniquity. For they shall soon be cut down like the grass, and wither as the green herb. Trust in the Lord, and do good, so shalt thou dwell in the land, and verily thou shalt be fed. Delight thyself also in the Lord: and He shall give thee the desires of thine heart. Commit thy way unto the Lord; trust also in Him; and he shall bring it to pass," [Psalms 37:1-5].*

Enemies come in different ways, shapes, and forms. At times, as well, we are our own enemy. Christ gave us an example of dealing with our enemies. Regardless of who that enemy might be, we have an advocate, the Just Judge of the World. The enemy that we face is the god of this world. All evil has its foundation in Satan. Just as the foundation, for Righteousness is in Jesus Christ, the Righteousness Judge.

Jesus tells us to pray for our enemies and those who misuse us. *"Dearly beloved, avenge not yourselves, but rather give place unto wrath: for it is written, Vengeance is Mine; I will repay, saith the Lord," [Romans 12:19].*

We as humans do not know how to pay. Christ does not want His people to have vindictive hearts; it is evil and takes away our ability to see. Vendetta becomes like a milky film hard to distinguish what is on the other side of it. It equals one wandering in an early pre-dawn mist; it is easy to lose your way. An enemy can cause a spiritual shipwreck. Our attempt to pay causes us to sink into sin and under the control of the devil.

Luke reminds us in *[Luke 18:1-8]* of the parable Christ gave of the Judge who did not fear God or man and the widow who came to him to be avenge of her enemies. At first, he would not but her continual coming would weary him; he avenged her. The unjust judged cared naught for her...her persistence bought about results ...just results. Our Savior loves and cares about His children, and is especially concerned about the poor, widows, and orphans. The unjust judge took notice only because he did not want to be worried about her case before him regarding her enemies. The quickest way to get rid of the situation before him – he avenged her.

Christ does avenge us in time (His time, not ours). It is not because He does not care but because He cares and bears long with us. We can never lose faith that if we continually lay our petition before His throne that He will help us. It may seem long to us, but God avenges His faithful children at the right time. He is never late; we are the ones in a hurry. Remember sisters God is merciful and compassionate unlike the unjust judge who had not the characteristics of mercy, compassion, nor was he longsuffering.

If we are faithful and trusting in His power, Jesus can make even our enemies be at peace with us, *"When the Lord takes pleasure in anyone's way, He causes their enemies to make peace with them," [Proverbs 16:7].*

This does not come [but] by faith. However, sisters, it is necessary that we wear garments of peace and not a spirit of vengefulness, which is usually a characteristic (vindictiveness) of the spirit and its intentions. Vengeance is an attitude of desiring or seeking. It is wise to conduct ourselves in the manner Christ gives us in *[Matthew 5th Chapter].* The Beatitude's Chapter describes the attitudes we should have the way we as His children should [Be].

It is not easy to get to this point; it is human nature to want to affect our revenge, this intent or attitude is not pleasing to our Lord and Savior. We are to have that child-like faith in Him trusting in His promises. We humbly go to God, the Publican did, and we will be justified *"I tell you; this man went down to his house justified rather than the other: for every one that exalts himself shall be abased; and he that humbles himself shall be exalted," [Luke 18:14].*

If we expect or desire mercy, we are to be merciful even to our enemies.

We have an enemy that is unconquerable by any measure man might imagine. We cannot appease him with nice words, treat him as if he is not aware, ignore him as if he is not there, and the most dangerous is thinking he is not dangerous [is] deadly to us physically and spiritually. Aligning ourselves with Satan makes a bad bedfellow. Satan is an enemy of God; therefore, he is the enemy of man because we are God's creation and will do anything he can to try to destroy and hurt God. He targets the people of God. His chief focus is destroying, *"The great dragon was hurled down that ancient serpent called the devil, or Satan, who leads the whole world astray. He was hurled to the earth and his angels with him,"* [Revelation 12:9].

This pre-existing condition has been, is, and will ever be a [pandemic], in the lives of people on earth. It has been since the beginning of time, the first violation of the commands that God gave the first of His creation. This [plague] only grows worse as time goes on as man encounters more of the pleasures in life that humans indulge in as their imaginations work overtime.

These pleasures and indulges are [contagious] and pulls at the heart and minds of humans even to the point that it becomes another battle of good and evil that exists. Satan continues to make available to humans, those attractive morsels, and tidbits, he knows are pleasing and attractive to them, and if they are not appealing enough he will embellish them more.

Christ suffered the most painful death we can imagine purchasing our Salvation. He fought the battle for humanity and won. Now we have that avenue and advocate helping us win that battle against Satan. We cannot be of those who refuse to accept change as the Pharisees and Scribes did even when they knew the Prophecy of the coming Messiah.

The points made in this chapter with them being the keepers-of-the-law, Nicodemus and Joseph of Arimathea came to the full knowledge of what was lacking in their belief and service that would be pleasing to God. They soon realized before them was the Messiah and the offer of something better than the law they had adhered to for centuries and did not reject the transformation, reformation, and regeneration Christ offered.

Regeneration, Reformation, and Transformation come in with the renewing of the mind and heart, which the Pharisees and Scribes refused to do because of fear, greed for power, and selfishness. We cannot be of those who fear, are power-hungry and selfish, but put our trust and faith in Christ Our Savior believing He can do all things, and Paul reminds us of the attitude each of us should have, *"I can do all things to Christ who strengthens me," [Ibid]*. We have a guarantee, to those who are of Christ and are faithful no one can separate us from the love of Christ, *"Who shall separate us from the love of Christ? Shall tribulation, or distress, or persecution, or famine, or nakedness, or peril, or sword? As it is written, For thy sake, we are killed all the day long; we are accounted as sheep for the slaughter. Nay, in all these things we are more than conquerors through Him that loved us. For I am persuaded, that neither death, nor life, nor angels, nor principalities, nor powers, nor things present, nor things to come, nor height, nor depth, nor any other creature, shall be able to separate us from the love of God, which is in Christ Jesus our Lord," [Romans 8:35-39]*.

The Pre-existing Condition....is not limited but requires being viewed from a universal concept...

CHAPTER ELEVEN

# THE PRE-EXISTING CONDITION: THE UNIVERSAL VIEW

We are all subject to this pre-existing condition regardless of who we are. We are not born Christian. We are born in innocence as children. Looking at this concept, from an earthly perspective, our babies are born in this world in a pure manner untouched by this world; they do not have the ability at that point to sin. Babies need care. Their total dependence is on their parents for every function necessary for their growth to maturity. Yet, at a certain point in life (their lives), accountability starts. We know they cannot remain a child for their entire life.

When raising children, we teach, train, warn, admonish, it is a looping process we start, it is like working a job in a sense. We get up every day and start the process over until they reach a point when we know they are to take responsibility for their actions after the proper training. They are no longer babies, have grown, and their attributes show, and personalities begin to form. We try as much as possible to put their feet on a path to use the guidance received as they grow into young adults. The day we are born physically, we are born into a world that has a pre-existing condition; there is no one exempt from this condition.

Webster defines pre-existing as, something being at or from an earlier time than (something) is.

There were demons (Satan) that were pre-existence to the flood. That brings us up to the moment when each one of us is born that pre-existing condition is here, we cannot escape this fact. That condition and man's interaction with its [father] had its birth in the Garden of Eden. The perpetrator of this condition was pre-existent to the Garden of Eden, Adam, and Eve's [first] act of disobedience. First is coming before all others, in time, order, earliest, and at the beginning. There is only one cure for the pre-existing condition and all other circumstances born from this underlying sickness and its infirmities are precursors to the errors into which humans fall. At this point, we recognize that we have this condition, or it has existed and need the doctor who has the ability, remedy, or treatment needed for the condition.

To take advantage of the treatment and keep the condition under control, we come to the Great Physician and put our lives and Spiritual health in His loving and capable hands because we know from Scripture, this condition will remain in this world until the end-of-time. Sisters, we cannot manage it alone but need the only begotten Son of God, Our Lord, and Savior Jesus Christ to help us deal with the struggles it causes and alleviate human error born from it.

I used the analogy of human experiences in dealing with Insurance Companies, in this day and time. When accidents or other tragedies befall us, find they (Insurance Companies), either refuse to cover your claim, put a frame-of-time on what they will, and will not pay within that time, balk at, drag their feet on paying, or questioned the period-of-time when it comes to pre-existing conditions in our health. In my experience, Physicians, when we move our medical care from one to the other want to know if there are any pre-existing conditions in our health, to determine what type of care they need to give or be aware of the care we received before they became our attending Physician.

We know in the medical field in this 21$^{st}$ Century, the type of care has gone from a universal manner of treating the sickness and diseases besetting humans to what scientist define as Precision Care…each patient is treated based on their individual needs and not on the condition in a global or universal sense.

The pre-existing condition of our health makes a difference in the medications, periods of time, and other treatments needed. Our pre-existing condition needs treating along with the other health outliers caused by that condition.

Concerning this condition, in a spiritual sense, there is a universal spiritual health care system for all. It treats everyone with this condition the same way, no matter what other spiritual maladies one might have, as time goes on we add more to our spiritual ailments, which are initiated by the condition that existed we cannot control.

There is one antidote/vaccine/treatment for the pre-existing condition of sin and that is the Salvation Jesus purchased with His Blood on the Cross. Christ's blood cleanses us from all sin once we are baptized into His Body, we are babes in Christ, and has at that point, a new beginning. Our Spiritual garments then are re-sized for growth and maturity with Christ's guidance, if we are willing to obey His Commands and follow His teaching. He knows the condition, He dealt with it at the beginning of time, and the battle continues. His war against it has gone on for centuries.

Christ does not ask about any pre-existing condition; He does not base His treatments on which medications to use either. Christ said, *"Come unto Me, all ye that labor and are heavy laden and I will give you rest. Take My yoke upon you and learn of Me; for I am meek and lowly in heart: and ye shall find rest unto your souls. For My yoke is easy, and My burden is light,"* [Matthew 11:28-30].

He takes all willing to come. We all come to Christ with the same Spiritual Pre-existing Condition, there is no level of it with Jesus all unrighteousness is sin, *"If we say we have no sin we deceive ourselves and the truth is not in us,"* [I John 1:8].

God sent only one remedy for the pre-existing condition of Sin, the Blood of Jesus Christ so that we might count all things lost to the world to gain Christ. Think of the remedy, for the people of Israel after God gave them victory and they did not keep their Vows.

God throughout time has provided a method of healing for His people if they are willing to accept that healing. He gave us Christ for our healing. An example of healing in the Old Testament is expressed by Moses lifting up the snake in the wilderness; all who were bitten by the poison Serpents, if they looked upon the brass serpent on the pole would be healed, *"And when King Arad the Canaanite, which dwelled in the south, heard tell that Israel came by the way of the spies; then he fought against Israel, and took some of them, prisoners. And Israel vowed a vow unto the Lord and said, If thou wilt indeed deliver this people into my hand, and then I will utterly destroy their cities. And the Lord hearkened to the voice of Israel and delivered up the Canaanites, and they utterly destroyed them and their cities: and he called the name of the place Hormah. And they journeyed from mount Hor by the way of the Red sea, to compass the land of Edom: and the soul of the people was much discouraged because of the way."*

And, the people spoke against God, and against Moses, *"Wherefore have ye brought us up out of Egypt to die in the wilderness? For there is no bread, neither is there any water; and our soul loathes this light bread. And the Lord sent fiery serpents among the people, and they bit the people, and much people of Israel died. Therefore, the people came to Moses, and said, "We have sinned, for we have spoken against the Lord and against thee; pray unto the Lord, that he take away the serpents from us. And Moses prayed for the people. And the Lord said unto Moses, Make thee a fiery serpent, and set it upon a pole: and it shall come to pass, that every one that is bitten, when he looks upon it, shall live,"* [Numbers 21:1-8].

Just think if they had refused the treatment or healing God gave they would suffer the consequences and loss of their lives, *"And Moses made a serpent of brass and put it upon a pole, and it came to pass, that if a serpent had bitten any man when he beheld the serpent of brass, he lived," [Number 21:9].*

In this, century, and all centuries, beginning in A.D. 33, the price Christ paid, the Cross; is lifted before man. His Blood ran backward and forward for the healing of the people. The same for healing in this century is as it was in the wilderness. We come to Jesus for our healing lifting our faith and belief in His Mighty Power, obeying His Commands. Christ does not operate in the abstract. Salvation or healing for humanity is not theoretical, something that is not applied or practical. Our Salvation is not concerned with or involving the theory of a subject or area of study, rather it is a practical application. God created the pattern for man's way back to Him and the treatment for the Pre-existing Condition that was already a factor at our birth. We cannot afford to refuse the healing that Christ offers.

God did not give us a shotgun remedy, for this universal pre-existing condition, by shooting into the crowd and see how many bullets of Salvation, will hit man as they scattered. We know that by shooting a scattergun (shotgun), the bullets will scatter because the pattern of a shotgun is widespread, which means not all of the pellets hit an intended target.

My husband, Timothy was a professional hunter and gun expert, i.e., with that said, I became a hunter. He taught me about the ability of each weapon and its power as well (hunting was in my blood from a child up. In addition, I hunted with my dad; at 12:00-4:00 a.m., on the coldest night in December as a little girl, rode on my 6'4" father's shoulders as we traveled more than a mile to the river behind our property to retrieve the Coons in the trap he set on the other side of the riverbank. He waded in his waist-high rubber boots and gear with me up in the air well wrapped to beat back the biting cold and retrieved the trap) with that bit of historical background for the statements about the power and spread of the bullets, is said to make my point.

My husband taught me to use a scattergun: the spread was enormous, and so was the kick of the gun, if you held it the incorrect way, but there are shots that always missed part of the target. This is the point I am making; God did not use a scattergun approach for the cure of this pre-existing condition.

95

In the medical field today, the initiative known as The Precision Medicine Initiative mentioned earlier is a long-term research endeavor, involving the National Institute of Health (NIH) and multiple other research centers, which aims to understand how a person's genetics, environment, and lifestyle can help determine the best approach to prevent or treat disease.

God does not need to take an assessment of our genetics, environment, or lifestyle to help determine the approach to treat the pre-existing condition humans suffer with, but has a precise treatment used for all. God gave us our gift of healing and cure for the sins man is guilty of and continues to be subject to in this world.

However, though the condition exists universally, there is a precision treatment for each person regardless of your environment, your gender, or your socio-economic status. It is designed to treat everyone who so desires to partake of the healing (as Moses' brass snake on the pole in the wilderness was). At this point, is where it gets precise, to come to the healing fountain that flows so freely, a propitiation for this disease, *"He is the atoning sacrifice for our sins, and not only for ours but also for the sins of the whole world,"* [I John 2:2].

The healing fountain is in single tense, there is not but one treatment that can heal in a precise way the sins that beset humankind; God gave us one way, one treatment (Christ's Blood), one facility (the Church), all through the same Lord and Savior Jesus Christ.

Since the beginning of time, we see the oneness of God in Scripture. The Garden of Eden had one entrance guarded by a Cherub to keep the way of the Tree of Life. The Ark had one door. The Kingdom of God has one way through Jesus Christ our Lord and Savior. Christ purchased one Church – the Church that bears His Name. Only one way to live in eternity with God through His beloved Son the same Lord and Savior who purchased our freedom from sin and death bridging the gulf between God and man created in the Garden of Eden that began with a single act of transgression and disobedience.

Our Savior gave His life (once) for all that we might have an avenue to use. Because without a doubt, sin was ushered into the world by disobedience and the perpetrator of sin is in the world and is alive and well. Death will be in the world until all are put under Christ's feet, sin causes death spiritually and physically it is the last enemy Christ will destroy, *"The last enemy to be destroyed is death,"* [I Corinthians 15:26].

Therefore, we, as Paul reminds us, are to conduct ourselves soberly with the awareness so that, *"Satan might not outwit us, for we are not unaware of his schemes," [2 Corinthians 2:11]*.

Satan's wiles are not a static force; they are evident by the force of impact in one's life. Because it is not noticeable, (evident) does not mean it has no long-term effect. Satan is effective at causing wounds, but has not the ability to heal … He only destroys – remember Eve and that fatal limb Satan led her on? When the God and Master of the universe called Adam and Eve to task for their defiance and lack of faith – Satan shrunk back because he knew the limited power he has before the Master of all creation including him …

Satan offered Eve a problem for God's solution for man's obedience. In essence, sister, we cannot dance with the devil; there is no might about his changing the dance steps he changes not only the steps; but also, the tune. Satan is a diabolical shadow rider – dark and operating outside of the light. Satan puts the yoke of sin upon man; Christ carried the yoke of sin to the cross on Calvary's Hill. David reminds us that God is willing to carry our burdens. Listen to his voice in the Psalms, *"Cast thou burdens upon the Lord and He will sustain thee: He shall never suffer the righteous to be moved," [Psalms 55:22]*.

Satan is not an honest broker (negotiator, advisor, or agent). He has no good to offer humans. In real-time, a broker intends to work for the client to negotiate for them the best deal or advise them in making the best decision. This does not describe the objective of our most dangerous adversary. Therefore, we cannot allow ourselves to fall under the illusion of his romantic overtures of love thereby deceiving you into thinking he desires to assist you, as he did Eve. Satan is disingenuous (deceitful, hypocritical, devious, untruthful); he will never tell you any truth nor is he kind or sympathetic; he cares for no one or nothing good; his every move is selfish and deadly, in both short and long-run scenarios.

He, in essence, convinced her, that, God was not being truthful or was hiding something that would help them, so he offered her his help to step in and fill in the gaps. That was deception on steroids. Satan's use of metrics (standards of measurement) in dealing with humans appears right but is in every way unrighteous and falls short of the God standard, the Plumb Line God used to define spiritual boundaries for man. Satan's metric standards do not have boundaries as he told Eve that eating the forbidden fruit would make her wise.

Sisters all the pleasures of the world are the conduit of Satan to trap man and pull them away from Christ and Salvation. Forewarned is forearmed. Christ warned us, the Old Testament warned us, The New Testament warns us; God, from the beginning to time warned man of the danger of defiance. He gave commands and patterns to live by; those warnings and commands apply to every generation until time ends.

The Rose is a beautiful flower used by man as a symbol of affection. Roses have thorns like the Blackberry Bush have briars, both can injure. They attach themselves to your skin and draw blood – Roses are beautiful and desirable used on special holidays for expressions of love. Yet the beauty of it is enthralling and deceptive, its beauty carries danger. They are given, for a sincere reason, yet at times, it is to manipulate or deceive for gain, which is dangerous. The same with the Blackberry Bush, the berry is sweet, but there is danger beneath, mostly unseen until it is too late. These are the deceptions the world provides; its insurance underwriter is Satan. He is still the same serpent he was in the Garden of Eden. This insurance policy of pleasure he sells is not redeemable; it has no benefit to your Soul. The pleasures of the world will pass away for they are temporary just as is his power.

Satan uses a three basic Utilitarian Principles for pushing his lie:

- Pleasure or happiness is the only thing that truly has intrinsic value.
- Actions are right insofar as they promote happiness, wrong insofar as they produce unhappiness.
- Everyone's happiness counts equally.

Sin has causation and association. Causation is the act or the process of causing…we know that sin has a long arm effect to it. The associations that are connected with the act or the process are without number. Satan has an enormous playbook each sin has attractive associates that look and appears innocent but are just as deadly as the cause.

When Satan goes before the Throne of God, he is bidding, for your soul to destroy you, not to help you. Consider the conversation he had with God about Job, "*Again there was a day when the sons of God came to present themselves before the Lord and Satan came also among them to present himself before the Lord.*" And the Lord said unto Satan, "*From whence comest thou?*" And Satan answered the Lord, and said, "*From going to and fro in the earth, and from walking up and down in it."* And the Lord said unto Satan, *"Hast thou considered my servant Job, that there is none like him in the earth, a perfect, and an upright man, one that fears God, and eschewed evil? And still, he holds fast his integrity, although thou moved me against him, to destroy him without cause,"* [Job 2:1-3].

I used this example and Scripture throughout Book 1, and Book 2. We are the Jobs of this Century sisters. Satan is still the same in every Century, as well as, bold. Remember he asked for Peter that he might shift him as wheat. His sifter has enlarged itself; he is running out of time; souls are important to him. He desires company, your (our) company where he is bound to spend eternity. We stand against Satan and stand for God as Job did. All of the things in what seemed like a moment in time done in his life, to his body, to his property, and the loss of his family, Job did not sin with his lips. Job's position was, *"And said, Naked came I out of my mother's womb, and naked shall I return thither: the Lord giveth, and the Lord taketh away; blessed be the name of the Lord,"* [Job 1:21].

In this light, listen to what Jesus said of Satan's followers, *"Ye are of your father the devil, and the lusts of your father ye will do. He was a murderer from the beginning, and abode not in the truth, because there is no truth in him. When he speaks a lie, he speaks of his own: for he is a liar and the father of it,"* [John 8:44].

Children learn early of the bogeyman under the bed, in the closet, just in the overall darkness. Those are fictional stories, there is no bogeyman it is imaginary in their little minds because of fear. All children are fearful in their young years of the unknown, as they grow they learn better. Hence, there is an actual bogeyman. We cannot see him but can see the results of his power here on earth. He is alive, well, and living out loud in our lives. He is everywhere at all times, he, and his minions. They are not a child-like fantasy of imagination, but a reality. Mommy and daddy protect children from the bogeyman in their imagination; they feel safe in their care and take their word when they say to them, "I scared him away. I will protect you." Our Lord tells us the same. He gives us a remedy for dealing with the bogeyman.

- *We take our parent's word when we are a child, can we not take Christ's word as adults and do His will for our lives and believe that he can protect us from the actual bogeyman?*

When it comes to the reality about Satan, the danger he poses to humans, notably the people of God when looking at the facts surrounding sin and evil needs a clear-eyed view. We are warned about the wiles of Satan; they are virulent (hostile, fierce, malicious) in nature. Allowing the fact that Satan is not visible (a spirit) to the naked eye does not lessen his danger. It increases his danger – "out of sight, out of mind" is also a dangerous ideology. This viewpoint clouds your spiritual vision – it shades issues of right/wrong, good/evil, me/them, I/you – it encourages an (I believe) mindset about Satan. He is evil and I am good he cannot hurt me, is the person with this attitude he goes after, simply put, at that point, your guard is down. We cannot see Satan but can see the effects of his nefarious (wicked) war on man and above all God said, "Satan is our enemy."

The pre-existing condition is an infectious and slow-moving disaster…

CHAPTER TWELVE

# THE PRE-EXISTING CONDITION
# A SLOW-MOVING DISASTER
# LACK OF DISCIPLINE

Sin is a slow-moving disaster in our lives; it can become unnoticed because of Satan's expertise to camouflage the deadly effects it leaves. Unawareness is also deadly…Satan uses a patchwork quilt approach in the pathway of human lives. What he purposes is so attractive man does not see it as sin. Sin is toxic. This pre-existing condition's appearance changes with each generation or even from person to person.

Ezekiel's described defiance and evil in this way with the warning from God to the King of Tyre who had a proud heart, functioned as if he was a god. He used his earthly wisdom and understanding to increase his wealth rather than serving the one and only God … God's warning included one who thought he was a god as well, proud, defiant, and wicked who he bought down and will do the same to any children of pride, *[Ezekiel 28:1-10]*.

Listen to God's message to Ezekiel of the one who exalted himself. He is still among us creating this slow-moving disaster as he encouraged the King of Tyre and others in defiance of the Commands of God.

The Word of the Lord came to me. Son of man take up a lament concerning the King of Tyre and say to him. This is what the Sovereign Lord says, *"You were the seal of perfection full of wisdom and perfect in beauty. You were in Eden the Garden of God, every precious stone adorned you carnelian, chrysolite, and emerald, topaz, onyx and jasper, lapis lazuli, turquoise, and beryl. Your settings and mountings were made of gold; on the day you were created, they were prepared. You were anointed, as a guardian cherub; for so I ordained you.*

*You were on the holy mount of God. You walked among the fiery stones. You were blameless in your ways from the day you were created till wickedness was found in you. Through your widespread trade, you were filled with violence, and you sinned. Therefore, I drove you in disgrace from the mount of God and expelled you guardian cherub from among the fiery stones. Your heart became proud on account of your beauty, and you corrupted your wisdom because of your splendor.*

*So, I threw you to the earth. I made a spectacle of you before kings. By your many sins and dishonest trade, you have desecrated your sanctuaries. So, I made a fire come out from you and it consumed you, and I reduced you to ashes on the ground in the sight of all who were watching. All nations who knew you are appalled at you; you have come to a horrible end and will be no more," [Ezekiel 28:11-15].*

This Scripture is a perfect description of Satan. God did not create any evil. Reading the above verses, we can see what the perfection of the God we serve looks like and then what wickedness looks like when it takes place growing and metastasizing until that evil is full-blown. We are facing that enemy who hates God and hates the people of God. He created the slow-moving disaster; the lie and all evil grew from that root.

Satan will conjure up (produce, materialize) any scenario in your life you so desire. I use the word conjure-up because its overtone is evil. Satan has not the ability to give anything positive in your life. He is a liar. He started at the beginning with a lie. He has the wherewithal to paint, color, embellish, smooth-over, misconstrue, deceive, or any other adjective Miriam Webster list that defines – describes his actions, to give willing participants the desires of their hearts. He promulgates the lie and continues to add to it; building it as a man who builds his house brick by brick.

Satan knows and understands the human propensity for folly. He uses this inherent weakness to further increase his power over the lives of men concerning the world and its ability to provide the needs and wants of humans that he knows, are against the laws of God that he pushes, making them attractive so humans, who unless are on their constant guard, will think they are okay. Attractive is drawing or alluring to humans, but appealing in reference to anything Satan puts before the insatiable desires of men is never okay. He will broadcast a lie that he makes attractive, so it is believable and ensure that man falls for it by disguising that falsehood, so it appears or sounds right.

Sisters the mirrors Satan has to reflect your reality is not yours it is his reality. Those trenches he digs for man only get deeper if you are living in his reality. He uses the mirrors of deceptive half-truths rather than the truth from Scripture.

Satan's lies and calculations I compared to a brothel (female) giving whatever pleasures you desire for as long as you desire. Tasting of the pleasures he offers is a Spiritual and physical deathtrap. I equate it to losing your footing on a weak area of a mountain and it tips you over the edge. You stumble, fall, and tumble seemingly unendingly so. The bottom is a long way down with a rocky treacherous descent. When you hit the bottom, there is no way to climb back up that mountain you fell off; because of the choice, you made the consequences are eternal.

Remember Jezebel in Revelation in the Church of Thyatira. She indulged in and led God's people into this type of lustful living and defiling actions to the displeasure of God, *"Notwithstanding I have a few things against thee because thou sufferest that woman Jezebel, which calleth herself a prophetess, to teach and to seduce My servants to commit fornication, and to eat things sacrificed unto idols. And I gave her space to repent of her fornication, and she repented not. Behold, I will cast her into a bed, and them that commit adultery with her into great tribulation, except they repent of their deeds,"* [Revelation 2:20-22].

He (Satan) is immune to the truth. The vaccine of defiance, disobedience, greed, and hunger for absolute power inoculates him against the truth; thereby, igniting this pre-existing condition in the world. Scripture describes Satan as a Lion; their hunger is deadly ravishing the life, of its victims.

In comparison, Satan will not only drain you of your life but also your soul. Wisdom dictates that our guards are always up, never for one minute let them down, walking with awareness, is using wisdom period. His soul is lost, and he is more than willing – able to assist you in living a life in direct defiance and disobedience to the commandments of God so you can lose yours along with his ... misery loves company.

Satan will take willing or unwilling participants ... The people of God cannot be spiritual Rip, Van Winkles, sleeping through the life God-gifted man and not serving Him. Satan is a totalitarian (one-party) he does not like to know that anyone serves God, Creator of all that exists. He wants absolute control over your life is why he uses all the tools and tricks of the trade to ensure he traps you eternally; thereby, joining him and his willing adherents separated from God for eternity.

Satan is a genius at causing spiritual carnage. Also, causing physical carnage because of the evil he perpetrates, affects the hearts and minds of humans that fall prey to his evil schemes. Saying or telling self he has no power over our lives is dangerous. "The devil made me do it" might sound like fun. This euphemism has a long-term eternal ramification and immediate danger to your heart and soul. It cost Eve a short-term loss of Paradise thrusting her into a world of evilness. He led her there with no safety net to use when she stepped over the truth line to take advantage of his lie.

Satan is in the world. He did not stop in her life at the garden but her first two children Cain killed Abel, the first human carnage because of envy (jealousy). It is a tool of his playbook to destroy humans the people of God beginning in the garden and has continued through every generation. Moses wrote, "*The Lord saw how great the wickedness of the human race had become on the earth, and that every inclination of the thoughts of the human heart was only evil all the time,*" *[Genesis 6:5].*

Cain's thoughts were evil. We cannot allow the evil thoughts and intents Satan pushes to mar, stain, or touch our garments of Christianity. We are of the Kingdom of our Lord and Savior Jesus Christ who provides the cleansing for the garments we wear when they are cleansed from sin through baptism when we contact His Blood through immersion.

Our garments both physical and Spiritual should communicate to those around us that we are people of the Kingdom of God. Our garments are to look like we are representative of the Heavenly Father. Appearance count in this era…as in every century that has passed, the appropriateness of our garments physical and Spiritual are important to God. Communication is important in the business world in body language, facial expression, verbal, and non-verbal communication. Businesses all require (demand) that dress be appropriate it is deemed as part of the key to success and what its message sends is important. As well, the garments we wear in our spiritual lives when we worship on Lord's Day show reverence to our Heavenly Father and speak to our focus, the people of God dress as if we are a child of God.

Satan morphs and shapes the lie to appear as truth. Man craves validation on what they want to do, so they allow Satan to coerce them. Reality and truth are hard to face on their face.

- *Why allow Satan to complicate your life by acclimatizing the truth through his lies and deceptions?*

Truth is not a can of Play-Doh man can shape and re-shape at his whim. Yet we see this happening every day. There is a glaring truth to the statement, "you cannot fit a square plug-in a round hole."

The statement, "You can't fit a square peg in a round hole" is an idiomatic expression, which describes the unusual individual who could not fit into a niche of their society. Smith (1804-1806) in a series of lectures at the Royal Institute reasoned this from the standpoint of Moral Philosophy. In a Spiritual sense, God's people cannot fit into the niche of the society Satan has created for man on this earth.

This is a picture of what Satan will have you do if you do not wear the garments of awareness, at all times.

Satan is an expert at articulating the lies he uses to deceive. He patterns that lie to your desires. He trims away the truth, taking away any choices like the lines on a pattern giving you a one-size choice, which boxes you in.

There is a space, (seemingly) between right and wrong; that is a conflict zone. In wars, there are always conflict zones. Taking both right and wrong and mating it together to be what one is comfortable and can live with, that space (conflict zone) is of man's devising. This equals rewriting right which is not allowable or acceptable to the Creator of all things. God gives us a choice of good/evil, life/death, right/wrong, *[Deuteronomy 30:15-20]*, which brings us back to the [If] condition, *"If you love Him, obey Him, and keep His Laws,"* *[Deuteronomy 30:16b]*.

Ducking will not help with sin, avoiding sin will. Satan does not stop hurling temptations at you. One of the key elements of Satan is vulnerability the arrow of temptation he shoots at you is lace with it. Satan's so-called help at the beginning is an active virus floating among humanity. He provides a ladder to the progressions of sins humans get pulled into. He does not overwhelm you with many sins at the same time, but slowly and progressively until you are overwhelmed; you become so mired down it is hard to pull yourself out of the quagmire. This is his number-one strategy.

Sin has ugly characteristics one of them is beastly – and we have physical and spiritual desires before us. The one that you concentrate on and put the most time into is important. The one that man places the uttermost importance on is the one that will win out. We cannot allow Satan to encourage us to feed the beast of sin. When that beast is well-fed and strong, it will turn and devour you.

Sin's current carries us along through life if we allow it to.

Sin never gets enough; it has the character of a leech it only wants you to give. The Preacher warns us of one with the characteristics of a leech, "*The leech hath two daughters, crying, Give, Give. Three things are never satisfied, yea, four things say not, It is Enough, the grave, the barren womb, land which is never satisfied with water, and fire, which never says,' Enough'!" [Proverbs 30:15-16].*

Because sin is so prevalent in today's society (21st-Century), we cannot allow ourselves to become insensitive to its effects. The fact that it has become commonplace in the world its evilness is overlooked far too much because of the atmosphere of familiarity man has put it in ignoring the Spiritual harm which factor will become eternal. Sin has destructive elements that are attractive when presented, but after the initial involvement can become additive and it will not be easy to rid your life of it —its grip is already reluctant to let go. Satan wants his number of participants to grow. The winds of time dispel all things memories, culture, generation, business, and numerous other physical elements of life. Truth is one absolute the winds of time cannot dispel, eradicate, or change. It is unchangeable because the Creator of the Universe and all therein is Truth because He does not change.

Sisters, Satan if allowed, will rock you to sleep on a train of complacency. While you get comfortable and become spiritually drowsy and not alert, the train of temporary harmony you are riding has an end-of-track. Hence, when life is smooth, things are going as planned in our days, finances are not perfect, but manageable, as well, stress levels are low, so life, we think, is good. Your guard is down at this point, Satan will attack you because he knows complacency has

set in. As the analogy goes, 'complacency is a thief of time." Chaos is his specialty, which affects our focus on God. Chaos is his entire mission because mistakes and errors are a possibility; both are by-products of contentment. It (complacency) affects our spirituality and faithfulness. Chaos is the foundation of losing control, chasing every little fire that breaks out around the once smooth day-to-day events in your life.

Sin will cause the othering of you…becoming someone other than the [you] God created. He wants you outside of the Salvation that our Savior died to purchase and gifted to humanity. Salvation is not a tealeaf reading process. We do not each have a different perception we can claim, this as well is a trick of Satan. God gave us the commonality (shared aims) of being a unified one this is the basic tenant of our Salvation. Salvation purchased through the Blood of Christ we contact through baptism.

- *Are these facts, ones you accept without question?*
- *On the other hand, do you alternatively, listen to the voice, of the enemy of God and man?*

Denialism or becoming a denialist has no place in reference to your soul, your salvation, an eternity of peace, or the Commandments if we want to spend an eternity of peace with God. The fact that Christ purchased our Salvation is indisputable. Denying that Christ is our Lord and Savior and has the power to decide what is best for man is dangerous to your soul. We cannot use the pattern of man to plot our course to eternity; that is, not one that is pleasing to God that will aid in you having an eternity of peace.

As stated more than once throughout the chapters in this book Scripture tells us, God does not change, man has to change. Jesus gave the most precious Pearls that will ever be, His life, His blood, and hung on that cruel cross for a [debt] He did not owe. Once again, we owed that debt. Eve signed a contract with Satan for a cost no man could/can pay. Sisters we cannot forsake God for anything in this world, our souls now and through eternity are important. If we abandon God now, there will be no eternity of peace for you only an eternity of misery that Satan and his followers will inherit.

We see every day the condition of man the Scripture describes. Paul wrote to Timothy of the coming danger, *"This know, in the last days, perilous times will come. Men will be lovers of themselves, lovers of money, boastful, proud, abusive, disobedient to their parents, ungrateful, unholy, without love, unforgiving, slanderous, without self-control, brutal, not lovers of the good, treacherous, rash, and conceited, lovers of pleasure, rather than lovers of God – having a form of godliness but denying its power. Have nothing to do with such people," [2 Timothy 3:1-5].*

Therefore, denying the inevitable is the most dangerous decision anyone can make, all for the pleasure put forth by Satan that will become acceptable to you if you allow it. He knows every 'trick' in the book. However, remember contracts are for a specific period, a one-time deal. Contracts are of man's creation and have the constraint of time and this world. God's Covenant with man is eternal.

- *The choice is yours. The choices are earthly contracts written by Satan or the eternal Covenant, purchased by Jesus Christ, what will be your choice?*
- *Both choices have consequences; which will you choose?*

Jesus set the standard for our life. He died for the Salvation of man. Spending that precious wealth listening to the voice of Satan is costly (a waste of your spiritual wealth). The individual, who listens to the defiant, as well as untruthful promises of Satan, ends in being spiritually broken, poor, homeless, destitute, hungry, and your life completely ravished. He attractively pushes greed, defiance, and all negativities. Keep in mind he is an expert and effective at what he does.

The dark patterns that Satan uses are not visible to man rather he makes them attractive and desirable as he had done over the centuries many times in the lives of humans, especially targeting the people of God. After your destruction, he will leave you out on that limb, on which he sat, to perpetrate the first lie he told. He misconstrued the Word of God and the commands He gave Adam. He used the Word of God against our Savior in the wilderness, and He is God. He will do the same thing to you, as is guaranteed by the Scriptures referenced in earlier chapters.

Satan can manifest and will manifest himself in any way he chose and will fulfill your desire according to your wants and needs.

Satan plays to the lowest common denominator in the lives of people. The lowest common denominator in colloquial terminology is a rule, proposal, or opinion simplified to appeal to the largest possible number of people. He knows the weakness of the flesh, insatiable human desires, and the attractiveness of the world. His footprints are all over the centuries of sin and defiance man is involved in. Those footprints are growing each day that passes.

- *Do you or I individually have to follow in the footsteps that look so attractive he leaves? No!*

The Commandments of God are unchanged; the truth is still the pattern we follow. Keeping in mind, he knows what your desires are; he knows your weakness, and he preys on your spiritual inactivity. Satan knows if he makes life attractive and comfortable enough you will lose your focus and fall into one of the multiple traps in his playbook.

He has the experience of making defiance attractive; remember his defiance is from the beginning of time. Defying God, he began to create the strategies of sin in that book. He adds pages to it each victory in humans (your) lives (life). Let reason dictate to us that he has a page for each of us, especially God's people. Satan led a coup d'état (violent seize) against the Creator of the Universe and was defeated.

- *His seizes in the lives of humans are violence against your soul.*
  *Satan defied God what do you think he will do to your life?*

Satan is an excellent [orchestrator] of his patchwork quilt sin process. He is the ultimate evil. It is wise to wake to this reality before it is eternally too late; we cannot allow the desires of our hearts or what we call our rights to become a misnomer. Man cannot know what is right or wrong; this is the idea that got us in this trouble with God – God identifies and decides what is right or wrong since we do not have that ability.

God does not give us a choice or the leave to re-write what His Commands are for our lives, nor decides what we think or how we are to be pleasing to him.

Satan has created this edifus system for man along with the weakness of the flesh. An edifus is an enormous conceptual structure. In the Spiritual sense, I used it to describe the enormous system of sin and deception he uses on humanity. Satan can influence humanity. He can cause them grief, spiritual and physical misery, and eventually eternal grief, which is separation from God.

This is due to man's lack of self-discipline and a willingness to obey the will of our Creator. Humans lack the humility in-and-of-themselves to be obedient to the Creator. God is the giver of all things in our lives and only through Him can learn humility.

As well, God is the creator of all including Satan!

We have the written Word, our Light to guide us down that correct path. Though we live in the world and sin exists, we are not of the world. We will not be able to claim ignorance at the Throne of God on Judgment Day. Satan's [playbook] increased in chapters every day. He adds and multiples; he does not subtract.

Satan pulls humans into his clutches, to sift them as wheat. We cannot allow ourselves to be pulled into his [playbook] of sinful desires that appears to be right but is not right in the sight of God and will cost us our souls. He will help you kick the can down life's road as far as you desire until you lose sight of your true spirituality.

*"Satan made all nations drink of the maddening wine of her adulteries,"* *[Revelation 14:8b].*

John the Apostle spoke of this, about the evil Roman Empire and the suffering of Christians as was the Babylonian Empire's evil against the people of Judah at that time, he reminds them of the same suffering. God's people suffered under the evil empires of the Babylonians and the Romans. Satan is still operating and has his beast of the sea and beast of the land with him in a three-fold effort to harm the people of God. Simply, evil surrounds us while living in this world, but we are not those who are of the world.

John wanted the faithful people of Christ (Christians) to be aware of the necessity of the Spiritual and Moral discernment God wanted His people to have at that time. Regardless of the difficulty and the evil that the empire was pushing upon the people, God is still in control and their spirituality was secure. The Holy Spirit was there as well. He is (our) seal of redemption. The Roman Empire had no moral compass but was evil and sinful positioning themselves against God and His people.

- *How does man regardless of who they are (an empire no matter the size) affront, God?*

I alluded to this in Book One of Dressed for The Kingdom. Scriptures tell us Satan tried challenging God and we see what the end was, (is). God is in control and no power on earth or in heavenly places has more control than the Creator of all things does, as well as, and including once again Satan.

110

When thinking of drinking the wine of maddening adulteries *[Revelation 14:8b]* just thinking of a scenario of this kind is frightening. Drinking indicates taking into one's system a liquid that permeates through the body. When we drink water – we know it lubricates every joint, tissue, vein, organ, hair, and nail of the body. According to *Dictionary.com,* lubricating is something that makes a process run smoothly. In another sense, it (strong drink) makes (that person/someone) convivial, friendly, and jovial. In essence, like alcohol, it takes away your rational abilities or expected normalcy of a coherent person, to the point John made about the maddening wine of her adultery.

Anything maddening is infuriating – it never stops – repeat and picks up one's life at that point, but then repeat, which is an annoying unending cycle or process; is exactly what Satan offers. God's people are to be aware of this lack of truth in the spiritual and moral behavior pushed by the adversary of the people of God. Drinking of maddening adulteries is more than one but many or anything in direct defiance of God's Word and desire for His people. The more humans take in the sins of this world, as a liquid does, it will lubricate every area of the heart, mind, and soul until they become completely infected with the sins Satan promotes as pleasures.

They (sins) become so enjoyable it (they) puts one in a state of happiness and unawareness. Just enough alcohol can make a person jovial, playful, and living outside of him or herself. They are not in a drunken stupor, but inebriated enough not to recognize they are walking down the wrong path. Satan does not want you drunk but high enough to like where you are in life and believe your soul is secure. Another of the fallacies he pushes. Satan's system of lather (wash), rinse, and repeat are deadly.

Satan's offers of pleasure are parasitical. If allowed the pleasure of that sin will latch on to you as a parasite does and drain the life out of your spirituality. It eats away at your heart and soul until it virtually consumes your life. The wiles of Satan are exploitative; he uses your desires for the pleasures of this world to take advantage of any weakness he discerns that you might have, and we all have them sisters is why we stay cognizant at all times. Daily we stay conscious that he is on the prowl – prowling is one of the characteristics of this slow-moving disaster.

Living as if we are in a spiritually semi-unconscious state while on our journey, in life, the outlay, in the end, is more expensive than we will want to pay. Satan is still serving humanity his cocktail of deceit, which feeds into the unawareness of man putting him in a drunken stupor to the guile he pushes. This type of obliviousness is a danger to our spirituality. He looks for any opportunity for the smallest of cracks to choreograph the fall of God's people, one at a time.

Satan, if allowed, will supplant, and continue to usurp the meaning of the Scripture in the lives of humans. He has a slavish playbook of meanings of the Word of God that he pushes that humans become subject to if they do not stay mindful and alert (Study). With the mass amount of information disseminated in this world about what is pleasing to God and who God is, it can become overwhelming. Choosing what sparkles is dangerous or putting in plainer language what is most popular, which is attractive to humans. There is always [the] truth in any attractive lie he (Satan) pushes. We cannot become spiritual slaves to his deadly wiles.

A lie, a single lie, and single defiance birthed this pre-existing condition. As long as the world stands, Satan will be here. Our garment sisters have to be of such that we can enter the battle prepared because it is a war. It is a cancer of the Spirit that can and will metastasize if it remains unchecked and that condition is not being treated by the Great Physician, though our sins are many there is only one treatment, *"Everyone who sins breaks the law; in fact, sin is lawlessness. But you know that He appeared so that He might take away our sins. And, in Him is no sin. No one who lives in Him keeps on sinning. No one who continues to sin has neither seen Him nor known Him,"* [I John 3:4-6].

John repeated what the Prophet Hosea said as well, *"My people are destroyed for lack of knowledge: because thou hast rejected knowledge, I will also reject thee, that thou shalt be no priest to Me: seeing thou hast forgotten the law of thy God, I will also forget thy children,"* [Hosea 4:6].

Words matter…Words:

- created the condition.
- created unprotected surroundings.
- created envy.
- created anger, which feeds the condition.
- created thirst for power; which elevated the condition; and
- Created a human weakness in belief, which created desires to know and defy God's Command to not touch or eat of the Tree in the midst of the Garden.

All words in the Garden of Eden spoken by our enemy, the animal in the tree, were deceitful and put man's feet on the path to the pre-existing condition each of us is born into…

Satan is armed and ready to swing you like a pendulum. My mother had a large clock with a pendulum, it moved constantly; that swing ensured the hands of the clock worked properly and it kept the correct time. His playbook has this type of swing (keeping your life according to his time and not God's). It is there to keep that person hanging taking away the ability to make solid decisions in their spiritual life. Trying to serve God and serve the desires of the pleasures of the world does not bode well. He makes the things we desire to do look so innocent and it seems okay when it is not.

Satan led Eve into that trap, and it cost not only Adam and her but also people for all generations until Christ came and paid the debt. Satan greases the wheels of sin so they will not squeak (noticeable) enabling man to fulfill his desires by making them easy and attractive to obtain.

Satan is the [author] of segregation between God and man.

Satan wiles are the [petri dish] for humanity. He cultivates the fungi and bacteria of the evil piloting his slow-moving disasters.

Satan is not an illusion (fantasy) but the full force of evil. We can see the results of the evil that he executes in the world. The evilness he implemented is on an ongoing basis as mentioned before, the pages and chapters in his playbook increases in number, intensity, and wiliness. Paul tells us *"Lest Satan should get an advantage of us: for we are not ignorant of his devices," [2 Corinthians 2:11].*

We know he is wily, yet man does not know all of his tricks and traps but knows they are there, and he is more than capable of tricking and trapping man; he has proved this down through the ages. This is a major reason why people of God are to walk [circumspectfully] at all times. God's people cannot let their guards down. At best we fall into his traps, but thanks be to God can recover or overcome those temptations through Christ.

Satan has a convenience store of pleasures. He makes whatever your heart desires convenient for you. He is the god of this world and uses his powers to persuade man. John reminds us, *"Love not the world, neither the things that are in the world. If any man loves the world, the love Father is not in him. For all that is in the world, the lust of the flesh, and the lust of the eyes, and the pride of life, is not of the Father; but is of the world. And the world passes away, and the lust thereof: but he that doeth the will of God abides forever," [I John 2:15-17].*

Each time we fall, rising from that fall is possible, and as a result, are wiser and stronger from experience and learn vigilance by wearing that armor. Satan is circling our spirituality at all times looking, for cracks in our armor, looking to sift us as wheat.

Sin and the pleasure of this world are like carrying a sack of heavy rocks; it can wear you down. That sack becomes a burden after a while giving the bearer a feeling that is backbreaking.

David tells us that sins are heavy burdens and displeases God and incurs His wrath. In his prayer, to God, David prayed for help with the burdens he bore, *"There is no soundness in my flesh because of thine anger; neither is there any rest in my bones because of my sin. For mine iniquities are gone over mine head: as a heavy burden, they are too heavy for me. My wounds stink and are corrupt because of my foolishness. I am troubled; I am bowed down gently; I go mourning all the day long," [Psalms 38:3-6].*

We realize as David did, *"The wages of sin is death and the gift of God is eternal life," [Ibid].*

Sisters, Christ died for all taking our burden of sin upon His self and His death was for us to have eternal life with God. At the risk of being redundant, Christ willingly gave His life for us to pay our sin debt. Sisters, Christ died for all taking our burden of sin upon Him that we have the gift. Sin changes our relationship with God.

Satan is the serpent wrapped around the foundation of the people of this world because he is the god of this world and the father of the lie. He birthed the lie into existence. He nurses the grudge and hate he has for God and the people of God. He feeds his multitude of lies to those willing to listen keeping them healthy and embellishes them (lies and deceit) to make them attractive so he can pull you in. His only motive is to destroy, not build, to cause division, not unity, to incite hate, not peace, to pull people away from God into his kingdom of lies, and not closer to God.

Hence, the same for us, his power still exists. Satan and his minions are alive and well.

All of this is under one umbrella of hate, and he is an expert at it. There is no possible way you can fight against Satan alone; you will lose the battle. Dealing with Satan at any level is flirting with danger. Any momentary thought of taking Satan up on his petri-dish of pleasure is a beginning of a loss of your footing spiritually. Again, he is a beauty and the beast in reverse.

We learn from history the ramifications of sin and adhering to the voice of our chief adversary. Climbing a mountain or driving up a mountain, cliffs are there. They are common or one of the various characteristics of a mountain.

- *If you know the cliff is there with inherent weakness, why walk too close to the edge?*

It is only one step too close or the rocks under your feet (foot) brake or you step on a weak spot, it only takes just one of these actions to tip you over the edge.

- *Sin is a cliff; Christians know the cliffs of sin exist why you would test your spiritual footing knowing sin weakens your life and it can cause one to tumble?*

The position one takes that it is fun to dabble into the unknown and learn and explore the things this life has to offer that are interesting and enjoyable this slow-moving disaster also a playbook favorite of Satan. The Scripture warns us we are, *"We are not unaware of his wiles,"* *[Ibid]*.

The Word of God is the tripwire that prevents the people of God from going over that cliff.

Judas Iscariot's greed led him to that cliff, *"Then saith, one of His disciples, Judas Iscariot, Simon's son, which should betray Him, Why was not this ointment sold for three hundred pence, and given to the poor? This he said, not that he cared for the poor, but because he was a thief, and had the money box; and he used to take what was put in it,"* *[John 12:4-6]*.

Judas' greed and love of money led him to do the ultimate, betrayed Christ for thirty-(30)-pieces of silver to the Sanhedrin who helped lead him to that cliff and the love of money (silver coins) push him over the edge. The worth of those thirty pieces of silver would value at less than $200 or equaling four working days for a man, defines the significance to him of the Salvation he knew Jesus came to purchase: And he, (Judas) said unto the Sanhedrin, *"What will ye give me, and I will deliver Him unto you? And they covenanted with him for thirty pieces of silver,"* *[Matthew 26:15]*.

The love of money, as the Scripture reminds us, is the root of all kinds of evil. It is necessary to keep in mind sisters that money and wealth are wonderful servants but cruel masters.

Demas's love of the world led him to that cliff. Paul reminds us, *"For Demas has forsaken me, having [loved this present world], and is departed unto Thessalonica,"* *[2 Timothy 4:10a].*

Eve's desire to "know" listening to the voice of Satan, led her to that cliff and when she tumbled off took Adam with her, *"Now the serpent was more subtle than any beast of the field which the Lord God had made."* And he said unto the woman, *"Yea, hath God said, ye, shall not eat of every tree of the garden?"* And the woman said unto the serpent, *"We may eat of the fruit of the trees of the garden: But of the fruit of the tree, which is in the midst of the garden, God hath said, Ye shall not eat of it, neither shall ye touch it, lest ye die."* And the serpent said unto the woman, *"Ye shall not surely die: For God doth know that in the day ye eat thereof, then your eyes shall be opened, and ye shall be as gods, knowing good and evil." And, when the woman saw that the tree was good for food and that it was pleasant to the eyes, and a tree to be desired to make one wise, she took of the fruit thereof, and did eat, and gave unto her husband with her; and he did eat. And the eyes of them both were opened, and they knew that they were naked, and they sewed fig leaves together and made themselves aprons. And they heard the voice of the Lord God walking in the garden in the cool of the day: and Adam and his wife hid from the presence of the Lord God amongst the trees of the garden. And the Lord God called unto Adam, and said unto him, "Where art thou?"* And He said, *" I heard thy voice in the garden, and I was afraid because I was naked; and I hid myself,"* *[Genesis 3:1-10].*

- **What has Satan contracted with you for that would pull you away from the grace and mercy of God?**

He only has failed promises and will not, nor cannot offer you mercy!

Human desires are "tests." Eventually, life tests each of us, up to, and including children. One's ability to resist the specific temptation defines the nature of the tests. If "I want," does not get in the way the test is easy, but if it is something we desire to do it is hard to reject the temptation. Each test you overcome is a victory for you and a defeat for Satan.

The desires of human hearts move them closer to that cliff of (I desire, I want). Each day we experience pleasures from our desires, they grow. It is like eating chocolate, one of the favorite delights in the world. Who does not like chocolate? There are many kinds: light or dark with nuts or without nuts. Humans visit a Willy Wonka Chocolate Factory each time they partake of the deliciousness of sin, as you eat your desire for it grows and its desire for you grows all the more. Remember Chocolate (sins) is pleasing to the palate.

The benefits of chocolate are there; it is a known antioxidant, at least the dark is, that is an advantage, even with the gain's chocolate might have; there are limits to those pluses. In contrast, there are no positives to sin. There are dangers in partaking of both (sin and chocolate), but the effects are not immediately known or felt. Each day you partake continuously; its effects are growing. Finally, with chocolate, weeks later the evidence of your enjoyment shows in your body, its size, and in your health. Indulgences in sin begin to manifest themselves in your spiritual and physical life in a negative way; becoming lackadaisical in your faithfulness to God is one of the first signs.

Sin, like chocolate, is enjoyable; however, when it has you in its clutches, in the end, leads you to that cliff, your footing lost, you tumble. Satan offered Eve his solicitude in the form of sympathy, *"Has God said? And ended with you will not die, but will know as God knows," [Ibid].* In other words, "I will help you and tell you even if He does not." He uses the 'you poor thing' mentality with Eve; another of his playbook wiles.

We should not desire or accept his twisted version of God's Word. It is a lie dressed in formal wear with gown, shoes, evening bag, and accessories; they sparkle so do all the lies he tells…that slow-moving disaster.

Satan's playbook is a perfect storm and we, unfortunately, without choice, are in the middle of his perfect storm. We have a shelter, as David tells us, *"He that dwells in the secret place of the most high shall abide under the shadow of the Almighty. I will say of theLord, He is my refuge and my fortress: My God; in Him will I trust. Surely, He shall deliver thee from the snare of the fowler, and from the noisome pestilence. He shall cover thee with His feathers; and under His wings, shalt thou trust: His truth shall be thy shield and buckler. Thou shalt not be afraid of the arrow by day nor: for the pestilence that walks in darkness; nor for the destruction that waste at noonday."*

*"A thousand shall fall at thy side, and ten thousand at thy right hand; but it shall not come nigh thee. Only with thine eyes, shalt thou behold and see the reward of the wicked. Because thou hast made theLord, which is my refuge, even the most High, thy habitation; there shall no evil befall thee, neither shall any plague come nigh thy dwelling, for He shall give His angels charge over thee, to keep thee in all thy ways."*

*"They shall bear thee up in their hands, lest thou dash thy foot against a stone. Thou shalt tread upon the lion and adder: the young lion and the dragon shalt thou trample under feet. Because he hath set his love upon me, therefore will I deliver him: I will set him on high, because he hath known my name; he shall call upon Me, and I will answer him: I will be with him in trouble; I will deliver him, and honor him,"* [Psalms 91:1-15].

The storm is not going away. The storms Satan brings into our lives do not pass over as hurricanes eventually do; he keep storms in our lives at all times. We are in this battle, suit up, and fight for the privilege of eternal peace with God and the right to live in that Mansion Christ is preparing for each of His faithful servants.

Paul gave us the key to that privilege and the results, *"For I am now ready to be offered, and the time of my departure is at hand. I have fought a good fight, I have finished my course, and I have kept the faith: Henceforth, there is laid up for me a crown of righteousness, which the Lord, the righteous judge, shall give me at that day: and not to me only, but unto all them also that love His appearing,"* [2 Timothy 4:6-8].

Finishing the race is the key and not falling into Satan's playbook of games becoming like the Hare and resting, but rather be like the Tortoise, who continued to plug along and reached the finish line and crossed it. We all know this childhood fable. It is a good analogy to use to make a point. Plugging along at a steady pace is the key. Not as the Hare that ran fast and suffered burnout and had to rest and because he thought he had time but did not.

We cannot take a spiritual break or rest under that spiritual shade tree on the way to eternity. Nor is it wise to buy into Hare's analogy. Being spiritually slothful is another trick Satan makes look so attractive: rather, we must keep moving. A 1st-Century-quote with a modern societal meaning makes that point, *"A rolling stone gathers no moss."* [Publilius Syrus 1st- Century B.C].

Satan will cause us to suffer stagnation in our Spirituality; keep moving regardless of the obstacles he places in your path, and he will place hurdles we need to get over there! We can overcome them, but only through Christ our Lord and Savior.

Satan will filter you as fined ground grain as Jesus told Peter, *"And the Lord said, "Simon, Simon! Indeed, Satan has asked for you, that he may sift you as wheat. But I have prayed for thee, that thy faith fails not: and when thou art converted, strengthen thy brethren," [Luke 22:31-32].*

Satan put Peter to the test, and he denied Jesus as He said. Peter was weak though he said he was ready to stand for Christ. This is an example for us to remember that we are all susceptible to His wiles. *"Without faith, it is impossible to please God," [Hebrews 11:6].*

This type of faith only comes through prayer.

Christ prayed for Peter that when his strength return he would strengthen his brethren, *[Luke 22:34].* Let us never forget Satan asks for us that he may try us as well. He will promise you the world, he did our Savior what do you think he will do to you? *"Jesus answered, "It is written: 'Man shall not live on bread alone." The devil led Him up to a high place and showed Him in an instant all the kingdoms of the world. And he said to Him, "I will give you all their authority and splendor; it has been given to me, and I can give it to anyone I want to. If you worship me, it will all be yours," [Luke 4:4-7].*

Prayer is our avenue of help from God. Satan is soulless. He does not understand moaning before the Throne of God, he rejects humility. He is prideful and defiant is what got him into the lost condition he is suffering knowing he has no hope for redemption. We are in a spiritual crisis in this world; sin is a spiritual crisis; it existed from the first defiance and is still existing…we are born into a pre-existing condition.

Our garments of prayer should be to our Heavenly Father to help us get through each day in the way that is pleasing to Him, for tomorrow is not promised, *"Sufficient unto today is the evil thereof," [Matthew 6:34].*

Each day is a precious jewel given to us by our Lord and Savior. Each day we wake again, we can count ourselves blessed to receive this gift and an opportunity to serve God and our fellowman as well while it is called today.

Sin is the anomaly – anomaly is defined as something that deviates from a standard normal or expected; it is an oddity, peculiarity, or abnormality. Sin is also a deviation or departure from the normal or common order, form, or rule. Sin is a malfunction on the curtain of our spirituality that does not fit the pattern of obedience and commands of God.

Sin causing cracks in the foundation of your spirituality is a playbook wile of Satan. Underestimating the chief adversary is eternally and spiritually deadly. He has no small guns in his arsenal for the war he makes…they are all "big."

The spirit of the world has a bent toward selfishness – selfishness is sinful. The fall of man began in the Garden of Eden is a glaring fact we cannot get around. Eve and Adam's act of defiance was selfish. The fallen man's desires and drives have piloted (guided) them to the point from the moment the defiant act of the eating of the forbidden fruit into a dark world and from that moment the darkness was encountered needed light and still needs a light, will forever need light until the day Christ returns.

God used a Herculean effort to save humanity. Webster Dictionary defines a Herculean effort as **a job, task, or activity that requires a huge amount of effort, energy, or physical strength.** In a Spiritual sense, with the definition above, and the conditions that would provide the avenue back to a one-on-one relationship with God no man could fulfill.

This extraordinary effort was universal requiring unchecked knowledge and the ability to preach the Gospel to draw man and assemble an army of warriors to lead the earthly battle His chosen (Twelve Apostles). It was an unbelievable effort, which took energy, and physical strength; Jesus was the only one to meet all the conditions, requirements, and do the work within three years which took an enormous amount of physical strength to bear up under what Christ (only God) could go/went through.

In the Book of Revelation, the scene John recorded he saw in Heaven the Lamb of God, Jesus Christ, was the only one worthy to break the Seal. As in that scene then and is now, was the only one worthy to walk the road to Calvary to purchase our Salvation and provide treatment, for the sins of man, *"And I saw in the right hand of Him that sat on the throne a book written within and on the backside, sealed with seven seals. And I saw a strong angel proclaiming with a loud voice, "Who is worthy to open the book, and to break the seals thereof?" And no man in heaven, nor in the earth, neither under the earth, was able to open the book, neither to look thereon."*

And *"I wept much because no man was found worthy to open and to read the book, neither to look thereon. And one of the elders said unto me, "Weep not: behold, the Lion of the tribe of Judah, the Root of David, hath prevailed to open the book and to break the seven seals thereof. And I beheld, and, lo, in the midst of the throne and of the four beasts, and in the midst of the elders, stood a Lamb as it had been slain, having seven horns and seven eyes, which are the seven Spirits of God sent forth into all the earth," [Revelation 5:1-6].*

Humans cannot allow faith and obedience to be the reverse anomaly. Sin is the anomaly; it is outside of God's plans for humanity. God created a perfect world. He made a perfect man and woman to live in this perfect world and placed them in a perfect garden. It was pure until the first bite of sin entered through the voice of an enemy of God and enemy of His people, an animal's voice in a tree bid the first bit, thought, action, touch, taste, and smell of defiance and disobedience, which was sin…ushering it (sin) into the world, at that moment.

Satan stokes human fires, of desire, daily. He adds more fat kindling of desire to your life. Wood tinder is fat, combustible, and causes a fire to burn out of control if not checked. Satan uses whatever kindling he knows will start human fires and makes what your desires are attractive until they are out of control.

See how fast a Forest of Pine Trees burns. The heat is so intense even getting near the fire is deadly. Sin is like tinder; it is deadly. Paul warns us, "Do *not handle! Do not taste! Do not touch!" [Colossians 2:21].*

We cannot touch a hot oven, of sin and expect the characteristics of it not to burn. When we purchase appliances, electric or gas stoves, those fire characteristics come with them. We know the fire characteristic is pre-existent to our purchasing them. We know fire destroys and burns; as well as does sin.

Satan wants man, as a whole, to continue using the Nero analogy: Fiddle, while Rome burns or in a spiritual sense [fiddle while your spirituality suffers] and not take advantage of the gift of Salvation Christ purchased for us. Using this analogy from the Spiritual sense, which is acting irresponsibly in the midst of the Spiritual and Salvation emergency we face. Time is short! No man knows the day or the hour of his final day on earth or how long this world will stand before the Savior of the World returns. We cannot ignore our Salvation and the serious matter of where we will spend eternity.

Satan pulls individuals into the throes of his playbook. He does not operate by pulling humans in – in a group way, but that pull is one at a time. He works his plan to ensure the fall of God's people also to prevent those who would come to God. We are in a spiritual, emotional, social, and even physical battle. Satan uses all or any of these characteristics in the human make-up to his advantage and against the individual. He preys on the weak areas in people's lives is why we are to put on the whole armor of God in a three hundred eighty degrees manner not leaving any opportunity for Satan to pull us in or attack our weakness; we all have them.

The pre-existing condition and its continual evolution have been in an osmosis (the process of gradual or unconscious assimilation of ideas, knowledge, etc.) manner. Satan's plan is a gradual accommodation of the desires of a man pushed by him as being right. Man has learned/acquired this ideology not from the source that God gives, the Holy Scripture: but from the desires that humans have to live life in the manner, they so wish and not according to God's desire for their life.

The facts are the presence of sin is not hidden; nor will it come upon one by surprise; we are aware it exists. The defining point is this: Satan uses the desires of man to rule his own life, as the tool, of which he leads man into destroying his soul by defying God.

Satan's playbook includes a: I came, I saw, and I conquered strategy; we cannot fall into that playbook strategy. We know that his only interest is in destroying our soul and preventing our chances of a peaceful and joyous eternity with the Father, the Son, and the Holy Spirit: the Trinity: the Triune God of Creation and Eternity.

He is seeking, circling, and prowling as *[Job 2:2]*, tells us, *"And the Lord said to Satan, "Where have you come from?" Satan answered the Lord, "From roaming throughout the earth, going back and forth on it."* Peter warns, *"Be alert and of sober mind. Your enemy the devil prowls around like a roaring lion looking for someone to devour," [I Peter 5:8]*.

Thinking of a Lion as stated enormous times, they are expert hunters. They target a victim's weakness or a weak victim. When looking at the National Geographic Channel (NGC), the Lioness identifies their victim and waits until that weak member of the herd is separate or lagging; at that point, that vulnerable member becomes their target because of that exposure.

A Lioness does not run into a herd of Water Buffalo. They would gore her to death. They protect their herd members. This is the same as with people of God is why God's people need to be close in a corporate way. The weaker members (vulnerable) have the strength of the entire congregation to lean on. Paul tells us, *"We who are strong ought to bear with the failings of the weak and not to please ourselves," [Romans 15:1].*

Finally, *"Be alert and of sober mind. Your enemy the devil prowls around like a roaring lion looking for someone to devour. Resist him, standing firm in the faith because you know that the family of believers throughout the world is undergoing the same kind of suffering," [I Peter 5:8-9].*

Satan is willing to lead your soul through a dry wilderness that ends in its destitution. Human desires are their weakest needs. Think of Eve's desire to know as God knows; as well, Lot's wife desires to possess both what is and what was; and Herodias' desire to fulfill her lust for life in every way.

Satan will take you as a willing or unwilling participant with the dark patterns he uses to deceive humans. We cannot be spiritual Rip Van Wrinkles … sleeping through our spirituality and not serving God.

Satan believes in totalitarianism (total control) we cannot fight against Satan alone – only through Christ our Savior can we avoid this slow-moving disaster he uses like the stalking and stealth of a predator upon his prey – Self Discipline is paramount.

We are to wear our garments of resistance to this pre-existing condition, but we cannot resist the wiles of Satan alone. Paul tells us we are to suit up, *"Put on the whole armor of God that you might be able to fight against the wiles of Satan," [Ephesians 6:11].*

We do not wear garments that Herodias and Salome wore. They used wiles from Satan's playbook to deceive one man and destroy another…a slow-moving disaster resulting in the death of a Prophet of God.

CHAPTER THIRTEEN

# WOMEN OF DECEIT GARMENTS OF HERODIAS AND SALOME THE DANCE OF THE SEVEN VEILS AND THE SILVER PLATTER

*For Herod had laid hold on John and bound him, and put him in prison for Herodias' sake, his brother Philip's wife. For John said unto him, it is not lawful for thee to have her. And when he would put him to death, he feared the multitude, because they counted him as a prophet. But when Herod's birthday was kept, the daughter of Herodias danced before them, and pleased Herod."*

*"Whereupon, he promised with an oath to give her, whatsoever she would ask. And she, being before instructed of her mother, said, 'Give me John the Baptist's head in a charger. And the king was sorry: nevertheless, for the oath's sake, and them, which sat with him at meat, he commanded it to be given her. And he sent and beheaded John in the prison. And his head was brought in a charger and given to the damsel: and she brought it to her mother,"* [Matthew 14:3-11].

*"For Herod, himself had given orders to have John arrested, and he had him bound and put in prison. He did this because of Herodias, his brother Philip's wife, whom he had married."* For, John had been saying to Herod, *"It is not lawful for you to have your brother's wife."*

*"So, Herodias nursed a grudge against John and wanted to kill him. But she was not able to, because Herod feared John and protected him, knowing him to be a righteous and holy man. When Herod heard John, he was greatly puzzled'; yet he liked to listen to him,"* [Mark 6:17-28].

The summer breeze and blue skies of peace, purity, obedience, and tranquility blew softly through the Garden of Eden in the daily lives of its inhabitants. Also, in their lives, came the unseen winds of change that were on the horizon. The winds of evilness, wickedness, disobedience, idol worship, and sins, of like kind, blew through Eden and have continued since, for centuries, marching like armies to war.

As the number of human inhabitants on earth increased, so did the evilness and wickedness until God destroyed the known world at that time with an earthly Deluge. Human nature did not change with the waters of the Flood. The nature of humans was sinful and in need of Salvation and a light to show them the way.

John the Baptist, a forerunner of Christ, was that voice of one crying in the wilderness preparing the way of the Lord, *"The voice of him that cries in the wilderness, Prepare ye the way of the Lord, make straight in the desert a highway for our God. Every valley shall be exalted, and every mountain and hill shall be made low: and the crooked shall be made straight; and the rough places plain: And the glory of the Lord shall be revealed, and all flesh shall see it together: for the mouth of the Lord hath spoken it. The voice said, Cry. And he said, "What shall I cry? All flesh is grass, and all the goodliness thereof is as the flower of the field: The grass withers, the flower fade: because the Spirit of the Lord blows upon it: surely, the people are grass. The grass wither, the flower fade: but the Word of our God shall stand forever,"* [Isaiah 40:3-8].

The strong winds of evilness and wickedness blew in the Palace of King Herod Antipas. They were the evils of malice and lewd behavior of Herodias and Salome and their mother/daughter conspiracy. Rejection of the light is not using wisdom, but trying to destroy the light or the bearer of the light is in direct defiance of God's Command.

The winds of change placed a great [gulf] between God and man, one that no human could span to fulfill the blood requirement to cleanse the sins of man in an acceptable manner. Herodias and her enthusiasts disregarded the message and destroyed the messenger, but not the message.

We read in the New Testament both versions given by *[Matthew and Mark]*, of the evil plot perpetrated by Herodias to kill John the Baptist. Though the New Testament writers used different descriptive wording, the descriptions, of the actions of two women that led to the death, of John the Baptist, are the same.

We see yet another example of a man (Herod Antipas) falling prey under the wiles of a woman.

Mothers tutor their daughters well by setting examples for them to follow. Herodias was a woman of questionable morals. She was Herod Phillip, Tetrarch of Ituraea's wife, but left her husband Phillip and entered into an adulterous illegal marriage to his brother Herod Antipas the King.

[I guess King is a little higher and makes one more important than being married to just a Tetrarch (governor)!]

I cannot think of what would possibly compelled her to leave her husband and live in a sinful adulterous situation with King Herod Antipas, except greed, power, and lust.

John the Baptist spoke against this sinful relationship. Naturally, Herodias did not want him preaching publicly and calling attention to this terrible sin, of which she indulged. The Scripture tells us, she nursed a grudge. When you nurse, one gives that person or thing life or health. In her case, it was a thing…the thing was her desire to destroy the voice that spoke against her pleasures and desires as sinful and defiant, of the Word of God. She was skilled in promoting and maintaining the health of this rancor, in short, she gave her bitter feelings life.

Herodias was desperate to silence the Prophet for speaking out against the outrageous flaunting of Herod's and her illicit relationship. She saw him as a threat to her pleasure and power.

In contrast, John the Baptist was feared by, and seemed to, fascinate (puzzle) Herod Antipas. He had respect and awe for him, considering him a Prophet and Holy man.

John the Baptist stood for what was right regardless of his impending imprisonment and death.

He was the witness sent by God to preach of the coming of the Light into the world. John the Apostle noted it in this way, "*There was a man sent by God whose name was John. He came as a witness to testify concerning that Light so that through Him all might believe. He himself was not the Light, he came only as a witness to the Light,*" [John 1:6-7].

The Light of Christ (The Word of God) exposes all manner of sins not approved by God. Jesus is the sum total of truth, knowledge, and moral purity: attributes which were lacking in the moral fibers of Herod Antipas, Herodias, and Salome: but especially Herod Antipas and Herodias – Herodias influenced the actions of Salome.

Dressed for the Kingdom of God

Wilson (1978) in his book, *On Human Nature*, wrote regarding the sexual actions and focuses of man, **"Human beings are connoisseurs of sexual pleasures. They indulge themselves by casual inspection of potential partners, by fantasy, poetry, and song, and in every delightful nuance, of flirtation, leading to foreplay and coition,"** [Pg141, P2].

History records that Salome was a Princess, the daughter of Herod Phillip and Herodias. Her name is not mentioned in the Bible, only that the daughter of Herodias danced to please Herod Antipas. Encouraged by her mother, and because she did not want John the Baptist speaking against her mother being married to her Uncle Herod Antipas and living in an adulterous relationship, joined in her scheme to get rid of the Prophet, agreeing with this ruse – she danced to please the King and fulfill her mother's wishes and his adulterous desires. History records it as, The Dance of the Seven Veils. It was an evil conspiracy, of a mother and her daughter.

Herod Antipas, Herodias, nor Salome regarded or had respect for the simple decency of morals when it comes to the sanctity of marriage or parent-child relationships. They did not view their pursuit of sexual pleasures or wickedness as wrong, only as an avenue to achieve the end they wanted to accomplish.

[The emphasis essential to this is not to get hung-up on whose daughter Salome is or is not. The pivotal point is that she did dance for the head of John the Baptist, a Prophet and faithful servant of God. Harking back to the example of Jezebel whose name has become a stigma in reference to a person's actions and evilness that were/is in direct defiance of God's commands in both sexual matters and wickedness].

- *Does this kind of sordidness provoke your spirit to stand even stronger for righteousness as John the Baptist did and against this type of flaunting of morals and integrity treating those types of turpitudes as an unacceptable way of living?*

History informs us, this type of interaction was common among the Herod family, yet not acceptable. John made the point of calling attention to this sin committed by Herodias, Salome, and Herod.

They were aficionadas of these types of pleasures. Herod was guilty of everything Christ described as adultery. Firstly, Herod was married to his brother,

Phillip's wife. Secondly, he lusted after Herodias' daughter Salome who was his niece; also, who he watched, and his thought processes became less than that of a King or a father figure; and thirdly and lastly, he served his own greed, lust, and desires given by the god of this world.

We keep in mind sisters that adultery begins with a thought process. The scripture tells us in one of the Sermons on the Mount, The Beatitudes Chapter, Jesus said, *"But I tell you that anyone who looks at a woman lustfully has already committed adultery with her in his heart,"* [Matthew 5:28].

A ricochet of Herod, Herodias, and Salome's actions is lust, which was then and is now adultery and fornication...sins that leads humans into living lives that are not pleasing to God our Father nor our Lord and Savior Jesus Christ and defiling the temple of which the Holy Spirit dwells.

Satan is always in the mix regardless of who you are, especially if God's people are involved. As a result, of John the Baptist speaking against Herodias' marriage to Herod Antipas, she plotted to destroy him with the very tool she knew would tempt her husband, her daughter Salome.

Herodias offered Salome to her husband who was Salome's uncle/stepfather to carry out an evil purpose, because of her selfish lust and bid to affect revenge, upon John the Baptist, which is more than unthinkable.

She knew Herod Antipas lusted after her young, beautiful, and tempting daughter; therefore, it did not take much to persuade Salome to dance for him. This point lends to the fact that Salome was also vain and egotistical, using the perceived beauty of self to tempt and deceive her uncle, in the same space, of time!

It was not just that Herodias offered her daughter, which is vile in-and-of-itself at any level, but this man (Herod Antipas) was her uncle.

*But then again, what loving, decent, caring, and moral mother would offer her daughter in a scheme to perpetrate evil by using the inference of sex?*

- *Even worse than that, of all things, what mother would involve her daughter with her husband knowing he lusted for her?*
- *Did the thought of protecting her daughter cross her mind once she learned that Herod lusted after her?*

Consequently, she provided the avenue to give the King what he desired. Which, of course, affected his reasonable thought processes, and he under this type of lustful coercion of physical and mental duress, promised to give her anything she desired without asking her the important question, "What?" was her wish for the dance that would prove to be fatal to John the Baptist, which would give Herodias his head on a platter.

Herodias and Salome were not aware, even though they killed the messenger, they could not kill the message. John the Baptist was to decrease, this was the prophecy coming to pass. Christ and the Message increased, as was written, and still, as it did then and now, is spreading throughout the world. Herod Antipas rejected the message John the Baptist preached to him to repent of the sins of which he indulged.

- **We could stretch our imagination momentarily and wonder if Herod Antipas like Herod Agrippa II, was almost persuaded to pull off that old man for the new man offered by the Prophet John, the Baptist or Paul, the Apostle of Christ?**

In rejecting the warning of John, the Baptist, Herod Antipas was rejecting God. God told Samuel when the people did not want God to reign over them but desired a King: they did not reject you, they rejected me, *"And the Lord said unto Samuel, Hearken unto the voice of the people in all that they say unto thee: for they have not rejected thee, but they have rejected Me, that I should not reign over them," [I Samuel 8:7].*

Herod's order to decapitate John the Baptist's head did accomplish his wife and niece's plot; however, yet in the same stroke of time, poured gasoline on an already burning fire.

John the Baptist did not fear Herod's power. He could put him to death. Of course, no one wants to die or be threatened; but John the Baptist knew Herod Antipas could only kill his body. On the other hand, John the Baptist knew whom he should fear, the One who has the power over life, death, and eternity. Christ reminds us, *"And I say unto you My friends, be not afraid of them that kill the body, and after that have no more that they can do. But I will forewarn you whom ye shall fear: Fear Him, which after He hath killed, hath power to cast into hell; yea, I say unto you, Fear Him," [Luke 12:4-5].*

In this, we are reminiscent of what God said through the Prophet Isaiah, *"So is My Word that goes out from my mouth: It will not return to Me void but will accomplish what I desire and achieve the purpose for which I sent It," [Isaiah 55:11].*

After John the Baptist's death, the Word of God grew and spread, and our Lord and Savior increased.

Herod Antipas regretted his promise of "anything," but it was too late at that point; the King's word had to stand or lose his respect before his subjects, so he heeded his wife's voice. Listen and hear her desperate bid for John the Baptist's death, "You promised before all your subjects my Lord and King, is it to be said that King Herod promises are like the mist that fades in the mid-morning sun?" Herodias and Salome are good examples of women of immorality. Their garments were of evilness, hate, adultery, fornication, incest, pre-meditated murder, trickery, and using Salome's wiles as a woman to tempt a man who was (one of the women's husbands and the other woman's uncle). It bears keeping these facts in mind of this evil triangle of three.

Wickedness in this scenario stood far above decency.

Their wickedness is in the same category as Jezebel, of the Old Testament, who destroyed God's Prophets, killed a neighbor Nabob so that she might possess his vineyard, and tried to tempt Jehu by painting her eyes. No doubt, sisters, no doubt, she was beautiful. Her beauty did not serve her with Jehu, a faithful servant, of God, who was not tempted by her female wiles. However, in contrast, Salome's beauty did tempt Herod Antipas.

Sisters, we, as the people, of God, do not wear the garments of evilness and revenge worn by Herodias and Salome.

The garments of a Christian Woman are modesty, humility, faithfulness, not of lust and mediocracy that was as recognizable in that century, as is in this one. Herodias and Salome both had debased minds. Herodias created this strategy using her husband's desire for her daughter to destroy a life to satisfy her desire for revenge because John the Baptist, Prophet of God, calling her sin of adultery to the public's attention. Just imagine, sisters, appearing before the judgment seat of Christ with this charge on your record.

If John, the Baptist, had gone to them in private and not exposed them publicly, their reaction, I am sure, would have been totally different.

Christ said, "*It is better that a millstone was hanged about his neck, and he cast into the sea than he should offend one of these little ones," [Luke 17:2]*. [He] describes/refers to whosoever offends or causes one of God's children pain and suffering.

John, the Baptist was a child of God. We are children of God and His little ones. We notice that he could have been free, yet he maintained his integrity and did not commit the sin of denying Christ the coming of the Savior by not speaking the truth, which would have been the results if had he not stood firm and strong, in the face of evil.

John did not speak with a double tongue, never flattering, or failing to call attention to their sins. He knew death [his decrease] was certain and could have acquiesced to the pressure to stop speaking publicly with fervor against the sin of adultery in their lives or telling them the truth, which meant remaining obedient to God's Word. John maintained his integrity. The Preacher tells us, *"The integrity of the upright guides them, but the unfaithful are destroyed by their duplicity,"* *[Proverbs 11:3]*.

Neither did he have a heart of disloyalty. He knew what was right and did not back up on the fact that the sins indulged in by Herodias and her devotee were against the Commandments of God, *"Thou shall not commit adultery,"* *[Exodus 20:14]*.

*"Thou shall not covet thou neighbor's house. You shall not covet your neighbor's wife, or his male or female servant, his ox or donkey, or anything that belongs to your neighbor,"* *[Exodus 20:17]*.

Thinking of John, the Baptist, and his refusal to abandon his integrity and continue to speak the truth to Herod Antipas and Herodias, I compare his integrity to that of Vashti, Queen of Persia. The King commanded her to appear before the banquet with the people of the kingdom great and small for them to see her beauty: for she was beautiful.

- **Why would she want to display or be on parade before hundreds of drunk, lustful, violent men at a party?**
- **What benefit would it be to her?**
- **Afterwards, how would she feel about herself?**
- **Would her maidens who served her continually have the same level of respect post her display?**
- **Would that bode well for the overall women of the kingdom?**
- **Would the husbands and others in authority expect women to display themselves because the Queen Vashti did it?**
- **We lead by example, Vashti did. It cost her; but to her integrity and morals were more important!**

Displaying her beauty before the King and his drunken male attendants was not comfortable for her, that display would violate her Honor and standing as Queen; therefore, she defied the commands of King Xerxes to appear. The decision she made was costly – it cost her – her position as Queen – cost her exile - cost her replacement by another they termed as better than her – *[Esther 1:1-21]*.

Sisters, we see this as an example of integrity and standing strong for your values and beliefs and not lowering your standards regardless of the price it will cost. Standing for God in the face of all odds no matter what they/who they are, requires strength, faith, moral integrity, discipline, and reliability. We gain and not lose when we stand for the truth of God as did John, the Baptist.

Christians cannot have waffling integrity; I will go along with the command if it does not violate something I want to do – is not an attitude a Christian can afford in our spiritual walk in Christ.

Herodias and Salome did not have the moral integrity displayed by Queen Vashti of Persia. Uprightness is an integral part of who the children of God are in their service. She did not flaunt her beauty or plot to destroy as did Herodias and her daughter hundreds of years later.

Questions to ask ourselves:

- *Integrity, in my viewpoint, how high does it stand?*
- *Am I using the checklist the Scripture gives to answer this question?*
- *Am I prepared to stand for the truth?*
- *Is my attitude toward this characteristic as it should be?*

Herod Antipas and Herodias committed the sins of adultery and coveting, in a televised manner. All the Roman Empire knew Herodias was Herod Phillip's wife and Princess Salome was his daughter (?). Coveting is a sin…Herod Phillip's household included his wife and daughter. Herod Phillip, even though he was his brother, was Herod Antipas's neighbor as well, *"If a man takes his brother's wife, it is* an unclean thing. He has uncovered his brother's nakedness. They shall be childless, " *[Leviticus 20:21].*

- *Do we read anywhere in the Scripture or history that Herod Antipas and Herodias had any children?*

John the Baptist knew his fate as a faithful servant of God. He believed the Prophecy that a Savior, the Prophetic Messiah would come into the world to redeem all humanity, of whom he announced His coming. *"He was the voice of one crying in the wilderness," [Ibid]*. Luke records that Christ said, *"The Law and the Prophets were until John: since that time, the Kingdom of God is preached, and every man presses into It," [Luke 16:16]*.

Therefore, we know and can be sure of our eternal home irrespective, of the fate we face that causes our death. John, the Baptist knew, he was to die.

Peter tells us that, *"Praise be to the God and Father of our Lord Jesus Christ! In His great mercy, He has given us new birth into a living hope through the resurrection of Jesus Christ from the dead, and into an inheritance that can never perish, spoil, or fade. This inheritance is kept in heaven for you, who through faith, are shielded by God's power until the coming of the Salvation that is ready to be revealed in the last time.*

Peter explains further that, *"In all this, you greatly rejoice, though now for a little while you may have had to suffer grief in all kinds of trials. These have come so that the proven genuineness of your faith–of greater worth than gold, which perishes even though refined by fire may result in praise, glory, and honor when Jesus Christ is revealed," [I Peter 1:3-7]*.

- *What will be your fate, especially if you did not correct your error (s) before you leave this world?*

We all have an opportunity to do so as did Herodias, Herod Antipas, and Salome. At that time, they could have obeyed the call of John, the Baptist to repent as others obeyed his call to action, for their souls. We have the same opportunity today through Jesus Christ – Jesus Christ died for all, but each one of us has to desire to hear the Word, and the key is to obey and then follow Jesus and turn from the world and sin. We have a **'call to action'** for our souls in this century as do all the future generations while the world stands.

- *Did Herod Antipas, Herodias, or Salome turn or repent?*

We read of another example of the character and like-mindedness of ones like Herodias and Salome. In the Church at Thyatira Christ said, *"nevertheless, I have this against you: You tolerate that woman Jezebel, who calls herself a prophet. By her teaching, she misleads My servants into sexual immorality and the eating of food sacrificed to idols," [Revelation 2:20]*.

**Hear what The Sovereign God says,** *"I have given her time to repent of her immorality, but she is unwilling," [Revelation 2:21].*

Herodias and Salome led Herod Antipas deeper into the sins of sexual immorality, lust, adultery, idolatry, and depravity of the mind and heart. They had time to repent during John, the Baptist preaching. [...]

Herod Antipas' use of sound reasoning of a leader seemed to elude him in his passion and desire for his wife's daughter. John tells us, *"All that is in the world is the lust of the eye, the lust of the flesh, and the pride of life," [I John 2:15-17].*

Herod Antipas was guilty of all three in the same frame of time. These three are a lock-step process and tools often used by Satan, to stoke the desires of humans.

Sisters our garments should have the look of Jehu's. His mind was not on the temporal physical beauty of a woman (which translates in this day and time to things and people of this world, no matter what they are, that tempt us and pull us away from God) but on the commands of God and his ultimate purpose for going to Jezebel's residence. God sent him as He sent John, the Baptist.

There are always those who are faithful who do not allow the temptations of this world to bring them to the point, of disobedience to God's Commands. We are all tempted with things of this physical world, and the needs of our bodies, we are human!

The scripture tells us, *"No temptation has overtaken you except what is common to mankind. And God is faithful; He will not let you be tempted beyond what you can bear. But when you are tempted, He will also provide a way out so that you can endure it," [I Corinthians10:13].*

We are to focus on what the finality of our lives will be. We are living in a temporal situation in this world. The world, I compared to a beautifully wrapped box, and the contents are Eternity with God. There is only one ribbon on that beautiful box, but the contents within are incalculable, which includes an eternal life of peace with God.

- *Which one is the most attractive to you?*
- *What is more important: the look of the box or the contents therein?*

As life has a sunrise, it also has a sunset. This world does not hold nor "is a be all to end all" life. We have eternal life waiting for us. Therefore, it is wise to do as Christ admonishes with the trials and tribulations we face and the needs and desires of things life holds in this world, *"But seek ye first the Kingdom of God, and His righteousness; and all these things shall be added unto you," [Matthew 6:33].*

What things! Those things that are necessary for life and survival while on earth.

Satan willingly affords you the desires of your heart providing you with whatever milieu (familiar social environment or things) to which, you are accustomed or ones that you desire. Satan keeps the bait as attractive and tempting for us as he did for Herod Antipas and Herodias.

A silver platter is waiting! Satan has one for each of us. [If] you fall into one of his traps, the head on that silver platter will be yours.

Unlike the garments of Herodias and Salome, Elizabeth, the mother of John the Baptist wore garments of faith, obedience, and humility.

CHAPTER FOURTEEN

# ELIZABETH
# GARMENTS OF THE MOTHER OF
# JOHN, THE BAPTIST

In a normal situation, women did not have babies past a certain age. In this modern society, with the aid of testing and with the increasing ability of the use of technology, women now have fertility drugs available to help with infertility that was common in women in Elizabeth's time.

A fertility drug treatment does not work overnight or sometimes it does not work at all for women young or mature. Fertility drugs have even had an unintended consequence in a woman or couple's life.

The uses of Fertility Drugs are to **enhance reproduction.** For women, the use of fertility medication stimulates follicle development of the ovary.

Infertility is the inability to get pregnant after one year of unprotected sex.

One of the main side effects of the drug, according to Medical News Today, deals with a decrease in insulin resistance. According to the Center for Disease Control (CDD) 12% of women, 15-44 years of age in this country (USA) experience difficulty in getting pregnant.

With the short overview of the age of women getting pregnant, and they are young, the elephant in the room, in Elizabeth's time was the medical field. At that juncture, did not know the cause of infertility in a woman, and knew nothing of it in a male.

This brings us to the point of Elizabeth, the Mother of John the Baptist, Jesus' cousin, Prophet, and teacher. Elizabeth, as the Scripture tells us, at that time, considered, a mature woman was past the childbearing age. God's plans for our lives are far from what we envision. Elizabeth had no idea I am sure, like Sarah, wife of Abraham, did not, that she would have a baby past the age which women normally do, pondered the question, "*Shall I have pleasure again past my childbearing age?*" Sarah was 90 years old when Isaac was born. Elizabeth, with a long stretch of today's mental age calculator, was 50 years old. Her husband Zechariah was older as well. In normal thoughts, in that century and at that time of life (her age) had passed for his wife to bear a child.

Before we continue with Elizabeth, a faithful servant of God, Scripture records that Hannah, in the Old Testament, suffered the same condition the Scripture defined as God closing the Womb. We know that giving a woman the ability to bear children is within God's Power. Hannah was a young woman and favorite (preferred) wife of Elkanah.

As Sarah was beloved by Abraham, Rachel was beloved by Jacob. Rachel is another example of a barren woman unable to conceive. This inability grieved these women as it does in our day and time. It is a painful thought to me or a female knowing you cannot bear children or conceive, or the male sperm cannot fertilize the egg. We know the heartache it causes supported by the fact women and men desperate for a family with children turn to doctors and fertility drugs.

Elizabeth and her husband Zechariah, Priest at that time did not have a fertility drug to turn to they knew that if it were God's will and through faith, He could do all things, that as well as the process as we see with Sarah, Hannah, Rachel, and Elizabeth, all conceived in God's time frame and not theirs.

Sarah and Elizabeth especially past childbearing age conceived and bore healthy sons whom God used in His plan to save man through His Word, "*The Word became flesh and dwelled among men," [John 1:1]* It was a miracle then, they conceived by God's chosen method. The Angel Gabriel announced the coming child to Elizabeth's husband, "*Zechariah, the father of John the Baptist, and husband of Elizabeth. He was a priest belonging to the order of Abijah. While he was offering incense in the Temple, the angel Gabriel appeared to him and told him that his wife Elizabeth who had been barren for many years would give birth to a son, and the son's name would be John," [Luke 1:5-2:20].*

Zechariah, by the way, doubted, and was struck dumb (unable to speak until the child was born) by Gabriel, but yet he went to his wife, and she conceived. God told Sarah as she stood at the door of their tent, on the Plains of Mamre, at an appointed time, that, she would bear a child. She laughed with joy at the thought, of pleasure again sexually and the promised son, "*Therefore Sarah laughed within herself, saying, "After I am waxed old shall I have pleasure, my lord being old also?" And the Lord said unto Abraham, Wherefore did Sarah laugh, saying, Shall I surely bear a child, now I am old? Is anything too hard for the Lord? I will return unto you at the appointed time next year, and Sarah will have a son," [Genesis 18:12-14].*

We know that Gabriel, six months later, after he announced to Zechariah of the coming birth of a son, went to announce to Mary, a virgin chosen by God, who had never known a man, to be the Mother of Jesus. We will discuss Mary, Mother of Jesus in another chapter. I can only imagine what Elizabeth thought when she realized she was with a child, not at her age. I know what I thought and felt when I was pregnant with both my sons, but I was a young mother, and the experience of the first one was different from the second. I felt joy, fear, happiness, amazement, anticipation, and wonderment at the changes my body went through even at the embellishment my pregnancy gave my hair the luster of a blackish-blue color, shimmering flowing down my back.

It must have been an overwhelming experience for Elizabeth especially when she knew that an Angel told her husband they would have a child after living 50+ years and she was beyond that time of life when normally a woman would conceive ... six months later her Mother's Cousin Mary, a virgin, was overshadowed by the Holy Spirit and conceived, *[Luke 1:26-38]*.

Elizabeth's child in her womb leaped for joy when He heard Mary's greeting, Elizabeth said, *"Why has the Mother of my Lord come to see me?" [Luke 1:43]*.

Mary's response to her question was of praise in a song of joy and thanksgiving known as the [Magnificat] Mary said, *"My soul doth magnify the Lord and my spirit rejoices in God my Savior, for He has been mindful of the humble state of His servant. From now on all generations will call me blessed, for the Mighty One has done great things for me, - Holy is His name. His mercy extends to those who fear Him, from generation to generation. He has performed mighty deeds with His arm; He has scattered those who are proud in their inmost thoughts. He has brought down rulers from their thrones but has lifted up the humble. He has filled the hungry with good things but has sent the rich away empty. He has helped His servant Israel, remembering to be merciful to Abraham and his descendants forever, just as He promised our ancestors," [Luke 1:46-55]*.

When she stood before Elizabeth the baby, when hearing the sound of Mary's voice, leaped in Elizabeth's womb. Mary praised the Lord for His choosing to bless the world through her. We are instruments of use in God's service as was Mary. Jesus was the Savior of Promise through a Virgin. Isaac, as well, was a son of promise through Abraham and Sarah. God did not accept Ishmael to father the Patriarch of the twelve tribes of Israel, Isaac was God's choice.

Christ was from the House of David as promised also in the genealogical line of the family of Abraham.

We know how both Mary and Elizabeth felt at that first twitch and recognize the first delicate flutter of life. Sometimes I wonder now if our children and all the roughhousing they do moving and kicking when we rub our stomach and talk to them it is a joy they feel when they hear mother's voice or dad's voice.

- *Sisters, have this ever made you wonder or consider this as a possibility?*

Zechariah and Elizabeth were overjoyed at the prospect of having a child. The news and fame of her carrying a child were noised everywhere with everyone knowing without question the thing was of God, no one wondered how, but felt joy as people do now when they know a loved one, cousin, or just another woman who is pregnant; we feel happy for our sister and her husband. We can put ourselves in their place, what joy and pride it gives both father and mother.

All things are possible with God. He can bring the dead back to life and give life where there was none before. Elizabeth lived all those years and was barren. Her being pregnant this late in life would be a miracle and all the people of God would know there is nothing impossible for God, as Sarah knew in her day at the age of 90 years old.

Women of the Kingdom with the same faith and attitude Elizabeth had are good examples for us to follow. She did not question God's will or God's power to work in her life at any age. We define people by the category of age they are in; this is understandable, but we cannot limit God's power to create and sustain life, because humans cannot. Elizabeth understood that neither time nor age could limit God; it only limits man.

The fact that we see these miracles recorded in Scripture should give us hope and assurance that there is nothing impossible for God to do; it is humans who have limits on what they can do; even with the things we as humans can do is only because of and through the grace and mercy of our God. These miracles show us an excellent expression of the power of God.

Remember that the Church, the Body of Christ, is the full expression of God!

CHAPTER FIFTEEN

# REMEMBER WOMEN OF GOD ...THAT

"*God appointed (placed) all things under His feet and appointed Him to be 'Head' over everything for the Church, which is His body, the fullness of Him who fills everything in every way,*" *[Ephesians 1:22-23]*.

Fullness refers to filling the Church with gifts and blessings. The Church should be the full expression of Christ. He wrote this to the full Church, not just individuals. Christ is the Head, we are the body...the human body is an excellent example...the body has arms, legs, eyes, ears, nostrils, finger, and toes, all have important functions that make the body operate as a whole, but the body has only one head.

Paul reminds us, "*And He is the Head, of the Body, the Church, He is the beginning and the Firstborn from among the dead, so His fullness dwells in Him,*" *[Colossians 1:18, 24]*.

Christ coming to labor and suffer for the Body, the Church paints us a portrait of what a servant looks like, sent by God to save humanity, and provide a way back to His Father to restore the relationship lost to all humans in the Garden of Eden.

Explicit to our Salvation is obedience to the Word of God. Jesus Christ is our model for obedience to God, "*The One who sent Me, is with Me; He has not left Me alone, for I always do what pleases Him,*" *[John 8:29]*.

Scriptures gives us the characteristics of Christianity among God's People:

- **We are to be hospitable one to another,** "*Offer hospitality to one another without grumbling,*" *[I Peter 4:9]*. We can use the gifts we have to help or serve one another.
- **We are to love one another**, "*This is My command that you love one another,*" *[John 15:17]*. Loving one another is a command and not an option.

- **We are to pray for one another,** "*The fervent effectual prayer of a righteous man avails much,*" *[James 5:16]*. God hears the righteous, "*For the eyes of the Lord are over the righteous, and His ears are open unto their prayers: but the face of the Lord is against them that do evil,*" *[I Peter 3:12]*. God listens. God hears everyone and sees everyone, and answers those who are living according to His will.

- **We are to confess our faults one to another,** "*If we claim (say) we have no sins we deceive ourselves and the truth is not in us. If we confess our sins, He is faithful and just to forgive our sins and purify us from all unrighteousness,*" *[I John 1:8-10]*. If we claim we have not sinned, we make God a liar, and His Word is not in us.

- **We are to consider one another,** "*And let us consider how we may spur one another on toward love and good deeds (works),*" *[Hebrews 10:24]*. We cannot cause our brothers to stumble by food, drink, or any other things that may weaken their faith. We are to support the weak…set the example, encourage (spur) our brethren in their efforts to serve God faithfully, and put their faith and trust in the His almighty power.

- **We are to exhort one another,** "*Exhort one another daily, while it is called today,*" *[Hebrews 3:13a]*. We may not get another opportunity, "*Lest any of you be hardened through the deceitfulness of sin,*" *[Hebrews 3:13 b]*, that kind (encouraging) word to a brethren might benefit them greatly, we never know where they are in their life…your words could be a lifesaver.

- **We are to comfort one another,** "*Rejoice with those who rejoice; mourn with those who mourn,*" *[Romans 12:15]*. Whenever our brethren are grieving from a loss whether it is a parent, child, friend, job, or just having difficulties we can comfort our brethren, considering ourselves we could/will [but] for the grace of God, be in that position at an unspecified point in our lives.

- **We are to be giving,** "*Give, and it will be given to you. A good measure, pressed down, shaken together, and running over, will be poured into your lap. For with the measure you use, it will be measured to you,*" *[Luke 6:38]*. We are to give of our material resources, of our time, of our energy, sharing our talents and abilities in the service of God and to others: sharing the attributes of the Fruit of the Spirit with all in whom we come in contact. We only gain when sharing and giving as Christ asked; we do not lose but God will bless us for our efforts. We cannot out-give God…His promises are firm and eternal, in this life and the next. He did not put a limit on what to give; only that we are to give, be generous with our blessing, with spreading the gospel, with comforting the sick and bereaved, and helping the helpless.

Sisters, we as women, have heavy responsibilities as wives, lovers, mothers, career women, taxi-cab drivers, coaches, referees, Physician assistants, friends, and the list goes on without end, which puts us in a fog sometimes. Satan will capitalize on our overloads and use the difficulty against us to his advantage and our disadvantage.

We have no snow days in our service to Jesus. Posting "closed" for a snow day on the windows or doors, in our service to God, and going home does not bode well, for people of God. Now, as in any generation, it is easy to become desensitized to living each day for our eternity. Life is busy, at times overwhelming, with the many tentacles of life pulling at us. However, it goes back to what Jesus said, *"He that loves father or mother more than Me is not worthy of Me: and he that loves son or daughter more than Me is not worthy of Me,"* [Matthew 10:37].

As well, it is wise to keep in mind what Joshua said to the Children of Israel, at that time, *"And if it seems evil unto you to serve the Lord, choose you this day whom ye will serve; whether the gods which your fathers served that were on the other side of the flood or the gods of the Amorites, in whose land ye dwell: but as for me and my house, we will serve the Lord,"* [Joshua 24:15].

The path we decide to walk is by choice. We cannot stumble our way through Salvation as a babe in Christ. The wiles of Satan are so dense they are as if one is wading through a fog. This concept makes it impossible to navigate the density of Satan's wiles alone. This is one of Satan's playbook strategies making it difficult to the point a person give-up that fight. Each time we face a difficulty (trial or tribulation), and we give up, is another win for Satan; it makes him smug. […].

He is an expert at tearing down our life or spirituality, one step at a time. We all know the dangers of fog when driving and the feeling of uncertainty that comes with the unknown of what is ahead. We proceed with caution, our fog lights are on, we reduce our speed, use windshield wiper, but we do not stop. We drive carefully until we get through the dense area of fog, but do not give up.

Translate this to trials and tribulations in our spiritual life, those times of dense thick fog. We have a guide, our light, our speed odometer, and windshield wipers, our Lord, and Savior Jesus Christ. Our faith gets us through trials and tribulations if we do not give up. In this life, so that we will reach our destination safely, sometimes we wait until the fog clears.

- *Why do we not have the same determination in our spiritual life, which ensures we face only clear days throughout eternity with Jesus?*

We wait until the fog clears without having a spiritual knee-jerk reaction, *"Be still, and know that I am God: I will be exalted among the heathen, I will be exalted in the earth," [Psalms 46:10].*

Life is not easy, Christ said, *"These things I have spoken unto you, that in Me ye might have peace. In the world ye shall have tribulation: but be of good cheer; I have overcome the world," [John 16:33].*

Our God is merciful though our pathways are difficult at times; hence, we have Jesus our Savior upon whom we can lean. Listen to the prayer of David and follow his example, *"I called upon the Lord in distress: the Lord answered me and set me in a large place. The Lord is on my side; I will not fear; what man can do unto me? The Lord taketh my part with them that help me: therefore, shall I see my desire upon them that hate me. It is better to trust in the Lord than to put confidence in man. It is better to trust in the Lord than to put confidence in princes," [Psalms 118:5-9].*

Mature Christian Women have a Spiritual biographical background when speaking with novices (babes in Christ) to help them in their walk toward Spiritual maturity. That journey is not easy, there is, but the one road; the one Jesus Christ left for us to walk to ensure an eternity with God and not away from God.

Mature women, in Christ, have the command from Scripture that the older women are to teach the younger, *"The aged women likewise, that they are in behavior as becomes holiness, not false accusers, not given to much wine, teachers of good things. That they may teach the young women to be sober, to love their husbands, to love their children, To be discreet, chaste, keepers at home, good, obedient to their husbands, that the Word of God be not blasphemed," [Titus 2:3-5].*

The word [older] does not necessarily mean age in chronological years or numbers, which is a part of it, but ones who are mature in Christ, have been a member of the Lord's Body for a while, and have leaned on the wisdom of the Scripture, and come to understand what God desires His children to do.

The mature Christian woman who has weathered a Spiritual storm comes out on the other side stronger and wiser. Those who can share their experiences with novice (younger) Christians can give solid advice on how to keep going, not giving up when times get tough, life gets hard, foggy days come and counsel them that when they are in the midst of trials and tribulations they do not dissipate as quickly as one would expect.

Sisters we use in our examples our prudence and decorum. When we are talking with our younger sisters, we use soberness (level-headedness) realizing they are in their novice period after baptism where we were at one time. Consideration (civility) for the situations they find themselves in at times takes prudence and decorum.

Sisters, we begin our journey in the shape of a pyramid. As we grow in the knowledge of God and faithfulness, each level defines our faithfulness and leaves behind the things of the world. Pyramids were built with a wide base; as the levels went up, they got smaller and smaller until they looked like a spear. Growth (building) upon our faith is a process that takes time and effort. As we study and understand what the will of God is, the basis of our faith gets stronger and more refined building endurance until we are firmly rooted and grounded in the Word of God and nothing can destroy that faith, which indicates we have reached that spear and understand what the will of God is for our lives.

I think of what Aristotle said in a quote, **"Men acquire a particular quality by constantly acting a particular way... you become just by performing just actions, temperate by performing temperate actions, brave by performing brave actions."**

Troubled times comes in each of our life without exceptions: tests, trials, and tribulations are inherent to this life. Jesus told us that, *"These things I have spoken to you, that in Me you may have peace. In the world you will have tribulation, but be of good cheer, I have overcome the world," [Ibid].*

Overcoming the world lets us know there is nothing in this world, we can go through that our Savior cannot help us with up to and including the most dangerous adversary we will face in life. He is the god of this world. Jesus warns, *"He was a murderer from the beginning, and abode not in the truth because there is no truth in him. When he speaks a lie, he speaks of his own: for he is a liar and the father of it," [John 8:44b].*

Satan birthed into this world all the sins (including the first sin of lying) we know of and all we do not know about. He has thousands of years of them in his playbook and they will sink humans into lower bases in life if he can entangle you in just one of them.

These trials and tribulations are part of life, they are not going away, but we have an Advocate to help us because He overcame the world, so can we. Christ showed us how. In this light, we cannot forget God tests His children as well; but not tempt us as Satan does. The tests are for our benefit. They make us stronger and more grounded in our faith. It builds our confidence in God's assurance, *"No temptation has overtaken you except what is common to mankind. And God is faithful; He will not let you be tempted beyond what you can bear. But when you are tempted, He will also provide a way out so that you can endure it," [I Corinthians 10:13].*

Scripture reminds us in the biblical account of Balaam, his interactions, rather him agreeing with the plot orchestrated by Balak King of Moab. Micah reminded the people, of God, of their disobedience. He used the example of Balaam's lack of obedience, humility, and faithfulness. However, he rather succumbs preferably to the pressures of the King and the opportunity, of worldly gain, rather than obedience to God, *[Micah 6:5].*

Sisters, we as people of God cannot have short memories (selective amnesia) and forget to be thankful to God in all the things He blesses us with, in good and bad times. Bad times (tests) in our lives does not by any mean indicate God has forsaken us.

Serving Christ is not in the abstract. Our service cannot be apart from the design of the pattern Jesus left us. We cannot serve in the abstract doing only certain parts of what Christ left for us to do. The way we conduct ourselves has to be in a manner pleasing to God. Serving in the abstract will cost us our souls and eternity with God.

When God calls, we listen. When we call, God will listen.

Zechariah reminds the people of their duty toward God. This is also applicable to us in this day and time, "*These are the things that you are to do: Speak the truth to each other; and render true and sound judgment in your courts; do not plot evil against each other, and do not love to swear falsely; I hate all this, declares the Lord,*" *[Zechariah 8:14-17]*.

We cannot reasonably expect of God what we do not do ourselves; especially, in those things we know are possible He has given us to do such as obedience, mercy, compassion, love, service, worship (in the correct manner), faithfulness, and believe without doubting. All things are possible with God; He is the Master of the Universe.

- *We ask ourselves do I (you) love to Worship?*

David, King of Israel, a faithful servant of God wrote about his love of worshipping God. One of the beautiful Psalms he penned said it in this way, "*I will wash mine hands in innocence: so, will I compass thine altar O Lord: that I may publish with the voice of thanksgiving, and tell of all thy wondrous works. Lord I loved the habitation of thy house, and the place where thine honor dwelleth,*" *[Psalms 26:6-8]*.

- *Do we embrace the attitude of David toward worship and our glorious Heavenly Father praising and adoring Him?*
- *What posture does your garment of worship show?*

Sometimes we as a human race take God for granted, turning our attention to ourselves, rather than remaining humble, merciful, thankful, and obedient before His throne. Intermittently remembering God is not pleasing to our Lord and Savior.

- *If you consider the statement above what would be the answer?*
- *Does God remember us and bless us on a sporadic basis, or does He remember His children constantly?*

Consider this fact, if God forgot us one Nanosecond of time, we would perish from the face of the earth.

- *What would happen if God showed no mercy?*
- *If God did not perform His promises (keep His word) what would your life look like on a day-to-day basis?*

We in-and-of ourselves have no power over the functioning of the world and all the power that exists.

- *Can we see or know what tomorrow will bring or be like? "Boast not thyself of tomorrow; for thou knows not what a day may bring forth," [Proverbs 27:1].*

On the other hand: we can choose to obey ... we can choose to be faithful ... we can choose to have unwavering faith in the power of God ... We can choose to serve Him in Spirit and Truth ... we can choose to practice the Beatitudes, [*Matthew 5:1-13*] ... we can choose to possess the Fruit of the Spirit, [*Galatians 5:22-23*] ... we can choose not to be of the world (we have no choice being in the world) ...we can choose not to be in defiance of God's commands, as we see in governments, ruling powers, pursuits of wealth, and greed, [*I John 2:15-17*]... and we can choose to gain Christ and be a loss to the world. All of these are choices we can make as Joshua reminds us, [*Joshua 24:15*].

As we continue to look at choices ... we can choose to have the attitude of Job, *"Though He slays me, yet will I trust Him," [Job 13:15]* ...we can choose to reflect the Light to the World by letting our light shine ...we can choose to be forgiving and merciful to those who injure us. The list goes on, the defining point sisters is, we follow the pattern Christ left for us, and walk the straight and narrow way. God will not leave us or forsake us, He promised. All of this comes through faith, [*Hebrews 11:1*] as Scriptures make crystal clear. If there is no faith in the ability of God, in our lives, we are the worse for it.

Running the race for eternity has rules and patterns that we are to follow. We cannot make up our own and be pleasing to God. As well, necessary to our walk, is the desire to follow Jesus and have the resolve to take part in the Salvation Christ purchased for humanity. All who desire can come and drink of the healing waters Christ offered flowing from the Spiritual Jacob's well. Mature Christian women can help in guiding the younger (babes) Christians through their examples, their faithfulness, actions, words, using their Biblical, as well as their secular wisdom.

The fact is, we need both Spiritual, and secular wisdom to know how to live in this world in a manner pleasing to God and resist the temptations Satan throws at humans. We get our strength and wisdom from the Bible, The Word of God. Paul tells us to, *"Study to show thyself approved unto God, a workman need not be ashamed rightly dividing the Word of Truth," [2 Timothy 2:15].*

We fashion our lives to the mandates of the Scriptures not the Scriptures to the dictates of our lives, which says, "If, it fits what my life decrees it is okay, then if it does not, I will decide what is and in this instant, will do what is best for me." Trying to live our lives outside, of the Truth of the Scriptures because it is inconvenient is a danger to our soul. We cannot allow the Word of God to become an inconvenient truth. This is a point older (mature) Christian women can make to the younger women of the Kingdom, God first everything else falls in line thereafter.

Mature Christian women have the training to assist their younger sisters. In this way, we as mothers, guide our babies in their growth, so they can avoid dangers in their little lives because, in their innocence, cannot recognize dangers, is the same approach mature Christian women can take with their spiritual novice sisters, in Christ.

The danger of standing historically ignorant about spirituality looms high in this 21st Century with so many changes in the social environment. It has a continuous pull on the lives of its people. History reminds us, "*Things written aforetime are written for our learning that we through patient and comfort of the Scripture might have hoped,*" *[Romans 15:4].*

We learn about the nature and righteousness of God through history. The people wandered in the wilderness for forty [40] years because of their rebellion. The people of God were in exile time after time because of idol worship and waywardness in every way. Sins were across the board in the lives of man in the Biblical Historical accounts we read. God punished the people for their flagrant defiance.

- *How often do we read about their falling back into the sins that caught them up repeatedly?*
- *Do you think that it is wise to heed the example and avoid the error Scripture records of their disobedience to and defiance of the Commandment of God?*

I used the phrase to [catch them up] because their (our) adversary will continually provide the avenue you so desire to traverse in your pursuit of worldly pleasures and its idol gods. He knows what works and what pitfalls to use to cause you to stray off the path of righteousness as he did the people of God in the Old Testament.

History secular or Biblical, at certain points, they record the same facts. We need to learn so the same mistakes our predecessors/ancestors made, we can avoid, and they saw the wrath of God and His promises of punishment come to pass. We can avoid the wrath of God and learn from the historical accounts and the end-results of non-compliance, *"It is a fearful thing to fall into the hands of the Living God,"* [Hebrews 10:31].

God is merciful, righteous, pure, holy, and does not change or overlook our desires to live in the world in the manner we so desire. His commands stand, and His warnings are true. God does not accept straddling the fence type of faithfulness or when it is convenient; inconvenient truth stands tall no matter the efforts of human denial that serving God in the manner you so wish is acceptable. God's commands are firm; they are too high to get over and wide to get around. Truth rejected, does not change God's commands for our lives. We cannot live in half-truths and think God will be pleased and will accept that lukewarm service to Him.

Humans live out their lives by patterns in all we do. The Scripture reminds us that, *"Whatever is has already been, and what will be has been before; and God will call the past to account,"* [Ecclesiastes 3:15].

Our lives in service to God our Lord and Savior implemented and fine-tuned ... the pattern [is] in place before the creation of the world; there is no room for changes. God's commands were not an afterthought (decided after He created the world, then man), it is, not but was, in place before He spoke the earth into existence. God said, *"I am the Lord thy God and I change not,"* [Ibid], and further, *"If you love Me keep my Commandments,"* [Ibid], also, *"I am the Vine and you are the branches said the Lord,"* [Ibid].

Christians come up the rough side of the mountain. Going forward in life in-and-of-itself is hard, coupled with the facts you choose and desire to serve God angers Satan and he doubles down on God's people and the road only gets rockier and the debris of life on the pathway thickens; in the end, affecting your ability to see.

The pain grows in the heart. You desire that all come to Christ, especially your family because you love your fellow man as Jesus loves each of us and the world knows us by our love for each other. He said, *"By this everyone will know that you are My disciples if you love one another,"* [John 13:35].

By being the example, practicing the Truth of the Spirit, learning, and practicing those Beatitudes is all in the struggle, as well as speaking the Biblical Truth. It is truly a cross to lift and carry; our Savior did so – so must we, as much as it is humanly possible, for each individual. God knows our strengths and weaknesses. The assurance that we have is this, we are not alone in this journey and battle; we have our brothers and sisters of the Kingdom for help and encouragement when that fog gets too thick.

But, above all, we have our Lord and Savior Jesus Christ who promises, "I will never leave you nor forsake you, "*Let your conversation be without covetousness; and be content with such things as ye have for He hath said, I will never leave thee, nor forsake thee. So that we may boldly say, The Lord is my helper, and I will not fear what man shall do unto me,*" *[Hebrews 13:5-6],* and "*Teaching them to observe all things whatsoever I have commanded you: and, lo, I am with you always, even*unto the end of the world," *[Matthew 28:20].*

Christ did not say it would be easy to climb that mountain, but it is doable. The Crown of Life awaits us at the end of the journey if we are faithful to God. Paul said, "*I have fought a good fight, I have finished my course, I have kept the faith: Henceforth there is laid up for me a crown of righteousness, which the Lord, the righteous judge, shall give me at that day: and not to me only, but unto all them also that love His appearing,*" *[2 Timothy 4:7-8].*

Christ is at the end of our journey. The Holy Spirit aids us on our journey and we will finally see God the Father in peace when all has been done and Christ presents His Bride to the Holy Father in Heaven. Satan has an alternate truth he will allow you only to see life through an artificial lens and not in real-time.

In this way, Satan peels off God's people, as one would the layers on an onion, one at a time. He and his angels are not groups or collective workers; they come to God's people individually. He has caused a slow bleed of the people of God, as one would peel the skins, off an onion.

In a letter to Timothy, Paul wrote this warning, "*This know also, that in the last days, perilous times shall come. For men shall be lovers of their own selves, covetous, boasters, proud, blasphemers, disobedient to parents, unthankful, unholy, Without natural affection, trucebreakers, false accusers, incontinent, fierce, despisers of those that are good, traitors, heady, high-minded, lovers of pleasures more than lovers of God; Having a form of godliness but denying the power thereof: from such turn away. For of this sort are they which creep into houses, and lead captive silly women laden with sins, led away with divers' lusts, ever learning, and never able to come to the knowledge of the truth," [2 Timothy 3:1-7].*

God knows and holds the past, present, and future in His hands. Everything, not somethings God tells us: have come, coming to past, and will come to past (past, present, and future). The Holy Spirit (God) guided the Apostles in the writing of the New Testament; therefore, it is what God said and not humans. The Holy Spirit, we continue to remind ourselves, is God. The Holy Spirit did the work in the creation; Genesis Chapter 1 supports this fact, *"In the beginning, God created the heaven and the earth. And the earth was without form and void, and darkness was upon the face of the deep. And the Spirit of God moved upon the face of the waters. And God said, Let there be light: and there was light," [Genesis 1:1-3].*

Christ said about the Holy Spirit, *"He is our teacher and guide."* He goes before our Savior putting our heart's desires and prayers with interpretations on our behalf, at His Throne with moaning we cannot, nor do we understand. The point here, after all, that is said, arguments made, the Holy Spirit had then/has now the authority to guide the Apostles in writing the New Testament and guiding the faithful servants of God into all righteousness because He is God, [The Spirit].

We can overcome the world through Christ if we do not give up; this life will not beat us. We can counsel our younger sisters in this wisdom giving them the benefit of our experience and journey in life on our way to eternity. Mature Christian women have the gravitas (sobriety) to go forward and help guide their younger sisters in their walk and service to God, in the manner so left us by our Lord and Savior.

Abstemiousness (self-discipline) is necessary when teaching and setting these examples. Considering, what Titus warns, that the older women are to teach; but they are also to live in the manner in which they tutor their younger sisters. We pick up the burden and go forward sisters as the Christian Women who left examples of faithful as the ones before them and not shirk that responsibility.

*"The aged women, likewise, that they be in behavior as become holiness; not false accusers; not given to much wine; teachers of good things; that they may teach the young women to be sober; to love their husbands; to love their children; to be discreet, chaste, keepers at home; good, obedient to their own husbands; that the word of God be not blasphemed," [Titus 2:3-5].*

My mother counseled me as I grew, "Nothing in life worth having is easy; there is always a cost."Salvation for us cost the life of Christ. It will cost us our life. We give up life, in the world, for life in His Kingdom, which is Salvation.

We, sisters are to be, women of good standing and character…A good name is more valuable than riches…riches can come and go but a good name does not: once it is gone it is hard to get back or live down that reputation.

Dorcas and Mary Magdalene were women of such reputation of good standing and character.

CHAPTER SIXTEEN

# WOMEN OF FAITH
# MARY MAGDALENE AND DORCAS
# (TABITHA)

Mary Magdalene was a woman of good standing and character. She was from the town of Magdala, a wealthy town known for its textiles and dye. She was a woman of means and supported Jesus from her living. Mary Magdalene played an important part in the life and ministry of Jesus.

She had seven demons, which caused her to suffer greatly. Mary's encounter with Jesus changed her life. He healed her of the demons as He did the man who lived among the tombs who was possessed with Legions of devils Jesus sent into a herd of three thousand swine and they ran off the cliff and perished in the sea.

I cannot imagine being possessed by demons and they control your every move; you have no peace within or without. Spirits haunted the individual they inhabited until they had no peace. This is a picture of Satan in our lives, as the demons were in Mary's life. Demons were usually associated with mental or physical illnesses.

Demons (evil spirits) were common in Biblical time, especially during Christ's three-year ministry. We have evil systems in our time with the lure of wealth and power. These examples of this evilness are everywhere in our society.

Babylon is an example of the people living in luxury and selfishness taking advantage and growing in wealth, power, living in comfort and pleasure. John describes the scene he saw, "*After this, I saw another angel come down from heaven. He had great authority, and the earth was illuminated by his splendor. With a mighty voice he shouted, "Fallen, Fallen Babylon the Great. She has become a dwelling for demons and a haunt for every unclean spirit, a haunt for every unclean bird, a haunt for unclean detestable animals," [Revelation 18:1-2].*

Only Christ could heal Mary of the demons. Evil can consume your life with every step. Seven is symbolic of completeness. Satan will exploit whatever illness we have sisters; he is ever waiting to take over your life, heart, and mind. After Jesus cured her, she became a disciple.

- *We learn from Scripture that Mary Magdalene was a faithful follower of Jesus after He cured her. When we come to Jesus and baptized into His body cleansing us from our sins, are we faithful followers?*

Mary was with Jesus every step of the way. Mary was first to the Tomb of Jesus wanting to take the body away when she discovered the tomb was empty asked the guards where have you laid him? Never thinking of herself as a woman to lift and take away the body of Christ put her fears and anxieties aside as she sought the body of Jesus. Love drives us to go beyond our fears in life, *"Now the end of the Commandments is charity out of a pure heart, and of a good conscience, and of faith unfeigned,"* [I Timothy 1:4].

- *Do we put aside fears and anxieties, seek, and follow Jesus regardless of what the world, our family, our friends, or others think?*

God can make us service ready and eliminate the fears and anxieties, *"Make you perfect in every good work to do His will. Working in you that which is well-pleasing in His sight through Jesus Christ to whom be glory, forever and ever: Amen,"* [Hebrews 13:21].

Comparably, Dorcas was also, a Christian woman living in Joppa – who Peter restored to life. Dorcas was wealthy in that she was a friend to the people. She was full of good works and did alms deeds. Tabitha (Dorcas) was a supporter of Jesus though she did not have the opportunity to follow Him during His earthly ministry. The people valued her wealth. She died and Jesus blessed her to live again…there is no limit to God's power even through man, *"This is a faithful saying and these things I will that thou affirm constantly, that they which have believed in God might be careful to maintain good works. These things are good and profitable unto men,"* [Titus 3:8].

The influence for good that Dorcas had on the people around her is an excellent example of what our reputation as a child of God should be [doers] of good works and alms deeds to those who are around us whether they are saints, widows, or our fellowman. James reminds us that, *"Pure religion undefiled before God and the Father is this: to visit the fatherless and widows in their affliction and keep himself unspotted from the world,"* [James 1:27].

154

Wealth comes in different ways and forms. God is the giver of them all. Dorcas had a wealth of heart. She was rich in benevolence made garments for all the women around her, "*Now there was at Joppa a certain disciple named Tabitha, which by interpretation is called Dorcas: this woman was full of good works and alms deeds which she did. And it came to pass, in those days, that she was sick, and died: whom when they had washed, they laid her in an upper chamber. And forasmuch as Lydia was, nigh to Joppa and the disciples had heard that Peter was there, they sent unto him two men, desiring him that he would not delay coming to them. Then Peter arose and went with them. When he was come, they brought him into the upper chamber: and all the widows stood by him weeping and showing the coats and garments which Dorcas made, while she was with them.*"

"*But Peter put them all forth, and kneeled down, and prayed; and turning him to the body said, "Tabitha, arise." And she opened her eyes: and when she saw Peter, she sat up. And he gave her his hand and lifted her up, and when he had called the saints and widows, presented her alive. And it was known throughout all Joppa, and many believed in the Lord. And it came to pass, that he tarried many days in Joppa with one Simon a tanner,*" [Acts 9:36-43].

We know from this Scripture sister Peter's work was not finished in that area because God sent him to Cornelius, the Centurion, who was a Gentile who his family and himself were devout and God-fearing and he was a generous giver, "*At Caesarea, there was a man named Cornelius, a centurion in what was known as the Italian Regiment. He and all his family were devout and God-fearing; he gave generously to those in need and prayed to God regularly,*" [Acts 10:1-2].

Sisters, the point is that God bless our efforts when we do alms deeds for those in need regardless of who we are and as we know from Luke's account of the life Cornelius lived pleased God and sent Peter to tell him what he must do to obtain Salvation. Only God knows the true hearts of men.

Tabitha (Dorcas) like Mary Magdalene was wealthy using her talents and abilities to supply the needs of people. She made garments. They thought her importance among them of such wealth and value to their hearts wept at her death, "*Give her the fruit of her hands and let her own works praise her in the gate,*" [Proverbs 31:31].

Peter answered the call of her friends as Jesus did Mary and Martha when Lazarus died. How important our loved ones are in our lives. Weeping shows deep pain and care. Weeping takes on a different connotation than crying…weeping is the pain of the soul…the pain reaches to the innermost parts of you. Weeping is such that the emotions so over-powers one as they express grief or sorrow.

Peter restored her life and as we think of the grief and sorrow, the same expression, weeping, and joy overcome the widows and saints that she aided while alive. *"I am the Vine, and you are the branches. He that abides in me and I in him the same brings forth much fruit for without Me you can do nothing. If a man abides not in Me he is cast forth as a branch and is withered and then gathered and cast them into the fire, and they are burned. If you abide in Me and My words abide in you, ye shall ask what ye will and it shall be done unto you. Herein is My Father glorified that ye bear much fruit so you shall be My disciple," [John 15:5-8].*

After her death and revival, the news of the miracle spread throughout Joppa bringing many to Christ. Peter tarried there many days, *"And it came to pass, that he tarried many days in Joppa with one Simon a tanner," [Acts 9:43].*

We know from the faithfulness of Peter that he continued to teach and strengthen the new converts.

- **Do we tarry with the new babes in Christ to help strengthen them?**

Our belief in Jesus and acceptance of Him as our Savior brings us from death to life through baptism…baptism is the final step before Salvation. We are then raised a new man, replacing our old man, pulling off the old garments, and putting on our new spiritual garments in Christ, *"In times past ye walked according to the course of the world, according to the prince of the power of the air, the Spirit that now works in the children of disobedience," [Ephesians 2:2].*

Tabitha lived a life of such that her alms deeds her friends presented to Peter tearfully. Tabitha's heart was evident in the way she lived her life. She used her talents to serve others. She used her gifts to glorify God and not selfishly [only] for herself, *"Above all, love each other deeply, because love covers over a multitude of sins. Offer hospitality to one another without grumbling. Each of you should use whatever gift you have received to serve others, as faithful stewards of God's grace in its various forms," [I Peter 4:8-10].*

Peter an instrument of use in the Kingdom of God; was given the power through Christ to restore Dorcas' life. *"I am the Vine, ye are the branches: He that abides in Me and I in him, the same brings forth much fruit: for without Me ye can do nothing,"* *[John 15:5]* We see the account of our Savior weeping. The news of his friend Lazarus being dead and the grief He saw through the moaning and pain of his sisters and the people around them grieved the Savior, *"Jesus wept."* *[John 11:35]* became overcome with grief and sorrow. Do we weep sisters when we lose one to the world (spiritually sick)? As well, do we feel joy when a spiritual sister, is restored to Christ! Joy overcame Mary and Martha when Jesus restored their brother's life as it did the friends of Dorcas when Peter restored her to life.

We read about Mary Magdalene and Dorcas and their faithfulness and work in the Kingdom there are other [Nameless] faithful followers of Jesus who worked in the Kingdom and are still working in the Kingdom because eternal life with God is the wealth we seek.

CHAPTER SEVENTEEN

# GARMENTS OF NAMELESS WOMEN
## EXAMPLES OF FAITH

*"Then I saw a great white throne and Him who was seated on it. The earth and the heavens fled from His presence, and there was no place for them; and, I saw the dead, great, and small, standing before the throne, and books were opened, another Book was opened; which is, the **B**ook of life. The dead were judged according to what they had done as recorded in the books," [Revelation 20:11-12].*

The Book of Revelation paints pictures for us as faithful servants of God the assurance that our names are written in the Book of Life. It was not deemed, necessary by the Holy Spirit to record every name of all the women who worked and works in the Kingdom supporting their brethren while they sought the lost and followed God's commands, but we know by faith their and our names are in the Book of Life because that is what Jesus promised the faithful until death.

Paul wrote the exhortation at the beginning of the book of Philippians about women who were his true companions. Women who worked in the Kingdom and their names are in the Book of Life, *"And I urge you also, true companion, help these women who labored with me in the gospel, with Clement also, and the rest of my fellow workers, whose names are in the Book of Life," [Philippians 4:3].*

Sometimes, most times, humans want recognition for what they do and have their names recorded somewhere in connection with the project or given accolades for the work done. In the Kingdom of God, we cannot allow pride to be an obstacle. The Kingdom has servants of God who have outstanding talents, as mentioned in Corinthians, *"Now about the gifts of the Spirit, brothers, and sisters, I do not want you to be uninformed. You know that when you were pagans somehow or other; you were influenced and led astray to mute idols. Therefore, I want you to know that no one who is speaking by the Spirit of God says, 'Jesus be cursed,'*

*And, no one can say, 'Jesus is Lord,' except by the Holy Spirit. There are different kinds of gifts, but the same Spirit distributes them. There are different kinds of service, but the same Lord. There are different kinds of working, but in all of them and in everyone, it is the same God at work. Now to each one the manifestation of the Spirit is given for the common good."*

And *"To one there is given through the Spirit, a message of wisdom; to another a message of knowledge by means of the same Spirit; to another faith by the same Spirit, to another gifts of healing by that one Spirit; to another miraculous powers; to another prophecy; to another distinguishing between spirits; to another speaking in different kinds of tongues; and to still another the interpretation of tongues. And all these are the work of one and the same Spirit, and He distributes them to each one, just as He determines," [I Corinthians 12:1-12].*

We are working for a crown in Heaven and not one (in name/popularity) on earth. We are seeking the higher calling of God and not recognition for what we do on earth, *"I press toward the mark for the prize of the high calling of God in Christ Jesus," [Philippians 3:14].*

We have a cloud of witnesses we can see that has successfully had their names written in the Book of Life, *" These were all commended for their faith, yet none of them received what had been promised since God had planned something better for us so that only together with us would they be made perfect," [Hebrews 11:39-40].*

*"Wherefore, seeing we also are compassed about with so great a cloud of witnesses, let us lay aside every weight and the sin which doth so easily beset us, and let us run with patience the race that is set before us; Looking unto Jesus the author and finisher of our faith; who for the joy that was set before Him endured the cross, despising the shame, and is set down at the right hand of the throne of God," [Hebrews 12:1-2].*

When we think of a cloud of witnesses, looking up at the heavens a cloud is expansive and immeasurable according to the standards we know. We are considering the faithful servants of God from the beginning of time until now. The world is thousands of years old and billions of people ago.

Moses spoke of the Book of Life during his time. His prayer to God about the people and intervened for them once more with God for their sins. This is an example of the level of care Moses had for the people of Israel to the point of willingness to sacrifice his own name not being listed in God's Book of Life, hear his plea, *"Yet now, if thou wilt forgive their sins; and if not, blot me, I pray thee, out of Thy Book which thou hast written. And the Lord said unto Moses, Whosoever hath sinned against Me, him will I blot out of My Book," [Exodus 32:32-33].*

Moses was willing to give his life and eternity of peace with God for the people. This was taking upon himself the errors and defiance of his people... Moses was willing to sacrifice and spend eternity away from God for his people. Jesus Christ was willing to give His life and die on the cruel cross of Calvary for the people so they would have the opportunity to spend eternity with God. We see these two seeds of leadership with the same fervent love for humanity, a selfless love taking on error and sin upon themselves.

- ***Do you know any people who would sacrifice their names being removed from the Book of Life, for a defiant sinful people?***

**About the Book of Life and the people of God, Daniel also prophesied concerning the end of time,** *"And at that time, shall Michael stand up, the great prince, which stands for the children of thy people. And there shall be a time of trouble, such as never was since there was a nation even to that same time: and at that time thy people shall be delivered, every one that shall be found written in the Book," [Daniel 12:1].*

Being concerned about whether your name is in the Book of Life and whether you are pleasing to God should be of uttermost importance to everyone. God has recorded names since the beginning of the time of those who were faithful and served Him under the Law, as well as those of us who serve Him under the dispensation of Grace. The gift of Grace – Christ purchased on the Cross of Calvary more than 2,000 years ago. We can have our names written in the Book of Life by obeying the Gospel and serving faithfully throughout our life.

Sisters, we live our lives now and it is paying it forward letting our light shine for all the Christian sisters who will come after us. Teaching by example the way Christian Women of the Kingdom of our Lord and Savior Jesus Christ are to be.

Our life, our examples, creates posterity in paying forward to the new babes in Christ and for those who are not as strong as you are (your name). God's work must continue with each generation that passes. We pick up that lantern of faith sisters and keep the light for Christ burning in our lives; so, they can pick up that lantern of faith and keep the light burning in their lives, for the next generation to continue paying it forward.

There are no "Envelope Please" moments in Christianity. There is only work and obedience for the Salvation Christ purchased until God calls us home. Our reward is in Heaven and not on earth.

We cannot wait to serve God while living pleasurably as if the Christian life is no longer of interest to us. Your decision, whatever it is will be costly. It is better that cost be a loss to the world and not a loss for Christ. Listen to what the Preacher says about pleasurable living as opposed to living for Christ.

Our youth years are a temptation to enjoy all the pleasures of this world. The Preacher warns it is all for naught and in vain. One of the warnings he phrases as thus, "*Rejoice, O young man, in thy youth; and let thy heart cheer thee in the days of thy youth. And walk in the ways of thine heart, and in the sight of thine eyes; but know thou that, for all these things God will bring thee into judgment,*" *[Ecclesiastes 11:9].*

There is only one [The] Book of Life, but the Scripture also speaks of Books were open as well. This brings to the forefront the wide and narrow way that Christ spoke of during His Ministry on Earth. He said, "*Enter ye in at the strait gate: for wide is the gate, and broad is the way, that leads to destruction, and many there be which go in thereat: Because strait is the gate, and narrow is the way, which leads unto life, and few there be that find it. Beware of false prophets, which come to you in sheep's clothing, but inwardly they are ravening wolves. Ye shall know them by their fruits. Do men gather grapes of thorns or figs of thistles? Even so, every good tree brings forth good fruit; but a corrupt tree brings forth evil fruit,*" *[Matthew 7:13-17].*

The Day of the Lord will be light and darkness. Light if we served Him faithfully until the end, darkness for those who were disobedient and followed their desires. We will all stand and answer for our deeds before the judgment seat of Christ – Christ is our Savior while the world stands but will be our judge on Judgment Day. We (no one) can escape the final judgment. Everyone will face his or her Judgment Day. We are not exempt because we are a member of the Body of Christ. The Israelites were of this opinion because they were God's people, listen to what Amos wrote, "*Woe unto you that desire the Day of the Lord to what end is it for you? The Day of the Lord is darkness, and not light as if, a man did flee from a Lion, and a Bear met him; or went into the house and leaned his hand on the wall; and Serpent bit him,*" *[Amos 5:18-19].*

In essence, everyone faces will face, have faced the Judgment Seat of Christ.

The fruit we bear in us and on our Tree of Service and the deeds we did or did not do will meet us, in eternity.

Our garments, of focus sisters, should be which [Book] our names, will appear on the Day of Judgment for all humanity Lydia was, this will also be the beginning of eternity!

CHAPTER EIGHTEEN

# GARMENTS OF WEALTH
# LYDIA, A SELLER OF PURPLE
# AND
# THE EXAMPLE OF
# THE RICH YOUNG RULER

Paul converted Lydia, from the city of Thyatira to Christianity. She was wealthy and the first European converted. She heard Paul preaching at Philippi. Lydia was a seller of purple...purple equates with royalty. The Roman Empire had specific uses for purple.

Lydia, after hearing the Gospel, obeyed the preaching of Paul she was baptized. Though she was rich, did not pull back as the Rich Young Ruler who came to Christ to ask what he lacked to be pleasing to God and have Salvation. He had kept all the Commandments from a child but was lacking one thing.

Paul preached to Lydia, she chose to obey and become a follower of Jesus. The Rich Young Ruler spoke directly to the Savior of the World, our Lord, and Savior Jesus Christ; but chose not to follow Him...but followed his riches. There is a noticeable contrast between the attitudes of Lydia and the Rich Young Ruler in reference to their choices. Jesus spoke of riches and the Kingdom of Heaven, *"And again I say unto you, It is easier for a camel to go through the eye of a needle, than for a rich man to enter into the Kingdom of God," [Matthew 19:24].*

Sunday, June 28, this year (2020), I heard Brother Harris preach. The title of his sermon was, "Do you Really Want God to Answer? He used the question the Rich Young Ruler asked. He reminded us, "God is not a phony." About the question, he asked Jesus, *"What do I lack?" [Ibid].* Christ told him, yet with all the right he had done, there was one thing he yet, needed to do. God does not sign off on what we want to do. We cannot do just enough to get into Heaven. God does not change His standards, *[Matthew 19:16-24].* Man has to change God does not change, deviate, or backup." *Dr. Loyd C. Harris, McAlmont Church of Christ, North Little Rock, Arkansas.*

Christ pointed out to the Rich Young Ruler clearly when he called to the Savior's attention quickly all the things he had done. *"What do I lack?" [Matthew 19:24b]*. Christ's response, *"Go and sell your possessions give to the poor and follow Me," [Matthew 19:21]*.

Christ gave him three things to do. He loved, but not enough. Selling all his possessions was the hardest; he had great wealth. His love for his wealth was stronger than his love for God. Christ wants our heart and not our wealth. God does not need our wealth. Nor can we bargain, purchase our Salvation, or get Him to change the structure of His Word to fit what we desire. God does not fit His Commands around our wants and desires; rather man fits their lives into the Commands of God. He is the Creator, not us.

Consider the eye of a needle its size and length. The Rich Young Ruler loved his riches more than he loved God. Christ said, *"It is easier for a camel to go through the eye of a needle than it is for a rich man to enter into the Kingdom of God," [Ibid]*.

He did not desire to give his life to God. We choose where we want the focus of our lives.

- **What comes first the material things of the world or obedience to God?**

The material possessions given to us are for our livelihood and enjoyment. We are not to worship gifts from God but worship the [Giver] of all good and perfect gifts. James reminds us, *"Every good gift and every perfect gift is from above, and cometh down from the Father of lights, with whom is no variableness, neither shadow of turning," [James 1:17]*.

*"Then Jesus said to His disciples, "If anyone desires to come after Me, let him deny himself, and take up his cross, and follow Me," [Matthew 16:24]*.

And *"Except a man be born again he cannot see the Kingdom of God," [John 3:3b]*.

Being born again is a change of hearts and minds, obeying the Gospel of Jesus Christ, and accepting Jesus as your Lord and savior. We are to hear, believe, repent, confess, and be baptized. Lydia did what Paul told her she must do to have eternal life and riches in Heaven without hesitation or a change of heart. She realized there were greater riches than this earthly wealth and obedience would not make her poorer but wealthy spiritually. *"Man cannot serve two masters: God and money," [Ibid]*.

Lydia's statement was different to Paul than the Rich Young Ruler's response to Christ. She said, *"If you have judged me to be faithful to the Lord, come into my house and abide there, and she constrained them," [Acts 16:15].*

Her desire to gain Salvation was evident. God opened her heart and Lydia obeyed the Gospel, she, and her household. We must make the effort as she did when we hear the truth spoken to us. Even after, we are a part of the Kingdom, especially if we fall into error, it must be a combination of teaching and our desire to want to make that change and then put forth that effort. We know what pearl of great price the Rich Young Ruler did not take advantage of the wealth Jesus offered him. We are to wear the garments of desire that Lydia had; she did not consider her wealth a greater treasure than the wealth of Heaven. Change comes from within.

God opens our understanding that we might comprehend and discern the Scripture. While the two disciples traveled on the Road to Emmaus their perceptions and understandings were open by Jesus, *"Then opened He their understanding, that they might understand the Scriptures," [Luke 24:45].*

We should wear those garments of desire to understand the Scripture that we may see and obey. God opens our spiritual eyes and then we can discern better with our physical eyes as well. Understanding is a powerful gift from God. The Preacher was wise enough to tell us, what the process is in getting the gifts of wisdom and understanding *"Wisdom is the principal thing; therefore, get wisdom: and with all thy getting get understanding," [Proverbs 4:7].*

Let us not forget knowledge is a factor as well as the result of one getting wisdom and understanding. Lydia understood the Rich Young Ruler did not. We still have the Law of Moses, the Prophets, and the Psalms of David. When we study them, we find our God is the same and He does not change His requirements if/because they do not fit our lifestyles. Christ fulfilled the Law. We must wear the garments of understanding that we obey Jesus not the Letter of the Law. When we accept Jesus as our Savior, we are sons of God and joint heirs with Jesus Christ; Lydia accepted this.

When Satan drives lives into a certain type of pleasure that seems harmless because he has painted it so innocent, it spreads like a wildfire almost causing a herd mentality as it gains participants (following the deceits of Satan).

Satan, at that point, has gained an advantage over you. There is one more thing (sin) he has presented that humans indulge in, and that indulgence pulls individuals further away from God and the Spiritual Integrity and Morality that is essential to Salvation. Again, God's standard does not change. Satan's effort does not change; he hates God and attempts (successfully) sometimes, but not always, to pull people away from the standards of God by his wiles. Paul reminds us *"In order that Satan might not outwit us. For we are not unaware of his schemes,"* *[2 Corinthians 2:11].*

Wisdom tells us we cannot be [deaf] in reference to Scriptural warnings but have deference for God's Word. Sin blinds our eyes. The foundations of sin Satan builds are on lies. Satan's insinuations to Eve were that God was keeping something (hiding) information from them they should know, "Go taste the fruit you will be like God." The Rich Young Ruler's mentality is dangerous as Scripture tells us what keeping the whole Law and offending in one point, we are guilty of all the Law, *"For whosoever shall keep the whole law, and yet offend in one point, he is guilty of all,"* *[James 2:10].*

We sisters should prefer immediately the mentality of Lydia. She upon hearing Paul's preaching did what he said, not ask what I am lacking? She understood what she was lacking. We can apply the example of *Luke 18*th Chapter of the Publican and the Pharisee in their prayers to God. The Pharisee took it upon himself to list those things, in a prideful tone he had accomplished in his life and compared it to the prayer of the Publican. In direct contrast, the Publican said, *"Forgive me a sinner."* He went down more justified. Listen to what Luke wrote of these two men, *"Two men went up into the temple to pray; the one a Pharisee, and the other a Publican. The Pharisee stood and prayed thus with himself, God, I thank thee, that I am not as other men are, extortioners, unjust, adulterers, or even as this Publican. I fast twice a week and I give tithes of all that I possess. And the Publican, standing afar off, would not lift up so much as his eyes unto heaven, but smote upon his breast, saying, God be merciful to me a sinner. I tell you; this man went down to his house justified rather than the other: for every one that exalts himself shall be abased; and he that humbles himself shall be exalted,"* *[Luke 18:10-14].*

We do not need to list anything before God – God is omnipotent, omnipresent, and omniscient. He knows, sees, and hears all [period]. Humility is an essentiality of integrity and morality. God's standards apply to everyone without exception to wealth, position, or power. We sisters cannot allow anything to place blinders on that understanding.

We wear the garments of Lydia and do not follow the example of the Rich Young Ruler.

The Woman at the Well was another with the Lydian mentality…

CHAPTER NINETEEN

# CHANCE, A WOMAN AT THE WELL AND OTHER'S GARMENTS OF A CHANGE

*"When therefore the Lord knew how the Pharisees had heard that Jesus made and baptized more disciples than John, Though Jesus himself baptized not, but His disciples,) He left Judaea and departed again into Galilee. And He must need go through Samaria. Then cometh He to a city of Samaria, which is called Sychar, near to the parcel of ground that Jacob gave to his son Joseph. Now Jacob's well was there. Jesus, therefore, being wearied with His journey, sat thus on the well: and it was about the sixth hour."*

*There cometh a woman of Samaria to draw water, "Jesus said unto her, Give me to drink." (For His disciples were gone away unto the city to buy meat.) Then said the woman of Samaria unto him, "How is it that thou, being a Jew, ask a drink of me, which am a woman of Samaria? For the Jews have no dealings with the Samaritans."*

*Jesus answered and said unto her, "If thou knew the gift of God, and who it is that said to thee, Give me to drink; thou would have asked of Him, and he would have given thee living water," [John 4:1-10].*

The Woman at the well when Jesus opened up the possibilities to her for eternal life to fulfill a need that would quench her spiritual thirst and change her life forever, her mind became a sponge.

A sponge is a piece of a soft, light, porous substance originally consisting of the fibrous skeleton of an invertebrate but is in this age usually made of synthetic material. The sponge absorbs liquid and is used for washing and cleaning.

Her mind became a sponge; she soaked up all of His words and immediately desired the living waters.

Jesus answered and said unto her, *"If thou knew the gift of God, and Who it is that said to thee, Give Me to drink; thou would have asked of Him, and He would have given thee living water," [John 4:10]*

The woman said unto him, "*Sir, thou hast nothing to draw with, and the well is deep: from whence then hast thou that living water? Art thou greater than our father Jacob, which gave us the well, and drank thereof himself, and his children, and his cattle?*" [*John 4:11-12*].

Jesus answered and said unto her, "*Whosoever drinks of this water shall thirst again: But whosoever drinks of the water that I shall give him shall never thirst; but the water that I shall give him shall be in him a well of water springing up into everlasting life,*" [*John 4:13-14*].

We can all drink the living water from the Spiritual Jacob's well. Christ made that cup of living water accessible to everyone including, but not beginning with the woman at the well. She drank of the spiritual water and it changed her life, so the same spiritual water will change our life.

Not only did she desire it for herself but went back to her village and shared the treasure she received and told the men of the village about the man who told her everything she ever did. She was changed at that point in her encounter with Jesus, though the men she talked to about her encounter went to check to verify the accuracy of what she said; she did not back off the message. Consider this as thoughts the men had of a woman in their village whose reputation, I am sure, was not the most upstanding.

Common-Law husbands were just as familiar in those times as they are now, human desires and needs seldom change; yet, however, sinful humans are, Jesus is the living water that can cleanse and make them whole. Christ offers us a new life in and through Him.

I cannot imagine what those residents said or thought when one of their community known for her immoral ways tells them the strange account of her encounter with Jesus.

I can imagine this question came to mind when the Samaritan Woman went into her village to tell her neighbors about Jesus, the man who told her everything she ever did.

- *Is not this the same woman whose life has been from one man to another why is this one different?*

They might have thought she is possessed with an evil spirit, and said, 'but let us go and see this wonderful thing of living water and a man who gives water that we never thirst again. To her, "We cannot take your word for this. He could be just another worker of magic tricks."

Change replied, "No he told me all things about myself, there was no way any man can tell one about everything they have done. He waits by our Father Jacob's well. He is a Jew."

"A Jew, and he talked with you, impossible. Let us hurry and see this great thing."

In the Samaritan woman's encounter with Jesus, she in ages past as we do in this age, think, in physical or earthly terms and not in the Spiritual sense.

In another account and encounter of a woman in adultery when Jesus returned to the temple again the next day, the Pharisees trying Him to see what judgment He would pass on a woman caught in adultery. The Law said she was to be stoned. Instead, Jesus put them to the test, *So when they continued asking Him, He raised Himself up and said to them, "He who is without sin among you, let him throw a stone at her first." Again, He stooped down and wrote on the ground. Then those who heard it, being convicted, by their conscience, went out one by one, beginning with the oldest even to the last. And Jesus was left alone, and the woman standing in the midst. When Jesus had raised Himself up and saw no one but the woman, He said to her, "Woman, where are those accusers of yours? Has no one condemned you?" She said, "No one, Lord." And Jesus said to her, "Neither do I condemn you; go and sin no more." Then Jesus spoke to them again, saying, "I Am the Light of the world. He who follows Me shall not walk in darkness, but have the Light of Life," [John 8:7-12].*

Jesus does not condemn us, nor did He condemn the woman caught in adultery, or the woman at the well with the six husbands who were not hers. However, there are "go and sin no more mandates." When we come to Him and receive forgiveness, we cannot go back into the life we once lived no more than these women could and be pleasing to God. It requires a change of heart and mind, which dictates a change in our actions...the key is, [change]! Christ gave us the [chance] to have eternal salvation and have once again that one-on-one relationship with God by His death on the Cross of Calvary.

Regardless of the sin sisters, our garments changes when we come to Christ, we cannot successfully go back to the condition of which we left... because of our encounter with:

Jesus our perfect example and man's revelation from God.

CHAPTER TWENTY

# JESUS IS.
# MAN'S REVELATION FROM GOD

Isaiah reminds us of who Jesus is, *"To whom shall ye liken Me, or shall I be equal? saith the Holy One. Lift up your eyes and behold who hath created these things that bringeth out their host by number, He calleth them all by their names by the greatness of His might, for that He is strong in power; not one faileth. Has thou not known? Hast thou not heard that the everlasting God, the Lord the Creator of the ends of the earth, fainteth not, neither is weary: There is no searching of His understanding. He giveth power to the faint, and to them that have no might He increaseth strength. Even the youths shall faint and be weary, and the young men shall utterly fail. But they that wait upon the Lord shall renew their strength' they shall mount up with wings as eagles; they shall run, and not be weary; and they shall walk, and not faint,"* [Isaiah 40:25-26, 28-31].

The word of the Lord came to me: *"Son of man how is the wood of a vine different from that of a branch from any of the trees in the forest? Is wood ever taken from it to make anything useful? Do they make pegs from it to hang things on? And after it is thrown on the fire as fuel and the fire burns both ends and chars the middle, is it then useful for anything? If it was not useful for anything when it was whole, how much less can it be made into something useful when the fire has burned it and it is charred?* Therefore, this is what the Sovereign Lord says: *"As I have given the wood of the vine among the trees of the forest as fuel for the fire, so will I treat the people living in Jerusalem. I will set my face against them. Although they have come out of the fire, the fire will yet consume them. And when I set my face against them, you will know that I Am the Lord,"* [Ezekiel 15:1-7].

*"And Jesus came and spoke to them, saying, "All authority has been given to Me in Heaven and on Earth,"* [Matthew 28:18].

Jesus is God's Covenant with the House of David. Christ is His promise to David one of his descendants would always sit on his throne. This Covenant is spoken of down through the ages. Amos the Prophet spoke to the people, *"In that day, I will restore David's fallen shelter. I will repair his broken walls and restore it ruins and will build it as it used to be so that they may possess the remnant of Edom and all of the nations that bear My Name declares the Lord,"* who will do these things, [Amos 9:11-12].

169

As did the Prophet Samuel … He wrote, *"The Lord declares to you that the Lord Himself will establish a house for you. When your days are over and you rest with your ancestors, I will raise up your offspring to succeed you, your own flesh and blood and I will establish His Kingdom. He is the one who will build a house for My name and will establish the throne of His Kingdom forever. I will be His Father and He will be my son," [2 Samuel 7:11-13].*

The vision came from God to Micah the Prophet of the coming Messiah. One who would rule over Israel, and has lived from the Ancient day, which means from before the creation of man and time. Christ is Eternal; He has no beginning and no end. He spoke of His birth in Bethlehem a small town. Everything Micah was told in the vision from God came to pass, *"But Bethlehem Ephratah, though you are small among the clans of Judah, out of you will come for Me one who will be ruler over Israel, whose origins are from of old from ancient times," [Michal 5:2].*

Micah, as well, spoke of the coming Messiah as the Shepherd of His people. This is another message using symbolism to get across the significance of the point God was making to His people. He would be a Shepherd for His people. A Shepherd leads the sheep, keeps them safe, takes care of their needs, and never leaves his sheep but is with them always. Micah told the people God said, *"He will stand and shepherd His flock in the strength of the Lord, in the majesty of the Name of the Lord His God and they will live securely, for then His greatness will reach to the ends of the earth," [Micah 5:4].*

Christ is the fulfillment of that promise.

We read in Peter's first Sermon, after the death, of Christ to the crowd, *[Acts 2:14-21]* of the fulfillment of the Covenant Samuel centuries before wrote about and continued in his sermon, *"Fellow Israelites, listen to this: Jesus of Nazareth was a man accredited by God to you by miracles, wonders, and signs, which God did among you through Him, as you yourselves know. This man was handed over to you by God's deliberate plans and foreknowledge, and you with the help of wicked men put Him to death by nailing Him to the Cross. But God raised Him from the dead, freeing Him from the agony of death, because it was impossible for death to keep its hold on Him."*

Peter continued: David said about Him: *"I saw the Lord always before me because He is at my right hand; I will not be shaken! Therefore, my heart is glad, and my tongue rejoices; My body will rest in hope because you will not abandon Me to the realm of the dead. You will not let your Holy One see decay. You have made known to Me the paths of life you will fill Me with joy in your presence," [Acts 2:22-36].*

Paul further reminds us in Ephesians of the fulfillment of the promise God gave to man. We see in Paul's letter, his explanation of the unity promised that One would come to earth to gather into one all things and they are under His subjection and rule, "*Wherein He hath abounded toward us in all wisdom and prudence; Having made known unto us the mystery of His will, according to His good pleasure which He hath purposed in Himself. That in the dispensation of the fullness of times, He might gather together in one all things in Christ, both which are in heaven, and which are on earth; even in Him: in whom also we have obtained an inheritance, being predestinated according to the purpose of Him who worketh all things after the counsel of His own will: That we should be to the praise of His glory, who first trusted in Christ," [Ephesians 1:8-10].*

Christ came from the Father to the Manger, from the Manger to the Cross-from the Cross-to the Grave, from the Grave to the Father. The word [from] is defined as indicating the source or provenance of someone or something, a journey, motion, or action starts. The word [to] is defined as approaching or reaching (a particular condition). [The synonym for the word (to) is (in route to or on the way)]. Christ came for a particular purpose that purpose was the Salvation of humanity. He said, "*I came forth from the Father and have come into the world; I am leaving the world again and going to the Father," [John 20:17].*

Jesus made a round trip, from Heaven to earth, and back. The plan was in place before time began for the redemption of man. Christ was reigning, did reign, and is still reigning Supreme Savior and God, "*I and My Father are One," [Ibid].*

We see above the relationship that Jesus had with the Father of which David spoke. We must strive to have an obedient relationship with Jesus who came to reconcile us back to God", [2 *Corinthians 5:15-21]*. Paul reminds us, "*Therefore if anyone is in Christ, the new creation has come. The old has gone, the new is here! All this is from God, who reconciled us to Himself through Christ and gave us the ministry of reconciliation that God and He have committed to us the message of reconciliation," [V17-19].*

God's love is our shelter in the storms that rage in our lives, "*He that dwells in the secret place of the Most High shall abide under the shadow of the Almighty. I will say of the Lord, He is my refuge and my fortress: my God; in Him will I trust. Surely, He shall deliver thee from the snare of the fowler, and from the noisome pestilence. He shall cover thee with His feathers, and under His wings shalt thou trust: His truth shall be thy shield and buckler. Thou shalt not be afraid for the terror by night; nor for the arrow that flies day," [Psalms 91:1-5].*

The promise included all people Jews and Gentiles. He tore down that middle wall of petition and Salvation is accessible for all who desire to follow Christ. God does not break His promises regardless of how long it takes – His promises have always come to pass.

**Jesus is:**

- **Yahweh Elohim, Jehovah: the unbreakable relationship between the Father and the Son,** "*God also said to Moses, "Say to the Israelites, 'The Lord, the God of your fathers-the God of Abraham, the God of Isaac, and the God of Jacob-has sent me to you.' "This is My name forever, the name you shall call me from generation to generation," [Exodus 3:15].*
- **Our source of truth***: Jesus answered, "I am the Way the truth and the life," - "I will ask of the Father and He will give you another Advocate to help you and be with you forever - The Spirit of Truth. The World cannot accept Him because it neither sees Him nor knows Him. But you know Him, for He lives with you and will be in you," [John 14:6, 17]. – "As for you, the anointing you received from Him remains in you, and you do not need anyone to teach you. But as His anointing teaches you about all things and as that anointing is real, not counterfeit – just as it has taught you, remain in Him," [I John 2:27]. – "I saw heaven standing open and there before me was a white horse, whose rider is called Faithful and True. With justice, He judges and wages war," [Revelation 19:11].*
- **God's Promises: God does not break promises,"** *For when God made a promise to Abraham because He could swear by no greater, He swore by Himself, saying, Surely blessing I will bless thee, and multiplying I will multiply thee. And so, after he had patiently endured, he obtained the promise. For men verily swear by the greater: and an oath for confirmation is to them an end of all strife. Wherein God, willing more abundantly to shew unto the heirs of promise the immutability of His counsel, confirmed it by an oath: That by two immutable things, in which it was impossible for God to lie, we might have a strong consolation, who have fled for refuge to lay hold upon the hope set before us: which hope we have as an anchor of the soul, both sure and steadfast, and which entered into that within the veil; Whither the forerunner is for us entered, even Jesus, made a high priest forever after the order of Melchisedek," [Hebrews 6:13-20].*

- Because God never breaks promises, we should strive for perfection, *"Therefore leaving the principles of the Doctrine of Christ, let us go on unto perfection; not laying again the foundation of repentance from dead works, and of faith toward God, Of the doctrine of baptisms, and of laying on of hands, and of the resurrection of the dead, and of eternal judgment. And this will we do if God permits. For it is impossible for those who were once enlightened, and have tasted of the heavenly gift, and were made partakers of the Holy Ghost, And have tasted the good Word of God, and the powers of the world to come, If they shall fall away, to renew them again unto repentance; seeing they crucify to themselves the Son of God afresh, and put Him to an open shame," [Hebrews 6:1-6].*

- **Our full authority in heaven and earth:** *"I Am the Way, the Truth, and the Life. No one comes to the Father except through Me," [John 14:6].*

- **Our high Priest: He has no beginning and no ending,** *"For He testified, you are a Priest forever after the order of Melchizedek," [Hebrews 7:17].*

- **Among us…Head of the Church purchased with His Blood,** *"He is the Head of the Body, the Church," [Colossians 1:18].*

- **Emerged throughout the Old Testament and burst into full view at God's appointed time as promised,** *"Therefore the Lord Himself will give you a sign: The virgin will conceive and give birth to a son, and will call Him Immanuel," [Isaiah 7:14].*

- **Described by Daniel, "Son of Man has dominion" Jesus will destroy death and Hades casting them into the Lake of Fire,** *"I saw in the night visions, and behold, one like the Son of man came with the clouds of heaven and came to the Ancient of days, and they brought Him near before Him. And there was given Him dominion, and glory, and a kingdom, that all people, nations, and languages, should serve Him: His dominion is an everlasting dominion, which shall not pass away, and His kingdom that which shall not be destroyed," [Daniel 7:13-14].*

- **Christ is the One who revealed the secrets of the Kingdom. The Spiritual truth is no longer a mystery; but known to all humans. God revealed His plan, for redemption through His Son who died that we might have Salvation (our Garden of Eden and the way back to the Tree of Life) lost by the first act of disobedience,**

**in that Garden,** *"He answered and said unto them, Because it is given unto you to know the mysteries of the Kingdom of Heaven, but to them it is not given," [Matthew 13:11].*

- **The Root of David,** *"Then one of the elders said to me, "Do not weep! See, the Lion of the tribe of Judah, the Root of David, has triumphed. He is able to open the scroll and its seven seals," [Revelation 5:5]…* **The source which David came from the Stump of Jessie,** *"A shoot will come up from the stump of Jesse; from his roots, a Branch will bear fruit," [Isaiah 11:1].*

- **The seed of the woman…He will be victorious,** *"And I will put enmity between you and the woman, and between your offspring and hers; He will crush your head, and you will strike his heel," [Genesis 3:15].*

- **God of all comfort,** *Blessed be God, even the Father of our Lord Jesus Christ, the Father of mercies, and the God of all comfort, Who comforted us in all our tribulation, that we may be able to comfort them which are in any trouble, by the comfort wherewith we ourselves are comforted of God. For as the sufferings of Christ abound in us, so our consolation also abounded by Christ."*

  *"And whether we be afflicted; it is for your consolation and salvation; which, is effectual in the enduring of the same sufferings, which we also suffer or whether we be comforted, it is for your consolation and salvation. And our hope of you is steadfast, knowing, that as ye are partakers of the sufferings, so shall ye be also of the consolation," [2 Corinthians 1:3–7].*

- **The Bright and Morning Star; as the one that appears at early dawn when the last hint of darkness is almost gone,** *"I Jesus, have sent mine angel to testify unto you these things in the churches. I Am the root and the offspring of David, [and] the bright and Morning Star," [Revelation 22:16].*

When riding early morning on my way to take my husband to Birmingham for his doctor's appointment, it is eerie, cold, and dark; there in the northern sky is the brightest star in the world, beautiful sparkling, and a promise that the breaking of the day (light) is imminent. Christ is the Morning Star at our most difficult and dark times in life, reminds us He is there for us and will not leave us alone.

This world and the situations get to be more than challenging sometimes, but we do not give up, rather keep looking to Jesus for the promise He made, "*I will not forsake thee or leave thee,*" [Ibid].

Jesus wants to be the desire of our hearts and the focus of our Spiritual eye: "*Seek ye first the Kingdom of Heaven and Its righteousness,*" [Matthew 6:33a].

Our garments of the heart should match what we portray with our garments we live each day before our fellowman as Jesus warned the Church at Sardis, "*To the angel of the church in Sardis write: These are the words of Him who holds the seven spirits of God and the seven stars. I know your deeds; you have a reputation of being alive, but you are dead,*" [Revelation 3:1].

Just having the outward appearance of righteousness is not sufficient it is sinful, and the garments of our spirituality are not clean. God wants our hearts to be true to Him regardless of what is taking place around us. Things go wrong in congregations of The Lord's Church; however, that does not mean we need to add to it or step away from being faithful to Christ.

We leave our first love and belief sometimes that is why we need awareness. It is easy to get off track before we realize it. The basic truth of God is where we need to be at all times. He does not change that truth or replace it with other truths there are no other truths but what Christ said, "*Jesus said unto him, I am the Way, the Truth, and the Life: no man cometh unto the Father, but by Me,*" [John 14:6].

All three is the path to Salvation, what we believe, and the light that reveals that truth; if any man walks in the light there is no darkness in him. We cannot sleep our way through life living as we are unaware thinking that God is different from His Nature described in Scripture, and He did not leave us a pattern to follow. Christ said to the Church at Sardis, they needed to wake up, "*Remember therefore how thou hast received and heard, and hold-fast, and repent. If therefore thou shalt not watch, I will come on thee as a thief, and thou shalt not know what hour I will come upon thee,*" [Revelation 3:3].

Getting comfortable in the pleasures of this world and losing your awareness is dangerous. No man knows the day nor hour of His return, just know He is coming. Spirituality and moral integrity are still paramount to God.

Christ is our Creator. The world begins with the Creation of Heaven and Earth, and it will end with a new heaven and earth, "*And I saw a new heaven and a new earth: for the first heaven and the first earth were passed away; and there was no more sea.And I John saw the holy city, New Jerusalem, coming down from God out of Heaven, prepared as a bride adorned for her husband.And I heard a great voice out of heaven saying, Behold, the tabernacle of God is with men, and He will dwell with them, and they shall be His people, and God Himself shall be with them, and be their God. And God shall wipe away all tears from their eyes; and there shall be no more death, neither sorrow, nor crying, neither shall there be any more pain: for the former things are passed away,*" [Revelation 21:1-5].

Everything will be new and there will only be joyfulness for an eternity.

Laodicea was a city where a wealthy church was located. Gold and cloth dying were  materials things that bought them wealth and they thought they needed nothing, but was poor, blind, wretched, and their relationship had fallen into lukewarmness. Self-sufficiency without God is dangerous and does not please God. Their spiritual eyes needed anointing (healing) so they could see.

He is an all-sufficient Savior who can supply all our needs, "*So then because thou art lukewarm, and neither cold nor hot, I will spew thee out of My mouth. Because thou says, I am rich, and increased with goods, and have need of nothing; and knows not that thou art wretched, and miserable, and poor, and blind, and naked: I counsel thee to buy of me gold tried in the fire, that thou may be rich; and white raiment, that thou may be clothed, and that the shame of thy nakedness do not appear; and anoint thine eyes with eye salve, that thou may see,*" [Revelation 3:16-18].

Indifference to God deprives one of their blessings. Indifference is an attitude with no humility or desire for God to be in your life or rule your life. We cannot insult The God of Heaven, Creator of all things, and think it will not cost us.

In summation, Jesus is our source of wealth, wisdom, strength, honor, glory, and praise – He is worthy of these in recognition of Him as we praise and worship Him. Jesus is Lion and Lamb – power and humility.

Isaiah spoke of the Messiah that would be born of a Virgin, "*Therefore the Lord Himself will give you a sign: The virgin will conceive and give birth to a son and will call*

*Him Immanuel. He will be eating curds and honey when He knows enough to reject the wrong and choose the right, for before the boy knows enough to reject the wrong and choose the right, the land of the two kings you dread will be laid waste," [Isaiah 7:14-16].*

*"Repent ye therefore, and be converted, that your sins may be blotted out. When the times of refreshing shall come from the presence of the Lord and He shall send Jesus Christ, which before was preached unto you; whom the heaven must receive until the times of restitution of all things, which God hath spoken by the mouth of all His holy prophets since the world began. For Moses truly said unto the fathers, A prophet shall the Lord your God raise up unto you of your brethren, like unto me; Him shall ye hear in all things whatsoever He shall say unto you. And it shall come-to-pass, that every soul, which will not hear that prophet, shall be destroyed from among the people. Yea, and all the prophets from Samuel and those that follow after, as many as have spoken, have likewise foretold of these days. Ye are the children of the prophets and of the covenant, which God made with our fathers, saying unto Abraham, "And, in thy seed shall all the kindred of the earth be blessed. Unto you first, God having raised up His Son Jesus, sent Him to bless you, in turning away every one of you from his iniquities," [Acts 3:19-26].*

God reveals Himself throughout History. We know the Old Testament is the beginning of the Revelation of God.

The word revelation has more than one definition. According to Vine [2005], it means an uncovering. The Holy Bible, the Word of God reveals the mystery and the purpose of God in this age, [*Romans 16:25*]. It is the communication of the Knowledge of God to the Soul. Paul's prayer for the Ephesians, "*I keep asking that the God of our Lord Jesus Christ, the glorious Father, may give you the Spirit of wisdom and revelation, so that you may know Him better,*" [*Ephesians 1:17*].

It is an expression of the mind of God for the instruction to the Church, "*Now, brothers and sisters if I come to you and speak in tongues, what good will I be to you unless I bring you some revelation or knowledge or prophecy or word of instruction?*"

"*What then shall we say, brothers and sisters? When you come together, each of you has a hymn, or a word of instruction, a revelation, a tongue, or an interpretation. Everything must be done so that the church may be built up,*" [*I Corinthians 14:6, 26*].

He is the Giver of what is soon to take place, the final judgment of God, *"The revelation from Jesus Christ, which God gave Him to show His servants what must soon take place. He made it known by sending His angel to His servant John, who testifies to everything he saw–that is, the Word of God and the testimony of Jesus Christ," [Revelation 1:1-2].*

John bore record of the *Word of God*, and of the testimony of Jesus of all that He said. Christ gave two Revelation to John:

1.) He gave a review of the seven churches of Asia and their service to Him and what things they needed to change (amend); and the faithful churches, He commended.

2.) He told John of the last day; final judgment allowed him to see a scene of the Throne of God when the books were open and then the Book of Life that only the Lamb of God was worthy to open.

In The Book of Revelation, John shows Christ as glorious and victorious overall. Revelation also helps us to know and understand more of the nature of God – to know who God, Jesus, and the Holy Spirit (Seven Spirits) are so that we can know [Them] better and have confidence in our ability to trust and rely on God and His Word.

The main themes in The Book of Revelation are love, power, justice as it is throughout Scripture from the Book of Genesis through The Book of Revelation, *"Blessed is the one who reads aloud the words of this prophecy, and blessed are those who hear it and take to heart what is written in it because the time is near."-" And from Jesus Christ, who is the faithful witness, the firstborn from the dead, and the ruler of the kings of the earth. To Him who loves and has freed us from our sins by His blood and has made us to be a kingdom and priests to serve His God and Father to Him be glory and power forever and ever," [Revelation 1:3, 5, 6].*

Revelation allows us to look at Christ, for who He is: our glorious Savior, Mighty God, and Maker of Heaven and Earth. Christ came to earth in humility for our benefit, not His. He needed no Salvation; He needed no Savior; He is the Savior. He wanted us to see and know Him and that, though He reigns King and Lord Supreme knows and understands the battles we face, in this world - in this fleshly tent, of which, we dwell.

We are to pass the Word of God on in a systemic way to all with whom we contact, and which enables them to teach the same Word. There was no doubt of this fact when John saw Jesus on Lord's Day during his exile on the Island of Patmos; He is Lord and Savior. Keep in mind sisters, John knew and lived with Jesus. He saw Him in the appearance of a man-eating, sleeping, laughing, caring, talking, and working miracles on this earth. John, then saw Him in His Glorified State on the Mount of Transfiguration, *"And after six days Jesus taketh Peter, James, and John His brother, and bring them up into a high mountain apart, And was transfigured before them: and His face did shine as the sun, and His raiment was white as the light. And behold, there appeared unto them Moses and Elias talking with him. Then answered Peter, and said unto Jesus, Lord, it is good for us to be here: if thou wilt, let us make here three tabernacles one for thee, and one for Moses, and one for Elias. While He yet spake, behold, a bright cloud overshadowed them: and behold a voice out of the cloud, which said, this is my beloved Son, in whom I am well pleased, hear ye Him. And when the disciples heard it, they fell on their face and were sore afraid. And Jesus came and touched them, and said, Arise, and be not afraid. And when they had lifted up their eyes, they saw no man, save Jesus only," [Matthew 17:1-8].*

Therefore, it was not hard for John the Apostle to recognize Him as the true Savior, pure and holy that he loved and lived with for three years. That is another reason why we avoid lowering our standards, compromising the truth, or doing just enough to get by. Christ is intolerant of sin. We have an opportunity to correct continuously the sins not approved by God; regardless of what the world might say or does including our family or friends around us, we cannot live our lives through the eyes of others.

The Prophets wrote of God and the coming of the Messiah. The way that He would manifest Himself through His only begotten Son, Jesus said, *"I and My Father are One," [John 10:30].*

When we know Jesus our Savior, we know God our Father.

In the 13th Chapter of Acts, Paul gave the people an exact timeline, of what the Scripture says of what the purpose of Jesus is and whom Jesus is beginning from the Old Testament to the New Testament, *"And after that, He (God) gaveunto themjudges about the space of four hundred and fifty years, until Samuel the Prophet."*

*"And after they desired a king; and God gave them Saul the son of Kish, a man of the tribe of Benjamin, by the space of forty years. And when He had removed him, He raised up unto them David to be their king; to whom also He gave testimony, and said, I have found David thesonof Jesse, a man after Mine own heart, which shall fulfill all My will."*

*"Of this man's seed hath God according to His promise raised unto Israel a Savior, Jesus: When John had first preached before His coming, the baptism of repentance to all the people of Israel?"*

*"And as John fulfilled his course, he said, "Whom do you think ye that I am? I am not He. But behold there cometh one after me, whose shoes of His feet I am not worthy to loose."*

*"And though they found no cause of deathin Him, yet desired they Pilate that He should be slain. And when they had fulfilled all that was written of Him, they took Him down from the tree, and laid Him in a sepulcher."*

*"But God raised Him from the dead: And He was seen many days of them, which came up with Him from Galilee to Jerusalem, who are His witnesses unto the people. And we declare unto you glad tidings, how that the promise which was made unto the fathers," [Acts 13:20-25 &28-32].*

Paul reminded the people of the freedom they had through the Savior of the World. The Law of Moses could not offer this freedom; through Christ Jesus, truth and grace, ushered in mercy and justification, *"Be it known unto you, therefore, menandbrethren, that through this Man is preached unto you the forgiveness of sins: And by Him, all that believe are justified from all things, from which ye could not be justified by the law of Moses," [Acts 13:38-39].*

Paul continues by explaining the reason Jesus came to earth. He is the fulfillment of the Prophecy of the sacrificial lamb for the sins of humanity and our assurance of an eternity with God: and to bring the Gentiles into the fold; thereby, creating one Body with no division. Without Jesus, man would forever be under that taskmaster that binds and hold him without hope, *"And the next Sabbath day came almost the whole city together to hear the Word of God. But when the Jews saw the multitudes, they were filled with envy, and spake against those things, which were spoken by Paul, contradicting and blaspheming."*

Then Paul and Barnabas waxed bold, and said, *"It was necessary that the Word of God should first have been spoken to you: but seeing ye put it from you, and judge yourselves unworthy of everlasting life, lo, we turn to the Gentiles. For so hath the Lord commanded us, saying, I have set thee to be a light of the Gentiles that thou should be for salvation unto the ends of the earth."*

*"And when the Gentiles heard this, they were glad, and glorified the Word of the Lord: and as many as were ordained to eternal life believed. And the Word of the Lord was published throughout all the region. But the Jews stirred up the devout and honorable women, and the chief men of the city raised persecution against Paul and Barnabas and expelled them out of their coasts. But, they shook off the dust of their feet against them and came unto Iconium. And the disciples were filled with joy, and with the Holy Ghost,"* [Acts 13:46-52].

God reveals Himself through all the beauty of nature, in storms, in the rain, the sun, and all the heavenly celestials that no man can create. We can only look in awe at its magnificence and power, which is a way of humans knowing our Awesome God and Savior. Paul explains to the citizens of Lystra and Derbe that, all the gods being worshipped, and their sacrifices were worthless, and those gods could not create or give them anything for survival or Salvation.

The elements that the God of Heaven gives, man derives needed benefits from the rain, the sun, as well as caring for the needs of the earth, *"Friends, why are you doing this? We too are only human, like you. We are bringing you good news, telling you to turn from these worthless things to the living God, who made the heavens, the earth, the sea, and everything in them,"* [Acts 14:15].

God reveals Himself in humans, *"And God said, Let Us make man in Our image, after Our likeness: and let them have dominion over the fish of the sea, and over the fowl of the air, and over the cattle, and over all the earth, and over every creeping thing that crept upon the earth. So, God created man in His own image, in the image of God created He him; male and female created He them,"* [Genesis 1:26-27].

God created man to worship and glorify Him in all our way, *"In all thy ways acknowledge Him and He will direct thy path,"* [Proverbs 3:6].

Even in this present time, people are still suppressing the Truth of God, ignoring His Commands because they do not want to get to the point where they know their lives have to change. Their focus has to be on the true God of Heaven and not on earthly gods man serves (money, wealth, power, success, I need, or I want).

There is no power but of God, and that is the truth man does not want to know. The One God requires we live in certain ways, following His Commandments and obeying the Gospel of Christ recognizing the death, burial, and resurrection of our Lord and Savior. God sits on His Throne, and we are to worship Him in Spirit and Truth.

Christ was both a human and divine God existing in one person. This creates the Christological basis for our belief. Presently, Christ is our King, Lord, and Mediator; however, on Judgment Day He becomes our Judge and then reigning King forever. The Scripture makes this clear in both of these before and after statements. Paul writes to Timothy, " For*there is*one God, and one *Mediator between God and men, the Man Christ Jesus,*" [I Timothy 2:5].

Christ will judge each man by the same words He offered us for Salvation, "*He that rejects Me, and received not My words, hath One that judges him: the Word that I have spoken, the same shall judge him in the last day,*" [John 12:48].

And He will reign as King forever, "*These shall make war with the Lamb, and the Lamb shall overcome them: for He is Lord of lords, and King of kings: and they that are with Him are called and chosen, and faithful,*" [Revelation 17:14].

"*The Lord is King forever and ever: the heathen are perished out of His land,*" [Psalms 10:16].

The flow of the Scripture, like a river, has no breaks in who God, the only God of the Universe is; His promises are certain. The plan, for the redemption of man, has come to pass. The future our Savior went back to prepare for us is ready. All of this, God did because of one word, "Love" for His creation. God put all the powers of Heaven behind the Herculean effort taken to accomplish the plan He gave to His Prophets to tell His people.

He sent His only begotten Son to purchase Salvation. Jesus is the Head of all other powers of Heaven and there is no one higher, but the Father, and they are one. Christ sent back the Holy Spirit to teach, guide, and help us who is also God the third of the God Head, the [Triune] God of the Universe; knowing this, should become for us a fierce urgency of "NOW." We cannot wait to take advantage of the Salvation, the Free Gift, we did nothing to deserve, that God gifted to humanity.

We cannot do anything to earn Salvation that is not in man's abilities we saw that in the Garden of Eden. Adam and Eve's actions tell us humans are never satisfied with "Now" what we have; but is always reaching for something usually that is not good for us, but we want it anyway.

- ***Do we think God would hold back from us those things that are good for us? The answer is no!***

God knows what is best for us even if we think it is not. We are the creature He is the Creator. We are the Play-Doh, He is the Artisan of Creation, of which He looked and said of each, "It is GOOD." After the creation of the sixth day was done God looked at the creation and said, "It is VERY GOOD." There is nothing beyond good in God's sight. We can use all the adjectives, adverbs, or any other wordy descriptions what God says is GOOD that is the best we get. In the end, when we stand before the judgment and have been faithful to the end will hear, "*Well done My [good] and faithful servant, take your rest,*" *[Matthew 25:21]*.

- ***How long will this rest be?***

We will spend eternity with the same Savior who purchased our Salvation, not a different one. He is the same Jesus who lived among humanity, promised an eternity of peace, a mansion, Salvation, hung on the Cross-was cruelly treated, spit upon, disbelieved, and rejected all because of man's desire to live in a way that so please them (humans).

Of course, the god of this world, Satan, who has been there from the beginning, and at the beginning, initiating the fall of man, stoked those fires and is still stoking those fires of desire.

Reject Satan's voice, his ideology, and his promises; they are like the morning mist that dissipates with the rising of the morning sun. When they encounter the light or heat of Salvation when it comes like the morning mist, they will not withstand the test. The promises of God have withstood, are withstanding, will withstand, all tests of time, and will continue to do so to the end of the world and through eternity.

Down through the centuries, prophets of God prophesied of His plan for the Salvation, of man. The Prophets of God made people everywhere aware of His power. The people knew of the God of Heaven, yet defied, denied, and disowned the God of Heaven and defended and recognized the ones they wanted to worship and upheld their right to do so.

• *Does that sound familiar?*

Becoming syncretistic in worship is dangerous. Jesus does not accept incorporating other forms or elements of paganism into our worship of Him. The Aesthetics (principles) of the worship is there but a closer look reveals a lack of total biblically based content. Jesus did not leave room for man to add any additional concepts to worshipping Him. When a man brings in other ideas that they want to append (additions) they think will make the service, more attractive does not get approval from God. We should ask ourselves who the audience is during our Worship. There are five steps of a true worship service: singing, praying, preaching, giving, and the Lord Supper (taking Communion).

Our doxologies (songs of praise) should be to God the Father, God the Son, and God the Holy Spirit for they too are prayers of the Heart singing with the melody in our hearts to God. Understanding the implication of these songs in our worship is to the praise glory and honor our God is due.

Paul reminds us that, Blood is the defining principle of the grace and mercy of God. We are justified through faith, *[Romans 51-9]. "This do in Remembrance of Me," [Ibid].* Christ wants us to reflect each moment on the reality of His being Lord and Savior and the Sacrifice made for the Gift of Salvation purchased with His Body and Blood. He left the emblems of bread and wine to remind humans of the cost of Salvation and why He hung on that cruel cross.

Christ wants us to reflect each moment on the reality of His being Lord and Savior and the Sacrifice He made so that we might have life and have it more abundantly. Reflecting reality, our memory does reflect reality, *"And He took bread, gave thanks, and broke it, and gave it to them, saying, "This is My Body given for you; do this in remembrance of Me." In the same way, after the supper He took the cup, saying, "This cup is the new covenant in My blood, which is poured out for you," [Luke 22:19-10].*

There is only one who justifies – that justification came through the Blood of Jesus Christ, not of man's devising but only God our Father who sent His only begotten Son to die for all that we might have the gift of life and a way back to Him lost in the garden.

Our worship is to the glory of God not to impress or make us (someone) happy. The joy should be there because we know our worshipping God in the right manner is pleasing to Him and beneficial to us. We do not worship to be entertained; God gives us sufficient time outside of worship service, for entertainments as well. All other things we do in the name of worship instead, of worshipping the one true God, are not acceptable to Him. Keep in mind it makes Satan happy.

We all have awareness and access to Salvation.

**Awareness:** In this 21$^{st}$-Century, we are aware of the plan of God; it has come to fruition. Christ came as promised and died as the sacrificial Lamb for the sins of humanity and to tear down that middle wall of petition so that Jews, Gentiles, bond, or free could partake of the Salvation Christ purchased.

**Access:** All of humanity has access to the Salvation Christ purchased without exception, *"For God so loved the world, that He gave His only begotten Son, that whosoever believeth in Him should not perish, but have everlasting life," [John 3:16].*

The Inconvenient Truth is like a bright shining light, from which man shy away. History records, for us, the power of God and the interaction with man and His wrath on the evil empires that worshipped idol gods and made shrines and other statues to worship instead of the one true God. The Babylon Empire, the Persian Empire, the Egyptian Empire, and lastly, the Roman Empire all were idol worshippers and at some point, in some ways, like the Law suppressed its people. Jesus took away the suppression of all people. The ultimate revelation of God was Jesus Christ and Salvation for all humanity.

Jesus is the one who searches and knows us, *"To the chief Musician, A Psalm of David. O Lord, thou hast searched me, and known me. Thou knows my down sitting and mine uprising; thou understands my thought afar off. Thou compasses my path and my lying down, and art acquainted with all my ways. For there is not a word in my tongue, but, lo, O Lord, thou knows it all together," [Psalms 139:1-4].*

Jesus is the one we cry to for help, *"Let my prayer be set forth before Thee as incense; and the lifting up of my hands as the evening sacrifice," [Psalms 141:2].*

Jesus is the Lion of Judah who opens the book and breaks the seven seals, *"And I saw a strong angel proclaiming with a loud voice, who is worthy to open the book, and to break the seals thereof? And no man in heaven, nor in the earth, neither under the earth, was able to open the book, neither to look thereon. And I wept much because no man was found worthy to open and to read the book, neither to look thereon. And one of the elders said unto me, Weep not: behold, the Lion of the tribe of Judah, the Root of David, hath prevailed to open the book and to break the seven seals thereof,"* [Revelation 5:2-5].

Jesus is the hope, joy, and desire of all ages.

The creation was in a perfect state until sin entered the world and it (man) fell from its perfect state. Humanity entered into bondage when sin entered the world. Christ freed us from that bondage and gave us hope for eternity with God. The Scripture describes the wait and hope of humanity for that birth of freedom is like, "pains of childbirth." Christians know that freedom is coming because Christ is coming back to carry His redeemed home where there is no sin, death, pain, only joy in the presence of God.

Romans the eighth chapter gives us a shining hope of the resurrection into a new eternal body. Paul begins with, *"There is now no condemnation for those who are in Christ Jesus because through Christ Jesus the law of the Spirit who gives life has set you free from the law of sin and death,"* [Romans 8:1-2].

We are heirs of God. Paul tells us, *"Therefore my brothers and sisters, we have an obligation – but it is not to the flesh, to live according to it. For if you live according to the flesh, you will die, but if by the Spirit you put to death the misdeeds of the body, you will live. For those who are led by the Spirit of God are the children of God. The Spirit you received does not make you slaves, so that you live in fear again, rather, the Spirit you received brought about your adoption to sonship. And we cry Abba Father. The Spirit Himself testifies with our spirit that we are God's children,"* [Romans 8:13-16].

Painted through these passages is a beautiful picture of hope-giving comfort for the people of God to have a strong faith. The people of God hoped and waited patiently for His promises to come to pass; that hope bought us Salvation – Salvation is immediate when we obey the Gospel of Christ – we do not have to wait, nor doubt that our Soul is secure because God's promises are without fail.

The unseen forces of Satan and his angels are fighting against God's people is a reality we need to be aware of so that we put our garments of faith and dependence in Jesus our Savior. He will not abandon us. This is our struggle, *"For we wrestle not against flesh and blood, but against principalities, against powers, against the rulers of the darkness of this world, against spiritual wickedness in heavenly places," [Ephesians 6:12].*

As mentioned before, we cannot see Satan with the naked eye, nor can we fight against him alone. We put our faith and dependence in the One who can, the Creator of the Universe. Satan cannot defeat God. Jesus promised that *"Upon this rock, I will build My Church and the gates of Hell shall not prevail against It," [Matthew 16:18].*

We cannot afford to have a, "well he is just the devil" attitude. He is unseen that is deadly to God's people. He tries to block your success in serving God and in your success in living a Christian life in every way he can; he and his demons (fallen angels as he is a fallen angel).

Each of us has a garment of allegiance…

- *What does your garment of allegiance look like?*
- *Does it have the look of Jesus Christ or the one that Bernice sported so proudly?*

CHAPTER TWENTY-ONE

# BERNICE WIFE OF HEROD AGRIPPA II AND HER GARMENT OF ALLEGIANCE

*"A few days later King Agrippa and Bernice arrived at Caesarea to pay their respects to Festus. Since they were spending many days there, Festus discussed Paul's case with the king. He said, "There is a man here whom Felix left as a prisoner. When I went to Jerusalem, the chief priests and the elders of the Jews brought charges against him and asked that he be condemned," [Acts 25:13-15].*

Bernice was a wife and companion of Herod Agrippa II, her brother. She also had a sister named Drusilla. Her father was Herod Agrippa I. She at one time, or before she was married to Herod Agrippa II was married to [Marcus]. She then married her brother Herod Agrippa II, her fathers' son. It seemed as if incestuous marriage relationships were common in the Herod family. As with Herodias to Herod Antipas, her husband Phillip the Tetrarch's brother who reigned in Ituraea.

They had two sons born of their marriage. Later, Bernice married Pomelo, King of Cicilia; and was a mistress, at one time, to Titus, a Roman Emperor. To say the least, she had a very prolific personality with an ingrained desire to freely associate with the ruling class of the Roman Empire.

One positive I can say of Herod Agrippa II and Bernice, they did not condemn Paul to death at that time, the decision of what to do with him was at Caesar's discretion. His incarceration and death were not at their hands. However, they did not do anything to prevent it; they passed the problem on to someone else. They, like Pilate, when the Jews chose Jesus over Barabbas to be crucified, washed his hands, as if he thought, it would wash away the guilt on his part of Christ's Crucifixion.

This is a portrait of selfishness on their part; a snapshot of the protean that surged through the veins of the hearts and minds of this family, as a life-giving agent, as blood surges through the veins of humans to give them life.

Herod was a paradox – cruel family...inappropriateness was a daily diet. The paradoxical family relationships seemed to begin with Herod the Great as history records him. Antipater, Father of Herod the Great, a Dictator installed by Rome also passed down the violence the Herod Family indulged in. Looking at the inherent culture of corruption and incest it is amazing the interactions that took place in the family's ongoing vicious cycle. The phrase 'keeping it in the family' stands waving from across the way. It calls attention to this sin, also committed years earlier by Herod Antipas and his brother's wife Herodias.

Christ forbids this type of sinful living. We see in the Old Testament, God forbad the intermingling or intermixing of even races of people at one time. This sin can never be pleasing to God. Moses wrote, *"Cursed is anyone who sleeps with his sister, the daughter of his father, or the daughter of his mother." Then all the people shall say, "Amen!" [Deuteronomy 27:22].*

What motivation drove them down this incestuous path in life is one only they could answer. This sisters is a prime example of the influence a family can have on their members' lives. We are, as they were, at times, victims of our environment…environments can either be good or bad. We teach by example. Mother told me when I was a child, "Little pictures have big ears," children see and hear what their adult parents say, as well as see what they do, and they mimic their ways and actions.

Lust for power can corrupt morals and integrity.

The Herod family made lust their god; they were connoisseurs of it. They continued to run around and around in this vicious circle like a dog chasing his tail. What does a dog do with his tail when he catches it if he catches it? He starts the chase again. This sin was deep-rooted in the Herod family. Each generation followed the same process bearing children that continued the same sinful practices. The Herod families were narcissists, the world revolved around them. Their practice of lawlessness was like a malignant daily diet. They adhered to no law except self.

In the days following their arrival, Paul stood before them to answer the accusations made against him. Herod Agrippa II knew the Jewish Law and the Prophecies as Paul pointed out to him they were lived for all the public to see. Paul stated, *"Especially because I know thee to be expert in all customs and questions which are among the Jews: wherefore I beseech thee to hear me patiently," [Acts 26:3].*

*"The King is familiar with these things, and I can speak freely to him. I am convinced that none of this has escaped his notice, because it was not done in a corner,"* [Acts 26:26].

After Paul defended himself and the Gospel, Agrippa said to Paul, *"Thou almost persuade me to be a Christian,"* [Acts 26:28].

Giving up the life he loved with his sister Bernice would have been required.

- **Can we count all things gained for Christ as a loss to the world?**

Yet, in that instance, it was counting all things lost to Christ as a gain for the world.

The spirit of altruism, about social conscience, was absent in Herod Agrippa II and Bernice's world. Regarding morals, it was not present in the Herod family period. Usually, it is the "powers to be" that has the greater influence on societal focuses...societal focuses, of what morals were, at that time, were out-of-the-fact, they were the ruling family, and others were out of fear, because they were a dangerous family, beginning with Herod the Great. He made a decree that all the children born in Bethlehem, at that time that were 2 years old and under killed in an attempt to destroy our Lord and Savior Jesus Christ.

He felt this Child a threat to his authority. There could be only one king and that king was he.

According to history, the enigma that described the Herod family was at best, cruel:

- Herod the Great murdered His wife and sons, which happened again in Bethlehem killing children in a cold-mannered attempt to kill our Lord and Savior Jesus Christ.
- His son Herod Antipas 33 years later killed John the Baptist, [Mark 6:14-29]; and then mocked Christ [Luke 23:7-12], it is dangerous to mock God as he learned at a very high price.
- His grandson Agrippa I, 14 years later killed James the Apostle, [Acts 12:1-2].
- His great-grandson Herod Agrippa II 16 years later was the King who Paul stood before and defended his faith [Acts 25:13-26:32]. [Halley Bible Handbook, P420].

There are no surprises, with this history, why Herod the Great's offspring inherited his cold-blooded cruelty and his taste for brutality. This Edomite came from a powerful line of Kings who controlled Judea. The word Paradox described by adjectives like absurd and inconsistent can explain the actions of this family. Looking at it from the point-of-view of his personality in everything we see… what we read in history's reasoning can, from an acceptable premise, lead to a conclusion that seems senseless, logically unacceptable, or self-contradictory.

I suggest this describes Herod the Great and seemed to flow down to his descendants and their family. The principle he used was based on logic and plots he concocted to remain in power, creating his own truth. His basic assertions were that whatever he decided was right.

A Paradox is contradiction, puzzle, anomaly, absurdity, error, oddity, nonsense, and enigma. The Herod family was like no other in history with the inter-mingling – inter-marrying, fornication, incest, and adultery; it was a puzzle with missing pieces; trying to put a puzzle together with missing pieces leaves too many gaps in it to the point it makes no sense and does not have any reasonable normal flow to it. The picture in the puzzle is not clear; it has an odd appearance, a broken look, as were their lives and morals. One trying to unravel the mystery that beset this family is like trying to determine, with the naked eye, where the rainbow begins and ends after it rains.

They were an oddity – abnormality…families do not conduct themselves in this manner as a ruling principle as the Herod's did. They were outlandish in their actions and thoughts. Their marrying each other was unnatural.

They were an enigma – the sixty-four-million-dollar question. The family, like the story of the Phoenix Bird, this perplexity continued rising from the ashes with each generation. Like the sphinx of Egypt, they had members with different characteristics, but the same paradox.

Hence, this brings us to Bernice who was from the same seed. There seemed to be no selfless spirit in Bernice and Herod Agrippa II, but rather the opposite they/she were selfish with no regard for her/their fellowman. Paul tells us that we are not to do anything to cause our brother to stumble, *"Be careful, however, that the exercise of your rights does not become a stumbling block to the weak,"* [I Corinthians 8:9].

The center of a selfish individual is self-indulging in and partaking of life's pleasure, as they wish, with no regard to how it looks – Bernice is an example of what we define in the 21ˢᵗ Century as living "out-loud". Her reputation, I am sure, was all around the known world at that time. She was a narcissistic egomaniac – as seems to apply to the Herod family as a whole. The family appears to have a resolute and strong emotional protean of devotion that was not discernable in a visible way, which did not allow others to comprehend this ever-changing interaction in this family, at best, it was egregious.

Jude reminds us of the dangers and ramification of ones in direct defiance to God's Universal Law there are no exceptions, *"Woe to them! They have taken the way of Cain, they have rushed to profit into Balaam's error, and they have been destroyed in Koran's rebellion," [Jude: 11].*

Cain murdered his brother Abel because of jealousy, *"And Adam knew Eve his wife; and she conceived, and bare Cain, and said, "I have gotten a man from the Lord." And she again bares his brother Abel. And Abel was a keeper of sheep, but Cain was a tiller of the ground. And in the process of time, it came-to-pass, that Cain brought of the fruit of the ground an offering unto the Lord. And Abel, he also brought of the firstlings of his flock and of the fat thereof. And the Lord* had respect unto Abel and to his offering: But unto Cain and to his offering he had not respect. And Cain was very wroth, and his countenance fell. And the *Lord* said unto Cain, Why art thou wroth? *And why is thy countenance fallen? If thou do well shalt thou not be accepted? And if thou do not well, sin lie at the door. And unto thee shall be his desire, and thou shalt rule over him."*

*"And Cain talked with Abel his brother: and it came to pass, when they were in the field, that Cain rose up against Abel his brother, and slew him. And the Lord said unto Cain, Where is Abel thy brother? And he said, "I know not: Am I my brother's keeper?" And he said, "What hast thou done? The voice of thy brother's blood cries unto me from the ground. And now, art thou cursed from the earth, which hath opened her mouth to receive thy brother's blood from thy hand; when thou tills the ground, it shall not henceforth yield unto thee her strength; a fugitive and a vagabond shalt thou be in the earth. And Cain said unto the Lord, My punishment is greater than I can bear."*

*"Behold, thou hast driven me out this day from the face of the earth; and from thy face shall I be hidden; and I shall be a fugitive and a vagabond in the earth; and it shall come to pass, that everyone that finds me shall slay me.* And, the Lord said unto him, *"Therefore whosoever slays Cain, vengeance shall be taken on him sevenfold. And the Lord set a mark upon Cain, lest any finding him should kill him."*

*"And, Cain went out from the presence of theLord, and dwelt in the land of Nod, on the east of Eden," [Genesis 4:1-16].*

Then we see the evil of Balaam who prophesied because he was greedy and not because he was a faithful servant of the God of Heaven. Greed and defiance, rather than humility and obedience stood in danger every hour because of his interactions with Balak the King who enticed him with wealth and he (Balaam) defied God, for the purpose, of garnering money and property, *[Numbers 22-24].*

Sin offends our God, as well; it separates us from God. Man fails to adhere to the truth, to hear the truth, and refuses to do righteousness. God is holy and righteous, and He is Truth, His Word is Truth. Isaiah says it in this way, *"So justice is driven back, and righteousness stands at a distance; truth has stumbled in the streets, honesty cannot enter. Truth is nowhere to be found and whoever shuns evil becomes its prey. The Lord looked and was displeased that there was no justice," [Isaiah 59:14-15].*

Evil and disobedience come, in all ways, shapes, and forms. Korah was destroyed in his rebellion against God's appointed leaders, railing against His Servants, and desiring power; both his objection and desire got him into trouble with God, *"Now Korah, the son of Izhar, the son of Kohath, the son of Levi, and Dathan and Abiram, the sons of Eliab, and On, the son of Peleth, sons of Reuben, took men: And they rose up before Moses, with certain of the children of Israel, two hundred and fifty princes of the assembly, famous in the congregation, men of renown. And they gathered themselves together against Moses and against Aaron, and said unto them, "Ye take too much upon you, seeing all the congregation are holy, every one of them, and the Lord is among them: wherefore then lift ye up yourselves above the congregation of the Lord," [Numbers 16:1-3, 4-35].*

As well, the examples Jude gave of humans conducting themselves in the manner they so wish or living their lives in a way that is in direct defiance to God's Commands, will eventually suffer at the hands of the living God.

The Herod family conducted themselves in the manner they saw fit with their way of living passed down from generation to generation to other members in their family. They had no regard for moral decency, the Commandments, or the lives of their fellow human beings.

This cruel family wielded their authority in any way they thought profitable to them and the desires they had for their life, which was, in every way, a defiance of God and violation of the Commandments.

The Hebrews writer warns us, *"How much more severely do you think someone deserves to be punished who has trampled the Son of God underfoot, who has treated as an unholy thing the Blood of the Covenant that sanctified them, and who has insulted the Spirit of Grace? For we know Him who said, "It is Mine to avenge; I will repay,"* and again, *"The Lord will judge His people." It is a dreadful thing to fall into the hands of the Living God," [Hebrews 10:29-31].*

It is difficult to produce enough thought to enable one to wrap their mind around this vicious circle Bernice was a part of, though they were part of the ruling class at that time. John the Baptist spoke against the selfish, incestuous, and defiant actions of Herod Antipas, Herodias, and Salome, his voice was still resonating in the reign of Bernice and she walked the same path as did her predecessors.

The garment she wore is not one accepted in society; it is unrighteous. The Scripture tells us, *"All unrighteousness is sin," [Ibid]* in God's eyes, *"For we have all sinned and fallen short of the Glory of God," [Romans 3:23].*

The Prophet Hosea gave the people the message from God, which was a formal accusation against them for their unfaithfulness, *"Hear the Word of the Lord, ye children of Israel: for the Lord hath a controversy with the inhabitants of the land, because there is no truth, nor mercy, nor knowledge of God in the land. By swearing, and lying, and killing, and stealing, and committing adultery, they break out, and blood touch blood. Therefore, shall the land mourn, and everyone that dwell therein shall languish, with the beasts of the field, and with the fowls of heaven; yea, the fishes of the sea also shall be taken away," [Hosea 4:1-3].*

We (humans) are the cause of why the blessings are withheld we would receive from God. God does not change. The formal accusation against unfaithfulness is there for us in this century as it was for the people of God in Hosea's prophetic era.

Regardless of what it is, Christ's Blood can cover our sins, if we repent and turn from that sin, *"If we confess our sins, He is faithful and just to forgive us [our] sins, and to cleanse us from all unrighteousness," [I John 1:9].*

As we read earlier in this chapter, recall the fact that after Paul defended his belief to the King and Bernice – King Agrippa II gave becoming a Christian serious consideration said to Paul, *"Almost thou persuade me to become a Christian,"* [Acts 26:28].

The Scripture records his (Paul's) response, *"And Paul said, I would to God, that not only thou, but also all that hear me this day, were both almost, and altogether such as I am, except for these bonds,"* [Acts 26:29].

Almost is not sufficient for Salvation, we are either almost or altogether we cannot be both as Paul expressed to Herod Agrippa II. It equates to standing at the finish line of a race you are in, and you got there first, you stopped at the finish line, but never stepped over that line; you lose the race. The rules state you win only if you cross the finish line. Using this in a Spiritual context, we cannot be almost a Christian, either we are, or we are not, a Christian.

The Herod family's indoctrination appeared to come at birth with this inexcusable allegiance, which seemed to be almost a brainwashing…the pre-existing condition is evident here and it has tentacles like an octopus with suctions cups pulling this family into that allegiance.

Our Savior has a specific way [Pattern] which we are to live that will be spiritually, emotionally, and physically healthy, and above all, pleasing to Him.

Agrippa's almost statement, in the end, left him, in the same condition before he made it…let us remember what that condition was! He stood, at that moment, on the Precipice of Eternity!

Sisters our garments should be of the thoughts that we are standing on the Precipice of Eternity at all times – we are approaching the finish line:

- *Will you stop and rest under a tree?*
- *On the other hand, do you stop at the line, or do you cross the line? It only takes one last step to be over the line, why stop at the line!*

CHAPTER TWENTY-TWO

# A PRACTICAL ANALOGY: THE NINTH INNING PRECIPICE OF ETERNITY

Americans, like the citizens of other countries around the world, are sports fans both men and women. We love sports in this country. As with every other activity people participate in, sports are seasonal.

To bring this to center stage, I use Baseball in this example to make my point. Baseball is normally a nine innings game. Sometimes the teams struggle at the beginning of the game, which is commonplace in sports and everyday life.

The game gets to the fifth inning, which is the halfway mark. The teams are still struggling as people do in life. The game is moving quickly toward the ninth inning. It finally reaches the bottom of the eighth into the ninth inning. At that point, the game is at a tie. The teams must play an extra inning to break that tie.

The winning team is finally apparent after the eleven innings.

To contrast this analogy with Christianity, we start our Christian journey as a new babe in Christ needing milk and not meat. Our digestive system cannot manage the solid Spiritual food because we do not have the Spiritual teeth to chew the solid foods of the Word of God.

As we grow or advance to the next inning or our sojourn toward eternity to our God or the ninth inning, our growth or maturity level should become evident by the fifth or sixth inning, first to us, and then to our brethren.

The flicker of a small candle as the liquidity of the wax increase should begin to burn brighter so others can see it from a distance. As we near the ninth inning, we realize or should realize that there are not tenth and eleventh innings in our life. Usually, the ninth inning in baseball is game over.

The Scripture tells us, "*the years in the life of man are threescore and ten (70 years) if peradventure we live to 80 years of age, we are under grace,*" *[Ibid]*.

During our life, we have no guarantee of a tenth or eleventh inning. Scripture reminds us God only promised today: James warns in this manner, *"Now listen, you who say, "Today or tomorrow we will go to this or that city, spend a year there, carry on business, and make money." Why you do not even know what will happen tomorrow? What is your life? You are a mist that appears for a little while and then vanishes. Instead, you ought to say, "If it is the Lord's will, we will live and do this or that,"* [James 4:13-15].

Sisters, even time has a fleeting aroma to it. We cannot afford to squander it away by our desires to partake of all the pleasures in this world. Rather we should use the time given us to glorify and honor God and our Lord and Savior Jesus Christ who came to earth with a thirty-three-year mission and completed that command of "go" within the appointed frame-of-time.

We have, through the mercy and grace of God, a promise of our appointed time of three scores and ten years. We do not know where within those years will be the allotted time God has for us – use it wisely. God alone, as stated before, decides the number of years of that promised time we will live. That old analogy applies here; wait (weight) broke (destroyed) the bridge, your chance for an eternity of peace.

James did not mince words in his letter...that ninth inning in our life is too close for us to drag our feet in doing what Christ left for us to do and the attitudes we are to have toward all people regardless of who they are because Christ loves all. If we are struggling, He gave us the solution for conquering our struggles, *"If any of you lack wisdom, let him ask of God, that giveth to allmen liberally, and upbraid not; and it shall be given him,"* [James 1:5].

In baseball terms, the ninth inning ends the game. We as well must learn to read the signs of the times Christ spoke about during His Ministry on earth. *"The Pharisees and Sadducees came to Jesus and tested him by asking him to show them a sign from heaven. He replied, "When evening comes, you say, 'It will be fair weather, for the sky is red,' and in the morning, 'Today it will be stormy, for the sky is red and threatening.' You know how to interpret the appearance of the sky, but you cannot interpret the signs of the times,"* [Matthew 16:1-3].

Jesus shined a spiritual and physical light on the Pharisees because they were not guiding the people in the right manner. They knew the Law but did not practice it themselves or tell the people what they needed to do to be saved and obedient to God.

Humans are easily misled; God cannot be. Eventually, times reveals the truth what is spoken in the dark (private) comes to the light, "*Meanwhile, when a crowd of many thousands had gathered, so that they were trampling on one another, Jesus began to speak first to His disciples, saying: "Be on your guard against the yeast of the Pharisees, which is hypocrisy. There is nothing concealed that will not be disclosed or hidden that will not be made known. What you have said in the dark will be heard in the daylight, and what you have whispered in the ear in the inner rooms will be proclaimed from the roofs," [Luke 12:1-3].*

Truth is what Jesus said it is not what we imagine, think, or understand. At times, man's truth is what affirms his beliefs and not what confirms what is true. Jesus said about truth, "*I am the Way, the Truth, and the Life,*" *[Ibid].*

Jesus warned the people that the Scribes and Pharisees locked up the Kingdom of Heaven. Knowledge of God is through Scripture, which both Scribes and Pharisees were misleading the people preventing them from understanding the things men should know about and of God, "*Woe to you experts in the law because you have taken away the key to knowledge. You yourselves have not entered, and you have hindered those who were entering*", *[Luke 11:52];* and "*Watch therefore, for ye know neither the day nor the hour wherein the Son of man cometh,*" *[Matthew 25:13].*

It becomes tragic when one allows their lives to be in spiritual bondage. The Pharisees and Scribes were guilty of trying to keep people in spiritual bondage.

The Pharisees knew prophecy; it was written (foretold), in the Law about the Messiah, the Savior, who would come into the world, not in fine Linens and kingly robes, but as a humble shepherd born of a Virgin into the House of David. Yet, they, the Pharisees, and Scribes, did not conduct themselves as if they knew this prophecy; Jesus called them hypocrites.

The Kingdom of Heaven was at hand, and they denied Him.

Our lives are from the first to the ninth inning. We are to live as if we are aware... we are to stay mindful and warn and teach others, so they are alert. No one knows when his or her ninth inning will come, or when our lives will end between the first and ninth inning. What we are to be, is ready. James puts forth the question and then answers it in the same sentence, and "*What is your life? It is even as a vapor which appears for a while then vanishes away,*" *[James 4:14].*

Christ spoke of the Pharisees and Scribes who did not tutor the people correctly…that warning is still current for us.

We learn to read the signs of the times by studying and learning what the Scripture tells us. We cannot take the chance of thinking we have large amounts of time even in our years as a novice on our Christian journey. We have an opportune time today [now] in our life to work out our Salvation in fear and trembling keeping in mind, everyone's maturity level is not the same, nor is their spiritual strength, but only in Christ, can we be strong, pleasing, and acceptable to God: not every Christian is spiritually strong…

When we are weak or struggling, our Savior bids us, "*Come unto me, all ye that labor and are heavy laden and I will give you rest. Take My yoke upon you and learn of Me; for I am meek and lowly in heart: and ye shall find rest unto your souls. For My yoke is easy, and My burden is light,*" *[Matthew 11:28-30]*.

Paul in his encounter with Jesus in the Third Heaven when he asked that He remove the thorn from him wrote, "*And He said to me, My grace is sufficient for you, for My strength is made perfect in weakness.*" Paul encourages us in this that he stated, "*Therefore, most gladly I will rather boast in my infirmities, that the power of Christ may rest upon me,*" *[2 Corinthians 12:19]*.

We cannot do anything about the thorns that come into our lives that try us; but through Christ, we can be strong, and those thorns can become a blessing for us so that we can be that "Epistles" read by men (letting your light shine) in your acceptance and handling of the thorn (test).

Christ does not tempt us, but He will test us as He did the Prophets before us evident by all we read written in Scripture, "*Things written aforetime are written for our learning that we through the patience and comfort of the Scripture might have hope,*" *[Romans 15:4]*.

We see the example of Ezekiel in the loss of his wife. God took her and told the Prophet not to grieve, moan, or pray but continue to preach His Word to the people of Israel they were disobedient children, "*Also the Word of the Lord came unto me, saying, "Son of man, behold, I take away from thee the desire of thine eyes with a stroke. Yet neither shalt thou mourn nor weep, neither shall thy tears run down.*"

*"Forbear to cry, make no mourning for the dead, bind the turban of thine head upon thee, and put on thy shoes upon thy feet, and cover not thy lips, and eat not the bread of men. So, I spoke unto the people, in the morning: and at evening, my wife died; and I did, in the morning as I was commanded; and the people said unto me, "Wilt thou not tell us what these things are to us, that thou doeth so?"*

Then I answered them, *"The Word of the Lord came unto me, saying, "Speak unto the house of Israel. Thus said the Lord God, Behold, I will profane my sanctuary, the Excellency of your strength, the desire 'of your eyes, and that which your soul pity; and your sons and your daughters whom ye have left shall fall by the sword. And ye shall do as I have done: ye shall not cover your lips, nor eat the bread of men. And, your turbans shall be upon your heads, and your shoes upon your feet: ye shall not mourn nor weep, but ye shall pine away for your iniquities, and mourn one toward another."*

*"Thus, Ezekiel is unto you a sign: according to all that he hath done shall ye do: and when this cometh, ye shall know that I am the Lord God. Also, thou son of man, shall it not be in the day when I take from them their strength, the joy of their glory, the desire of their eyes, and that whereupon they set their minds, their sons, and their daughters," [Ezekiel 24:15-25].*

It is unwise to put anything or anyone before God regardless of whom it is or what it is. We cannot value our children, spouses, parents, homes, or any other form of wealth above our Savior. He is God ... our God is jealous. We cannot have any other god before Him or above Him. Our focus should be on Him and the commands for our lives in worship and service to Him. The fact that Ezekiel was a faithful servant of God, and his wife was taken, "the desire of his eyes" tells us following the commands given to us by God is necessary [essential]. Taking care to remember that He is first in our lives is paramount. It is better for us to [get] the point than for our God to [make] the point to us concerning disobedience and putting things and others before Him.

Our God is a Sovereign God...He alone decides those five questions mentioned in an earlier chapter that we use in modern societal business management and communication, "Who, what, when, where, and why." To decide our fate, that right belongs only to our Sovereign God. He is the Creator of all things. Paul reminds us that, *"For in Him we live, and move, and have our being; as certain also of your own poets have said, for we are also His offspring," [Acts 17:28].*

Christ sets our boundaries, determines our life, and accomplishes what He desires for us as His children, *[Ibid]*.

We are facing the Precipice of Eternity...to face or be on the brink can be compared to a rock, mountain, bluff, cliff, crag, height, sheer drop, or steep climb.

[To Face] is to come up against something, be confronted by, or our life as a Christian we brave the tides of the requirements of Salvation. We [face] the challenge set before us as we would a cliff to climb so that we achieve our goal.

### *What is that goal?*

This goal describes in one sentence: To inherit eternity and live in peace throughout eternity with God.

In Book 1, I wrote the account of traveling to Mount Rainier in the State of Washington and being on the Precipice of that Mountain. The cliffs on both sides of the road were steep and a drop would have been deadly. Yet, to reach the 4,000 feet level of our goal; we had to use balance (stay in the middle of the road).

The road driving up the Mountain was on a precipice of danger – the danger of a steep drop-off and death.

The danger was present both going and coming it was an ever-present danger. It was only one way up and one way down, which brings us to Salvation, and the ninth ending. We only have one way to live in peace for an eternity with God. The way is the one that Christ died for on the cruel cross of Calvary. Christ died to purchase our Salvation. He is the Head of the Body, His Church; it bears His name. Paul writes to the Church at Colosse, *"And He is the Head of the Body, the Church: who is the beginning, the first-born from the dead; that in all [things] that He may have the pre-eminence,"* [Colossians 1:18].

As Salvation was only in the Ark God instructed Noah to build, and the people were safe only in the Ark, in this dispensation our spiritual safety and Salvation are in the Body for which Christ gave His life. In the Biblical account of the Ark, only eight people believed God and were saved, Peter reminds us of this fact, *"Which sometime were disobedient when once the longsuffering of God waited in the days of Noah, while the Ark was a preparing, wherein few, that is, eight souls were saved by water,"* [I Peter 3:20].

The Plan of Salvation in place for man now is our Noah's Ark and there is room for all. God sent His only Son to sacrifice His life, the Blood of the Lamb that took away the sins of the world. Christ is our High Priest, Prophet, and Savior promised from the beginning. He stood on the precipice of that mountain we were to climb and won the battle and the war against sin.

Now, each of us has the opportunity to brave the tides and work out our Salvation in fear and trembling. The frontier of our sojourn is before us whether you think of it as the precipice or the brink of eternity. We cannot storm the gates of Heaven but get there through the way purchased with The Precious Life of our Lord and Savior Jesus Christ, also our Perimeter (boundary).

We only have to the ninth ending or less to work and serve God and take advantage of the Salvation He purchased so that we might live with Him. A tenth or eleventh ending is not promised, *"It is appointed unto man once to die then after that the judgment," [Hebrews 9:27].*

No humans are living who can predict or tell you how long you will live or what will be tomorrow. When it comes to the question of our life spans or tomorrow, it is dangerous to put our confidence in humans. Asking those who think they can look into the future is a deception pushed by Satan. The predictions of man are too leaky a vessel in which to place any confidence: our only assurance in every area of our life and what we will or will not do can only come from God, who holds the keys to tomorrow and eternity!

Sisters, our garments should be those of balance – balance is only found in Christ.

We cannot fall prey to the importune pressures of Satan and the evil wickedness of his desire for your life and desperation to separate you from God.

Sisters those pressures are like skating on a frozen lake.

CHAPTER TWENTY-THREE

# THE FURNACE OF REALITY
# THE PRE-EXISTING CONDITION
# AND THE FROZEN LAKE
# PART I

Taking the temperature of this condition is what is on the top ten lists of "things to do." The temperature of this pre-existing condition is compared to a furnace with fires started at a low burn. As you add wood or kindling, it gets hotter until you can feel the effect from a distance to the point of melting (destroying) anything that comes within that boundary.

I think of the Biblical account of Shadrach, Meshach, and Abednego thrown into the furnace because they refused to worship an idol god, the intensity of the heat killed the guards that threw them into the fire when they got near it.

King Nebuchadnezzar made an image of gold of himself, everyone in the province was to bow down and worship it, *"Now when you hear the sound of the horn, flute, zither, lyre, harp, pipe, and all kinds of music, if you are ready to fall down and worship the image I made, very good. But if you do not worship it, you will be thrown immediately, into a blazing furnace. Then what god will be able to rescue you from my hand?" [Daniel 3:15].*

Shadrach, Meshach, and Abednego replied, *"King Nebuchadnezzar, we do not need to defend ourselves before you in this matter. If we are thrown into the blazing furnace, the God we serve is able to deliver us from it, and He will deliver us from Your Majesty's hand. But even if He does not, we want you to know, Your Majesty, that we will not serve your gods or worship the image of gold you have set up," [Daniel 3:16-18].*

Their statements were of strong men, faithful men, and even when they refused, were respectful of Nebuchadnezzar's authority and position, he is the King they are in service also, but he was not their God.

*"Then Nebuchadnezzar was furious with Shadrach, Meshach, and Abednego, and his attitude toward them changed. He ordered the furnace heated seven times hotter than usual and commanded some of the strongest soldiers in his army to tie up Shadrach, Meshach, and Abednego and throw them into the blazing furnace. So, these men, wearing their robes, trousers, turbans, and other clothes were bound and thrown, into the blazing furnace. The king's command was so urgent and the furnace so hot that the flames of the fire killed the soldiers who took up Shadrach, Meshach, and Abednego, and these three men, firmly tied, fell into the blazing furnace," [Daniel 3:19-23].*

Then King Nebuchadnezzar leaped to his feet in amazement and asked his advisers *"Weren't there three men that we tied up and threw into the fire?"* They replied, *"Certainly your Majesty."*

He said, *"Look! I see four men walking around in the fire, unbound, and unharmed, and the fourth looks like a son of the gods."*

Nebuchadnezzar then approached the opening of the blazing furnace and shouted, *"Shadrach, Meshach, and Abednego, servants of the Most High God, Come out! Come here!"*

*"So, Shadrach, Meshach, and Abednego came out of the fire, and the satraps, prefects, governors, and royal advisers crowded around them. They saw that the fire had not harmed their bodies, nor was a hair of their heads singed; their robes were not scorched, and there was no smell of fire on them."*

Then Nebuchadnezzar said, *"Praise be to the God of Shadrach, Meshach, and Abednego, who has sent His angel and rescued His servants! They trusted in Him, defied the king's command, and were willing to give up their lives rather than serve or worship any god except their own God. Therefore, I decree that the people of any nation or language who say anything against the God of Shadrach, Meshach, and Abednego be cut into pieces and their houses be turned into piles of rubble, for no other god can save in this way."*

*"Then the king promoted Shadrach, Meshach, and Abednego in the province of Babylon," [Daniel 3:24-30].*

- **Sisters, at this point, we need a station identification break: King Nebuchadnezzar recognized that there is a higher God. Why do you think it takes him having to become like an animal to convince him of the fact in actions and not words only?**

The effects of sin are scary, it will destroy everyone it touches, or encounters, especially by adding fuel to an already hot furnace. That furnace is hot when we are born, the fires of it are blazing, and the concentration of the heat does not cool down rather the deadly effects of it increases, as time goes on.

Shadrach, Meshach, and Abednego did not bow down to this fiery error and worship another god that would have been a sin. They knew the furnace fires were hot but had faith in the ability of their Lord and Savior to save them and would remain faithful regardless of the outcome.

We can each take our faithfulness temperature during the condition of which we are subject. The Scripture gives us the process/steps to take to avoid adding more fuel to that already raging furnace fire and stay strong as did Shadrach, Meshach, and Abednego. The Old Testament warns us, of the furnace fire the people of Israel were told by God's Prophet what committing sins would cost as Moses warned them to "*Hear O' Israel*",*[Deuteronomy 6:4]*. Amos, the Prophet said, *"The Lord will roar like a lion from Jerusalem. His loud voice will sound like a growl from Jerusalem. The green pastures of the shepherds will become dry. Even Mount Carmel will dry up,"* *[Amos 1:2]*.

This process/step lends to the fact that being life-long students of the Scriptures are necessary. There is never a safe time to let down your shield of faith, take off your armor, or get comfortable in our day-to-day walk. Paul warns us, *"See then that ye walk circumspectly, not as fools, but as wise, redeeming the time, because the days are evil; wherefore be ye not unwise but understanding what the will of the Lord is,"* *[Ephesians 5:15-17]*.

Redeeming the time is essential, using the time, you have to obey and remain aware of your environment by avoiding the traps, and wiles of Satan, are important. The Scripture warns that the days are evil not one, all are laced daily with evil by our adversary. When it comes to our redemption, we must take advantage of the time each day with which we receive His blessing and mercy to live and serve God according to His will, for our lives.

Satan's time is counterclockwise to reality. His efforts are to make you believe that time is a friend and not an enemy in reference to how long we have on earth. We have no guarantee – youth, wealth, health, neither are a guarantee of longevity, which has its grace but no guarantee. The time to serve God is now. Thinking we have the time we want to fulfill our desires and wishes in life and time to live as long as we want, are fallacies of Satan in another trench.

Keep in mind redeeming is also compensating for someone's fault, the ability to save people from sin, error, or evil. Christ paid the price; He redeemed us so that we could have salvation and fulfill the Blood requirement of God our Father. He gives us time to work out our Salvation. Paul reminds us in this manner, "*Therefore, my dear friends, as you have always obeyed-not only in my presence, but now much more in my absence-continue to work out your salvation with fear and trembling,*" [Philippians 2:12].

We are to be obedient and faithful to God. We are not here for an eternity. We are only promised three scores and ten years (70 years old), David, the Psalmist wrote, "*The days of our lives are seventy years; And if by reason of strength they are eighty years, Yet their boast is only labor and sorrow; For it is soon cut off, and we fly away,*" [Ibid].

After that, the judgment, "*And as it is appointed unto men once to die, but after this the judgment,*" [Ibid].

If peradventure, we live past the appointed time of (70 years) we are under the Grace of God. Listen to what David said, "*Or if due to strength, eighty years, yet their pride is but labor and sorrow;for soon it is gone, and we fly away. Who understands the power of your angerand fury, according to the fear that is due to you? So, teach us to number our days,that we may present to you a heart of wisdom,*" [Psalms 90:10b-12].

We have the opportunity and time God gave each of us; it is to our advantage and with wisdom use that time prudently. We are to seek God when the opportunity is before us and not wait until it is too late, "*Seek ye the Lord while He may be found, call ye upon Him while He is near,*" [Isaiah 55:6].

Further, heed the day you hear His voice as the Scripture tells us, "*The day you hear His voice do not turn away but heed His will,*" [Ibid].

God loves man and wants all saved and not lost. God gave us the time we need. Christ redeemed it for us; paid the price for sin, a debt He did not owe. We owed the debt. He paid the debt, how much plainer is it than that?

Think of it in this way, you owe $250,000. We will be reasonable; this amount of debt is what an average person can accumulate or acquire easily with just the purchase of a home and vehicle together.

Use your imagination, if one morning, you awakened, and go to pay both these monthly notes, when you arrive at the Bank and is next in line, the Teller says to you, "Your debt for your home and your car has been paid in full, you should receive your Deed and your Title within 4-6 weeks." What a blessing, first you stand astonished, then in wonderment wanting to know who would be that kind and why are you so deserving of someone paying your debts.

You will have that money you saved to focus on other parts of your life. You have the time as well to spend with your family and friends, to do those things in life you never dreamed you would be able to do.

Bucket list here you come!

- *You stand in awe of that person how loving and caring they are, knowing that you did nothing to deserve this blessing, so why?*

Christ paid our debt.

- *Do we think of His sacrifice for us in the same way you did the man/woman who paid the enormous debt you accumulated?*
- *Do you use that time to know Him, serve Him, and spend time with His Spiritual Family, and taking advantage of the time He purchased for you?*
- *Do we look at His sacrifice with the same awe?*
- *Do you tell people how you feel about the expensive sacrifice He made for you individually and for us collectively?*

Our deeds are rewarded after our life is over; that reward is to live in that Mansion for an eternity He went away to prepare for us. We can live with surety on our journey of this promise through the Salvation purchased on the Cross.

Christ, died for us at an enormous price, as the example of the person who paid your physical debt, loves his fellowman. Christ paid man's sin debt. He loved and loves us individually and collectively. In the Chapter of Love, in the Scripture, Paul writes to us of the three greatest things in the world, there is faith, hope, and love/charity...the greatest of these three is Love, *"And now abides faith, hope, charity, these three; but the greatest of these is charity,"* [I Corinthians 13:30].

Yes, that individual who paid your home and car off gave you hope and inspired your faith probably again in humanity, which is low or non-existence in our environment at times, but that person loved you and spent their hard-earned money or inheritance on you, why? More than anything, they loved and cared about your future, your ability to survive because they saw the possibility in you and allowed you to focus on an important aspect of your life, your retirement years.

Christ did all of this for your eternity years, as well as living and surviving here in the earthly kingdom of Satan, keep in mind, *"He is the god of this world and a liar and the father of it. He was from the beginning," [Ibid].*

Every day, our garments sisters should reflect wisdom, awareness, obedience, as well, a faithful appreciation for the debt Christ paid for us, *"Redeeming the time because the days are evil," [Ibid].*

That furnace of sin that Satan makes attractive to humans leads to Spiritual death. One of the characteristics of the effects of sin is the unintended consequences of the desensitization of the human ability to recognize – distinguish - with constant contact – what will be the end product sin is having on your perspective (life) that has become your normal. Satan indulges in this backdoor strategy. The effects of the sin appear to come in piles – those piles come upon you without warning and as a thief in the night. It steals your vision of what is good or bad…yet the saying stands, "all that glitter is not gold." Additionally, sin is as if a skater looking at a frozen Lake tries to determine what part of that Lake has the thin ice and what part of that lake where the ice is frozen. The deceptive look of sin resembles a frozen lake with the water near the bank, which is shallower than the water in the middle of the lake. Would that not stand to reason? Therefore, it freezes solid first.

The skater starts by evaluating the solidity of the Lake, as the skater works forward and finds each area he tried thus far is solid; with each of those tries, it raises his confidence and lowers his awareness, which is a (built-in) deception. The further the skater goes out on the Lake the more confident he is the entire lake is frozen solid.

Finally, the skater begins to wonder how many more times he will chance to go further onto the lake before it will become problematic and serious trouble;

not realizing, at this point, it has already become problematic each time he took the chance to go a little further toward the middle. However, sure the middle of the Lake is solid, and because he is not aware of the problem, decided to go further toward the middle of the Lake. He, at this point, is confident in his reasoning because every try thus far has been successful. Using weak rational rather than supported facts, decided to take a quick run to assess its solidity, off he goes with conviction and surety in tack, then disaster strikes.

He reaches the middle of the Lake, the ice crumbles and he falls through a weak area into the water with a temperature below zero (<0), with no way to get back; suffering hypothermia, a condition of having an abnormally low body temperature, typically one that is dangerously low because of (overexposure). Sin's water temperature drops when it has you in its clutches, which leads to spiritual hypothermia. Satan leads man into these dangerous waters of sin. You can no more get across a frozen lake with a strong guarantee you will reach the other side safely than you can indulge in sin with the solid guarantee that you will not suffer the burns of unintended consequences.

At this point, the man began suffering unforeseen results, for the purpose, of evaluating the middle of that frozen Lake. It looks solid and safe like the areas closer to the bank...sin has these deceptive looks about it...we cannot afford to wear garments of chance not with sin; the characteristics, of it, is, like the fires of a furnace heated seven times hotter...

Relatedly so, remember Eve and her first bite; the fact it yielded the knowledge of good and evil, led her to inspire Adam down the same path of disobedience she took.

When my husband and I owned a farm, we had along with the other livestock pigs in pens on slabs. Also, I remember when my husband fed them anything like onions, peppers, or something that they would not eat on a normal basis, would stop chewing to see if it burned. They seemed almost to listen to what their sensors of danger were telling them. My father told me the same thing when I was growing up as a child on my parents' farm: that pigs, senses danger of anything that might be strange that is not part of their normal diet. His pigs used to get in the garden, they loved to eat the onion and hot peppers, they would stop chewing to see if it burned, which it did, and they would run away screaming.

We as humans have God-given instincts and the abilities to read danger, if we stop, look, and listen. Our parents raised us on this analogy. At the crossing of a railroad track, we are motivated to stop, look, and listen even though we have the signals on the track; it is by instinct we know that trains are dangerous and deadly. We proceed with caution at every track, as animals know when something is hot like peppers or onion; humans know furnaces, stoves, fires, and any of this kind are dangerous. I could note things that burn (or sins that are dangerous) on a list longer than my arm and still would not have half of them. Translate these examples into a Spiritual comparison and the multiplicity of sins that are in the world and growing each day.

Sin, like fire in a furnace, is destructive and dangerous. Man cannot stand against this fire without assistance. As firefighters need fire retardant outfits to fight forest fires that are too intense to approach without being charred; we also need fire retardant garments to fight the fires of sin. Our fire-retardant garments are the Word of God giving us the ability to be in this battle on our way to eternity and our mansion Jesus prepared for us. He purchased Salvation for humanity, but we have to earn our place in eternity with God by, "*Working out your Salvation in fear and trembling,*" *[Ibid].*

Be afraid first of the fires of sin; they do not bode well for us; it teaches us to avoid them and know their danger.

A glass half full or a glass half empty. We cannot look at sin in this way. A glass half full or glasses half-empty, in reality, add up to the same thing it is dependent on the perspective of the person you are asking. No two people's frame of reference in any given situation is the same, even what they consider sin.

A low burning flame is less likely to be deadly than a fully kindled furnace, of course, it is, but there is where the danger lies in this perspective. When we see intense fires, furnaces burning out of control, and forest fires we do all we can to avoid this danger because we know they are deadly even from a distance the human body is unable to withstand the intense heat; we run the other way!

Then again, the low burning fires that we consider are not dangerous, so we hug-up to those fires, move around freely with no fear of a burn, not even over-heating, yet sisters, those are the most dangerous and most deadly. In the Spiritual sense, the blatant sins that stick out like a sore thumb we readily identify and avoid. However, it is those low-burning little fires (sins) we do not notice that are more deadly than any raging forest fire (blatant sins) out there.

One of the wiles of Satan is slipping in little tempting morsels that lead us to sin because it sounds innocent, like things we say. James warns about the tongue though the smallest member of the body, can be deadly, destructive, burn down empires, destroy families, and destroy reputations; words are dangerous if not used correctly, *"Not many of you should become teachers, my fellow believers, and because you know that we who teach will be judged more strictly. We all stumble in many ways. Anyone who is never at fault in what they say is perfect, able to keep their whole body in check. When we put bits into the mouths of horses to make them obey us, we can turn the whole animal. Or take ships as an example; although they are so large and are driven by strong winds, they are steered by a very small rudder wherever the pilot wants to go."*

Sisters this is the overarching point, *"Likewise, the tongue is a small part of the body, but it makes great boasts. Consider what a great forest is set on fire by a small spark. The tongue also is a fire, a world of evil among the parts of the body. It corrupts the whole body, sets the whole course of one's life on fire, and is itself set on fires by hell. All kinds of animals, birds, reptiles, and sea creatures are being tamed, and have been tamed by man; but no human being can tame the tongue. It is a restless evil, full of deadly poison,"* [James 3:1-8].

There are things and actions we never think about, like humility: one of the attributes or characteristics of the Fruit of the Spirit, *"But the fruit of the Spirit is love, joy, peace, longsuffering, gentleness, goodness, faith, meekness; temperance: against such there is no law. And they that are Christ's have crucified the flesh with the affections and lusts. If we live in the Spirit, let us also walk in the Spirit. Let us not be desirous of vain glory, provoking one another, envying one another,"* [Galatians 5:22-26].

Provoking others requires the use of words and actions together. Actions do not always define what we are thinking, or one may not be sure that the actions are what they seem to portray. However, words we can be sure of because we hear them coming from the person's mouth supported by their body language. Words hurt, destroy, discourage, injure, cause division, and a multitude of other irreversible damages. We cannot take words back.

The tongue is like a [send] button or symbol on a technical instrument, once you hit that send button the message is gone you cannot erase it someone got those words before you were able to delete them on your end; even if we can delete it on our end, the words are out there and irretrievable. It is the same with the tongue, though we might regret what we say cannot take back words we say, run ahead of them to cut them off, or erase them from a person's memory.

James asked the questions about sweet and bitter words coming from the same heart/mouth, *"Doth a fountain send forth at the same place sweetwater and bitter?"* [James 3:11].

Jesus said defilement comes from within, *"But those things which proceed out of the mouth come forth from the heart; and they defile the man,"* [Matthew 15:18].

Our prayer to God should as be David's *"Set a watch, O Lord, before my mouth keep the door of my lips,"* [Psalms 141:2].

We are reminded that a lying tongue is one of the seven abominations God hates," *[Proverbs 6:17b]*. Evildoers will be destroyed, *"The tongue devises mischief, like a sharp razor working deceitfully; Thou love all devouring words, o thou deceitful tongue,"* [Psalms 52:2, 4].

When we are caring for our fellow man, being humble, seeking God with a thirst and hunger out of a pure heart, trying to live peacefully with all men, and standing up for God, no matter the ridicule we receive, for serving are all pleasing to God.

- **Do we focus on the things in our lives and around us that are not as pronounced and do not have that big fire appearance?**

If not, this question needs serious consideration …

The Sermon on the Mount Christ gave in the Gospel of Matthew known as the Beatitudes, addresses the subjects above. It is a blessing in our lives when we conduct ourselves in the manner spoken by our Savior, *"And seeing the multitudes, He went up into a mountain: and when He was set, His disciples came unto Him: And He opened His mouth, and taught them, saying: Blessed are the poor in spirit: for theirs is the kingdom of heaven. Blessed are they that mourn: for they shall be comforted? Blessed are the meek: for they shall inherit the earth. Blessed are they, which do hunger, and thirst after righteousness: for they shall be filled. Blessed are the merciful: for they shall obtain mercy."*

*Blessed are the pure in heart: for they shall see God. Blessed are the peacemakers: for they shall be called, the children of God. Blessed are they, which are persecuted: for righteousness' sake: for theirs is the kingdom of heaven. Blessed are ye, when men shall revile you, and persecute you, and shall say all manner of evil against you falsely, for my sake. Rejoice, and be exceeding glad: for great is your reward in heaven: for so persecuted they the prophets which were before you,"* [Matthew 5:1-12].

We cannot see the forest for looking at the trees is another well-known expression man uses to describe physical blindness or their perspective on certain issues or points. We see the small portrait and not the big picture. Looking only at the situations in your face is never wise. Tunnel vision is costly. Thinking outside the box gives a broader discernment. There are always underlying factors in any situation.

Satan has many wiles, no two are alike, and he patrols or monitors our environment looking, planning, and circling for the attack. He is good at identifying human weakness and we as humans have flaws, which we are not aware of until a tragedy of the occurring situation or incident calls them to our attention. Burning furnaces are facts of dangers we recognize…however, the hidden dangers lie in the little fires we hug close and the frozen lakes we skate to the middle of with weak areas in the ice.

This goes back to my analogy in Book One of the hidden dangers in the BlackBerry patches that grew along fence lines on my family's farm. The lusciousness of the berries is attractive and appetizing to the point the berries with the little nibbles on them people ignore, and the dangers are not recognized, but the Rattle Snakes are still present and deadly. It is a hidden danger. Once you reach your hand to pluck the fruit of the vine he strikes with deadly precision, swiftness, efficiency, and effectiveness. Satan's skills are just as the Rattlesnakes in the Blueberry Patches that grow along the fence line, on the side of highways, and other places, they like Satan are everywhere and have a hidden danger that is just as deadly.

Hidden dangers are perfect traps of Satan. Remember God's question to Satan when the Sons of God came to present themselves Satan was among them, *"One day the angels came to present themselves before the Lord, and Satan also came with them. The Lord said to Satan, "Where have you come from?" [Job 2:1-2a].*

- ***This brings to one's attention did the Sons of God recognize this enemy of God?***

Satan answered the Lord, *"From roaming throughout the earth, going back and forth on it," [Job 2:2b].*

Satan seeks whom he may devour. The word "[may]" in this context stands out as a possibility; everyone in Satan's preview is a possibility he can pull in with his collection of wiles. His disguise was of such, the angels of power and might did not recognize him neither will we without the Scriptural sight God provided as our armor and magnifying glass.

Satan is an expert architect, builder, and supplier of materials of temptation. He will draw the plans your heart desires, build the house of your dreams, including supplying the materials, and the initial cost to you will be zero (<0). Dealing with Satan is like living in a 'beauty and the beast' world but in a reverse manner. He starts as the prince and not the beast when he has completely pulled you in, and your enjoyment of the first kiss of the pleasures he provided for you he changes into the fiery beast that stokes the fires of that furnace of reality, which can destroy on the first contact.

Satan has the capital to support any pleasures you desire. He will finance your desires for you, but be aware financing requires repayment. His interest rates are at 100%. We cannot let Satan re-draw the lines in the sand that God drew before time began. He set the standards for our lives. Satan will create those standards that fit that mental scenario you desire. Satan will lead you into a spiritual desert void of the food and water need for your spiritual survival. Sisters we cannot wear garments of willful blindness nor ignorance to what the god of this world pushes, but rather, "*Desire the sincere milk of the word that we might grow thereby,*" *[Ibid]*.

Once he traps you in his wiles and you become beholding to him he uses the nail in the coffin type strategy, you are locked in.

Our garment of faith and walking wisely is the only fire-retardant garments that will keep us safe from Satan wiles, "*We are not unaware of his wiles,*" *[Ibid]*, as Paul, the Apostle, reminds us.

It is wise to live in [real time] and not be caught up in his trap of rationalizing our choices in life to fit our desires…no more than it is wise to become over-confident that the middle of a frozen lake is frozen, solid.

CHAPTER TWENTY-FOUR

# THE FURNACE OF REALITY AND LIVING IN REAL-TIME PART 2

The furnace of the reality of this pre-existing condition burns hot, we are wise when we stop, look, and listen is a continuous effort; it is neither seasonal nor sporadic.

The Furnace of Reality burns in Real-Time. You cannot borrow from the future but can secure the future in eternity by taking to heart the fact that sin is not an area of your life in which you can take risks. It takes strength, resolves, conditioning of heart and mind for serving God in Spirit and Truth; however, this is done with self-control, bringing our body, heart, mind, and soul under subjection to the will of our Lord and Savior Jesus Christ, *"Submit yourselves then to God. Resist the devil and he will flee from you,"* *[James 4:7]*.

Paul further states, *"But I keep under my body, and bring it into subjection: lest that by any means, when I have preached to others, I myself should be a castaway,"* *[I Corinthians 9:27]*.

Paul reminds us we cannot serve God by yielding to the demands of the flesh, *"The mind governed by the flesh, is hostile to God. It does not submit to God's law, nor can it do so. Those who are in the realm of the flesh cannot please God,"* *[Romans 8:7-8]*.

Christ sent the Holy Spirit back to earth, for our spiritual comfort on our journey to help us to understand what is the will of God, for our lives; it is wise to listen to the Holy Spirit, our teacher, and guide.

Christ promised, *"When the Advocate comes, whom I will send to you from the Father the Spirit of Truth who goes out from the Father-He will testify about Me,"* *[John 15:26]*.

The Holy Spirit is our teacher, and we follow His guidance, as the Apostles and others followed Jesus' teaching while He was among them, *"For if we sin willfully after that we have received the knowledge of the truth, there remains no more sacrifice for sins,"* *[Hebrews 10:26]*.

John further reminds us of Christ's promise, *"However, when He, the Spirit of Truth, has come, He will guide you into all truth; for He will not speak on His own authority, but whatsoever He hears He will speak; and He will tell you things to come," [John 16:13].*

Christ's promises are firm, we see evidence of this every day, *"I will not leave you as orphans; I will come to you," [John 14:18].*

Also, the promise includes, *"But the Helper, the Holy Spirit, whom the Father will send in My name, He will teach you all things, and bring to your remembrance all that I said to you," [John 14:26].*

The prophecy as well of the Spirit among us Nehemiah being instructed of God wrote, *"You gave your good Spirit to instruct them, Your manna You did not withhold from their mouth, and You gave them water for their thirst," [Nehemiah 9:20].*

The Spirit also goes before Jesus' Mighty Throne on our behalf and interprets our prayers with groaning we in our finite minds cannot begin to comprehend, *"In the same way, the Spirit helps us in our weakness. We do not know what we ought to pray for, but the Spirit Himself intercedes for us through wordless groans," [Romans 8:26].*

God knows every aspect of what we will suffer here, the adversary we face, the trials, and tribulations we go through, and just the day-to-day challenges of this life. He has the plan and pattern in place. Like lines on a dressmaker's pattern or an engineer's plan for a building, for the pattern or plan God put in place to work for us, we must follow the lines of the pattern. This plan is, as I mentioned, in this and earlier chapters cover the people of God in an individual as well as a collective manner.

Real-time is Reality. We learn from the past but cannot live there; it is only for learning spiritually even in the secular world, we call it history of the past. We learn from secular as well as Biblical History – History, or things written aforetime are for our learning, *"For whatsoever things were written aforetime were written for our learning, that we through patience and comfort of the scriptures might have hope," [Romans 15:4].*

In secular history, it translates to humans learning from their physical ancestors' mistakes. Both of these scenarios bring us to the same conclusion that, history, Biblical or secular bears itself out, human mistakes are costly, we see this with wars, misnomers, disobedience, defiance of God's Command, straying off the path, worshipping idols gods, and the list goes on endlessly. [...].

Listen to what the people said to Isaiah when he confronted them with the message of God, "*Leave this way, get off this path, and stop confronting us with the Holy One of Israel,*" *[Isaiah 30:11].*

We cannot embrace the attitudes of the people of God that spoke to Isaiah. We are to follow His pattern each day we live; rejecting the message of Christ is as Isaiah describes when the people of God rejected the message he gave them.

God answered in this way to them, and that answer applies to us as well, "*Wherefore, thus, said the Holy One of Israel; Because ye despise this word and trust in oppression and perverseness, and stray thereon; therefore, this iniquity, shall be to you as a breach ready to fall swelling out in a high wall whose breaking cometh suddenly at an instant. And He shall break it as the breaking of the potters' vessel that is broken in pieces; He shall not spare: so that there shall not be found in the bursting of it a sherd to take fire from the hearth or to take water withal out of the pit,*" *[Isaiah 30:12-14].*

God will take away our blessings with us having the attitudes of the people Isaiah gave His answer to…it will leave us lacking and wanting for just the bare minimums in life and without God's hand to guide us, protect us, or help us. A breach is a division. We cannot afford to be without God for a second in our lives, let alone refusing to hear or wanting one to speak to us of the oracles of God.

We are to submit to Christ as the ruler of our lives for He is the Chosen One of God Our Father as King and Savior before He takes away everything, all blessings, even our lives.

In Biblical history, the sins of the people were costly. God Does Not Change. He is Righteous; a Just God; Pure and Holy; we can only be pleasing to Him if we follow the pattern shown on that Spiritual Mountain and are obedient to His Commands, keeping in mind, we are not perfect. God also gave us the Blood Sacrifice to satisfy the sin debt against man; therefore, we are born again through Baptism into His Holy Kingdom, and we live according to the Pattern He left for us. We put on our garments of armor; it is a war sister. We enter this war with different battles we face during our journey; yet in all our errors and missteps, Christ does not leave us alone if we remain faithful, ever striving for the mark of the higher calling of God.

We are to live in real-time in this respect. The stealth of a Lion is hard to match. This analogy equals what humans trying to deal with Satan in this world will be like without Jesus in their lives. Satan is surreptitious; that roaring Lion God warns us about.

In addition, the Hebrew writer tells us, "*The day you hear My voice, harden not your heart as in the days of temptation in the wilderness.*"

Still, the Hebrews writer tells us the Holy Spirit says, "*Today if you hear His voice do not harden your hearts as you did in rebellion during the time of testing in the wilderness, where your ancestors tried Me, though for forty years they saw what I did.*"

The Hebrew writer repeated this warning twice; it expresses the importance of the strong warning he gives us about our under-handed adversary. He warns us to heed the voice of God do not turn away; we have a perfect example in Scripture of what the people of God suffered in the wilderness because of disobedience. They tested God and incurred His wrath. We do not want God to declare in His anger against us as He did against the people of Israel at that time, "*They will never enter my rest,*" [Hebrews 3:7-9].

Further, "*See to it brethren and sisters that none of you has a sinful unbelieving heart that turns away from the living God; but encourage one another daily as long as it is called "Today" so that none of you may be hardened by sins deceitfulness. We have come to share in Christ, If indeed we hold our original conviction firmly to the very end,*" [Hebrews 3:12-14].

A pause and thought, Scripture does not specifically say who wrote the Letter of Hebrews; however, as I read, it sounds so much like the Apostle Paul. The way he penned his phrases, the acute analogies made, the sound of his voice resonates in the Book of Hebrews. Hebrews ends, in the same manner, Paul ends all his letters, "*Grace be with you all;* **Philemon**: *Grace of the Lord Jesus Christ be with your Spirit;* **Titus**: *Grace be with you all;* **Timothy**: *The Lord be with your Spirit; Grace be with you all,*" [Ibid].

Indulging in the attractive morsels of the world that Satan dangles before you is like playing Russian roulette with your soul and an eternity of peace. The pre-existing condition is the gun, the attractive morsels are the bullets of sin, and it only takes one bullet to destroy your life. Each time you pull the trigger, and another empty chamber goes around with your enjoying those tasty morsels gets you one chamber closer to that bullet that will take away (destroy) your opportunity to return to Christ.

Every time one tries another enjoyable morsel, and nothing happens as the skater on the frozen lake, going a little further each time the last skate achieved success, which equals not knowing what chamber that deadly bullet is in the gun. The last temptation, (Satan always saves the best for last when he is about to close the trap door), is the most attractive…you try it…that morsel is the one that is the deadliest. Up to this point, he has made sin for you as En Vogue, as your heart desires.

Reality is knocking at our door, Christ, or Satan.

• *The question is with which one will you spend eternity?*

Christ stood in the breach and closed it between God and man. Satan sat in a tree and caused the breach between God and man. His only ability is to cause human breaches with God. We as people of God cannot declare a spiritual "détente," with God's Word; it is neither negotiable nor open for the people of God backing off the truth. […].

Lethargic and overwhelmed are two of sins' powers; sin can cause humans to become lazy in a way they are unaware of in the sense of being overwhelmed in a spiritually unmindful way. Becoming reckless, being overly confident of your Salvation, and stop taking every precaution to ensure continued faithfulness and awareness of the wiles of Satan, is dangerous.

Sin is systemic, not episodic. It is a fire stoked by the god of this world (Satan). Sin's pre-existing tide is one against which we cannot swim. The stream of Christianity flows downstream not upstream. Disobedience is swimming against the tide; all unrighteousness is sin. We are conscious of sin – its awareness is like a built-in warning system that we rather "*Hear O' Israel*" than partake of its evilness. The fires that stoke this condition are the things of the world, "*The lust of the flesh, the lust of the eye, and the pride of life," [Ibid]*.

Solomon expressed the pride of life in this manner, "*Pride goes before destruction and a haughty spirit before a fall," [Proverbs 16:18]*.

James warns in this way, "*But He giveth more grace. Wherefore He said, God resists the proud, but giveth grace unto the humble," [James 4:6]*.

When we think we are sure of our Salvation and service is pleasing to God, we let our defenses down then sudden destruction befalls us. Another of those dangers is mental Torpidity, which affects the spirit. The more spiritual inactivity we get into after a while overwhelms one to the point it is hard to get out of the rut of which Satan has led you.

Consider looking at sin in the same light as the Law of Diminishing Returns, the more you encounter things in the world that are sinful the more sinful returns you get. Keep in mind, sin overlaid with attractive jewels, of pleasure, is enjoyable, but that overlay has hidden dangers to it, and the attractiveness of it causes an overwhelming desire to continue... In the Economics Classes, I teach at the University, we discuss the Law of Diminishing Marginal Utility in business. The law states, 'the marginal utility of a good decreases as more of it is consumed in a given period.' Looking at this Law from the Spiritual perspective, the more you ingest and internalize the sinful nature of the world, the less attractive or beneficial it should become until it nauseates you.

- *We, as humans, can understand and apply this in business. Why is it so hard to understand it in a spiritual sense?*

Consider this analogy with this example in mind: You have five whoppers fully loaded before you. The first one is delicious, its deliciousness increases your desire to eat another one; you begin eating the second one, it tastes okay but not as tasty as the first one. The second one began to lose its tastiness, even though you consume the entire burger. Yet, you tried the third one the first bite was somewhat okay, but not very good. The second bite makes you nauseous to the point you almost lose the first two you consumed.

The utility of consuming those burgers you immediately become aware of has lost their benefit; actually, it did after the first burger, but not its attractiveness. This is what sin is like, Satan continues to push the things you desire and have an appetite for, which can overwhelm you ... you become inactive not knowing what to do.

Paul reminds us, *"We see and know his wiles," [Ibid]*.

Paul reiterates that this awareness of Satan's wiles should engender (stimulate) more confidence not less confidence in the Salvation and Promises of God. Think about the Chapter of Faith, *[Hebrew 11]* we read of the roll call of champions of faith in the Scripture. Even that reading does not mention all the names of the champions of faith, but we know they are there. Our names will be there as well. Whether we are champions of faith, as the Hebrew writer tells us is determined, by, our faithfulness to God, while living on earth.

- *What book will your name appear in?*

Revelation mentions 'Books' (more than one) or in the Book (one) that will be opened at the Judgment Seat should be important. It is wise of you to be concerned with whether you are living a life pleasing to God and not allowing the temptations of this world provided by its god to pull you in and overwhelm you to the point of becoming lethargic.

Everyone will stand before Christ's Throne on Judgment Day this is a reality. We are not exempt because we are a member of the Body of Christ. The Israelites were of this opinion because they were God's people though defiant and disobedient hoping for God to rescue them from all the worldly ills. Listen to what Amos wrote. No one will escape judgment, *"Woe unto you that desire the day of the Lord to what end is it for you? The day of the Lord is darkness, and not light. As if a man did flee from a Lion, and bear met him; or went into the house, and leaned his hand on the wall, and a serpent bit him," [Amos 5:18-19].*

We should live each day as if we know Judgment Day is coming (whether that day is while living here on earth or the final judgment) and Jesus is our Savior now; furthermore, He will be our Judge on that day, a day of pain and suffering if we die outside of Christ…

Garments of a Christian Woman should not have the appearance of a Spiritual détente, playing Russian roulette, or a frozen lake about them; but rather their appearance should be of living in and with Spiritual reality in real-time. The pre-existing condition of sin is alive and well, its physician, Satan, nurses it constantly, thereby, keeping it healthy.

Our garments, sisters should have the look of the resolve to serve Christ, being firm in our faith in God, speaking the truth, and standing against our foe and adversary, Satan. We cannot allow his wiles to encourage us to agree with anything that has the appearance of being unrighteous or that will compromise the truth as he presents it or can and will present it. Jesus Our Savior warns us, *"He was a murderer from the beginning, and abode not in the truth because there is no truth in him. When he speaks a lie, he speaks of his own: for he is a liar and the father of it," [John 8:44b].*

Women in service to Christ wear garments of "more being and more doing" which eliminates lethargies as Christians in the Kingdom of God.

The experience in our lives and their impacts help shape who we are…

CHAPTER TWENTY-FIVE

# THE COLORS OF A PRISM
# RELATIONSHIPS AND EXPERIENCE
# THOSE MOMENTS OF IMPACT
# GARMENTS OF THOUGHT

Solomon in his God-given wisdom wrote, *"I applied my heart to what I observed and learned a lesson from what I saw,"* *[Proverbs 24:32]*

Experiences shape who we are in our lives. The paths that experience puts one on shapes them like a piece of cloth cut without a pattern or like a picture painted by an artist without a model. There are no straight paths in life; they all at certain intervals curve.

Experiences are like looking through a prism. What variety of colors do you see? The colors depict pictures of our experiences and the impact they have on our future.

We know that the red areas, in our lives, warn us about the danger that exists. At times, it feels like we live our lives in a vacuum. Human nature, now and again, puts us in awkward positions with the path that our experiences lead us.

Ghosts of the past occasionally cross our path. They are colors from that prism of experiences in our lives another moment of impact. Those ghosts are standing, pointing, trying to push us back past that impact that was so positive in our lives. Carefully we thread that path to get past that ghosts and shadow that impacted us so strongly, lest we feel ourselves slipping – slipping as if we are on a mountain of ice falling back – back into the impact of the past when our human nature did not allow us to take a positive path where the impact changed our lives.

Good or bad experiences can affect what path we take in life. *"Not only so, but we also glory in our sufferings, because we know that suffering produces perseverance; perseverance, character; and character, hope and hope does not put us to shame, because God's love has been poured out into our hearts through the Holy Spirit, which is given to us,"* *[Romans 5:3-5]*.

A Prism is a solid geometric figure with two end faces that are similar, equal, and parallel rectilinear figures, and with the sides that are parallelograms. Think of this as an example of the paths in life that is open to us, but which one should we take in this complicated life is always before us. Choosing wisely is as complicated as the geometric figure.

Our experiences are deep within us, entwined into our souls. They are different but also connected. They inhabit our soul that inner being where the greatest impact takes place.

Prisms of glass are superficial. When they are looked through the color changes, but not those experiences embedded deep within us are where the impact is the strongest do not change; however, does have the power to change us positively or negatively!

Experiences can change our lives. The way we use them is the way they influence us, *"And let us consider one another to provoke unto love and to good works not forsaking the assembling of ourselves together as the manner of some is but, exhorting one another: and so much the more, as ye see the day approaching,"* [Hebrews 10:24-25].

Relationships are an impact; how a relationship starts affects the future, of that relationship. Relationships in life start like an empty wagon.

An empty wagon makes noise. As time goes on, and the relationship progresses those experiences and moments of impact enrich that relationship and fill those empty places. The relationship becomes more solid; as solid rocks fill an empty wagon and soon the noise is gone, *"Whatever you do, work at it with all your heart, as working for the Lord, not for human masters,"* [Colossians 3:23].

Moments of impact decide the road we take in our relationship. Sometimes it even takes us down the well-traveled path and other moments of impact take us down the road seldom traveled. When we take a road in life that we have never/seldom travel is a moment of impact, a strange territory if you will. New relationships on an unfamiliar road are strange territory, sometimes even on that well-traveled road.

- *How we manage a new relationship will determine the level of that moment of impact in our lives; will that impact be a color from a prism (superficially), or will that impact be one that will affect us deep within our being (soul)?*

We cannot throw away love in a physical or spiritual marriage. Sisters, we as humans sometimes repeatedly take love for granted. It appears to be an inherent characteristic in the make-up of humans, who gets comfortable where they are, and forget that love is fragile, because of the emotional side of being human beings. We do not take advantage of the beauty of love –but is, at times, careless treating love as a common thing – however, when we realize what we have it is too late, the person has lost interest, or the pain is too great in the heart to want to continue in that relationship.

We also cause our Savior pain because of our unfaithfulness and lack of love. Nor will God wait forever for us to obey His will and be faithful (continue to willfully sin). When our focus is on everything and everyone except who we are in a relationship with, is not fulfilling the covenant we made and is in danger in both spiritual and physical senses. There is always a day of reckoning.

God gave us rules for faithfulness. He created the Standards we are to live by in our marriage relationships whether they are physical or spiritual. We cannot add nor take away from the established pattern lest we find ourselves outside of the commands and our choices are willfully defiant to our Creator. There are only two people in a marriage, in reference to the Church, it is Jesus and you, and in respect to marriage, it is your spouse and you. A third person or god is not acceptable. Our relationships rise or fall based on our willingness to follow the rules.

Building our relationships on earth is crucial; on the other hand, building our relationship with Christ is more important than any other aspect of our lives. We must have that foundation found only in Christ; it is only then can we be successful. We will then know how to build relationships with others and our spouses.

Sisters, sin changes our relationship with God. We strive for righteousness daily and make every effort to avoid sinning and if we do sin, take steps to correct it immediately and seek forgiveness through repentance and humility before the Throne of God. Do not forfeit your justification as Demas and others did by being disobedient and not walking in the light, "*But if we walk in the light, as He is in the light, we have fellowship with one another, and the blood of Jesus, His Son, purifies us from all sin,*" *[I John 1:7]*.

Nor do we want to damage our relationship with our Father by denying our sins. If we ignore our sins, we deny our sins, as if they did not happen or we are not guilty of sinning we become a liar as well, *"If we claim to be without sin, we deceive ourselves, and the truth is not in us. If we confess our sins, He is faithful and just and will forgive us our sins and purify us from all unrighteousness. If we claim we have no sin, we make Him out to be a liar and His word is not in us,"* [I John 8-10].

Lest we forget, Satan is our adversary and continues to fight against us – he is the orchestrator of that slow-moving disaster of which we are born. We strive to keep our relationship with God on a firm foundation with our Lord and Savior Jesus Christ.

Carpe Diem, [siege the day]. The Pharisees failed to siege the day. Christ came according to the Prophecy. They knew the Prophecy but ignored it when it came right down to being faithful leaders of the people; desired or chose to stay stuck in time. I see this as the actions of those who are scoffers; people who say nothing changes when the change was before them. They put Jesus on trial because of the fear of change, fear of loss of power, and fear the Roman Empire would take away their Synagogue. They were comfortable to the tune of being complacent; let things stay the same; do not fix it if it is not broken (but it was incomplete, broken) thereby sacrificing a relationship with the Savior of the World.

[T]he plan was never broken. God does not deal in broken plans; He never put a broken plan in place but a progressive successive one. The change was that all nations of people would be included in His plan. They too are His creation. God's plan continually unfolded with each generation and those plans [pre-structured] before creation including the prophecies that foretold the changes to move forward until the birth of our Savior. Christ coming to earth transformed our lives. We begin living in the light, not darkness, and building our relationship with Jesus.

Christ gives us the chance to siege the day [Carpe Diem]. Hebrews reminds us, *"Therefore, as the Holy Spirit says: "Today, if you will hear His voice, do not harden your hearts as in the rebellion, in the day of trial in the wilderness. Where your fathers tested Me; tried Me; and saw My works forty years,"* [Hebrews 3:7-10].

God desires a relationship with His people; those moments of impact had the Pharisees sieged them, would have continued, and further enriched their relationship with God. They knew the prophecy that the Messiah would fulfill the Law.

Without exception, sisters, we all have one or more skeletons in the closet. We have made decisions that we learned from and done things in life we would not do again. Once we came to Christ – Christ takes away all the guilt that once existed against us as the old man. We have become a new man (transformed).

The closet, where those skeletons are, lock the door and throws away that key. Continually languishing and mourning that past life when those skeletons are dead is a tool, of Satan. He wants you to continue to go back and pick up that old man with the skeletons and drag them along. He uses the consciousness of man and the inherent ability it has to feel pain and guilt. Any relationship with Satan makes a bad marriage; he does not play by the rules – any rule.

Lot's wife fell into the trap of languishing and mourning what was past and it destroyed her and changed the relationship of her family forever.

Most certainly, Satan does not compromise; any compromise, he makes with you, is to his and not your advantage. You lose every time you try playing by his rules. It is necessary to remind ourselves constantly we are new creatures in Christ, and we left our past behind. We have shed our (old garments) sisters and we now have new lives in Christ (wearing the fresh garments) of Salvation.

Allow Christ to assist with this weak area in your lives. At times, we all go back to that guilt we felt and to those skeletons we locked away. Each time we resist Satan's attempts to tempt us to moan their death again make us stronger.

Each day we live turns another page in our life. Each page turned, gets us a little closer to eternity. We cannot add any pages to our journals of life; on the other hand, we can fill up the pages (time) in the journals we have with work, good deeds, and living for God each day. As these pages turn, we mature with the experience of continually putting off the garments of that old man and putting on the garments, of the new man, growing to be a strong servant of God in desire, attitude, and actions. Our garments of Christianity are evident if we are living in the light.

Seeing the example Jesus left us of the relationship He has with His Father; we build a relationship with God and its impact before we can fully understand the relationship we are to have with our fellowman. Our Savior is an all-powerful, omniscient, omnipotent, and omnipresent God. Christ is worthy of our respect, love, and honor, which is due to Him, and only then will we understand how to love and respect others.

If the relationship between God and you is not right, other relationships will suffer. Scripture reminds us, *"Anyone who claims to be in the light but hates a brother or sister is still in the darkness. Anyone who loves their brother and sister lives in the light, and there is nothing in them to make them stumble. But anyone who hates a brother or sister is in the darkness and walks around in the darkness. They do not know where they are going, because the darkness has blinded them," [I John 2:9-11].*

Jesus is light. We treat our fellow Christians and others in the manner which we want to be treated, practicing [the] Golden Rule, *"Therefore all things whatsoever ye would that men should do to you, do ye even so to them: for this is the law and the prophets," [Matthew 7:12].*

We cannot foster positive relationships with God or man when we walk in darkness. Darkness blinds one's eyes. Whether we are loving God or loving our brother; we cannot love one without loving the other. *"Loving God with all our heart and soul is the greatest Commandment"* and the second like unto it. Christ tells us to, *"Love our neighbor as we do ourselves," [Ibid].* We try to avoid doing anything that will hurt ourselves and take particular care with our lives and survival why not our neighbor whosoever they might be; *"Thou shaltlove thy neighbor*as thyself. There is none other commandment*s greater than these," [Mark 12:31, Leviticus 19:18].*

We are to view the Scripture in a textualist manner, it says what it says; it will not change for our convenience. Scripture is superlative, it says the same things to everyone who reads and studies it. Our knowledge of God's Word helps us in the building of relationships with both God and man.

Christ has given us the tools we need to meet the moment, this moment, your moment. We all have that moment in our lives, *"The Day you hear His voice harden not your heart," [Ibid].*

Then those who have advantaged that moment you are in the room, you filled your lamp, then took additional oil so your lamp will not go out (if the Bridegroom delays His coming). We are in the room sisters, there is no reason to leave and go back to a life once lived. Christ the Bridegroom has everything we need. The wedding feast is complete; there is sufficient Spiritual food for all to partake who hear the invitations and attends. The bread and wine are ready. Jesus thought of everything needed for this marriage reception.

Sisters our mansions are waiting. We are now packing, sending ahead those pearls of faithfulness so our mansions are sufficiently furnished. When we arrive, all we do is live forever with our Lord and Savior Jesus Christ, God the Father, and God the Holy Spirit in peace, joy; all pain and heartache have ended there will only be tranquility in the presence of God.

The witnesses we have in Scripture allow us to soar. There are witnesses to the faithfulness of God's promises. They believed God, walked as He asked them. They were strong in their faith and did not doubt God, but continuously built their relationships with Him and their fellow man, as we should each day because it impacts all our lives; theirs and ours. Obedience, faith, good deeds, faithfulness, and love are furnishing our Mansions and it will be ready for that "Great Day."

**"Every moment and event of every man's life on earth plants something in his soul." Thomas Merton**

A Close relationship with Jesus; the impact that changes lives, it did for Martha and Mary.

CHAPTER TWENTY-SIX

# GARMENTS OF SISTERS OF FAITH MARY AND MARTHA

Martha and Mary are examples of women of faith close to Jesus here on earth as well as spiritually. Lazarus their brother was a friend of Jesus and close to His heart. Jesus loved Martha, Mary, and their brother. Scripture describes Jesus' close relationship with this family.

They believed that Jesus could do all things including raising the dead, *"Lord, "Martha said to Jesus, "if you had been here, my brother would not have died," [John 11:21]*.

She reaffirmed her belief, *"But I know that even now God will give you whatever you ask," [John 11:22]*.

Christ said, *"Your brother will rise again."* Martha answered, *"I know he will rise again*

*in the resurrection on the last day."* Jesus **said** to her, *"I am the Resurrection and the Life; the one who believes in Me will live, even though they die," [John 11:23-25]*.

Mary was a common name in Biblical times. There were more than one disciple named Mary following Jesus. They were friends of Jesus even one who Jesus cured. The name Mary means beloved.

This example of the relationships they had can be a teaching pattern from these two women and their care for Lazarus their brother and Jesus, their friend.

What we focus on and whom our focus is on is important. We read about both, but Mary has a better focus on what is necessary for life, those things essential, for survival and hospitality both are important. Mary as Jesus pointed out, chose the better way. She sat at His feet and listened while Martha busily prepared the food as told in Scripture. When she identified her concern to Jesus, she was working while Mary sits and listens. *"But Martha was distracted by all the preparations that had to be made."* She came to Him and asked, *"Lord, don't you care that my sister has left me to do the work by myself? Tell her to help me!"; "Martha, Martha," the Lord answered, "You are worried and upset about many things, but only one thing is needed. Mary has chosen what is better, and it will not be taken away from her," [Luke 10:40–42]*.

Think about your day-to-day activities' sisters are we so busy with what we as a mother, wives, homemakers, career women do that is vital for our family survival and well-being, which is serving God, that we forget to serve God, in the way, most needful? Martha busied herself with the preparation of food and Mary sits at Jesus' feet as He taught, "*And she had a sister called Mary, which also sat at Jesus' feet, and heard His word," [Luke 10:39].*

Now Martha's service was just as important in this setting, Jesus was the friend and visitor of Lazarus and his sisters. When visitors come to our home, we show hospitality to them. Therefore, we let our light shine so all can see Jesus in our actions. We face moments in our lives, when one service outweigh the other, though all service in God's Kingdom is important times and instances come when it is necessary to put the most important one above the other as Mary did.

We are to show hospitality to all regardless of who they are. The Hebrew writer reminds us that we are to, *"Keep on loving one another as brothers and sisters. Do not forget to show hospitality to strangers, for by so doing some people have shown hospitality to angels without knowing it," [Hebrews 13:1-2].*

Indeed, if it is important to show generosity to strangers we encounter how much more so to our fellow brothers and sisters of the faith.

- *Do they see the friendliness, love, and care we have for our fellow man in our actions?*

We are looking at two sisters who are excellent examples of faithful Christian women. Both helped Jesus in their way using their skills and talents in His service.

- *Take a moment and imagine Jesus as a guest in your home, how would you welcome Him as Mary and Martha did?*
- *How would your heart look to Jesus? Like Mary's?*

We have Jesus as a guest in our home now sisters, not just Jesus our Savior, but God the Holy Spirit our teacher who is the promised gift, who lives with us and in us each day.

Mary also means bitterness. Martha and Mary would see bitter times. Their beloved brother Lazarus fell sick and died. When Lazarus became ill, Mary met Jesus to make her plea in pain and heartache. This is the only place recorded in Scripture where we see the overwhelming emotions of our Savior about His friend, *"Jesus wept," [John 11:35].*

His heart was broken for His friends because death is final on earth. When we lose a loved one, it is painful. Love is the most beautiful concept in our lives. As well, love can be the most painful emotion we can experience if we lose a loved one whether to life or death. Jesus loves us as He did Mary and Martha, and it does break His heart when we choose to love others more than we love Him.

Martha loved Jesus and had strong faith believing He could do all things evident by her statement, "*Lord if you had been here our brother would not have died,*" *[Ibid]*.

Faith in Christ's ability to raise Lazarus from the dead is the most important point in this chapter. Mary and Martha's faith in the Savior of the world is remarkable though Lazarus' death caused bitterness and His resurrection bought Joy because their brother, though dead, was alive again, Christ said, "*I am the Resurrection and the Life though they are dead will rise again,*" *[Ibid]*.

Mary and Martha's faith is impressive, as were the faith of others during that time. The Scripture tells us, "*Weeping may endure for a night, but joy comes in the morning,*" *[Psalms 30:5b]*.

The things we suffer are temporal and only for a moment compared to the Eternity we have before us. Bitterness, weeping, and suffering are part of our journey to Eternity, as it was, for these two sisters.

Christ tasted the bitterness of the journey to Jerusalem. He knew He would be rejected by the Chief Priest and Scribes, deserted by His people (the people of God), and die there. The worse bitterness He experienced was, separation from His Father.

***Do you stop to consider what it would be like to spend moments separated from God?***

It is scary just the contemplation of it. Mary and Martha's faith was solid and grounded in their Savior.

They had hope and faith as Scripture reminds us, "*Faith is the substance of things hoped for and the evidence of things not seen,*" *[Hebrews 11:1]*.

They believed Jesus was all-powerful and whatever He asked of God, He would grant him.

### *Do we have that level of faith and trust?*

God does not change nor does our Savior. The Scripture did not indicate these sisters ever doubted the power of Jesus. The evidence of their faith was alive and well with Lazarus in their lives again, *"Then Jesus six days before the Passover came to Bethany, where Lazarus was, which had been dead, whom He raised from the dead. There they made Him a supper, and Martha served: but Lazarus was one of them that sat at the table with Him. Then took Mary a pound of ointment of spikenard, very costly, and anointed the feet of Jesus, and wiped His feet with her hair: and the house was filled with the odor of the ointment,"* *[John 12:1-3].*

Jesus prayed all night before He chose His Apostles, *"And it came to pass in those days, that He went out into a mountain to pray, and continued all night in prayer to God. And when it was day, He called unto Him His disciples: and of them, He chose twelve, whom also He named Apostles,"* *[Luke 6:12].*

The emphasis on prayer brings us to real-time the extreme importance of praying. The Scriptures tells us the significance of prayer in our lives, *"Ask and it shall be given,"* *[Ibid].*

Of course, this is if your request is according to the will of God. Though we ask, the request might not be His will for our lives. However, we continue to pray as always talking to God about our needs, praising, glorifying His Holy Name, giving thanks: for His grace, mercy, and blessings in our lives. Thanking God for sending the Holy Spirit, our Comforter, to guide us into all righteousness, who intercedes with interpretations of those prayers before the Throne of God with groaning we cannot understand.

Prayer still changes things, Christ being God, prayed to His Father. God is still our Father and Christ is our Savior. Hence, praying to God brings about change, whether it is situations, hearts, governments, administrations, or each of us.

- ### *Do we doubt the power of God?*

God works through faith and not doubt. Martha and Mary had that faith without doubting. It takes a strong person to withstand trouble and never doubt that God can do as He promised. God's ear is not heavy; His arms are not short, and He has never broken a promise.

The book of Revelation depicts events we read about throughout the Bible of the power and might of God from both the Old Testament and the New Testament.

Mary, Mother of Jesus another example of innocence, faith, and belief… she was a servant of God who birthed the Savior of the world … joy was born into her life as was bitterness … bitterness which led her to the Foot of the Cross of Jesus…

CHAPTER TWENTY-SEVEN

# GARMENTS OF INNOCENCE SERVANTS OF GOD: MARY MOTHER OF JESUS

*"Unto you first God, having raised up His Son Jesus, sent Him to bless you, in turning away every one of you from his iniquities," [Acts 3:26].*

At times [many] of the things God asks us to do are difficult for us to understand. Mary was young and innocent when she received the announcement from the Angel Gabriel she would carry the Messiah (Savior) of the world.

I am sure, Mary, chosen by God, as the earthly Mother of the His Son was the most honored part of her life, yet the most difficult. God never gives us more than we can carry. He has a perfect plan for our lives. Mary submitted humbly to His will for her life, obedience is necessary to serve God.

Mary, a relative of Elizabeth, husband Zechariah, was a Priest from the division of Abijah. Elizabeth lineage was of Aaron tribe of Levi. Aaron was Moses' brother...the two families of whom the Savior was born descended from priests and kings. Joseph, the husband of Mary, is a descendant of David the King. The Prophecy fulfilled. Jesus is Priest and King.

Living in the times of Mary Mother of Jesus was as closely monitored community of people as ever was...there were certain or set standards that guided communities. The Rabbi was the religious leader in that Synagogue and followed the Law according to the pattern God gave them in the Torah.

Thinking of Mary and Joseph's marriage, if the betrothal or what we know as engagement, were violated both the guilty parties were taken outside of the camp and stoned stamping out the evil from among God's people.

Marriage at that time was a two-step process, as it is in the 21st-Century (there is a step skipped at times).

However, the betrothal was a step above an engagement they had a marriage ceremony and after a fashion of time the second step, the celebration, and the consummation.

Then as now, a union was a sacred event because it was as pleasing to God then as it is now. Mary was very young, maybe 18 years of age when she became Joseph's betrothed. He was a descendant of David, the King, which is traced back to the Tribe of Judah, *"The Scepter shall not depart from Judah, nor a lawgiver from between His feet until Shiloh come; and unto Him shall the gathering of the people be,"* *[Genesis 49:10]*.

What must have been Mary's state of mind when a heavenly being (Gabriel) awakened her with the news, first, her cousin Elizabeth would bear a child at her advanced age past what they knew as the age a woman at that time could bear a child. Then Gabriel told her an even more wonderful event would take place in her life, she would also have a child. The Holy Spirit would overshadow her, and the Child would be the Holy One of Israel.

This was perplexing then, as it would be now because she knew no man at that point though betrothed to Joseph of the lineage and House of David. Being young, just beginning adulthood, and realizing you have the responsibility of life, especially the Son of God, the Messiah, the Anointed One to be Savior of the world born to die for the sins of man, was a heavy responsibility. This announcement would be a bit overwhelming for a mature woman over 40 years old to accept, just think how unnerving this must have been for this innocent young woman of the small village of Nazareth. She was well known and well regarded…by all.

I am sure she felt frightened and alone. How to tell her mother that a messenger from God told her she would bear a child and the news of her cousin Elizabeth also six months pregnant. Just put yourself in her mother's place - knowing what the Law said about women in this condition without a husband considered defilement among the people of Israel and stamping it out was the Law; adultery was a sin. Her mother, apparently a woman of faith, believed her daughter. She knew of her innocence and faithfulness to God, stood in support of her child, her only child.

There is no record of Mary having siblings, only a sister-in-law, Mary wife of Cleopas, who was the brother of Joseph. All that Mary said the Angel Gabriel told her, came-to-pass. Elizabeth was with child and in her sixth month, *"And in the sixth month the angel Gabriel was sent from God unto a city of Galilee, named Nazareth, to a virgin espoused to a man whose name was Joseph, of the house of David; and the virgin's name was Mary. And the angel came in unto her, and said, "Hail, thou that art highly favored, the Lord is with thee: blessed art thou among women.And when she saw him, she was troubled at his saying, and cast in her mind what manner of salutation this should be. And the angel said unto her, "Fear not, Mary: for thou hast found favor with God. And behold, thou shalt conceive in thy womb and bring forth a son, and shalt call His name Jesus. He shall be great and shall be called the Son of the Highest: and the Lord God shall give unto Him the throne of His father David: And He shall reign over the house of Jacob forever; and of His Kingdom, there shall be no end."*

*"Then said Mary unto the angel, "How shall this be, seeing I know not a man? And the angel answered and said unto her, "The Holy Ghost shall come upon thee, and the power of the Highest shall overshadow thee: therefore, also, that holy thing which shall be born of thee shall be called the Son of God.And behold, thy cousin Elisabeth, she hath also conceived a son in her old age: and this is the sixth month with her, who was called barren. For with God nothing shall be impossible. And Mary said, "Behold the handmaid of the Lord; be it unto me according to thy word. And the angel departed from her," [Luke 1:26-28].*

Telling Joseph, I am sure, if we put ourselves in her place would know how she felt telling your betrothed she was carrying a child conceived without being with a man. Joseph hearing this news must have been strange to him especially since he knew the baby was not his and then her telling him. How perplexing and torn he must have felt. Joseph was a strong man who did not desire to expose Mary to public scrutiny. God's plan for our lives is solid and He does not forsake His children. Adultery, fornication, or any error (sin) of this level was certain death by stoning to both the male and female participants.

Joseph followed the instructions of God. An angel told him of the Child Mary, his betrothed carried, *"But after he had considered this, an angel of the Lord appeared to him in a dream and said, "Joseph son of David, do not be afraid to take Mary home as your wife because what is conceived in her is from the Holy Spirit. She will give birth to a son, and you are to give Him the name Jesus because He will save His people from their sins," [Matthew 1:20-21].*

God can do all things, nothing is impossible, for our God to do. Christ was the Prophecy to be born of a Virgin. In *[Luke 1:26-38],* we read of the Virgin birth.

Webster Dictionary defines Innocence as, a lack of guile or corruption, purity. Looking at similar words [virginity] and][chastity] are comparative to innocence. Mary was submissive to God. Whatever God's desire for her life, she would obey. She knew her reputation would be on the line if the people of the village knew, she would be stoned, but she trusted God though she knew no man.

In contrast to the morals of Mary, Mother of Jesus, Herodias, Salome, and Bernice's integrity and morals were in direct defiance to the Commands of God; women of God, nor women on a whole, cannot embrace these type characteristics and be pleasing to God. […]

Mary's truth was seen when her Son, Our Savior, was resurrected from the dead and all the miracles He performed, *[Luke 1:26-38]*.

Mary was highly favored, in the sight of God. Sisters, just imagine being highly favored by God. We know that we, *"All have sinned and fallen fall short of the Glory of God," [Romans 3:23]*.

No one is perfect. Mary had the characteristics of innocence desired by God our Father, the purity of mind, heart, and soul. She could have protested or objected in her human way, but instantly complied whatever His will is, it be done.

- *Can we be as trusting sisters in our God?*
- *Do we trust Him to take care of the situation because we are humbly obedient as was Mary?*

The future we cannot see, so there is an element of mystery there and we are a little apprehensive, probably more than a little apprehensive. Yet, we like Mary trust God … God does not break His Word, or leave us out on a limb of uncertainty, we can be sure what He says will come to pass. Joseph being of the House of David also knew the Prophecy. I am sure it never entered His mind, though he knew, the Messiah would come through the lineage of King David of the Tribe of Judah, of which he was a descendent, he would be the earthly parent of the Savior of the World.

Every word and prophecy happened from conception to birth; to the lineage in the house of David is where the King comes from, the birthplace in Bethlehem, the star guiding the wise men, the census, and being born in a stable. Mary was from a humble village and Joseph was a Carpenter (working with hands, mind, ingenuity, precision, understanding, carefulness, planning) are all elements in the field of carpentry (Joseph had a humble profession). Humility is what God desires of each of us. Jesus our King pulled off His Heavenly Robes and submitted to the plan of God for man's redemption and came to earth, lived in a human body, and purchased our Salvation by dying for our sins.

- *Is it too much to ask that we make sacrifices and serve Him in Spirit and truth as Mary and Joseph did?*

Jesus is the promised Messiah, King, and Savior.

Sisters, we see Mary's garments of humility, faithfulness, patience, innocence, obedience, and thankfulness. Are we humble as she was to the will of God? Scripture tells us that the dangers the people of God are in if they are, disobedience to His will. We cannot be ones that Christ said, *"To what can I compare this generation? They are like children sitting in the marketplaces and calling out to others: "'We played the pipe for you, and you did not dance; we sang a dirge, and you did not mourn,"* [Matthew 11:16-17].

Sisters, we know the great responsibility or burden that the children are that God has given us as gifts and blessings. How much greater this concern must have been upon Joseph and Mary knowing they were raising the Only Son of God born into this world to bring Salvation, grace, truth, and mercy.

Mary as Jesus' mother, as we are mothers, felt the larger obligation. We as mothers have so much more weight in raising our children, as did Mary, Mother of Jesus. The burden that I speak of is not in a negative way, but that child's safety, health, future, conduct, knowledge, teaching, moral characteristics weigh heavily upon a mother. Mary was no different though she knew the child she carried and would rear was the Holy One of God still had all the anxieties of a young inexperienced mother.

She felt like a mother, worried like a mother, cared for Him as a mother, kissed His little worries away, rocked Him to sleep at night, smiled and played with Him, was kind and loving to Him. He was a happy child playing at the feet of his mother and earthly father and learning the art of carpentry from his father Joseph.

Just to know this Child was in the world for another reason than them raising Him to be productive in society, serve God, continue the next generation as children normally do, and above all to live and function in this world was a different experience and fact I am sure they had not considered.

I also think of Joseph, we do not know when he died, but do know that he lived a long life; they had four sons after Jesus was born. I know as any father would if Joseph had been alive during the three years of Jesus' Ministry and then His persecution in the last days would have fought anyone that tried to hurt his child. Although he knew Jesus was born at the Will of God to be the Savior of the World – love dictates, we want to protect the ones we love.

I cannot imagine standing at the foot of the Cross of Christ as Mary did and watch her son suffer and then die, pain Joseph did not experience. I can imagine the sword of pain that he felt that pierced his heart knowing he left his faithful loving wife alone in this world, with the knowledge she would have to suffer the pain of watching Jesus denied, beaten, and crucified with that sword of pain piercing her heart. Just imagine our Father in Heaven – the level of pain He suffered, turned away from His Son at His crucifixion when taking on the sins of the world.

God suffers as our parent, as did He on the day His Only begotten Son died. When we sin and defy God's Commandments, it pains God because of the sin and the fact that Jesus died for us. We are to be mindful of insulting the Spirit of Grace and counting the Blood of Christ as a common thing or nothing as if it is not important.

We cannot be of those whose garments of hearing and obedience turn a death ear to the calling of our God and Savior. Our garments of innocence are to become as a child trusting God, depending on God, waiting for His will for our lives to be revealed and then to come to pass, and pray for forgiveness, guidance, understanding, wisdom, and all the while grow in the knowledge and understanding of His word (will) as did Mary and Joseph.

We obey God and receive a new life through the Spiritual cleansing waters of the Jordan

CHAPTER TWENTY-EIGHT

# SPIRITUAL AND MORAL LEPROSY FAITH, TRUST, AND THE CLEANSING WATERS OF THE JORDAN RIVER

Leprosy is a chronic slowly progressive illness that is treatable today. Left untreated, it can cause death after years of being ill with the disease. It was common in Old Testament and New Testaments times; but; unlike today; it was untreatable by man, but not by God as we read with Moses first encounter with God, *"Then the Lord said, "Put your hand inside your cloak." So, Moses put his hand into his cloak, and when he took it out, the skin was leprous–it had become as white as snow," [Exodus 4:6].*

Another example, Miriam the sister of Moses and Aaron, became a person with leprosy, *"When the cloud lifted from above the tent, Miriam's skin was leprous, it became as white as snow. Aaron turned toward her and saw that she had a defiling skin disease," [Numbers 12:10].*

Lastly, to Naaman, the example in this chapter and his final submission to the fact that he would not be healed unless he followed the pattern given him for his healing, *"Now, Naaman was commander of the army of the king of Aram. He was a great man in the sight of his master and highly regarded because through him the Lord had given victory to Aram. He was a valiant soldier, but he had leprosy," [2 Kings 5:1].*

The books of Matthew, Mark, and Luke describe leprosy: *"And it came to pass, when He was in a certain city, behold a man full of leprosy: who seeing Jesus fell on his face, and besought Him, saying, Lord, if thou wilt, thou canst make me clean. And He put forth His hand, and touched him, saying, I will: be thou clean. And immediately leprosy departed from him," [Luke 5:12–13]; [Matthew 6:3; Mark 1:42; Luke 17:15; Matthew 10:8; and Luke 4:27].*

Christ spoke of the cleansing of Naaman. There were people with leprosy in Israel, but not all of them were healed. Naaman was blessed to receive the healing from this terrible disease, *"And many lepers were in Israel in the time of Elisha the prophet; and none of them was cleansed, saving Naaman the Syrian," [Luke 4:27].*

Sisters, we are wise to take advantage, of the healing that Christ offers even though Naaman's' method of healing came through Elijah, the power to heal came from God. As Naaman finally took advantage of the method of healing Elisha gave him, so must we obey the way Christ gave us, for the healing of sin so that we might inherit Eternity?

Faith, like a muscle, grows stronger with use and exercise. Muscles atrophy if you do not use them. As with your faith, lack of use, it gets weak or never materializes; finally, in the end, becomes useless to your Salvation. In Naaman's situation, learning to have faith was the road to his Salvation.

The Jordan River did/does not have the cleanest water. During harvest time, it overflows its banks. John baptized Christ in the Jordan River. The Jordon River was a prominent part of the Old and New Testament.

*"The people of God carried the Ark across the Jordan River parted, so they could cross to the promised land, "And it came to pass, when the people removed from their tents, to pass over Jordan, and the priests bearing the Ark of the Covenant, before the people; And as they that bare the Ark were come unto Jordan, and the feet, of the priests, that bare the Ark were dipped in the brim of the water, (for Jordan overflowed all his banks all the time of harvest)."*

*"That the waters which came down from above stood and rose up upon a heap very far from the city of Adam, that is beside Zaretan: and those that came down toward the sea of the plain, even the salt sea, failed, and were cut off: and the people passed over right against Jericho. And the priests that bare the Ark of the Covenant of the Lord stood firm on dry ground in the midst of Jordan, and all the Israelites passed over on dry ground until all the people were passed clean over Jordan," [Joshua 3:14-17].*

Elijah struck the Jordon River with his cloak and the waters parted so Elisha and he could cross, *"Fifty men from the company of the prophets went and stood at a distance, facing the place where Elijah and Elisha had stopped at the Jordan. Elijah took his cloak, rolled it up, and struck the water with it. The water divided to the right and to the left and the two of them crossed over on dry ground," [2 Kings 2:7-8].*

Naaman, a man of authority and a Leper, desired healing from this debilitating disease. Elijah sent word by his servant Elisha to him with what he needed to do to cure his Leprosy: *"go and dip seven times in the waters of the*

*Jordan Rivers" [2 Kings 5:13-15]*, (we know from Scripture, seven [7] is symbolic for perfection).

When John Baptized in the waters of Jordan River the water was not an issue with the people as it was with the Leper. They wanted baptism, by John, for the forgiveness of their sin. They went in unclean and came out clean with a new birth to live a new life through John's Baptism.

- *Do we consider the waters we are in or the effect that those waters have on our Salvation?*

The Holy Spirit attends our baptism and re-birth. Naaman lacked faith; our re-birth is faith-based.

Jesus cleansed a Leper giving him a chance for a new life, *"When He was come down from the mountain, great multitudes followed Him. And behold, there came a leper and worshipped him, saying, Lord, if thou wilt, thou canst make me clean; and Jesus put forth His hand, and touched him, saying, I will; be thou clean; and immediately his leprosy was cleansed. And Jesus said unto him, "See thou tell no man; but go thy way, show thyself to the priest, and offer the gift that Moses commanded, for a testimony unto them," [Matthew 8:1-4].*

Leprosy, like a parasite, eats away at the skin destroying all sensation and nerves until there is no feeling. As Leprosy can physically destroy; so, can spiritual Leprosy deaden the senses, eat away at your soul and mind, as it does physically. Spiritual Leprosy is still common among men. Sin is ever-present.

The Leper came to Jesus because he desired freedom from this terrible disease eating away at him bodily, so we need to come to Jesus for our Spiritual Leprosy for that terrible disease of sin that eats away at our Spirituality. The Leper recognized it was beyond his ability to choose to heal himself. Our spiritual leprosy is beyond our ability to heal ourselves as well.

Healing from Leprosy was not common in Biblical times; there were communities designated for the ones to live who suffered from this devastating condition. Leprosy was not only an enfeebling disease, but it was a contagious disease as well. Sin is of this nature; it is crippling both emotionally, mentally, and spiritually. The point is, humans cannot heal themselves and requires assistance from the Great Physician who can heal all illness of man physical, spiritual, emotional, or mental.

We have the opportunity to come to Jesus for healing, as did the Leper who said, *"If you are willing."* God sent Jesus to heal our sins morally, spiritually, and physically. He took upon Himself our sins and died for them. John Baptized in the waters of the Jordan River flowing cleansing the sins away of all who desired to come to God. He was baptized with water only. Our baptism is with water and with the Holy Spirit.

God healed Miriam of Leprosy, after being outside of the camp for a while because she spoke against Moses' marriage to Zipporah and God punished her for speaking against His Prophet, *"When the cloud lifted from above the tent, Miriam's skin was leprous-it became as white as snow. Aaron turned toward her and saw that she had a defiling skin disease, [Numbers 12:10].*

Naaman, commander of the Army of King Aram, a valiant soldier, was also a person with leprosy, was healed in the Jordan River. However, not without questioning the instructions sent to him for healing by the Prophet Elijah. He asked why the dirty waters of the Jordan and not the clean waters of the other rivers in the Damascus area, *[2 Kings 5:1-26].*

There are spiritual and moral Jordan Rivers in our walk to eternity. One of the first that comes to mind is Sacrifice. In our service, to God sacrifice is necessary as a Christian; did Christ not sacrifice His life for humanity? No matter the sacrifice, Christ asks us to make it is ultimately working for our good, *"And we know that in all things works for the good of those who love God, who have been called according to His purpose,"* [Romans 8:28].

As Christ said, *"I am willing to heal you."* Are we willing to come to Christ and ask for healing for the spiritual and moral leprosy (sin) that besets us in our lives; we cannot manage that healing on our own. Miriam was healed after she repented of her sin, so will we be healed upon repentance and allowing Jesus to heal us and turn and live for Him. When we come to Jesus and the Jordon River He has for our cleansing, we wear garments of faith and acceptance not one of questioning and doubt. The scripture reminds us of what God said about those who do not have faith (doubt), *"But without faith, it is impossible to please Him: for he that cometh to God must believe that He is and that He is a rewarder of them that diligently seek Him,"* [Hebrews 11:6].

We, as Naaman, finally did, need to go outside our comfort zone (step-down) and realize ego can impede our blessings, which is, the Salvation Christ purchased for us. The rivers were cleaner in Damascus and the river in Israel was not clean but had the healing needed and desired by Naaman. Christ's blood purchased our healing.

- ***Can God wave His hand or speak the word and save us?***

He could have, just as the Prophet could have given Naaman a different healing method (sent him to a clean river in Damascus), but since we cannot heal ourselves, we accept the method given by the power from God through His tools of healing and Salvation. Once again, Naaman realized that his cleansing was in the Jordan River and not the clean rivers of Damascus.

It equals us telling the oncologist which therapy is best to treat the different cancers that beset humans rather than the one they know works better. We cannot treat ourselves medically or spiritually. We need an experienced Physician on earth for our physical illness; and [The] experienced Physician, Jesus our Savior for both Spiritual and Physical healings.

- ***We all stand at the spiritual Jordan River for our healing, or do you choose the clean waters of Damascus (one that you decide) the way of the world?***

The message Christ sent to John in his question whether He was the one or should he look for another said, *"Go back and tell John what you hear and see. The blind receive sight, the lame walk, those who have leprosy are cleansed, the deaf hears, the dead are raised, and the good news is proclaimed to the poor," [Matthew 11:4-5].*

There were then, as now, so many physical illnesses, and there was (is) not one Jesus could not cure.

God does not change; now as He was then, is our spiritual and Physical Jordan River – all cleansing comes through Jesus Christ [God, the Savior of the World].

Looking from the perspectives, of The New Testament, and the three [3] years Christ were on earth healing, cleansing, and spreading the Good News, we see Salvation through Paul's description of the death, burial, and resurrection of our Lord and Savior Jesus Christ, *"Now, brothers and sisters, I want to remind you of the gospel I preached to you, which you received and on which you have taken your stand. By this Gospel, you are saved, if you hold firmly to the word I preached to you. Otherwise, you have believed in vain. For what I received I passed on to you as of first importance: that Christ died for our sins according to the Scriptures, that He was buried, that He was raised on the third day according to the Scriptures," [I Corinthians 15:1-4].*

We see what Paul said about the Good News, *[I Corinthians 15:1-4]*. However, before he became a follower of Christ he was found to be fighting against God, *"And when we all had fallen to the ground, I heard a voice speaking to me and saying in the Hebrew language, 'Saul, Saul, why are you persecuting Me? It is hard for you to kick against the goads," [Acts 26:14].*

Fighting against God is a battle we cannot win, as Paul discovered, in his encounter with Jesus; as well, it is dangerous. A goad is a sharp stick with spikes on the end of it to move cattle along in the manner the owner so desires. My father had a goading stick for our cattle and my husband, and I had cattle prods; instruments with batteries in them to send shocks when it touched the hips of the cattle to move them especially when they were resistant. The black Brahma Bull we owned was overly stubborn and would charge if you were not careful; my husband stopped him with the cattle prod: it was hard for him to resist the sting it carries with it, as it is for us to fight against the God of Heaven and Savior of the World.

Christ is reigning now on His Throne of Eternity seated at the right hand of God. Stephen made this point at his stoning, *"Look," he said, "I see heaven open and the Son of Man standing at the right hand of God." At this, they covered their ears and, yelling at the top of their voices; they all rushed at him, dragged him out of the city, and began to stone him. Meanwhile, the witnesses laid their coats at the feet of a young man named Saul," [Acts 7:56-58].*

He saw the heavens open and Christ standing observing the torment and torture he went through for His Name's sake. When we suffer for the Name of Christ, we are blessed. Jesus still stands (He stood in our place and took our sins upon Himself) when He sees His faithful servants persecuted for righteousness. He suffered for our righteous and we will suffer because we chose to live righteously and not suffer from spiritual leprosy (sin) that destroys our eternal place with God.

Stephen's stoning brings to mind what the Scripture says that we are not to attack another, assault with any weapon of any kind. Those who helped stone him and the ones who stood by agreeing with them are all guilty of that [egregious] sin because He spoke the [Truth] because of that [Truth] he died. They killed the Savior of the world because they, like their ancestors, were uncircumcised in heart and mind, *"Lay hands suddenly on no man, neither be partaker of other men's sins: keep thyself pure,"* [I Timothy 5:22].

We know Jesus our Savior loves us and will heal us spiritually, morally, and physically if we ask and if it is according to His will. Luke points this fact out... granting us with the gift of the Holy Spirit, *"Which of you fathers if your son asks for a fish will give him a serpent instead? Or if he asks for an egg will give him a scorpion. If you then, though you are evil know how to give good gifts to your children, how much more will your Father in Heaven give the Holy Spirit to those who ask Him,"* [Luke 11:11-13].

We have healing of our physical illness through human doctors, which is temporary, but the Holy Spirit healing is eternal. If we suffer from the leprosy of sin without healing, it will cost us an eternity without God. The cleansing waters of the Spiritual Jordan are ready at all times, Christ does not give us a serpent (evil) or a scorpion (death) but grants us through the Second Person of the God Head: life, forgiveness, and strength to be faithful.

Our faithfulness increases with time, because of the weakness of the human flesh we have to learn to follow the teaching of Jesus and trust His Word. However, as Naaman finally realized, after a fashion of the time, there is but the one way, and that way is God's and this is faith that we believe and trust Him; now, as it did then, for Naaman will bring about our spiritual healing and strength.

God's blessings of healing, grace, mercy, and compassion are evident in our lives today. As well as it was the day that the man, lame from birth was healed through Peter with the power of God resting upon him, *"And, a certain man lame from his mother's womb was carried whom they laid daily at the gate of the temple, which is called Beautiful to ask alms of them that entered the into the temple. Who seeing Peter and John about to go into the temple, asked alms; And Peter fastening his eyes upon him with John said,"* Look on us. And *he gave heed unto them, expecting to receive something of them. Then Peter said, Silver and gold have I none; but such as I have given I give thee: In the name of Jesus Christ of Nazareth rise up and walk,"* [Acts 3:2-6].

As our garments, if faith grows in the knowledge of God, we grow stronger becoming grounded in our belief that God can do all things, including rid us of spiritual leprosy *"Surely the arm of the Lord is not too short to save, nor his ear too dull to hear," [Isaiah 59:1].*

Christ freed humanity from the curse of the Law and imparted the gift of grace and blessings from God.

- *Under which do you live?*

Abraham's Children are people of faith

TWENTY-NINE

# START WITH THE FLESH...END WITH THE SPIRIT!
# THE LAW AND GRACE

*"You foolish Galatians! Who has bewitched you? Before your very eyes, Jesus Christ was clearly portrayed, as crucified. I would like to learn just one thing from you: Did you receive the Spirit by the works of the law, or by believing what you heard? Are you so foolish? After beginning by means of the Spirit, are you now trying to finish by means of the flesh? Have you experienced so much in vain–if it really was in vain? So again, I ask, does God give you His Spirit and work miracles among you by the works of the law, or by your believing what you heard? So also, Abraham "believed God, and it was credited to him as righteousness." Understand, then, that those who have faith are children of Abraham," [Galatians 3:1-7].*

Humans begin with the flesh and should end with the Spirit. Paul warned the Galatians about their reverting to obeying the Law. Law and grace we look at through two different telescopes of reasoning. We cannot do both; we cannot live by the Spirit and in the same stroke of existence obey the law is impossible to do. The letter of the Law Christ took them upon Himself at the Cross of Calvary, Paul wrote, *"Blotting out the handwriting of ordinances that was against us, which was contrary to us, and took it out of the way, nailing it to His cross," [Colossians 2:14].*

This, I compared to one trying to obey both Old Testament and New Testament in the same stroke of time, which is Law and Grace.

We are looking through the first-century telescope lens, which was a long time ago, but the encouragement we find there to serve God even unto death (possible loss of life in our service) and the crown will be there for those who serve God in the 21st-Century as well.

The Apostle Paul went into specific details about the dangers of trying to live under the Law after Christ has fulfilled its requirements and paid our account before Our Heavenly Father and God. He repeated at length the cons of the Law and the pros of Salvation, which are grace and mercy through Jesus Christ our Lord and Savior.

Dressed for the Kingdom of God

Jesus blotted out these charges against us. When thinking of something blotted out is to make obscure, insignificant, or inconsequential...wiping out, destroying. Christ washed our sins away with His blood and gave us the chance to begin again...a fresh start.

- *Ask yourself, is faith alone too easy, and my confidence level so low in putting my trust in serving God through faith that I have to drag the law along with it as a prop?*

We cannot have it both ways. We cannot get close to God by obeying rules and regulations. The people of the Old Testament served under the Law, and they were not pleasing to God, because they disobeyed the [Letter of the Law] constantly.

We can study to show ourselves approved of God, but that alone is not enough putting that faith into action is also required. The Scripture tells us Christ sent the Holy Spirit (the third person of the Godhead) to assist, help, and guide us in our faith. Without the Holy Spirit involved, we are not doing as Christ asked. However, we can be secure, in our Faith that God is a God of His Word when we listen to our Teacher and Guide here on earth. We listen and learn from the Holy Spirit. If we are not listening and go our own way then we have transgressed against the will of God for our lives. We cannot be guilty of wearing garments of feigning ignorance, acting as if we do not know what is right or wrong in God's sight or that we are transgressing His Commandments. We cannot afford to allow [pretending] to be part of our lives it will lead to the destruction of our souls.

Christ nailed the Law to the Cross thereby purchasing our Salvation enabling us to live through Him with the grace and mercy Salvation affords. The Holy Spirit is our seal, our guarantor.

- *Consider the following question: are the (Law) rules or regulations more profitable than living by Faith?*

We must ask ourselves this question as Paul asked the Galatians. With all the evidence of Salvation before them, why do they still try to obey the Law? *"Faith is the substance of things hoped for and the evidence of things not seen,"* [Hebrews 11:1].

Living by Faith and [dependence] upon God and the only way we get close to God is through the Holy Spirit operating in our lives since we serve God in Spirit and Truth.

Again, Scripture reminds us of what Paul said to the Galatians, *"Have you experienced so much in vain-if it really was in vain? So again, I ask, does God give you His Spirit and work miracles among you by the works of the law, or by your believing what you heard? So also, Abraham "believed God, and it was credited to him as righteousness," [Galatians 3:4-6].*

Faith (belief) in God is righteousness. God accounts it to us as He did Abraham, *"So also Abraham "believed God, and it was credited to him as righteousness," [Ibid].*

Living under the Law, we are cursed; because, man cannot continue in the things of the Law, *"For all who rely on the works of the law are under a curse, as it is written: "Cursed is everyone who does not continue to do everything written in the Book of the Law." Clearly no one who relies on the law is justified before God, because "the righteous will live by faith," [Galatians 3:10-11].*

No one living by the Law or attempting to so in this day and time, as it was after 33 A.D., is justified before God, *[Ibid].*

The third chapter of Galatians paints a perfect picture, for us to see, the contrast of living by Faith and trying to obey the letter of the Law. The Law is not based on Faith, *[Galatians 3:12].* Christ was the cursed One hanging on a tree, *"Christ redeemed us from the curse of the Law by becoming a curse for us, for it is written: "Cursed is everyone who is hung on a pole," [Galatians 3:13].*

He redeemed us [Gentiles] that we might not be apart from them [Jews] but receive the blessings given, *"He redeemed us in order that the blessing given to Abraham might come to the Gentiles through Christ Jesus so that by faith we might receive the promise of the Spirit," [Galatians 3:14].*

- *Why do we then try to travel back beyond that cruel cross and reinvent for ourselves that curse again?*

We cannot serve God under an umbrella with both Law and Grace.

- *Why do humans continue to try to drag the Law along with the freedom Christ gave us in the Grace that comes with the purchase of Salvation?*

The Law offered no grace – only the letter of the Law; it was not merciful. Cramming too much of anything into one area is not efficient in any situation.

The two crammed together equals putting new wine in old bottles, *"And no man puts new wine into old bottles: else the new wine doth burst the bottles, and the wine is spilled, and the bottles will be marred: but new wine must be put into new bottles,"* [Mark 2:22].

Also, trying to put a new cloth with old will cause a rip or tear. I know this is a fact from experience as a seamstress. If you put a piece of new cloth with old, the elasticity in the new cloth is stronger than the elasticity of the old cloth and the strength or the pull of the new cloth will tear the old cloth. When I grew up as a child, if my mother mended a piece of clothing, she would wash the piece of new material several times letting it dry each time before she sewed it with the old material. She never sewed new cloth with old without properly preparing the new cloth to mend the rip or tear. This method worked for my mom it was necessary since my parents could not afford to buy new outfits.

God's plan, for our Salvation, does not include the Law. Christ fulfilled the Law. It is our tutor to bring us to Christ; as well, it gives us comfort and hopes that God keeps His promises. We have Faith in Christ it is the substance…Hope comes from this substance.

God cannot be in our lives under the conditions of the Law. There is no continuous sacrifice of the blood of bulls and goats, or a Priest from the Levitical Priesthood to intercede for us so that sacrifice is pleasing to God… God sent that perfect sacrifice once and for all, for our redemption so that we might live by Faith.

We cannot base our faith on what is seen or touched. However, it is essential that faith is because we believe what we cannot see and has evidence that the written Word of God is true.

Heaven is where we cannot see it with the naked eye either but know through Faith, Jesus went to prepare a place for us that we might be where He is for an eternity when our time on earth is over, *"Let not your heart be troubled; you believe in God, believe also in Me. In My Father's house are many mansions; if it were not so, I would have told you. I go to prepare a place for you. And, if I go and prepare a place for you, I will come again and receive you unto Myself; that where I am, there you may be also. And where I go you know, and the way you know"*, [John 14:1-4].

In contrast, eternity without God is there, as well. Jesus said to all those who do not obey his commands. To avoid an eternity without God first we obey the Gospel, *"Moreover, brethren, I declare unto you the gospel which I preached unto you, which also ye have received, and wherein ye stand; By which also ye are saved, if ye keep in memory what I preached unto you unless ye have believed in vain," [I Corinthians 15:1-2].*

Secondly, go into the vineyard and work, *"They also will answer, 'Lord, when did we see you hungry or thirsty or a stranger or needing clothes or sick or in prison, and did not help you?' "He will reply, 'Truly I tell you, whatever you did not do for one of the least of these, you did not do for me.' "Then they will go away to eternal punishment, but the righteous to eternal life," [Matthew 25:44-46].*

We know this because He said it…we also know Hell is there because He said it. Some were under the Law who died separated from God because of disobedience and unbelief. We sit and consider these facts….

We were prisoners under the control of sin. The Law was the Guardian until Christ came. Now, He has provided a pathway away from this control.

- *No longer are we under that cruel taskmaster, Christ freed us why would we want to be under the taskmaster of the Law?*

There is no justification before God when humans try living under the Law, *"But Scripture has locked up everything under the control of sin, so that what was promised, being given through faith in Jesus Christ, might be given to those who believe. Before the coming of this Faith, we were held in custody under the law, locked up until the faith that was to come would be revealed. So, the law was our guardian until Christ came that we might be justified by faith," [Galatians 3:22-24].*

The Law was good until the Seed came God promised Abraham. Think of the workplace there are instances when the supervisor, managers, etc. you work under are cruel and unrelenting sometimes simply because they can or is in a position of authority.

The Law was that authority Christ nailed to the Cross. That Law came through angels or a mediator. Now we are under His authority but have grace, mercy, and His Precious Blood covering our sins. Christ is not a harsh and merciless taskmaster. Think of how much better off we are than under a specific letter of the Law. Every jot and tittle of the Law must be obeyed, or a consequence follows. Specificity was definitely in every moment of Israel's lives under the Law, "do it or."

Consider these facts....

**We are Abraham's seed if we are people of Faith.** Those who belong to Christ are people of Faith according to the promise. God does not break His promises. God's Word is Truth, He does not promise and then does not back up those promises, "*God is not a man that He should lie; neither the son of man that He should repent: hath He said, and shall He not do it? Or hath He spoken, and shall He not make it good?"[Numbers 23:19].*

God is all-powerful, "*Surely the arm of the Lord is not too short to save, nor His ear too dull to hear," [Isaiah 59:1].*

He is a God of His Word, "*So shall my word be that goes forth out of my mouth: it shall not return unto Me void, but it shall accomplish that which I please, and it shall prosper in the thing whereto I sent it," [Isaiah 55:11].*

**We are no longer under the tutorship of the Law,** "*Now I say, that the heir, as long as he is a child, different nothing from a servant, though He be Lord of all, but is under tutors and governors until the time appointed of the father. Even so we, when we were children, were in bondage under the elements of the world: But when the fullness of the time was come, God sent forth His Son, made of a woman, made under the law, to redeem them that were under the law, that we might receive the adoption of sons and because ye are sons. God hath sent forth the Spirit of His Son into your hearts, crying, Abba, Father; wherefore, thou art no more a servant, but a son; and if a son, then an heir, of God through Christ," [Galatians 4:1-7].*

**The Law was our custodian until grace and mercy came.** Until then were slaves. Sin bought the Law of God into being. The falsehood perpetrated by Satan ushered in disobedience because of the thirst for knowing what God knows. We, as children or heirs to Salvation and Eternity of peace with God, need supervising, as our children need supervising until at the appointed time of adulthood when they come into their own. We as parents keep a close watch on their lives and what they are learning, who they associate with, all this in training them so they can eventually make reasonable and hopefully rational decisions.

God kept man under the Law until that appointed time He set for Jesus to come into the world through the flesh and live among us that we may know Him and believe that He is God, all-powerful, all-knowing, and all-seeing He loves us as His little brothers and sisters, yet He is our Savior. The spiritual forces of the world at that time, as is now, are still working against us in high places.

We are no longer under the Law but fight the good fight of faith daily because the forces of evil that work against us are present, our adversary (underwriter) and his adherents are alive and well. We come out of the world into the Kingdom of Christ though the evil still exists and we have a Six Star General leading our charge against these forces.

He provides the armor we need to fight this battle. Christ is General of the Armies (GAS) in our spiritual battle as the General are in the physical, are (five) star Generals or GAS.

History states that George Washington was the only Six-Star General in the memoirs of this nation. The point is there was only one that ever existed. At this point, Christ is the only Savior that we will ever have – God is a God of oneness.

As God is one, Jesus led the charge to purchase us from the terrible jaws of sin, which ushered in the Law. We no longer need the trainer. Jesus sent the gift of the Holy Spirit once we obey the Gospel as our teacher and guide. He dwells with us and in us that we might know how to be pleasing to God.

Christ is the only Six Star General of the Spiritual world.

Now, we know God and is known by God; we are no longer slaves but are free. We are Christians, people of Christ. The Law was weak, and life was miserable under its instruction. Our focus should be on seeking the Kingdom of Heaven and its righteousness not on trying to dig up the Law and its infirmities, *"Howbeit then, when ye knew not God, ye did service unto them which by nature are no gods. Now, after that ye have known God, or rather are known of God, how turn you again to the weak and beggarly elements, whereunto ye desire again to be in bondage? Ye observe days, and months, and times, and years,"* [Galatians 4:8–10].

The teacher [Law] did not bring joy. The Galatians seemed to have lost their joy. We cannot turn back to our former life. The characteristics of that life are still there; they bring heartache and misery. We cannot meet the expectations of people or religious day celebrations and times that were done away with on the cross. It is easy to lose your footing on a slippery slope is what the world and the Law offer with no one to catch you but your adversary. The fall is endless and when you reach the bottom of the slope you are broken, injured beyond repair, or it will take a lifetime to recover from all the spiritual surgeries and broken bones.

Sisters, garments are worn using this rule of conduct is akin to treading a slippery slope. Satan is waiting for life and this world to crush you, which gives him a decided advantage. Paul's concern for the Galatians is also his concern for us today. The world does not care about you or about your suffering; it is of little concern to it. We cannot be callous and uncaring. We are part of the Body of Christ.

Jesus gave us the command to care for our fellow man as He did when He was among us. He cared for the sick and broken, we are to do the same. We are no longer under the controlling authority of the Law and the values of the world, but received a gift of Salvation from God through Christ who nailed it to the Cross. He can heal all illnesses, care for the sick, and comfort the grieving.

The people of Christ are ambassadors standing in His place, in regard, to our fellowman. Jesus' response will be completely different to those who were faithful in all things while they worked out their salvation in fear and trembling; as well as, carrying out His commands to love and obey during our time here on earth, *"Then the King will say to those on His right hand, 'Come, you blessed of My Father, inherit the kingdom prepared for you from the foundation of the world. For, I was hungry, and you gave Me food. I was thirsty and you gave Me a drink. I was a stranger, and you took Me in. I was naked and you clothed Me. I was sick and you visited Me. I was in prison, and you came to Me."*

Matthews continued furthermore, *"Then the righteous will answer Him, saying, "When did we see You a stranger, take you in, or naked, and clothe You? Or when did we see You sick, or in prison, and come to You?' Also, the King will answer and say to them, 'Assuredly, I say to you, inasmuch as you did it to one of the least of these my brethren, you did it to Me,"* [Matthew 25:34-40].

We are children of promise the free woman Sarah not under that formally recognized tool but children of promise. Paul writes, *"Tell me, you who want to be under the Law, are you not aware of what the Law says? For it is written that Abraham had two sons, one by the slave woman and the other by the free woman. His son by the slave woman was born according to the flesh, but his son by the freewoman was born as the result of a divine promise. These things are being taken figuratively. The women represent two covenants. One covenant is from Mount Sinai and bears children who are to be slaves: This is Hagar."*

*"Now Hagar stands for Mount Sinai in Arabia and corresponds to the present city of Jerusalem because she is in slavery with her children. But the Jerusalem that is above is free, and she is our mother. For it is written, "Be glad, barren woman, you who never bore a child; shout for joy and cry aloud, you who were never in labor; because more are the children of the desolate woman than of her who has a husband." Now you, brothers, and sisters, like Isaac, are children of promise," [Galatians 4:21-28].*

Being justified by the Law alienates us from Christ for the circumcision is of the heart (faith) and not the flesh. We cannot be pleasing to God by living and observing the teachings of the Old Testament. Paul warns if this is what is being done the hands of time are turned back; we have fallen from grace, *"Again I declare to every man who lets himself be circumcised that he is obligated to obey the whole law. ⁴You who are trying to be justified by the law have been alienated from Christ; you have fallen away from grace," [Hebrews 5:3-4].*

When our hearts are hardened to Jesus' sacrifice and blood, it insults the Spirit of Grace. By desiring to maintain the practices through the dead sacrifices of the symbolic blood of bulls and goats, we are [living] outside of Christ, *"Of how much sorer punishment suppose ye, shall he be who hath trodden under-foot the Son of God, and hath counted the Blood of the Covenant; wherewith He was sanctified an unholy thing and hath done despite unto, the Spirit of Grace?" [Hebrews 10:29].*

Each of us is to have the determination and resolve not to allow anyone to interrupt our race for eternity. Jesus provided life through the Spirit and is not led by the tutor, *"For in Jesus Christ neither circumcision avails anything nor uncircumcision; but faith which works by love," [Galatians 5:6].*

One cannot say they walk by the Spirit and satisfy fleshly needs, for the flesh and the Spirit are contrary to each other; in essence, they are in constant conflict.***How can we serve God sisters straddling the fence?***

If we walk by the Spirit we walk as Christ said and not the world if we follow the Spirit we are not subject under the Law, *"For, brethren, ye have been called unto liberty; only use not liberty for an occasion to the flesh, but by love serve one another. For all the Law is fulfilled in one word, even in this; Thou shalt love thy neighbor as thyself. But if ye bite and devour one another, take heed that ye be not consumed one of another. This I say then, Walk in the Spirit, and ye shall not fulfill the lust of the flesh. For the flesh lusts against the Spirit, and the Spirit against the flesh: and these are contrary the one to the other: so that ye cannot do the things that ye would. But if ye be led of Spirit ye are not under the Law," [Galatians 5:13-18].*

Paul was concerned in references to the Galatians, as well as us in this century, about the vices of Satan. These concerns are also written for our benefit, *"Now the works of the flesh are manifest, which: are these, Adultery, fornication, uncleanness, lasciviousness, Idolatry, witchcraft, hatred, variance, emulations, wrath, strife, seditions, heresies, envying's, murders, drunkenness, reviling's; and such like: of the which I tell you before, as I have also told you in time past; that they which do such things, shall not inherit the kingdom of God," [Galatians 5:19-21].*

Paul also reminds us we know the virtues of the Spirit, *"But the fruit of the Spirit is love, joy, peace, longsuffering, gentleness, goodness, faith, meekness, and temperance: against such, there is no law. And they that are Christ's have crucified the flesh with the affections and lusts. If we live in the Spirit, let us also walk in the Spirit. Let us not be desirous of vain glory, provoking one another, envying one another," [Galatians 5:22-26].*

We are new creations in Christ, wearing the garments sisters, of a new creation, or new women, with spiritually focused thoughts and desires, caring for the poor, sick, and disadvantaged of this life. If we live by the Spirit let us walk by the Spirit. Sacrifice is a difficult level to reach. It is not realized overnight, rather a triumph is over time eliminating consistently all those sins that have kept us under bondage so that we might practice selflessness.

Sacrifices that are more difficult to make than others are the ones our adversary focuses on in our life making the pathway difficult filled with temptations hard to overcome because we continue to dragging along or falling back into the curses of the letter of the Law. Christ overcame, so we can through the Spirit, for He is God sent to lead and guide us in all righteousness.

Studying the Word of God widens the lens of who God is, what He did to provide Salvation; why Christ came to earth; and lived in a human body for [33] years to purchase salvation for humanity. When the timeline God put in place over the centuries came to past as God said and what all prophets preached for centuries as at the point in which God's promises.

When the appointed time arrived, the promised Messiah was there and died on the Cross fulfilling the promise in the Garden of Eden. He will crush his head and he will bruise his heel, *"And I will put enmity between you and the woman, and between your offspring and hers; He will crush your head, and you will strike his heel," [Genesis 3:15].*

When we as a child or even potential child of God before obedience and acceptance of the Salvation Christ purchased, use the wider lens of the Word of God, Salvation, and the one body unified body will understand what God plan was from the beginning.

A Prodigal People....Servants of Christ.

CHAPTER THIRTY

# A PRODIGAL PEOPLE
# COUNTING ALL LOSS AS GAIN
# PART II

The Book of Luke gives another example of the price one pays for choosing the pleasures of this world over the treasure of the Kingdom of God, *"Jesus continued: There was a man who had two sons. The younger one said to his father, 'Father, give me my share of the estate.'* So, he divided his property between them, *"Not long after that, the younger son got together all he had, set off for a distant country, and there squandered his wealth in wild living. After he had spent everything, there was a severe famine in that whole country, and he began to be in need. So, he went and hired himself out to a citizen of that country, who sent him to his fields to feed pigs. He longed to fill his stomach with the pods that the pigs were eating, but no one gave him anything," [Luke 15:11-16].*

The Scripture reminds us, *"The love of money is the root of all kinds of evil."* We cannot serve God and Mammon. Christ said, *"No man can serve two masters either you will hate one and love the other or you will be devoted to the one and despise the other. You cannot serve both God and money," [Matthew 6:24].*

This was not only a warning (advice) from Christ to the Church at Laodicea *[Revelation 3:14-22,* and their lukewarmness which made Him sick; but, also for us today, whether it is an individual or a congregational, the application is the same. Further, we are counseled by Paul in his letter to Timothy, *"For the love of money is the root of all evil: which while some coveted after, they have erred from the faith, and pierced themselves through with many sorrows," [I Timothy 6:10].*

This love of earthly wealth can cause so many problems. Our Savior gave a list of griefs to the Church at Laodicea that He sees not in each of the members' life, but in the entire congregation; they were all guilty, being neither hot nor cold before His Throne making him sick. We know how it feels when our children go so far out into the left field with the activities in their lives doing things we as parents raised them to know are not acceptable. To hear or know what they do in these instances makes us nauseated and sick in heart and mind at what they are doing.

We counsel our offspring trying to get them back on track again. Christ gave all for us. He reminds us to consider that we count things lost to Him when we gain in things in the earthly realm, [i.e., wealth] and put them before our God, we are losing our chance at Salvation and neglecting to serve Him because our focus is on the earthly wealth and the lives that wealth provides us. We cannot serve both (choices have consequences). Christ warns we will always love one more than we love the other. It takes a strong person, faithful to God, and desires to be pleasing to Christ to put Him before their wealth. God blesses us with those gifts that enable us to serve him and serve others, because there will, always be on this earth, those who need assistance.

Christ said, "*For ye have the poor with you always, and whenever ye will ye may do them good: but Me ye have not always,*" *[Mark 14:7; Matthew 26:11].*

Christ expects us to continue the work He started and left for us to do while we are here.

- ***What garments or examples are you wearing?***

Our garments set the archetype while we sit on the banks of life for all to see. We are Ambassadors for Christ; members of the Body of Christ and through our actions and us are how people in this world see Jesus.

Sisters, we are at the top of the hill of choice, there is no ladder or bridge to use to get us over the choice of counting loss or gain. It comes down to the world (what we want) or Jesus (what is necessary to be pleasing to God). There is always a valley or an unknown path we walk in this life; however, walking with and trusting Christ can help us navigate any unknowns in life we encounter. Choices in this life are not always the easiest thing to make; however, through Christ, we can have that confidence in our choices.

The simple things in life like choosing food for health benefits even those choices, at times, are not easy for us to make. It is hard not to eat that doughnut or ice cream with all the toppings, or the 6-ounce steak, just to name a few. However, none of the three named food items with continual partaking of the pleasure they give to our taste buds will yield, in the end, a healthy body, or lifestyle. In the short run, it does not seem to make that much of a difference to our health, so we continue to indulge and enjoy the decadence of the taste.

Six months later or less, the results begin to manifest themselves in how our clothes fit, and the different areas of our bodies are re-shaped. The scales tell us we are off-track. In a short time, and ultimately our lifestyle changed, we look and feel different, it can produce stress and set off a battery of bad habits taking one down another path than intended all because of the choices we made to indulge in a little too much enjoyment to satisfy our appetites.

Translate this example into a Spiritual one. Those simple little things of this life in which we indulge do not seem harmful at the time. This is another short-run choice. "I can give it up anytime I want." This statement sounds familiar; one that is used so much among humans. In the long run, the more you partake, the more enjoyable it becomes like the ice cream with all the toppings. Our Spiritual bodies began to take an alternate shape or feelings become confused when pulled in two different directions.

There is no bridge or ladder to get you across that valley. If we try to cross it by climbing down and walking across the dangers, we will not be successful. There are too many traps and dangers Satan has set along the path to prevent your success. We choose while we are at the top of the hill when the choice is clear, at an unspecified point in our lives, we are counting loss and gain.

Once Satan's victim is in one of his traps, sin's cancer metastasizes quickly. He continues to add attractive traps leading one deeper and deeper into sin without any way back. Man (humans) cannot outwit Satan. It is wise to keep in mind he, (Satan) wrote the rules, and they are dangerous. Our Savior warns us, "*Satan is the god of this world and the father of the lie,*" *[Ibid]*. How stauncher warning does humans need to recognize they are playing in a game that they are guaranteed to lose – part of the illusion is that those activities you engage in that are so pleasant are his main snares used to trick man. James reminds us to, "*Resist the devil and he will flee from you,*" *[James 4:7b]*.

We are all bitten by the elements of sin regardless of who/whom we are, "*For all have sinned and fallen short of the Glory of God,*" *[Romans 3:23]*.

There is an idiom mother used when we were growing and learning from a particular experience, "Once bitten, twice shy." Essentially, sisters, avoid that particular sin and add it to your column of success in your journal of the experience. In the future avoid that sin; its teeth are just as dangerous as the first time it bit you. Runaway if it is still a temptation flee from the devil and his attractive lies and alternative truth he pushed on Eve. In essence, he told Eve, 'Here's the thing, you will not die; but, become knowledgeable, you will be like God."

Satan is a god of emotions, thoughts, and desires; remember at the beginning, the world was not that old. God destroyed the known world at that time with a flood because the imaginations and intents of the heart of man were evil continually. He (Satan) will work on your mind with insinuations of the desires and pleasures you want in your life. Keep in mind sisters, he hangs around and is not visible to the naked eyes, but the evil results are visible he brings about through man.

Choices are hard, we cannot have both in this life, like the food we eat if we want healthy bodies, it is necessary to choose those foods that will promote good health. Physical health means mental and emotional health. The choices we make have a total effect on us. If we want Spiritual health, we chose the path to walk Christ left for us to follow.

- *Do we choose Christ and count the gains as a loss to the world or do we choose the world and all its attractions, pleasures, and count that as a loss to Christ?*

One counting leads to an eternity of peace and the other counting leads to an eternity apart from God and in pain and suffering, including our lives before we leave this world.

Either choice we make trials and tribulations are a part of it in the short run; however, in the end, is where we see the benefits; whether positive or negative the choice requires leaving things behind. The Rich Young Ruler desired to be saved, *"And a certain ruler asked him, saying Good Master, what shall I do to inherit eternal life?" [Luke 18:18]* – Jesus told him what he needed to gain eternal life, *"Jesus said to him, "If you want to be perfect, go, sell what you have and give to the poor, and you will have treasure in heaven; and come, follow Me," [Matthew 19:21].*

The choice Christ gave the Rich Young Ruler was difficult for him to make. Jesus told the followers and onlookers, *"And again I say unto you, it is easier for a camel to go through the eye of a needle, than for a rich man to enter into the Kingdom of God.," [Matthew 19:24, Mark 10:17-3].*

The Rich Young Ruler went away sad because he had great wealth. Gaining Jesus and Salvation cost. Gaining the world and all its pleasures cost. We are either followers or onlookers the choice is ours. God is not willing that any should perish, but all are saved, *"The Lord is not slack concerning His promise, as some count slackness, but is longsuffering toward us, not willing that any should perish but that all should come to repentance," [2 Peter 3:9].*

The statement Jesus made was hard for not only the Rich Young Ruler but also those of who heard him say "Eat of His Body and drink of His Blood was a hard saying *"From that time many of his disciples went back and walked no more with him."* Then said Jesus unto the twelve, *Will ye also go away? Then Simon Peter answered him, Lord, to whom shall we go? Thou hast the words of eternal life. And we believe and are sure that thou art the Christ, the Son of the living God." Jesus answered them, "Have not I chosen you twelve, and one of you is a devil?" [John 6:66-70].*

The Rich man had enormous treasure here on earth. Christ offered him an opportunity to lay up treasure where it would be eternal. Eternal treasures would not rust or eventually fade away or be lost to him. We cannot allow the material things of this earth that are necessary for our survival to be what we concentrate solely on but seek the greater treasure of Heaven and Eternity. No man can steal the treasures we lay up in Heaven by serving God and doing His will.

Here on earth at any moment, any time, all the material possessions humans work hard for can be taken away, stolen, we can lose them, the Stock Market, Banks, and the economy can all fail without notice. When these things falter in life resources dry up. All the resources of comfort we have can disappear virtually overnight. When we leave this earth, whatever treasures we have accumulated here, stays here, we cannot take them with us. The sage saying, "I have never seen an armored car following a hearse," is a true statement no one has ever taken the earthly wealth with them; although the Pharaohs, of Egypt, hoarded their riches and put them in their pyramids or tombs, in the end, could not take them beyond this earth. Those riches were [are] still there to be [have] been discovered and taken away by man to either enjoy in a museum or to sell to provide them the pleasures of this life.

There is a place where the treasure we lay up will never fade away or thieves can come in and steal. We work for that treasure while here on earth. Jesus' promises are solid and eternal. No one can take the individual treasure we work for by being obedient to God and doing His will for our lives, because they are spiritual, not physical. Hear what Jesus said, *"Lay not up for yourselves treasures upon earth, where moth and rust doth corrupt, and where thieves break through and steal. But lay up for yourselves treasures in heaven, where neither moth nor rust doth corrupt, and where thieves do not break through nor steal for where your treasure is, there will your heart be also,"* [Matthew 6:19-21].

God's plan predestined us according to His will, *" He predestined us for adoption to sonship through Jesus Christ, in accordance with His pleasure and will to the praise of His glorious grace, which He has freely given us in the One He loves,"* [Ephesians 1:5-6].

The Father in heaven had a purpose for our life. That purpose is not to live for ourselves, fulfilling earthly desires and dismissing the will of our Father in Heaven and the price Jesus paid for our Salvation. Our Spiritual blessings are in Christ chosen by God in Christ before He created the world, *"For He chose us in Him before the creation of the world to be holy and blameless in His sight. In love, He predestined us for adoption to sonship through Jesus Christ, in accordance with His pleasure,"* [Ephesians 1:4-5a].

Christ gave all for us because He loves us. He provided redemption for us through the blood sacrifice of His life. Christ counted the loss of His people to the world as a gain for Him to come and fulfill the plan of God and the redemption of His people as important. He acted on that desire to have us with Him for eternity. We must ask ourselves if we (act) on or (accept) the Salvation Christ purchased for us!

Paul reminds us, *"In Him, we have redemption through His Blood, the forgiveness of sins, in accordance with the riches of God's grace that He lavished on us. With all wisdom and understanding, He made known to us the mystery of His will according to His good pleasure, which He purposed in Christ to be put into effect when the times reach their fulfillment – to bring unity to all in heaven and on earth under Christ,"* [Ephesians 1:7-10].

We must realize, as Paul did, that Christ is the beginning and the end of life on this earth and is the Master of eternity. No human can offer you the certainty of anything in the present or the future; each of our lives every moment are at the will of God and not of our own, *"For in Him we live, and move, and have our being; as certain also of your own poets have said, For we are also His offspring. Forasmuch then as we are the offspring of God, we ought not to think that the Godhead is like unto gold, or silver, or stone, graven by art and man's device.And the times of this ignorance God winked at; but now commanded all men everywhere to repent," [Acts 17:28-30].*

Jesus came to seek and save the lost.

- *Are you counting from the hill or counting trying to cross the valley?*

Think about the Chapter of Faith *[Hebrews 11:1-40]* and all the ones that counted the gain of Christ and eternal Salvation more worthy than that of the pleasures of the world. Our service to God requires obedience and faithfulness holding Jesus' hand and letting Him lead us. He is the only bridge or ladder that will get us to an eternity of peace.

Christ bridged that gap between God and man lost to him in the garden where the first choices of gain and loss occurred made by Adam and Eve. As well, through them came the first defiance and disobedience of the Commandments of God. Every command, law, or instruction is given man by God is for our benefit. However, He does, in those commands and instructions give us a choice. Gain or loss, the choice is ours to make.

- *What does your garment of choice look like?*
- *What choice will you make, passing pleasure or eternal peace, joy, and happiness in the presence of God, Jesus, and the Holy Spirit?*

We seek God while He may be found, not after a lifetime of living, and in the interim becoming callous and hardened through sin and pleasure; thereby, creating a separation from God. He does not let sin abide in His presence.

We cannot use ignorance to excuse our sins before God, but rather we are to confess our sins and ask for forgiveness and help from Jesus, *"We all sin and fall short of the Glory of God"*, *[Romans 3:23].*

*"Repent ye therefore, and be converted, that your sins may be blotted out when the times of refreshing shall come from the presence of the Lord. And He shall send Jesus Christ, which before was preached unto you: Whom the heaven must receive until the times of restitution of all things, which God hath spoken by the mouth of all His holy prophets since the world began," [Acts 3:19-21].*

In 2004, I heard a sermon preached by Brother David Myers. He made the point in his sermon the profitability of counting all things lost to gain Christ, said, "Everything important to you spiritually comes from God our source of power on the way to something else." [Minister Azalea City Church of Christ, 2004].

*"As for other matters, brothers, and sisters, pray for us that the message of the Lord may spread rapidly and be honored, just as it was with you. And pray that we may be delivered from wicked and evil people, for not everyone has faith. But the Lord is faithful, and He will strengthen you and protect you from the evil one. We have confidence in the Lord that you are doing and will continue to do the things we command. May the Lord direct your hearts into God's love and Christ's perseverance,"* [2 Thessalonians 3:1-5].

- Paul knew he was dependent upon God's power.
- Paul knew he was dependent upon God's patience.

Jesus is waiting with open arms to welcome His children back into the fold. Think of the example of the Prodigal son and his desire to leave his father and go into the world. After a fashion of the time, he discovered what he had at his father's house is where he had everything but found no place or friends in the world after all his riches were gone; he spent it all on riotous living and pleasure, left alone, and no one cared.

He went from wealthy to feeding swine, which was an abomination to the Jews. Going after the things of the world is in direct conflict with our Father's will. After burning that candle at both ends, returned home and his father greeted him with gladness and joy because a son who was lost returned to the fold!

- ***Do we realize sometimes we burn our candles, at both ends?***

He walked out of that fog he seemed to be in and realized he had the best of both worlds with his father *"When he came to his senses, he said, "How many of my father's hired servants have food to spare, and here I am starving to death! I will set out, go back to my father, and say to him, "Father, I have sinned against heaven and against you. I am no longer worthy to be called your son; make me like one of your hired servants,"* [Luke 15:17-20a].

The Prodigal Son, for the first time, thinking rationally, acted!

He left his pride and quest for independence behind, *"So he got up and went to his father, but while he was still a long way off, his father saw him and was filled with compassion for him; he ran to his son, threw his arms around him, and kissed him. "The son said to him, 'Father, I have sinned against heaven and against you. I am no longer worthy to be called your son,"* [Luke 15:20b-21].

The Prodigal Son returned home before it was too late. Experience is the best teacher. Attending the [University of Hard Knocks] paints reality for us as nothing else will. When we learn this hard lesson and come home, no one can convince us to leave again. I am sure the Prodigal Son did not. Pride is a dangerous characteristic of human makeup. To lean into its desires can lead humans into thinking they can make it without the God of Heaven. It is good to be independent but in the right context, not when it comes to our God and Savior.

Sisters, in this Scripture notice, that his father did not speak harshly to him. Nor did he say you wasted my money on riotous living why should I take you back? *"But, the father said to his servants, bring forth the best robe, and put it on him; and put a ring on his hand, and shoes on his feet. And bring hither the fatted calf, and kill it, and let us eat, and be merry: For this, my son was dead, and is alive again; he was lost and is found, and they began to be merry," [Luke 15:22-24].*

He counted the loss of pleasures of the world and fulfilling his desires and counted going home to his father as gain. We sisters can stray, there is always that possibility; anyone can get off-track. The paths, on the cliffs of life, which we walk, are still narrow and it is easy to slip if we allow the pleasure of the world and our desires to pull us away from our Father's House.

Jesus welcomes the children of His Kingdom home with celebration and joy, *"I say unto you, that likewise, joy shall be in heaven over one sinner that repents, more than over ninety and nine just persons, which need no repentance," [Luke 15:7].*

- *Just think of the joy that it brings to heaven; God and His angels celebrate because one came home. Can we identify with this feeling when our straying children come back to the fold after they have gone out into the world and learned only trouble is there and safety is with God?*

I recall something my mother told my siblings and me as we grew, "If you love someone/something set it/them free. If they/it returns to you it/they were yours and if it/they do not it/they were never yours from the beginning." That statement made by my mother has proved over time to be very true. God set us free from sin and He gives us the gift of choice. In the Old Testament Book of Joshua, the people of God assembled to hear a message from God through Joshua. He reminded them of the blessing God had given them since their freedom from bondage in Egypt.

Joshua then added, *"If it seems good to you to serve the gods on the other side of the river then do that, but as for me and my house we will serve God," [Joshua 24:15].*

We have a choice, as did the Prodigal son. His father set him free; he finally realized that he had the best of both worlds in his father's house and returned to him. Sometimes we conduct ourselves in the same manner. Although, I am sure his father did not want him to leave but honored his request to give him his portion of the riches. God does not make us do anything (He does have the power, let us not forget that point) but gives us freedom of choice; however, like the father of the Prodigal son, will welcome His repentant child back into the fold.

We can be Prodigal Daughters as he was the Prodigal Son. When we stray, we realize it and Christ desires us to get back on track. We have everything we need in our Father's house and abundance. We either live for Jesus and leave the world behind or live in the world and leave Jesus behind, one or the other has to count as a loss. We cannot straddle that fence. We can only serve one master at a time, *"No man can serve two masters," [Matthew 6:24a].*

Satan is always angry when we overcome another temptation and we repent and return to the fold. We win those battles through Jesus and His promises to forgive us.

Paul said, *"I have fought a good fight, I have finished my course; I have kept the faith: Henceforth there is laid up for me a crown of righteousness, which the Lord, the righteous judge, shall give me at that day: and not to me only, but unto all them also that love His appearing. Do thy diligence to come shortly unto me: For Demas hath forsaken me, having loved this present world, and is departed unto Thessalonica; Crescens to Galatia, Titus unto Dalmatia," [2 Timothy 4:7-10].*

Paul using every minute of his last days because he knew his time was at hand *"For I am already being poured out as a drink offering, and the time of my departure is at hand", [2 Timothy 4:6].*

- ***Do your garment of faith, work, and obedience choose the Kingdom of God over the world look like that of Paul's?***

He worked for the eternal food of salvation. The Scripture tells us, Jesus answered, *"Very truly I tell you, you are looking for Me, not because you saw the signs I performed but because you ate the loaves and had your fill. Do not work for food that spoils, but for food that endures to eternal life, which the Son of Man will give you, for on Him God the Father has placed His seal of approval," [John 6:26-27].*

Further, *"Our ancestors ate the manna in the wilderness; as it is written: 'He gave them bread from heaven to eat.'"* Jesus said to them, *"Very truly I tell you, it is not Moses who has given you the bread from heaven, but it is my Father who gives you the true bread from heaven. For the Bread, of God is the bread that comes down from heaven and gives life to the world,"* [John 6:31-33].

*"But here is the bread that comes down from heaven, which anyone may eat and not die. I Am the Living Bread that came down from heaven. Whoever eats this bread will live forever. This bread is my flesh, which I will give for the life of the world,"* [John 6:50-51].

Remember the words of our Savior in response to Mary about her brother Lazarus, *"But I know that even now God will give you whatever you ask."* Jesus said to her, *"Your brother will rise again."* Martha answered, *"I know he will rise again in the resurrection on the last day."* Jesus said to her, *"I am the resurrection and the life. The one who believes in Me will live, even though they die,"* [John 11:22-:25].

The Prodigal people of God are willing to count all loss to gain Christ. Sisters, we are aware we cannot go to the world where there is no dependable help from the world; all that is there is temporary. Peter and the Apostles knew there was nowhere to go except to Christ, *"Will ye also go away? Then Simon Peter answered him, Lord, to whom shall we go? Thou hast the words of eternal life; and we believe and are sure that thou art that Christ, the Son of the living God,"* [John 6:66-69].

After His resurrection Christ showed Himself to His Apostles; His hands had the nail prints of His Sacrifice on the cross for our Salvation, so there would be no doubt that as He said, *"Because He was teaching His disciples. He said to them, "The Son of Man is going to be delivered into the hands of men. They will kill Him, and after three days He will rise,"* [Mark 9:31].

The nail prints are still in His hands for each century or generation that passes. We cannot ignore the Sacrifice Christ made and expect that we are pleasing to Him. We are to abide in the Doctrine of Christ. We cannot speak beyond what the Scripture teaches, at that point, we are no longer pleasing to God, and we build a wall that cuts us off from God, *"Whosoever transgresses and abides not in the Doctrine of Christ hath not God. He that abides in the Doctrine of Christ has both the Father and the Son,"* [2 John 1:9].

As members of the Body of Christ, we engage in both individual and congregational evangelism using the skills and talents God blessed us with to continue to build His Kingdom, plant, and water those seeds of the Gospel, and God gives the increase.

Jesus' name is sweet to the spiritual taste buds.

- *How far or high will you climb above the worldly pleasures and demands on your life for Jesus Christ Lord and Savior of the world?*

Zacchaeus, a Tax Collector, hated by all for his profession, climbed up the Sycamore Tree to see Jesus though small in stature did not allow that to stop him from seeing the Savior of the World, *"Jesus entered Jericho and was passing through. A man was there by the name of Zacchaeus; he was a chief tax collector and was wealthy. He wanted to see who Jesus was but because he was short, he could not see over the crowd. So, he ran ahead and climbed a Sycamore-fig tree to see him, since Jesus was coming that way. When Jesus reached the spot, He looked up and said to him, "Zacchaeus, come down immediately. I must stay at your house today." So, he came down at once and welcomed Him gladly," [Luke 19:1-6]*

He was so inspired, climbed as high as possible.

- *Do we desire, as Zacchaeus did, to see Jesus and then do what it takes to come to Him?*
- *We do not have Sycamore Trees physically to climb to see Jesus. However, does that burning desire exist within your spirit to serve God, leave the world behind, and become a Member of the Body of Christ?*

It requires moving to a new residence from a physical one to the spiritual one, and a change in our lives. The sweet nectar of Salvation is flowing free for all to drink of, become renewed and refreshed, regenerated, and lubricating your heart, mind, and soul.

The Zealots of Jesus' day were religious and pious. They thought of themselves living for God and serving him. They looked for the earthly King that would fight the Romans who shed the blood of their people (Israel). Christ did not come to earth to wage war, not with weapons of swords, spears, clubs, or threats, but with the Sword of the Word of God. He came to wage a war against sin, to fight the battle against the god of this world, to purchase Salvation with His life.

The pageantry of kings in our day and time, even in a movie is always a sit-up and notice moment. Looking for this type of king was also prevalent in Biblical times as well; however, the King we serve did not come in that manner, but as a man born of woman, who lived and functioned as a human does, experienced what humans do in this tent we inhabit but is yet God.

Christ stepped off His Throne and put on the robe of humility to purchase our salvation. Let us not forget Christ is our reigning King now and forever, not on earth but reigns in Heaven, where we will spend eternity. All earthly Kings died, as Biblical history tells us. Christ is a King forever.

He is a King, has been the King, and will forever be King, death has no hold on Him as it did David, Asa, Uzziah (Azariah), Solomon, Hezekiah, and all others that have come and gone from the time of the first earthly king, Saul. In this century, as with centuries past, we (people of God) are looking for Christ to return for His Bride, the Church, to present her to His father as a Bride without spot or blemish. Then He will reign as Lord, Savior, and King forever. He purchased His Bride so she (we) could reign with Him for eternity.

Christ came to call the sinners to repentance and bridge that gulf between God and man – created by man. Jesus Christ won the battle and the war on the Cross of Calvary and tore down the middle wall of petition to bring many sons to repentance and God.

Simon, the Zealot, finally realized the war was not a physical one and became a follower and an Apostle of Christ. The Zealots truly had lots of zeal, but not according to the pattern, Christ gave us.

Paul said about their zeal, *"Brethren, my heart's desire, and prayer to God, for Israel is that they might be saved. For I, bear them record that they have a zeal for God but not according to knowledge. For they being ignorant of God's righteousness and going about to establish their own righteousness have not submitted themselves unto the righteousness of God," [Romans 10:1-3].*

The Zealots were believers in the Law that Law no longer was what Jesus wanted them to live by, but under the new dispensation, He established through righteousness. Paul further says to them, *"Christ is the end of the Law for righteousness to everyone who believeth. The righteousness Moses described, the law, he who do the law, live by it," [Romans 10:5].*

Jesus established the righteousness of the heart and not keeping the Law. The Scriptures tells us, "*For with the heart man believeth unto righteousness and with the mouth, confession is made to Salvation,*" *[Romans 10:10].*

As Philip told the Ethiopian Eunuch, in *[Acts 8:36],* after teaching him when he asked, "*What hinders me from being baptized?*" And Phillip said, "*If thou believeth with all thine heart, thou may.*" And, he answered and said, "*I believe that Jesus Christ is the Son of God,*" *[Acts 8:37].*

All the examples in this chapter about the Prodigal Son give us hope that we can also be prodigal daughters/sons that return to the fold of Christ and He welcomes His repentant children back wrapping His loving arms around them that they might receive strength, knows that He loves, and forgives. We can walk in the newness of life as the Ethiopian Eunuch did...Paul in *[Romans 6:1-11]* reassures us what richness we will dwell in – in our new life in Christ on our journey to eternity with God.

- *What does your count look like?*
- *Are you counting losses or counting gains?*
- *Our choices are the world or Christ; which one will you choose?*

We have Scriptures as our source for encouragement and reassurance.

CHAPTER THIRTY-ONE

# Scriptures to remember. Givers of courage and reassurance

*"In the beginning, God created Heaven and earth," [Genesis 1:1]*

**We have a guarantee there is no condemnation to those in Christ,** *"There is therefore now no condemnation to them which are in Christ Jesus, who walk not after the flesh, but after the Spirit. For the law of the Spirit of life in Christ Jesus hath made me free from the law of sin and death. For what the law could not do, in that it was weak through the flesh, God sending his own Son in the likeness of sinful flesh, and for sin, condemned sin in the flesh: that the righteousness, of the law, might be fulfilled in us, who walk not after the flesh, but after the Spirit. For, they that are after the flesh do mind the things of the flesh; but they that are after the Spirit the things of the Spirit."*

**As well, we have new life in Christ through the Spirit,** *"For to be carnally minded is death; but to be spiritually minded is life and peace. Because the carnal mind is enmity against God, for it is not subject to the law of God, neither indeed can be. Then they that are in the flesh cannot please God. But ye are not in the flesh, but in the Spirit, if so be that the Spirit of God dwells in you. Now if any man has not the Spirit of Christ, he is none of his. And if Christ be in you, the body is dead because of sin; but the Spirit is life because of righteousness. But if the Spirit of Him that raised up Jesus from the dead dwell in you, He that raised up Christ from the dead shall also quicken your mortal bodies by His Spirit that dwells in you," [Romans 8:6-11].*

**The only promise we have is today; we can only get through one day at a time,** *"Take therefore no thought for the morrow: for the morrow shall take thought for the things of itself. Sufficient unto the day is the evil thereof," [Matthew 6:34].*

**We can say nothing to ridicule God, listen to what Hezekiah said,** *"And Hezekiah prayed to the Lord, "Lord the God of Israel, enthroned between the Cherubim you alone are God over all the kingdoms of the earth. You made heaven and earth," [II Kings 19:15].*

**Solomon recognizes that God is Our Creator and no place in the universe can confine the Almighty God,** "*But will God really dwell on the earth? The heavens, even the highest heavens, cannot contain You. How much less this temple I built,*" *[I Kings 8:27].*

**Scripture parallels show our God does not change and no man can confine the mighty God,** "*God who made the world and everything in it is the Lord of Heaven and earth and does not live in temples made with human hands,*" *[Acts 17:24].*

**Nebuchadnezzar came to this realization after God humbled him,** "*We are the peoples of the earth and are regarded as nothing. He does what he pleases with the powers of heaven and the peoples of the earth no one can hold back His hand or say to Him what have you done?*" *[Daniel 4:35].*

**All creation should worship God. We praise Him individually and collectively. What harmony of praise His people give him in unison and the sound is like a symphony with members of His Body praising and exalting Him on High with thanksgiving and humility,** "*Let them praise the name of the Lord, for His name alone is exalted; His splendor is above the earth and the heavens,*" *[Psalms 148:13].*

**The magnificence of God is not comprehendible; the power of the beauty of God humbled Ezekiel and it will as well humble you!** "*Then there came a voice from above the vault over their heads as they stood with lowered wings. Above the vault over their heads was what looked like a throne of Lapis Lazuli and high above the throne was a figure that of a man. I saw that from what appeared to be His waist and up looked like glowing metal, as if full of fire, and that from there down looked like fire; and brilliant light surrounded Him. Like the appearance of a rainbow in the clouds on a rainy day, so was the radiance around Him. This was the appearance of the likeness of the Glory of God. When I saw it, I fell face down, and I heard the voice of one speaking,*" *[Ezekiel 1:25-28].*

**God is a compassionate creator – He spoke this to Jonah,** "*But, the Lord said, "You have been concerned about this plant, though you did not tend it or make it grow. It sprang up overnight and died overnight. And I should not have concern for the great city of Nineveh in where there are more than a hundred and twenty thousand people who cannot tell their right hand from their left – and many animals?*" *[Jonah 4:10-11].*

**Jesus is the [ONLY] way to God!** *"In the beginning was the Word and the Word was with God, and the Word was God. He was with God in the beginning. Through Him all things are made without him nothing was made that has been made. In Him was life, and that life was the light of all mankind. The light shines in the darkness and the darkness over it," [John 1:1-5].*

*"Jesus is the true Bread from Heaven. Do not work for the food that spoils, but for food that endures to eternal life, which the Son of Man will give you for on Him, God the Father has placed His seal of approval."* **Jesus said to them,** *"Very truly I tell you it is not Moses who gives you the true bread from heaven. For, the Bread of God is the Bread that comes down from Heaven and gives life to the world. I am the Bread of Life," [John 6:27, 32, 35].*

*"I am the good Shepherd. The good Shepherd lay down His life of His sheep. The hired hand is not the shepherd and does not own the sheep. So, when he sees the wolf coming he abandons the sheep and runs away. The wolf attacks the flock and scatters it. The man runs away because he is a hired hand and cares nothing for the sheep. I am the good Shepherd, I know my sheep, and they know me – just as the Fathers know me and I know the Father and I lay down my life for the sheep."*

*"I have other sheep that are not of this sheep pen. I must bring them also. They will listen to my voice and there shall be one flock and one Shepherd. The reason my Father loves me is that I lay down my life – only to take it up again. No one can take it from me, but I lay it down of my own accord. I have the authority to lay it down and the authority to take it up again. This command I received from my Father," [John 10:11-18].*

*"Do not let your hearts be troubled. You believe in God believe also in Me. In my Father's house are many mansions, if it were not so would I have told you that I am going away to prepare a place for you. And if I go away and prepare a place for you, I will come again and receive you unto Myself: that where I am there you may be also. And whither I go ye know, and the way ye know," [John14:1-4].*

**Jesus our Savior is the image of the Father in Heaven,** *"I Am the Way, the Truth, and the Life. No one comes to the Father except through Me – if you really know Me, you will know My Father as well. From now on you do know Him and have seen Him," [John 14:6-7].*

**We have the promised Gift of the Holy Spirit,** *"If you love Me keep My Commandments. And I will ask the Father, and He will give you another Advocate to help you and will be with you forever – the Spirit of Truth. The world cannot accept Him, because it neither sees Him nor knows Him, but you know Him, for He lives with you and will be with you," [John 14:15-17].*

**The Holy Spirit is our Advocate and Teacher,** *"But very truly I tell you it is for your good that I am going away. Unless I go away, the Advocate will not come to you, but, if I go, I will send Him to you. And He comes He will prove the world to be wrong about sin, righteousness, and judgment, about sin, because people do not believe in me, about righteousness because I am going to the Father, where you can see Me no longer, and about judgment because the prince of this world now stand condemned.*

*"But when He, the Spirit of Truth, comes, He will guide you into all truths. He will not speak on His own; He will speak only what He hears, and He will tell you what is to come," [John 16:7-11, 13].*

**Christ prayed to God for His Apostles and us,** *"My prayer is not for them alone, I pray also for those who will believe in Me through their message, that all of them any be one Father just as you are in Me and I am in you – may they also be in Us so that the world may believe that you have seen Me," [John 17:20-21].*

**We are dwelling under the Secret of the Most High,** *"For the Lord watches over the way, of the righteous but the way, of the wicked, leads to destruction," [Psalms 1:6].*

**The power of Our God is unmatched,** *"One thing I ask of the Lord, these only do I seek: that I may dwell in the House of the Lord all the days of my life to gaze on the beauty of the Lord and seek Him in the Temple. For in the day of trouble He will keep me safe in His dwelling; He will hide me in the shelter of His sacred tent and set me on high upon a rock," [Psalms 27:4-5].*

*"Trust in the Lord, and do good, so shalt thou dwell in the land, and verily thou shalt be fed. Delight thyself also in the Lord: and He shall give thee the desires of thine heart. Commit thy way unto the Lord; trust also in Him, and He shall bring it to pass. And He shall bring forth thy righteousness as the light, and thy judgment as the noonday," [Psalms 37:3-6].*

*"The heart is deceitful above all things and beyond cure. Who can understand it? I, God, search the heart and examine the mind to reward each person according to their conduct, according to what their deeds deserve," [Jeremiah 17:9-10].*

**Our mutual faith is a comfort yielding fruit of our Salvation,** *"For I long to see you, that I may impart unto you some spiritual gift, to the end ye may be established; That is, that I may be comforted together with you by the mutual faith both of you and me. Now I would not have you ignorant, brethren, that oftentimes I purposed to come unto you, (but was let hitherto,) that I might have some fruit among you also, even as among other Gentiles," [Romans 1:11-13].*

**Baptism of the Holy Spirit and water baptism, both are required for Salvation,** *"Do not leave Jerusalem, but wait for the gift my Father promised, which you have heard me speak about; for John baptized with water, but in a few days you will be baptized with the Holy Spirit," [Acts 1:4b]*

**Stephen's warning to the people as they stoned him; truths are like well driven nails; killing the messenger does not change the truth or the message,** *"The words of the Preacher, the son of David, king in Jerusalem. Vanity of vanities, said the Preacher, vanity of vanities; all is vanity. What profit hath a man of all his labor which he taketh under the sun?" [Ecclesiastes 1:1-3].*

*"You stiff-necked people your heart and ears are still uncircumcised. You are just like your ancestor. You always resist the Holy Spirit: was there ever a Prophet your ancestor did not persecute? They even killed those who predicted the coming of the Righteous One. And now you have betrayed and murdered Him – you who have received the Law that was given through angels but have not obeyed it," [Acts 7:51].*

*"For I am not ashamed of the Gospel it is the power of God unto Salvation to everyone who believes, first to the Jews then the Gentiles. For in the Gospel, the righteousness of God is revealed - a righteousness that is by faith from first to Jews and then the Gentiles. For in the Gospel the righteousness of God is revealed – a righteousness that is by faith from first to last, just as it is written, the righteous will live by faith," [Romans 1:16-17].*

*"Abraham believed God and it was credited to him as righteousness," [Romans 4:3b].*

**The Gentiles come into the fold.** Cornelius a God-fearing man and his family were devout. God accepts all who are obedient, loves, and serves Him out of a pure heart. We are to share the good news as Peter did – he shared with Cornelius the steps of Salvation! *"About the ninth hour of the day, he saw clearly in a vision an angel of God coming in and saying to him, "Cornelius!" And when he observed him, he was afraid, and said, "What is it, lord?" So, he said to him, "Your* *prayers and your alms have come up for a memorial before God. Now send men to Joppa and send for Simon whose surname is Peter. He is lodging with Simon, a tanner, whose house is by the sea. He[d] will tell you what you must do." And a voice spoke to him again the second time, "What God [has] cleansed you must not call common," [Acts10:4-6, 15].*

*"And when he had found him, he brought him into Antioch. And it came to pass, that a whole year they assembled themselves with the church and taught many people. And the disciples were called Christians first in Antioch," [Acts 11:26].*

**We see the fruit of the Spirit; Paul reminds us at all times our attitudes should always be, of the desire to promote unity; it creates synergy among God's people,** *"I, therefore, the prisoner of the Lord, beseech you that ye walk worthy of the vocation wherewith ye are called, With all lowliness and meekness, with longsuffering, forbearing one another in love; Endeavoring to keep the unity of the Spirit in the bond of peace," [Ephesians 4:1-3].*

**Unity in the Body of Christ,** *"There is one Body and one Spirit, one God and Father of all, who is over all and through all and in all. There is one Lord, one Faith, and one Baptism," [Ephesians 4:3-6].*

**The Body and Blood of Jesus Christ: Do this in Remembrance of Me, and the Night Christ was betrayed,** *"And He said unto them, I have eagerly desired to eat this Passover with you before I suffer: For I say unto you, I will not any more eat thereof until it is fulfilled in the Kingdom of God. And He took the cup, gave thanks, said, take this, and divide it among yourselves: For I say unto you, I will not drink of the fruit of the vine until the Kingdom of God shall come. And He took bread, gave thanks, breaks it, and gave unto them, saying, this is My Body, which is given for you: this do in remembrance of Me. Likewise, also, the cup after supper, saying, and this cup is the New Testament in My Blood, which is shed for you. But behold, the hand of My betrayeriswith Me on the table," [Luke 22:15-21].*

**Paul reminds us, to examine ourselves and take The Body and Blood of Christ in a worthy manner that we may not be guilty of His Body and Blood,** *"For I have received of the Lord, that which also I delivered unto you, that the Lord Jesus the same night in which He was betrayed took bread: And when He had given thanks, He brake it, and said, Take eat this is My body, which is broken for you: this do in remembrance of Me. After the same manner, also, He took the cup, when He had supped, saying, this cup is the new testament in my blood: this do ye, as oft as ye drink* *it, in remembrance of Me. For as often as ye eat this bread, and drink this cup, ye do show the Lord's death till He comes. Wherefore, whosoever shall eat this bread, and drink this cup of the Lord, unworthily, shall be guilty of the body and blood of the Lord."*

*"But let a man examine himself, and so let him eat of that bread, and drink of that cup. For he that eats and drinks unworthily, eats and drinks damnation to himself, not discerning the Lord's body. For this cause, many are weak and sickly among you, and many sleep. For, if we would judge ourselves: we should not be judged. But when we are judged, we are chastened of the Lord, that we should not be condemned with the world. Wherefore, my brethren, when ye come together to eat, tarry one for another. And if any man hunger, let him eat at home; that ye come not together unto condemnation. And the rest will I set in order when I come," [I Corinthians 11:23-27].*

**The Son of God is Supreme,** *"Christ is the Head of the Body, which is His Church," [Colossians 1:18].*

*"The Son is the image of the invisible God. The firstborn overall creation. For in Him all things were created, things in heaven and on earth, visible and invisible whether thrones, power, rulers, or authorities. All things have been created through Him and for Him. He is before all things and by Him all things exist," [Colossians 1:10-18].*

*"Salvation is found in no other; there is no other name found under the heaven whereby men might be saved," [Acts 4:12].*

*"For God so loved the world that He gave His only begotten Son that we might through Him live," [John 1:17].*

**Live as an example for the world and not by the world's example,** *"Be not conformed to the world, but be transformed by the renewing of your mind. Then you will be able to test and approve what God will is - His good, pleasing, and perfect will," [Romans 12:2].*

**We speak in a manner acceptable in due season and to God,** *"A man hath joy by the answer of his mouth: and a word spoken in due season, how good is it!" [Proverbs 15:23].*

*"The heart of the righteous studies to answer but the mouth of the wicked poured out evil things," [Proverbs 15:28].*

*"He that hath a forward heart finds no good: and he that hath a perverse tongue falls into mischief," [Proverbs 17:20].*

*"He that hath knowledge spares his words: and a man of understanding is of an excellent spirit. Even a fool, when he holds his peace, is counted wise: and he that shuts his lips is esteemed a man of understanding,"* [Proverbs 17:27-28].

*"Death and life are in the power of the tongue: and they that love it shall eat the fruit thereof,"* [Proverbs 18:21].

*"Those who guard their mouths, and their tongues keep themselves from calamity,"* [Proverbs 21:23].

**We are to serve humbly in the Body of Christ**, *"By the grace given me I say to every one of you: Do not think of yourself more highly than you ought, but rather think of yourself with sober judgment in accordance with the faith God has distributed to each of you,"* [Romans 12:3].

*"I Am the Light of the world,"* [John 8:12].

*"And Jesus said unto them, I am the bread of life: he that cometh to Me shall never hunger; and he that believeth on Me shall never thirst,"* [John 6:35].

*"Trust in the Lord with all thine heart and lean not to thy own understanding in all your ways submit to Him and He will make your path straight. Do not be wise in your own eyes, fear the Lord, and shun evil. This will bring health to your body and nourishment to your bones,"* [Proverbs 3:5-6].

*"There is a time for everything and a season for every activity under. Whatever is has already been and what will be has been before and God will call the past to account,"* [Ecclesiastics 3:1, 15].

**Humans have value because we are in the image of God**, *"For in the image of God has God made mankind,"* [Ecclesiastics 9:6b],

*"A good name is rather be chosen than fine riches and the day of death better than the day of birth,"* [Proverbs 22:1].

**No matter what we do while on earth, enjoying life whether with the purpose of a defined path or if there is not a definite path, God will judge everything in our life on Judgment Day - whether we obeyed His Commandments and lived a life that was pleasing to Him.**

**Solomon gave us the measuring stick to use that we might meet the standards of God. The conclusion is to** "*fear God and keep His Commandments*" **no matter what else we do during our lifetime. What are your focuses in life, passing pleasures or eternal value? Solomon made a well-driven point of youth and old age; without drawing close to God in your youth is costly in old age (mature years) when the body begins to fail and trials of age beset mankind; it will, in some way if you live long enough,** *There words of the wise are like goads, their collected sayings like firmly embedded nails – given by one Shepherd. Be warned my son of anything in addition to them. Of making of many books, there is no end, and much study wearies the body. Now all has been heard, here is the conclusion of the matter, fear God, and keep His commandments for this is the duty of all mankind. For God, will bring every deed into judgment, including every hidden thing, whether it is good or evil," [Ecclesiastics 12:11-14].*

*"And many other words die He testify and exhort saying, save yourself from this UN-toward (crooked) generation," [Acts 2:40].*

*"The fear of the Lord tends to life: and he that hat it shall abide satisfied: he shall not be visited with evil," [Proverbs 19:23].*

*"I counsel thee to buy of me gold tried in the fire, that thou may be clothed, and the shame of thy nakedness may not appear, and anoint with eye salve that thou may see," [Revelation 3:18].*

*"Do not judge or you will be judged, and with the measure you use, it will be measured to you." Why do you look at the speck in your brother's eye and pay no attention to the plank in your own eye? How can you say to your brother, "Let me take the speck out of your eye when all the time there is a plank in your own eye? You hypocrite, first take the plank out of your own eye, and then you will see clearly to remove the speck from your brother's eyes," [Matthew 7:1-5].*

*"For everyone born of God overcomes the world. This is the victory that has overcome the world, even our faith. Who is it that overcomes the world only the ones that believe Jesus is the Son of God," [I John 5:4-5]?*

*"Anyone who claims to be in the light but hates a brother or sister is still in darkness. Anyone who loves their brother and sister lives in the light and there is nothing to make them stumble. But anyone who hates a brother or sister is in the darkness. They do not know where they are going because the darkness has blinded them," [I John 2:9-11].*

*"If we claim to be without sin, we deceive ourselves and the truth is not in us,"* [I John 1:9].

**We cannot lose heart God keeps His promises, Christ paid the price therefore we look to Him for all we need to make it to the end of our race for eternity. We have a cloud of witnesses cheering us from the sidelines, "you can make it do not quit,** *"Therefore since we are surrounded by such a great cloud of witnesses, let us lay aside every weight and sin that besets us, and let us run with perseverance the race set before us, looking to Jesus the author and finisher of our faith; who for the joy that was set before Him endured the cross, despising the shame, and is set down at the right hand of the throne of God. For consider Him who endured such contradiction of sinners against himself, lest ye be wearied and faint in your minds,"* [Hebrews 12:1-3].

*"Endure hardship as discipline; God is treating you as His children. For what children are not disciplined by their fathers? If you are not disciplined – and everyone undergoes discipline – then you are not legitimate, not true sons and daughters at all. Moreover, we have human fathers who disciplined us, and we respected them for it. How much more should we submit to the Father of spirits and live! They disciplined us for a little while as they thought best, but God disciplines us for our good, in order that we may share in His Holiness."*

**As well,** *"No discipline seems pleasant at the time, but painful; later on, however, it produces a harvest of righteousness and peace for those who have been trained by it. Therefore, strengthen your feeble arms and weak knees - make level paths for your feet, so that the lame may not be disabled; but rather healed,"* [Hebrews 12:7-12].

*"But you have come to Mount Zion, to the city of the living God, the heavenly Jerusalem. You have come to thousands upon thousands of angels in joyful assembly, to the Church of the Firstborn, whose Name is written in Heaven. You have come to God, the judge of all, to the spirit of the righteous made perfect, to Jesus the Mediator of a New Covenant, and to the sprinkled blood that speaks of a better word than that of Abel. See to it that you do not refuse Him who speaks. If they did not escape when they refused Him who warned us from Heaven?"* [Hebrews 12:22-25].

**The Kingdom of Christ is unshakeable He purchased with His blood. The Kingdom of Christ stands when others fall (did fall),** *"At that time, His voice shook the earth, but now He has promised, "Once more I will shake not only the earth but also the Heavens. The words once more, indicating the removing of what can be* *shaken – that is, created things so that what cannot be shaken may remain. Therefore, since we are receiving a Kingdom that cannot be shaken, let us be thankful, and so worship God acceptably with reverence and awe," [Hebrews 12:26-28].*

**Everything not of God or dedicated to God will be consumed in His fiery wrath. Fire is deadly and final, as we know it now, how much more so is the fire of God. God promised Noah never to destroy the earth with water. Peter reminds us,** *"But the heavens and the earth, which are now, by the same word are kept in store, reserved unto fire against the day of judgment and perdition of ungodly men," [2 Peter 3:7]*

*"For our God is a consuming fire," [Hebrews 12:29].*

**The navel is the center of the human body as it gives balance, the fear of God and His presence in your life should be its center as well. Marrow is the life substance of the body and promotes growth and health, so will the Word of God and obedience to His Commands,** *"Trust in the Lord with all thine heart and lean not unto thine own understanding. In all thy ways acknowledge Him, and He will direct thy path. Be not wise in thine own eyes fear the Lord and depart from evil. It shall be health to the navel, and marrow to thy bones. Honor the Lord with thy substance and with the first fruits of thine increase," [Proverbs 3:5-9].*

*"The fear of the Lord is the beginning of wisdom. A wise man will hear and increase learning: and a man of understanding shall attain into wise counsel," [Proverbs 5, 7].*

**"And unto man, he said,** *"Behold the fear of the Lord that is wisdom and to depart from evil, is understanding," [Job 28:28].*

*"Every good and perfect gift is from above and cometh down from the Father of Lights, with whom is no variableness, neither shadow of turning. Of His own will beget He us with the Word of Truth, that we should be first fruits of His creations," [James 1:17-18].*

*"Come unto Me all ye that labor and are heavy laden, and I will give you rest. Take My yoke upon you and learn of Me for I am meek and lowly in heart and ye shall find rest unto your souls. For My yoke is easy and My burden is light," [Matthew 11:28-30].*

**There is but one conduct we should have, Holy!** *"But He that hath called* *you is Holy, so be ye holy in all manner of conversation; because it is written be ye Holy, for I am Holy. And if ye call on the Father, who without respect of person judges according to everyman's work pass the time of your sojourning here in fear,"* [I Peter 1:15-17].

*"Examine yourselves, whether ye be in the faith; prove yourselves. Know ye, not that Jesus Christ is in you, except ye be reprobates?" [2 Corinthians 13:5].*

*"Abstain from all appearances of evil," [I Thessalonians 5:22].*

**Humility among God's People**, *"Feed the flock of God, which is among you, taking the oversight thereof, not by constraint, but willingly; not for filthy lucre, but of a ready mind; neither as being lords over God's heritage, but being examples to the flock. And, when the Chief Shepherd shall appear, ye shall receive a crown of glory that fades not away. Likewise, ye younger, submit yourselves unto the elder. Yea, all of you be subject one to another, and be clothed with humility: for God resists the proud, and giveth grace to the humble," [I Peter 5:2-5].*

**We are to be one in the body with no schism**, *"Now, I beseech you, brethren, by the name of our Lord Jesus Christ, that ye all speak the same things and that there be no division among you, but that ye be perfectly joined together in the same mind and the same judgment," [I Corinthians 1:10].*

*"Cast not away, therefore, your confidence, which hath great recompense of reward. For ye have need of patience, that, after ye have done the will of God, ye might receive the promise. For yet a little while, and He that shall come will come, and will not tarry. Now the just shall live by faith: but if any men draw back, My soul shall have no pleasure in him. But we are not of them who draw back unto perdition, but of them, that believe to the saving of the soul," [Hebrews 10:35-39].*

*"I would not have you ignorant brethren concerning them which are asleep, that ye sorrow not even as others which have no hope. If you believe that Jesus died and rose again, even to them also which sleeps in Jesus will God bring with Him," [I Thessalonians4:13]!*

*There hath no temptation taken you, but such as is common to man: but God is faithful, who will not suffer you to be tempted above that ye are able; but will with the temptation also make a way to escape, that ye may be able to bear it," [I Corinthians 13:10].*

*"Charity suffers long and is kind; charity envies not; charity vaunts, not itself, is not puffed up," "Love never fails. But where there are prophecies, they will cease; where there are tongues, they will be stilled; where there is knowledge, it will pass away." And, so now, faith, hope, and love abide, these three, but the greatest of these is love," [I Corinthians 13:4, 8, 13].*

*"Study to show thyself approved of God, a workman need not be ashamed rightly dividing the Word of Truth," [2 Timothy 2:15].*

*"The wages of sins is death, and the gift of God is eternal life," [Romans 6:23].*

*"And they, continuing daily with one accord in the temple, and breaking bread from house to house, did eat their meat with gladness and singleness of heart, Praising God, and having favor with all the people. And the Lord added to the Church daily such as should be saved," [Acts 2:46-47].*

*"Know ye not, that so many of us as were baptized into Jesus Christ were baptized into his death? Therefore, we are buried with Him by baptism into death: that like as Christ was raised from the dead by the glory of the Father, even so, we also should walk in newness of life. For, if we have been planted together in the likeness of His death, we shall be also in the likeness of His resurrection," [Romans 6:3-5].*

**Death is a reality,** *"If after the manner of men, I have fought with beasts at Ephesus, what advantages it me, if the dead rise not? Let us eat and drink; for tomorrow we die," [I Corinthians 15:32].*

**All will be changed, Jesus conquered the grave,** *"Behold, I show you a mystery; we shall not all sleep, but we shall all be changed, in a moment, in the twinkling of an eye, at the last trump: for the trumpet shall sound, and the dead shall be raised incorruptible, and we shall be changed," [I Corinthians 15:51-52].*

**Our eternity abides with Jesus Christ our Lord and Savior now and our Judge when eternity begins and we all stand at the judgment seat and answer for our deeds while we were on earth,** *"And when I saw Him, I fell at his feet as dead. And He laid His right hand upon me, saying unto me, Fear not, I am the First and the Last: I am He that lives, and was dead; and behold, I am alive forevermore, Amen; and have the keys of hell and death," [Revelation 1:17-18].*

**Singing with the instruments of our heart and mouth, not using mechanical instruments, but the one Christ gave us is pleasing and approved**

**of God,** *"Let the Words of Christ dwell within you richly with all wisdom; teaching and admonishing one another in psalms and hymns and spiritual songs, singing with grace in your heart to the Lord,"* *[Colossians 3:16].*

**Living in peace with each other,** *"He died for us so that, whether we are awake or asleep, we may live together with Him. Therefore, encourage one another and build each other up, just as in fact you are doing. Now we ask you brothers and sisters to acknowledge those who work hard among you, who care for you in the Lord, and who admonish you. Hold them in the highest regard in love because of their work; live in peace with each other,"* *[I Thessalonians 5:10-13].*

**Paul reminds the Corinthians to love at all times and this is a reminder for us of this day and time as well. All we give means nothing, if it is not given with and, in love,** *"Though I speak with the tongues of men or of angels, and have not charity, I have become as sounding brass or a tinkling cymbal. And though, I have the gift of prophecy and understand all mysteries and all knowledge, and though I have all faith so that I could remove mountains, and have not love, I am nothing. And though I bestow all my goods to feed the poor, and though I give my body to be burned and have not love, it profits me nothing,"* *[I Corinthians 13:1-3].*

**Paul reminds us to give as we prosper that the work of God will continue and we fulfill the mission of "Go" and take hold of the [Responsibility] Jesus left for us,** *"Now concerning the collection for the saints, as I have given order to the churches of Galatia, even so, do ye. Upon the first day of the week let, every one of you lay by him in store, as God hath prospered him, that there be no gatherings when I come. And when I come, whomsoever ye shall approve by your letters, them will I send to bring your liberality unto Jerusalem,"* *[I Corinthians 16:1-3].*

*"Will a man rob God? Yet ye have robbed Me, but ye say wherein have we robbed Thee? In tithes and offerings!"* *[Malachi 3:8].*

**The New Jerusalem will have the wealth of peace and righteousness in the Spiritual City. There is no wealth in the world that can compare to the wealth of the New Eternal Jerusalem,** *"All the flocks of Kedar shall be gathered together unto thee, the rams of Nebaioth shall minister unto thee: they shall come up with acceptance on mine altar, and I will glorify the house of My glory,"* *[Isaiah 60:7].*

**We as children of God are to promote peace and not confusion, as did Diotrephes because he wanted preeminence among brethren. We are all the**

same in Christ; there is no one above another. God is no respecter of person. God adds to the Church, not man. He gives no one authority to decide who can and cannot be in His Body, *"I wrote unto the Church, but Diotrephes, who loves to have the preeminence among them, receives us not. Wherefore, if I come, I will remember his deeds which he doeth, prating against us with malicious words, and not content therewith, neither doth he receive the brethren and forbids them that would, and caste them out of the Church. Beloved follow not that which is evil, but which is good. He that doeth good is of God, but he that doeth evil hat not seen God," [3 John 9-11].*

We can come to God through our High Priest Jesus Christ. His blood atones for our sin, and we become sinless before God through the Blood of Christ, *"Having therefore, brethren boldness to enter into the holiest by the blood of Jesus. By a new and living way, which he hat consecrated for us, through the will, that is to say, his flesh. And having a high priest over the house of God. Let us draw near with a true heart. In full assurance of faith, having our heart sprinkled from an evil conscience, and our bodies washed with pure water. Let us hold fast the profession of our faith without wavering: for He is faithful, that promised. And let us consider one another to provoke unto love and to good works. Not forsaking the assembling our ourselves, together, as the manner of some is not exhorting one another and so much the more, as you see the Day approaching," [Hebrews 10:19-25].*

Salvation does not come through any work that we can or will do. We know as humans that ego will get in the way, and we begin saying, "Look what [I] did." We are saved by grace…we are children of Abraham, children of faith. Christ did the work, and paid the price for the gift of grace, *"And you hath He quickened, who were dead in trespasses and sins; Wherein in time past, ye walked according to the course of this world, according to the prince of the power of the air, the spirit that now works in the children of disobedience: among whom also we all had our conversation in times past in the lusts of our flesh, fulfilling the desires of the flesh and of the mind; and were by nature the children of wrath, even as others."*

*"But God, who is rich in mercy, for His great love wherewith He loved us, Even when we were dead in sins, hath quickened us together with Christ, (by grace ye are saved;) And hath raised us up together, and made us sit together in heavenly places in Christ Jesus: That in the ages to come He might show the exceeding riches of His grace in his kindness toward us through Christ Jesus. For by grace are ye saved through faith; and that not of yourselves: it is the gift of God: Not of works, lest any man should boast. For we are His workmanship, created in Christ Jesus unto good works, which God hath before ordained that we should walk in them," [Ephesians 2:1-10].*

**Our Savior, as expressed by Isaiah, was a Man of Sorrow, acquainted with the grief, because of the sins of man, and knowing He would suffer for humanity was a heavy burden; Christ is a picture of Love, Isaiah asked,** *"Who hath believed our report? And to whom is the Arm of the Lord revealed? For He shall grow up before Him as a tender plant, and as a root out of the dry ground. He hath neither form nor comeliness, and when we shall see Him; there is no beauty that we should desire Him. He is despised and rejected of men; a man of sorrows and acquainted with grief: and we hid as it were our faces from Him; He was despised, and we esteemed Him not. Surely, He hath borne our griefs and carried our sorrows: yet we did esteem Him stricken, smitten of God, and afflicted. But He was wounded for our transgressions, He was bruised for our iniquities: the chastisement of our peace was upon Him, and with His stripes, we are healed," [Isaiah 53:1-5]*

**Jesus willingly went to the cross for our sins. He lay His life down and He took it up; no man could take it from him. A Lamb to the slaughter; we know lambs are humble animals and offer no resistance,** *"All we like sheep have gone astray; we have turned everyone to His own way, and the Lord hath laid on Him the iniquity of us all. He was oppressed, and He was afflicted, yet He opened not His mouth: He was led as a lamb to the slaughter, and as a sheep before her shearers is dumb, so He opened not His mouth. He was taken from prison and from judgment: and who shall declare His generation? He was cut off out of the land of the living: for the transgression of my people was He stricken. And He made His grave with the wicked, and with the rich in His death; because He had done no violence, neither was any deceit in His mouth," [Isaiah 53:6-9].*

**Christ is our offering for sin, the [perfect] Lamb of God; His blood is [our] payment for sin,** *"Yet it was the Lord's will to crush him and cause him to suffer, and though the Lord makes His life an offering for sin, he will see his offspring and prolong his days, and the will of the Lord will prosper in His hand. After He has suffered, he will see the light of life and be satisfied; by His knowledge, my righteous servant will justify many, and He will bear their iniquities. Therefore, I will give Him a portion among the great, and He will divide the spoils with the strong, because He poured out His life unto death, and was numbered with the transgressors. For He bore the sin of many, and made intercession for the transgressors," [Isaiah 53:10-12].*

**God adds to the Church such as should be saved. Those being saved having all things in common,** *"And they continued steadfastly in the Apostles' doctrine and fellowship, and in breaking of bread, and in prayers. And fear came* *upon every soul: and many wonders and signs were done by the Apostles. And all that believed were together, had all things common; sold their possessions and goods, and parted them to all men, as every man had need. And they, continuing daily with one accord in the temple, and breaking bread from house to house, did eat their meat with gladness and singleness of heart, Praising God, and having favor with all the people. And the Lord added to the church daily such as should be saved," [Acts 2:42-47].*

**Think on those things that bring peace,** *"Rejoice in the Lord always and again I say rejoice. Let your moderation be known unto all men the Lord is at hand. Be careful for nothing, but in everything by prayer and supplication with thanksgiving let your requests be made known unto God. And the peace of God, which passes all understanding, shall keep your hearts and minds through Christ Jesus."*

*"Finally, brethren, whatsoever things are true, whatsoever things are honest, whatsoever things are just, whatsoever things are pure, whatsoever things are lovely, whatsoever things are of good report; if there be any virtue, and if there be any praise, think on these things. Those things, which ye have both learned, and received, and heard, and seen in me, do and the God of peace shall be with you."*

*"But I rejoiced in the Lord greatly, that now at the last your care, of me hath flourished again; wherein ye were also careful, but ye lacked opportunity. Not that I speak in respect of want for I have learned, in whatsoever state I am, therewith to be content. I know both how to be abased, and I know how to abound: everywhere and in all things, I am instructed both to be full and to be hungry, both to abound and to suffer need," [Philippians 4:4-12].*

**There is no justification for us living under the Law,** *"As it is written, there is none righteous, no, not one: There is none that understands; there is none that seeks after God. They are all gone out of the way, they are together become unprofitable; there is none that doeth good, no, not one. Their throat is an open sepulcher; with their tongues, they have used deceit; the poison of asps is under their lips: Whose mouth is full of cursing and bitterness: Their feet are swift to shed blood: Destruction and misery are in their ways: And the way of peace have they not known: There is no fear of God before their eyes. Now we know that what things whatsoever the law said, it said to them who are under the law: that every mouth may be stopped, and all the world may become guilty before God. Therefore, by the deeds of the law, there shall no flesh be justified in his sight: for by the law is the knowledge of sin," [Romans 3:10-20].*

**God takes care of the birds of the air and the lilies of the field; likewise, He will take care of us,** "*Therefore, I say unto you take no thought for your life, what ye shall eat, or what ye shall drink; nor yet for your body, what ye shall put on. Is not the life more than meat, and the body than raiment? Behold the fowls of the air: for they sow not, neither do they neither reap nor gather into barns; yet your heavenly Father feeds them. Are ye not much better than they? Which of you, by taking thought can add one cubit unto his stature? And why take ye thought for raiment? Consider the lilies of the field, how they grow; they toil not, neither do they spin: And yet I say unto you, that even Solomon in all his glory was not arrayed like one of these. Wherefore, if God so clothes the grass of the field, which today is, and tomorrow is cast into the oven, shall he not much more clothe you, O ye of little faith? Therefore, take no thought, saying, what shall we eat? Or what shall we drink? Or wherewithal shall we be clothed?" [Matthew 6:25-31].*

**Our focus should be on today,** "*Take therefore no thought for the morrow: for the morrow shall take thought for the things of itself. Sufficient unto the day is the evil thereof," [Matthew 6:34].*

**We are in the world not of the world,** "*Therefore, "Come out from them and be separate, says the Lord. Touch no unclean thing, and I will receive you," [2 Corinthians 6:17].*

**God is the source of our strength,** "*I can do all things through Christ which strengthens me," [Philippians 4:13].*

**God delights in His people being good,** "*The steps of a good man are ordered by the Lord, and he delights in his way. Though he falls, he shall not be utterly cast down for the Lord upholds him with his hand. Mark the perfect man and behold the upright: for the end of that man is peace," [Psalms 37:23-24, 37].*

**We are to wait on the Lord...He is our redeemer,** "*Wait on the Lord, and keep His way, and He shall exalt thee to inherit the land: when the wicked are cut off, thou shall see it. But the Salvation of the righteous is of the Lord: He is our strength in the time of trouble. And the Lord shall help them and deliver them: He shall deliver them from the wicked, and save them because they trust in Him," [Psalms 37:34, 39-40].*

And "*Our soul waits for the Lord: He is our help and our shield. For our heart shall rejoice in Him because we have trusted in His Holy Name. Let thy mercy, O Lord, be upon us, according to as we hope in thee," [Psalms 33:20-22].*

**David's Prayer for the forgiveness of his sins, petition for help, and cry for mercy from His loving and giving God applies to people of God for all generations who love and serve Him. Acknowledging our sins before Him and being truthful when we fall into error can receive complete forgiveness and restoration is blessed. God is love...**

*"Blessed is he whose transgression is forgiven, whose sin is covered. Blessed is the man unto whom the Lord imputeth not iniquity, and in whose spirit there is no guile. When I kept silence, my bones waxed old through my roaring all the day long. For day and night, thy hand was heavy upon me, my moisture is turned into the drought of summer. I acknowledged my sin unto thee and mine iniquity have I not hid. I said, "I will confess my transgressions unto the Lord, and thou forgave the iniquity of my sin. For this shall everyone that is godly pray unto thee in a time when thou mayest be found, surely in the floods of great waters they shall not come nigh unto him. Thou art my hiding place; thou shalt preserve me from trouble, thou shall compass me about with songs of deliverance.*

*God promises, "I will instruct thee and teach thee in the way which thou shall go. I will guide thee with mine eye. Be ye not as the horse, or the mule, which has no understanding: whose mouth must be held in with bit and bridle, lest they come they come near unto thee. Many sorrows shall be in the wicked: but he that trusted in the Lord mercy shall compass him about. Be glad in the Lord, and rejoice, ye righteous: and shout for joy, all ye that are upright in heart," [Psalms 32:1-11].*

David later wrote the fifty-first Psalms, which mirrors the thirty-second Psalms in his cry for mercy, forgiveness, and thanksgiving for the blessing and love of a merciful God. Sisters, we can all be recipients of that love and mercy when we love and serve God in humility and obedience.

CHAPTER THIRTY-TWO

# GARMENTS OF SYMBOLISM AS TOOLS OF LEARNING AND CHANGE

Symbolism is defined as natural objects or facts. Scripture uses symbolism frequently. The usage is there to help humans understand the meanings God applies to the Commands He gives us. Christ used symbolism in the Parables He spoke. The Book of Revelation has symbolistic examples given by John the Apostle, to the people of God because, of suppression by the Roman Empire.

Domitian, the Emperor of Rome, exiled John to the island of Patmos. John wrote to the people symbolically, giving them hope that the time would not be long until their bondage would end. The Christians understood the symbolism used by John, the Romans did not.

The Parables Christ spoke were earthly examples with a heavenly meaning. Man can identify with [what] they are familiar. God is not the author of confusion. He planned a way for humans to understand and have the wisdom needed to serve Him in righteousness, humility, and obedience.

God gave Amos a vision of judgment for His people. He used the symbol of the locust, fire, and a plumb line. Locusts destroy everything in their path. They only leave residue marching like armies and flying in swarms darkening the sun. Then again, fire destroys as well leaving a path of destruction in its wake, everything charred into dust and ashes; yet to plot a straight line, to build, or set a foundation needs a plumb line (God's Pattern).

A wall that is built, if it is not on the straightness of the plumb line, it will not stand long, or the foundation if not level will cause the structure built on it to collapse with time. This is symbolic of the power of God and the judgment He did not relent from bringing to pass, because of their constant disobedience after the multiple warnings He sent them through his Prophet Amos, "*Thus He showed me: and behold, the Lord stood upon a wall made by a plumb line, with a plumb line in His hand. And the Lord said unto me, Amos, what seest thou? And I said, a plumb line. Then said the Lord, Behold, I will set a plumb line in the midst of my people Israel: I will not again pass by them anymore: And the high places of Isaac shall be desolate, and the sanctuaries of Israel shall be laid waste; and I will rise against the house of Jeroboam with the sword," [Amos 7:7-9].*

Using God's plumb line is the only way we can be pleasing to Him. We cannot use our version of a plumb line to draw the pattern for our service to Him. He is standing on the mountain with it in His hand. We can translate this to the Scripture we use as our guide to be pleasing to Him. We build our foundation of faith on the Word of God our plumb line for Salvation.

In this day and time, as with the people of God as then, God sent warning His people by Prophets of the dangers of disobedience and defiance was grace and mercy for His people. Today we have the Scripture to warn us; they are God's gift of grace and mercy to His people of the cost of disobedience.

In the Master of Communication Degree program at the University of South Alabama (USA), one of the required courses was The Art of Film Making. In that class, during the semester the importance of the use of symbolism and its relation to making movies, and what it communicates through non-verbal scenes was thoroughly taught.

The students in the class were taught the correct method of setting up a scene and what symbolistic props to use. We made a short five-minute movie trailer, cut the film eliminating unnecessary scenes, adding music to the short film, adding a title at the beginning of the movie, and then the participants (producers) at the end. The movie was on key; the professor pleased, yielded the committee and me an 'A' for the class.

The lists of criteria required for the success of the movie must-haves were water, a symbol of (power), greenery, a symbol of (life), smoke/mist, a symbol of (mystery), light, a symbol of (success), and darkness, a symbol of (danger). Included in this criterion, there was to be no motion with the camera, which required a sturdy hand. The only motion allowed was if it was the prop or part of the scene. I filmed the scene for the movie from thirty-five stories high on one of the RSA Towers at the sphere. The wind was blowing 35-40 miles per hour to the point it blew me around. Regardless of the difficulty we met, the project had to be completed. We submitted the project and the criteria to the Professor by the deadline and could not change it; he did not accept a redo for any reason.

Jesus gave us the criterion for Salvation to finish the course as Paul said, *"For I am already being poured out like a drink offering, and the time for my departure is near. I have fought the good fight, I have finished the race, and I have kept the faith. Now there is in store for me the crown of righteousness, which the Lord, the righteous Judge, will award to me on that day-and not only to me but also to all who have longed for His appearing,"* [Ibid].

God does not change the Commands He put in place. He is our Lord and Master. Once we become a member of the Lord's Body [His Church], we obey the requirements in place. He does not change His Plan about what is necessary for our Salvation. He does not modify it on a person-to-person basis.

It was the same with the professor; He did not amend the rules because we chose a project we could not complete. He made sure the projects were possible to finish; he was an expert; a former Hollywood Producer.

Christ did not give us a Salvation in which the requirements were so difficult we could not be successful in serving Him or pleasing Him. It takes hard work, determination, desire, fortitude, understanding, knowledge, and wisdom that come from above if we ask. Symbolism is part of our life, and we need to understand how it applies to our salvation.

Every action or inaction in which humans are involved has a basis. Either the basis is the pattern God gives for our obedience or the wiles put forth by Satan that appears harmless or good. The Foundation of Salvation is rooted and grounded in is our Lord and Savior Jesus Christ. When we trust in the true Foundation the one true Foundation, our souls and eternity are secure. Satan pushes a false foundation. When tried on those sands of deceit he pushes with the weight of sins that are inherent to it – it crumbles.

The foundations Satan builds are akin to what God told the Children of Israel about their promises; Satan's promises of security, are as, bitter weeds springing up in a freshly plowed field. Listen to what Hosea said, *"They make many promises, take false oaths, and make agreements, therefore lawsuits spring up like poisonous weeds in a field,"* [Hosea 10:4].

About our Salvation and Satan's interactions in our lives once we are baptized and the Lord adds us to the Body (Kingdom) our lives, at that point, is like a newly plowed field and Satan is the bitter weeds. Sisters, we all know what a newly plowed field looks like. The rows are straight, new soil has been turned by a plow to the top; no weeds exist at that time. The soil looks and smells fresh, even moist when at one time, it was dry before the plow turned the soil (our hearts), and it is fresh and ready for the planting of the new seeds (The Word of God) which can continue growing and feeding on the nutrients in the soil.

Our adversary is standing ready to sow seeds of disobedience and defiance in the heart of the new convert, after a while, the seeds of Salvation began to grow, so does the bitter weeds of Satan ready to suck the energy and nutrients from the plant (Christian novice) is what Satan does. He has one engine of deception: ready, set, go when a new Christian is born. He plants bitter weeds (attractive idle promises) alongside the good seeds of righteousness in each area of your life from that day you obey the Gospel of Christ forward.

However, there is a bright spot in this analogy. As the seeds of righteousness grow stronger and the light of the Son of God shines, the Word of God waters and fertilizes the seed. The seed grows stronger, and the roots grow deep in the new soil. It is difficult for the bitter weeds to survive, though they might still grow, they are not strong enough to overcome the positive growth to destroy or smother it out.

As we get stronger in our service to God and our knowledge of the Scriptures increases so does our ability to withstand Satan's attacks, because, we know we have an Advocate promised by our Savior who helps us, guides us, and teaches us. His promises assured us of a Helper. The Holy Spirit is our down payment guaranteed by our Loving Savior before He returned to the Father, *"I will not leave you comfortless, but will send back a Helper to guide you into all righteousness," [Ibid].*

I have focused on the different garments about serving God. The examples I used, are facts based on Scripture, which gives us the ways that are pleasing to God and win us an eternal crown, and those who are not willing to please Him will yield an eternity without God.

We cannot allow God, rather our service to God to be a footnote – a reference when needed and not our complete focus.

My point here sisters is, God used symbols to train the minds of His people for the coming Messiah (Lamb for the Slaughter). Their enemies, the Romans of course, did not understand the symbolism and its connection. There are always those familiar with every aspect of the Law, as were Herod Agrippa II, whom Paul stood before and defended his belief.

There were those who were blind living in darkness because they said they could see, did not see, nor wanted to see (the Pharisees) who claimed they were righteous and refused to accept the Savior, though they knew the Prophecy of His coming. For those who were blind Christ came to give sight and take away sight from those who said they were not blind and could see.

Paul said the foolish things of the world confound the wise, *"But God hath chosen the foolish things of the world to confound the wise; and God hath chosen the weak things of the world to confound the things which are mighty," [I Corinthians 1:27].*

The Parables and symbolistic saying are still there for us to learn from, understand, and apply to our lives. Without a clear understanding of the Salvation Christ purchased, we are in spiritual danger. The world lived in darkness until the light came. Christ is that light. We understand the misery and dangers of darkness. Environments void of light are unbearable at times then and even now. Humans need light in their life; it is virtually impossible to function without it. Light is beneficial for spiritual, physical, mental, and emotional health.

Light is reflective of God. Christ is the Light of the World. Looking up at the beauty of the Moon at night when it is shining in its full strength is breathtaking. However, we know the Moon has no light of its own but reflects light from the sun. We like the moon, people of God, are symbolic lights in the world reflecting that light from Jesus Christ [the Light of the World], *"Neither do men light a candle, and put it under a bushel, but on a candlestick; and it giveth light unto all that are in the house. Let your light so shine before men, that they may see your good works, and glorify your Father which is in Heaven," [Matthew 5:15-16].*

We use symbolism in instructing our children. We are God's children, and the training came from God, maker of heaven and earth. Humans readily understand when explained to them in terms and with things, objects, or facts of which they can identify.

Darkness (the world), light (Christ) –are symbolistic. We are the [sheep] of His Pasture – He is our [Shepherd], *"For He is our God, and we are the people of His pasture and the sheep of His hand. Today if ye will hear His voice, Harden, not your heart, as in the provocation, and as in the day of temptation in the wilderness: When your fathers tempted Me, proved Me, and saw My work,"* [Psalms 95:7-9].

God is the author and finisher of our faith, not us. We cannot successfully pull it apart and shape it to our satisfaction by categorizing the Commands Christ left for us to follow. When we are ready to enjoy the pleasures of the world pull it and roll it into a shape that ultimately fits our desires. When we are through enjoying ourselves for that period put the ball of pleasure back into the cans of [sometimes] and put the top on it until the next time. We cannot conduct ourselves in this manner when serving God in spirit and truth.

God is not a Caricature Artist of Salvation. He did not draw a different plan for each individual, as a Caricature Artist would do. The artist draws an illustration of the human model of the individual they see in real-time.

The plan of Salvation God painted as an artist would on a canvas, to picture everyone there who desires to be part of the Kingdom Christ purchased, and the canvas is large enough for the artist to continue to add another soul with each stroke of His eternal brush.

Christ did not die for and purchase a piecemeal Salvation for us. His death purchased a unified body of believers, Jews, Gentiles, bond, slave, and free into One Sheepfold.

We cannot conduct ourselves as if Christianity is a Play-Doh religion; it is not! Nor can we shape and re-shape our Salvation in a way that is convenient for us. Watching a child use Play-Doh, they shape it to their ideas. Then tear it into small pieces and make little weird-looking Play-Doh statues. Once they are finished playing with it for that period press it back into the can and put the top on it.

Change is not without pain God endured the pain of watching His Son suffer and then die. Christ suffered the pain for thirty-three [33] years knowing He came to the world to take on sins of humanity ... [the sins of humanity are multiple sisters], and then die on the Cross. His death was heart-rending but bought about change – change gifted us Salvation – Salvation ensures our eternity of peace with God. Choosing to accept this gift (symbol) of Salvation requires a change – change is not without grief and agony – agony because we chose to leave friends, family, loved ones, and desire a new way of life not continue in living without God in our life, and taking advantage of and accepting, the gift of Salvation Jesus Christ purchased.

We can partake of the gift from the God of Heaven given an undeserving people because He loves us so much that He sent His only begotten Son to purchase our Salvation and way back to Him lost by the first sin of defiance and disobedience in the Garden of Eden. Change begins with pain and can end in an eternity of joy and peace.

We, as people of God, cannot allow the sins that are so attractive to crouch in our lives. If it stays in that fixed position too long, it takes over your soul. The idea of hunkering down is symbolic of staying in place for a time, as a predatory animal does…the slayer waits for their victim to come into their perimeter, and they advantage themselves by taking its life. Satan will do the same to you if you allow sin to squat for long or short periods in your life without amending the error.

Change is necessary – change is hard – change is painful – change takes time – change brings resistance – change can bring success – change equals swimming against the tide. It is like paddling in white water rapids. The ride is bumpy making the waters difficult to row; it is a virtual wild ride. When I think of swimming against the tide, I think of Salmon jumping over the tide to reach their spawning beds.

It takes an enormous amount of roaring power to get through white water rapids. Salmon can jump over the raging waves, we cannot. We paddle through the rough waters of this world (working out our Salvation). Christ paddled through the rough waters. We cannot jump over the Commandments and the path to eternity Christ left, we get our spiritual muscles ready for the roaring of the waters, or the sinful wiles of Satan will consume you!

- *Sisters, do not accept the defeatist mentality Satan pushes – "if I make it difficult enough they will give up" can you not hear his voice?*

Life cannot conquer you if you do not feed that beast – consider Job – consider what Christ did to ensure victory – we have victory, in our Lord and Savior. He did not say easy and smooth, but we are to put our mental, physical, emotional, psychological, and spiritual muscles to work – it is a journey worth taking. Trusting in our Savior to help us overcome – we enter the furnaces in this life that try us – preparing us for our reward - that reward is dwelling with the Triune God, for all eternity.

Christ left symbolism, as a tool of learning for us to become successful in our faithfulness…we are lights to those in our range of influence through the things we do, the lives we live, and the words we say. All these reflect the love, mercy, grace, and kindness of our Lord and Savior – let your garments of light shine brightly…

We use symbolism in our everyday lives, which makes understanding the symbolistic examples in the Word of God easier to navigate.

No matter, our knowledge or understanding, remain aware of sin; it leaves a residue…

CHAPTER THIRTY-THREE

# LIKE PLAY-DOH ON A SURFACE
# THE RESIDUE OF SIN AND ITS EFFECTS

Each time a child plays with the Play-Doh, it leaves a residue on the surface. The parent(s) will not know it is there or how much; it is not noticeable with the naked eye, unless you look closely, run your hand over the surface, or wipe the area with a paper towel.

Every trace of residue left on a surface means that less Play-Doh goes back into the can each time until finally the ball is smaller and does not fill the container any longer; it becomes necessary to replace it with a new container and throw the old one away.

Sin, like Play-Doh, each time you participate in the pleasures of it – it leaves a residue in your life. It, like the Play-Doh, is not discernible with the naked eye, nor can you run your hand over the surface, or wipe it with a paper towel, to see the amount of residue accumulated there. Sin does take away a little more from your spirituality each time you indulge. It, like the Play-Doh, on the surface, causes your spirituality and faithfulness to lessen and grows weaker over time, almost unobserved by you.

Sin also leaves scars and when we successfully come out on the other side of that challenge when that particular sin is before us, that scar should remind us never to go there again. When I was a girl, maybe between 7-8 years of age, I was not sure of the exact age at this point; however, I was very tiny. One of my brothers rode me on the handlebars of his bicycle on an asphalt highway ingrained with small rock pebbles. While we were riding he sped up and I fell off the handlebars onto the highway. As I went down, I broke my fall with both hands to keep from scaring my face, but my knees suffered, especially my left knee. It had a large lesion and scar on it. The wound was painful for a long time. After it healed over the years the lesion became smaller, but the scar is very visible.

That scar is very evident no matter what I do. When I look at my knee, it reminds me why and how I got that scar. When we overcome that particular sin we were caught up in, the scar from that sin, and like the residue left by Play-

Doh, reminds us how we overcame that sin and what efforts it took to achieve this success. I have hated riding a mobile bike since that time. Subsequently, from that time to the present, I changed my bike riding to a stationary bike, which has its dangers if you do not follow the instruction for use, but the chance of me falling off it is zero to none.

- ***Do you hate the sin you recovered from and never want it to be part of your life again?***

Sin is like a thief, it comes in the backdoor, the side window, the roof, or any other way not as guarded. We usually guard our front door, and that door faces everyone else's house so people can easily see. Thieves come in the less guarded entrance or area not as visible to the naked eye.

Finally, indulging has cost you spiritually and in faithfulness, you become weak, your faithfulness [like Play-Doh disappears in smaller amounts at a time] in your service to God. The residue of sin grows each time you partake and ultimately changes your life by adding another layer until the residue is not easy to wipe away with a towel like Play-Doh.

We cannot play in the pleasures of the world and think it will not have a long-term effect on our spirituality, as the build-up of the Play-Doh on a surface if not wiped each time, sin will continue to get thicker with each layer until finally, the pleasures of the world have replaced your faithfulness to God. There is counting in both the world and the Kingdom of God for losses or gains.

Our garments of counting sisters will be either: for the world or Christ, we cannot count both. Christ said, *"No man can serve two masters," [Ibid]*. Our garments of counting should add up to gain for Christ and loss to the world. Both are eternal in the end, one with God, and one without God. Joshua reminds us, *"Choose ye this day whom you will serve," [Joshua 24:15a]*.

Jesus died to purchase our right to the Fruit of the Tree of Life once again that was lost in the Garden of Eden.

- ***Why would you continue to pick the fruit of destruction from the Tree of Knowledge of Good and Evil?***

Though the fruit (pleasures of the world) are delectable and attractive to the taste buds and eyes, it is temporal and deadly.

The Scripture warns us in the Love Chapter of the Bible, about knowledge, tongues, and prophecies, *"Charity never fails but whether there be prophecies, they shall fail; whether there be tongues, they shall cease; whether there be knowledge, it shall vanish away. For we know in part, and we prophesy in part: but, when that which is perfect is come, then that which is in part shall be done away. When I was a child, I spoke as a child, I understood as a child, I thought as a child: but when I became a man, I put away childish things," [I Corinthians 13:8-11].*

The Word of God is from everlasting to everlasting. *"The Word became flesh and dwelled among man," [John 1:1].*

We are to speak God's Word in the times of light, times of darkness, in tribulation, and persecution it will not change, man has to make the change: God does not.

His dominion is an everlasting Dominion and no power on earth can destroy His Kingdom. Death cannot stop the Kingdom of God. Jesus said, *"Upon this rock, I will build My Church and the gates of Hell will not prevail against It," [Ibid].*

The great and terrible day of the Lord is at hand, repent, and flee from its wrath.

Sin is embellished by the grim reaper our most deadly adversary. His promises only end in the graveyard of misery and pain. Satan's promises are like aberrations – a temporal irregularity – think of Eve and Adam their basking in [knowing] only lasted a short time (morning to evening concept) when God walked daily in the Garden in the evening with His creation.

- *He called them to task for their defiance and disobedience, "Who told thee thou was naked?" [Ibid].*
- *"Have you eaten of the fruit of the tree of which I told you not to eat," [Ibid]?*

Sin cannot abide in the presence of God. He is holy and just. God expelled Adam and Eve from the Garden of Eden their [Earthly Paradise] and barred the way the Tree of Life lest they put out their hands, eat of the Tree of Life, and live forever in sin without hope.

Our Garments should be of praising God for His Grace and Mercy that He would not allow His creation to live forever in this condition. God knowing the weakness of the flesh planned before the creation of the world the way back to him. A way back to the Garden of Eden and the Tree of Life and in the end, have an opportunity to spend [Eternity] with God and for that [Eternity] the pleasure of partaking of the Tree of Life and its healing effects for all nations.

However, Satan will fertilize and water any tree from which fruit of pleasure you desire to partake.

Christ is our Tree of Life. He hung on a [tree] that we might have that [eternal] right. Christ purchased our Salvation with cost to Himself, not to man. It is an [Gift] of God. Christ came to earth and laid down His life voluntarily because of Love and because there was no sacrifice man could offer that would pay the blood debt in the way our Father God required it paid through a perfect lamb without spot or blemish nor hint of sin.

Christ laid down His life for us and He took it up again.

The offer Satan made to Eve in the Garden was an opportunity to "know" a privilege he did not create, and the man paid an awful price for Eve's choice. Satan's promises to man were vain in the Garden of Eden and his promises are still vain whereas his strategies have changed and are even more deceptive. It appears good on the surface; however, his offers are broken.

I think of a cake made to appear unbroken because it is supported by beautiful icing, when cut into is still broken. Satan is the Father of the lie as John the Apostle reminds us of what our Savior said about Satan, *"Ye are of your father the devil, and the lusts of your father ye will do. He was a murderer from the beginning, and abode not in the truth, because there is no truth in him. When he speaks a lie, he speaks of his own: for he is a liar and the father of it,"* [John 8:44].

Satan will take you for a wild ride of pleasure undergirded by lies and deception. Yet remember, Satan's train of pleasure has an end-of-track. His trickery steered Eve out on that limb he sat on with the first deceptive morsel of pleasure offered to man. God made man in his image and Satan hates God; He is an enemy of God. Satan hates God's creation and makes every effort he can to destroy the soul of man because he cannot destroy God.

Satan, like man, was created by God, *"But who are you, a human being, to talk back to God?" Shall what is formed say to the one who formed it, 'why did you make me like this?" Does not the potter have the right to make out of the same lump of clay some pottery for special purposes and some for common use?"* [Romans 9:20-21].

Though Satan is not human, the principle applies; he made a choice, like we, make choices. He just happens to make the wrong one. The Scriptures tells us [to know] is to *"Seek ye first the Kingdom of Heaven and its righteousness and all these things will be added unto you," [Matthew 6:33].*

What things! The things necessary for life and survival in this world; God can supply all our needs. Those first things are what God said seek not what we desire. Man seeks things of the world first and not the things of Heaven and righteousness. God has to come first. We cannot indulge in the pleasures of life to our fulfillment and when our desires, for the attractions of the world have diminished; then we seek Him!

This is man's way without evidence of the use of wisdom in this choice, which leads to spiritual destruction in the end; also, a tool of Satan. The pleasures of the world that blind our minds are as well, a tool of Satan. Sin leaves a residue like Play-Doh, each time one enjoys its pleasures, finally becomes a film hard to remove after it hardens with each added layer.

The pre-existing condition is a reality and not an illusion, and its master [Satan] is alive and well.

The people of Christ are right in the middle of his deceptive mastery but cannot allow the residue of sin to be part of their lives. We are, as Paul reminds us, have protective armor from this dangerous systemic condition. We are to put on the *"whole armor of God," [Ibid]* to fight against the wiles of Satan.

We cannot fight alone. However, with our armor [the Word]) and our Savior, we can continue to win the battles we have with the sins existing in the world. Allowing Christ to take the lead is a guarantee of success. There is only one bulwark against Satan, Jesus Christ our Lord and Savior, and the armor He provided through His death for our protection. A bulwark in Biblical times was a strong wall built around the city so when attacked by an enemy they were not able to penetrate its strength.

Trying to protect ourselves against this nemesis any other way is like waving a red flag in front of a bull. It gives him the [go] signal at your soul and life because he knows the weaknesses of man and we should never deceive ourselves into thinking we are stronger than he is. Satan is the god of this world. Satan deceived himself into thinking he could challenge God and win! Did he? Think about it …God is overall … the Master of the universe and all that exists in heaven and on earth.

I think of the analogy of the canary in the cold mine about this foe, we know he is here, he exists, he is evil, and he is prowling looking for souls. The dangers of this combatant were told by Prophets sent by God to His people and warned them down through the ages, of the evil deceit he wears like a garment.

- *Shall I mention once more of the many times, the first deception of humans started in the Garden of Eden?*

However, through whatever trials and tribulations we face on our Sojourn here on the road to an Eternity of peace with God, we encounter difficulty; but it is worth the count: gains of Eternity or gains of the world or losses of Eternity or losses of the world, the choice is each of ours to make.

We cannot live our lives trying to shape and reshape the Commandments of God as a child does Play-Doh.

Our choices will determine what our encounter with Jesus will be like in this world and the world to come.

CHAPTER THIRTY-FOUR

# WOMEN TAKEN IN ADULTERY ENCOUNTER WITH JESUS

Women, like Rahab, made their living from this profession by choice or because they did not have a choice or because of the pleasure and income derived from their choosing to indulge. Their survival, like Rahab's in the Old Testament, was Prostitution; a profession looked upon in the most negative sense. When caught in this act, the people stoned them to death for bringing that sin among them.

Adultery, one of the Ten Commandments under the Law was a sin and applies to us in this day and time; it is still a sin, *"Thou shall not commit adultery,"* *[Exodus 20:14].*

*"Flee from sexual immorality. All other sins a person commits are outside the body, but whoever sins sexually, sins against their own body,"* *[I Corinthians 6:18].*

*"Therefore, to him, that knoweth to do good, and doeth it not, to him it is sin,"* *[James 4:17].*

As we read examples in Scripture, Adultery is condemned by our Heavenly Father, *"Thou shall not covet thou neighbor's house, wife, maidservant, or anything that is thou neighbors,"* *[Exodus 20:17].*

It was hard for a single woman to make a decent living in those times. Women then were more of the homemakers, a helpmeet to their husbands not working outside the home. Jobs were not as lucrative for women then, as it is, in our day and time. Single women in this day and time are homemakers working and supporting themselves, but they have that option.

Hence, with jobs, for women were not as prevalent in Biblical times, so their incomes were dependent upon the men who desired their company. Of course, this profession rendered women a negative reputation in their villages. As was the woman at the Well, who up to that point, had five men who were not her husbands, and the sixth one she has at the time when speaking with Jesus, was not hers. He said, *"For thou, hast had five husbands; and he whom thou now hast is not thy husband: in that said thou truly,"* *[John 4:18].*

Jesus is the Light of the World. Whosoever follows Him will not walk in darkness; because they are following the only light we have to guide us through life, *"Then spake Jesus again unto them, saying, I Am the Light of the world: he that follows Me shall not walk in darkness, but shall have the Light of Life," [John 8:12].*

When we are in the world and separated from God we are walking in darkness as were the women caught in adultery or prostitution. Jesus forgave all of them who repented and desired to change their lives. Jesus did not condemn them (her) as their fellow citizens who did not consider their sins only the prostitute or adulterer they caught in the act. We see this in the reference John made when a woman caught in adultery encountered Jesus, *"So when they continued asking Him, He lifted up Himself, and said unto them, He that is without sin among you, let him first cast a stone at her," [John 8:7].*

The Scripture describes Jesus' encounter with three women in His ministry known as prostitutes or adulterers had mercy on each of them. The men wanted to stone them, which makes one wonder if they were of them that were her daily or weekly visitors and were as guilty of the sin as the ones caught in adultery! The Scriptures warns us to, *"Flee fornication; every sin that a man doeth is without the body; but he that commit fornication sins against his own body," [Ibid].*

Jesus encountered the woman with the Alabaster of Ointment who anointed His feet tell us of the heart of our Savior for all humanity. Jesus did not just come to save one nation of people but all people and be the sacrificial lamb for our sins, *"And one of the Pharisees desired Him that He would eat with him. And He went into the Pharisee's house and sat down to meat. And behold, a woman in the city, which was a sinner. When she knew that Jesus sat at meat in the Pharisee's house, brought an alabaster box of ointment, and stood at His feet behind Him weeping, and began to wash His feet with tears, and did wipe them with the hairs of her head, and kissed His feet, and anointed them with the ointment.*

*Now when the Pharisee which had bidden Him saw it, he spake within himself, saying, This man, if He were a prophet, would have known who and what manner of woman this is that toucheth Him: for she is a sinner. And Jesus answering, said unto him, Simon, "I have somewhat to say unto thee." And he said, "Master, say on." There was a certain creditor, which had two debtors: the one owed five hundred pence, and the other fifty. And when they had nothing to pay, he frankly forgave them both. Tell me, therefore, which of them will love him most?"*

Simon answered and said, *"I suppose that he, to whom he forgave most." And He said unto him, "Thou hast rightly judged." And He turned to the woman, and said unto Simon, "See thou this woman? I entered into thine house; thou gave Me no water for my feet: but she hath washed My feet with tears and wiped them with the hairs of her head. Thou gave Me no kiss: but this woman since the time I came in hath not ceased to kiss My feet. My head with oil thou didst not anoint but this woman hath anointed My feet with ointment. Wherefore I say unto thee, her sins, which are many, are forgiven; for she loved much: but to whom little is forgiven, the same loves little" And He said unto her, "Thy sins are forgiven."*

*And they that sat at meat with Him began to say within themselves, who is this that forgives sins also? And He said to the woman, "Thy faith hath saved thee; go in peace," [Luke 7:36-50].*

The woman with the Alabaster of Oil name is not mentioned, as well, neither is the Samaritan woman at the well, her name remains – unidentified. Jesus made the point there was no difference in the sin committed, *"All unrighteousness is sin," [Ibid]*.

Jesus looks at the heart something man cannot do. He did not ignore the fact she was an adulterer (prostitute). Jesus came to the world to purchase Salvation for humanity that included Jews, Gentiles, slaves, bond, or free, including women living this kind of lifestyle. The Salvation Jesus purchased, without exception, includes everyone.

However, our choice to obey and take advantage of this gift of Salvation is up to each individual. Jesus' statement, we see is to anyone, not just the women caught in adultery (it is not the only sin that exists) but after our cleansing too, *"Go and sin no more," [Ibid]*.

Jesus gave them a command upon His saying your sins are forgiven required a turning from the old man and putting on the new man. We see a change of heart or a tender heart in the example given in *[Luke 7:36-50]*, she recognized Him as the Savior, which the Pharisees sitting at meat in Simon's house did not. Her silent tears, kissing Jesus' feet, and anointing them with oil, drying them with her hair, tells us much more about her heart and desire to know and follow Jesus than any word she can speak.

The Pharisees sit in the judgment seat and thought themselves above her... she tainted their environment because of the life she lived. Mercy, pity, kindness, and forgiveness we see none of this in their dealing with this woman. As well, they questioned and challenged Jesus on what He was telling them. If indeed, it is possible to challenge our Savior! Endless questions and a rigid mindset left little or no room for them to accept Jesus' Words. They knew from Prophecy the coming of the Messiah who would save people from their sins. A woman of her reputation seemed to recognize Christ as above a normal man. Her actions spoke of her heart and their words revealed the thoughts of their hearts, out of the issues of the heart the mouth speaks, "*Keep thy heart with all diligence; for out of it are the issues of life,*" *[Proverbs 4:23]*.

The lives of these women caught in adultery changed after their encounter with Jesus. Everyone's life changed at his or her encounter with Jesus whether we continue to walk in the light is each individual's decision. Sisters, we wear garments, of change in the Kingdom of God and turn from our sins, allowing Jesus to help us in our day-to-day lives to overcome our sins and continue to grow as these women did. Jesus had mercy on all of them and will have mercy on us as well.

Then again, at the temple in Jerusalem, a woman was bought to Jesus caught in adultery, "*And early in the morning He came again into the temple, and all the people came unto Him, and He sat down, and taught them. And the Scribes and Pharisees brought unto Him a woman taken in adultery; and when they had set her in the midst, they say unto Him, "Master, this woman was taken in adultery, in the very act. Now Moses in the law commanded us, that such should be stoned: but what says thou?"*

*Jesus stooped down, and with His finger wrote on the ground, as though He heard them not. So, when they continued asking Him, He lifted up Himself, and said unto them, "He that is without sin among you, let him first cast a stone at her."*

*And again, He stooped down and wrote on the ground. And they, which heard it, being convicted by their own conscience, went out one by one, beginning at the eldest, even unto the last: and Jesus was left alone, and the woman standing in the midst. When Jesus had lifted up Himself and saw none but the woman, He said unto her, "Woman, where are thine accusers? Hath no man condemned thee?" She said, "No man, Lord." And Jesus said unto her, "Neither do I condemn thee: go, and sin no more,"* *[John 8:2-11]*.

Jesus' response remains the same with each of these encounters. He did not have respect of persons in any of the cases of adultery, prostitution, or any other sin of which those who came to him were taken in by…

Each of us, when we come to Jesus is guilty of sin. It may not be adultery, prostitution, stealing, lying, or any of these named sins it could be worshipping other gods of mammon, lack of humility, not helping those less fortunate, regardless it is sin, and we are guilty of something that is why we come to Christ that we might have help and forgiveness as the unnamed women in Scripture.

Salvation, the fragile fig….it is precious, purchased with the precious blood of Jesus Christ our Lord and Savior…

CHAPTER THIRTY-FIVE

# FINAL THOUGHTS ON SALVATION AND A BIBLICAL FRUIT THE FRAGILE FIG

A strong wind blew through the Garden of Eden because of Adam and Eve eating the forbidden fruit [Fig]. Satan produced a wind of defiance; at that moment, the two inhabitants fell prey to his deceit. Let us not join in the actions Adam and Eve involved themselves nor the exploits of the tribes of Ephraim and Dan in their defiant and idolatrous ways committed against our Holy Father.

The One Hundred Forty-Four Thousand (144,000) symbolic number of the tribes of the faithful to God, we see these two tribes (Dan and Ephraim) are not listed in John's account of his vision in *[Revelation 7:5-8]*. They were in the original Old Testament Twelves Tribes of Israel – but in the final judgment, as those who were faithful to God John's accounting did not include them.

Symbolically looking at *[Revelation 7:5-8]* the tribes of Dan and Ephriam who are not mentioned in the twelve tribes (144,000) listed because God was not pleased with their faithfulness we can know this can apply to us today in the last counting of that multitude described who were wearing white.

- *Ask yourself, will I (we) be in white in the last counting?*

Left out, left behind, displeasing to God will be in our eternal future if we are found at the judgment of having been displeasing and unfaithful to God.

Sisters, Figs are fragile fruit and easily knocked off the tree or if a sudden impact to the tree happens; they will fall. My mother had Fig Trees. The Figs constantly fell if a disturbance happened. We were picking up Figs off the ground continuously, including the ones that were not ripe that fell due to the impact.

Our Salvation can be symbolically compared to the fragile Fig… we face so many forces in this world after we come to Christ that we often need to pick up affected area of our faithfulness and continue to go forward strengthening our resolve to avoid that error again.

Strong winds of change and challenges instituted by our adversary are the underlying reasons for the weaknesses of the human flesh aided by the numbers of attractive choices that he dangles in front of us in this world are all in the scented potpourri pot of our lives. The people of God have forces to fight against and a multitude, of which, causes enormous levels, of fear and doubt.

Salvation cannot be looked at in an on-and-off light switch-like manner starting and stopping are not a part of Salvation; when I need it –it is convenient but inconvenient when I have a pleasure I want to indulge in I switch it off. We cannot run in and out of Salvation no more than we can be a light switch Christian, on and off, "Jesus said, *"No one who puts a hand to the plow and looks back is fit for service in the Kingdom of God," [Ibid]*.

Our life and service to God should not be in a footnote manner.

We strive constantly to keep our lights as bright as possible. We all have dimmer switch moments in our life; however, we continue to strive to reach our goal, *"We all sin and fall short of the glory of God," [Ibid]*; And *"If we say we have not sinned, we make Him a liar and the truth is not in us," [I John 1:10]*.

In our striving to be faithful, which is necessary we are not alone; Jesus is with us at all times. Everything or anything this world has to offer cannot compare to what we have in the promises of our Lord and Savior. Solomon tells us that it is all, *"Vanity of vanities, saysthe Preacher, vanity of vanities! All is vanity. Whatdoes man gain by all the toil at which he toils under the sun?" [Ecclesiastics 1:2-3]*.

There is no benefit to gaining the world; in the end, you lose everything. As mentioned before, it is like a wheel rolling downhill: it is hard to stop the wheel before it gets to the bottom even then it continues rolling on flat land before it hits an object to stop it.

We cannot live all our life in pleasure and when pleasure is no longer an attraction; we want to offer God what is left. Even the leftover foods are not attractive or tasty to the human palate; neither is spending the best part of your life in pleasure without any interest in serving God. Solomon also warns, *"Remember now thy Creator in the days of thy youth, while the evil days come not, nor the years draw nigh when thou shalt say, I have no pleasure in them," [Ecclesiastics 12:1]*.

Paul reminds us, no matter how difficult Satan makes our service to God; the Holy Spirit is God's seal of faithfulness for His people while we are living. Even though we may suffer different levels of persecution on earth during our journey, our souls are secure. The suffering is not for naught; our faithfulness to God will be a blessing with an eternal reward of being in His presence as long as He lives. Paul reminds us, *"In whom ye also trusted, after that, ye heard the Word of truth, the gospel of your salvation: in whom, also after that, ye believed, ye were sealed with that Holy Spirit of promise, which is the earnest of our inheritance until the redemption of the purchased possession, unto the praise of His glory,"* [Ephesians 1:13-14].

There are only two seals: the one of God and the one of Satan. There is not an alternative seal out there. Satan wants you to think it is. He presents it as [you] having a choice if you do not want to choose God or him. Nevertheless, be mindful, making the choices this world offers for your life is a choice for him. Let us remember, he is the master of deception; you cannot out-think, out-smart, or outwit Satan: whichever of these you prefer using as a description, Jesus is the only solution to the alternatives Satan makes so attractive to humans.

- *Satan is a spirit – we are flesh. How do you physically fight something you cannot see?*

Recalling my earlier analogy about him, he has the characteristics of a Lion (prowling and seeking) as Scripture describes in *[Job 1:6-11]*. We know, in this fleshly form we cannot kill a Lion with a stick.

James emphasizes to Christians why being mindful is so vital. We are subject to fall prey to Satan's destructive wiles. Being careful and avoiding a fixed attitude that 'we cannot fall, is the first danger.' We are all at risk with a chance of being caught in the clutches of the sins of this world, staying aware is key. If we sin, we acknowledge them before God's Throne then ask for forgiveness, and repent. We cannot become complacent in our Salvation, *"Let no man say when he is tempted, I am tempted of God: for God cannot be tempted with evil, neither tempts, He any man: But every man is tempted, when [he] is drawn away of [his] own lust and enticed. Then when lust hath conceived, it brings forth sin: and sin, when it is finished, bring forth death,"* [James 1:13-15].

After we sin, for so long, Scripture warns of the danger of becoming hardened losing the desire to change our hearts and return to God. We do not want to lose our moral compass and fall into immorality – immorality does not happen all at once; it is a slow-moving process unnoticed, as mentioned in previous chapters. When we are tempted, humans tend to fool themselves into thinking; I can rid my life of that temptation at any time.

Too many tomorrows come and go in our lives; humans are people of habit. After that sin (habit or desire) is so fixed in our lives, we cannot or do not want to change the habit that plagues our lives. It does not seem harmful; yet it [sin] is separating us from God each day that passes and we pander to its inviting arms of delight, and finally, the last thread is broken, and destruction is in our eternity.

John, the Apostle, in his vision, wrote, "*The rest of mankind who were not killed by these plagues still did not repent of the work of their hands; they did not stop worshiping demons, and idols of gold, silver, bronze, stone, and wood–idols that cannot see, hear, or walk. Nor did they repent of their murders, their magic arts, their sexual immorality, or their thefts,*"

[Revelation 9:20-21].

Satan wants you to worship other gods; he makes them seem innocent.

- *In our daily walk, we are to consider at every point, decisions we make, and every step of every action taken should ask ourselves, "Would Jesus approves of this?"*

We can easily know by studying the Word of God and rightly dividing the Word of Truth. John also reminds us, "*All that is in the world is the lust of the eye, the lust of the flesh, and the pride of life,*" [Ibid].

Therefore, we know what the world offers.

I do not think there can be enough said about the dangers of Satan and his wiles [they are plural, more than one]. The wiles of Satan compared to a cube four-square, all sides are equal with no escape. They are traps for the souls of humans. Once he traps you, there is no door to a foursquare cube; he and not you draw the lines of ownership.

The world offers us only pain and heartache, conforming to the world and its temporal state and the material things it offers is not pleasing to God. We are to transform not conform. Changing our way of thinking is necessary for this transformation so that we might present our bodies as a living sacrifice that will be holy and acceptable to God.

We are duty-bound [our reasonable service] to offer our body and lives as living sacrifices to our Lord and Savior. Christ offered His body and life as a sacrifice for our sins, we have that responsibility to do no less for Him if we want to inherit Heaven, Paul tells us, *"I beseech you therefore, brethren, by the mercies of God, that ye present your bodies a living sacrifice, holy, acceptable unto God, which is your reasonable service. And be not conformed to this world: but be ye transformed by the renewing of your mind, that ye may prove what is that good, and acceptable, and perfect, will of God," [Romans 12:1-2].*

I love you – these three little words are not hard to say to our children, parents, friends, or spouses. We say them to all these people and then prove it by our actions along with those words. Then again, Jesus said, *"If you love, Me keep My commandments," [Ibid].*

- ***Why is saying I love you to Jesus so easy, but proving it by our actions is so hard?***

The [If] condition, is there as mentioned, in previous chapters.

I love you creates an intimate personal relationship. You and I are personal pronouns. They give us focus and do not put that individual in a group setting. We each have a personal relationship with our Savior and Him with us. Christ said, *"I love you,"* and proved His love by the actions taken.

We can never give up on that relationship with our Savior and God. When my husband called me at work to tell me about his appointment with the Doctor to get the test results from his Bone Marrow test that the diagnosis was Multiple Myeloma, [Bone Marrow Cancer] is the day our world changed forever. Life was not easy-going anymore – the outlook became so dismal. That diagnosis changed everything for us even to the way we ate, what we ate, and especially for him. There were downhill days after his diagnosis. Life became even more important and his care a matter of urgency.

We tried cramming as much living into the days we had after his diagnosis as possible and enjoying as much as we could of the blessings God afforded us. I saw him many days suffering in every way, but never complained, not one of them. He had a quiet strength about him I never knew he had, not at the level I saw. My husband desperately tried comforting and reassuring me. He worried about me often whether I was eating, resting, or doing too much. He wanted me to stop teaching at two Universities and working an eight-hour-a-day job in a high-stress environment. There were days we awoke wondering what the next step would be! There was no certainty in life day-to-day regarding his care. On a daily, sometimes weekly basis, the doctors changed his medications and care, and the expenses mounted.

The cost of his care was paramount, so quitting any job was not practical at that time; it took every penny to keep us going, keep him going, pay the bills, buy his medications, and nourishing blood-building foods. He was in the hospital so much with blood issues, dehydration, Pneumonia, low iron count, and blood pressure instability problems until it was almost a weekly routine. He had days when his pressure dropped, yet he had a cheerful outlook with each of these setbacks, as much as was possible.

I know he was depressed at times but did not want me to worry so he tried to hide it. It was hard enough that his appetite was gone with the Chemotherapy given to him to fight this terrible disease and the added depression further intensified the situation. Yet, still added to that was the pain I witnessed during his bone-marrow test and how much he hated the pain piled upon pain he was already experiencing, was heartbreaking.

He would grip my hands to the point of almost breaking them because of the pain during the Bone Marrow Test. The days were heart-rending sitting with him for his Chemo treatments – yet in all of this he maintained a cheerful outlook, continued to say, "I am fine baby don't worry." The Velcade, also known asBortezomib, was so strong it affected his spine, the bones became fragile, and he had a hairline fracture after a few months rendering him having to wear a brace and use a walker to keep himself mobile. Yet, he never stopped.

We had a ramp built so it would help him navigate easier and not continually try climbing the three steps to the den door. He went to worship as long as he could until his health would not allow him to attend anymore. He was tired in April 2012, two months before he died. He said to me three weeks before his death, June 2012, "He wanted to stay with me but could go ahead and start enjoying Paradise with Jesus and he would wait for me there."

The point is that my husband never lost faith, he never gave up, and he was more concerned about me than he was about himself. All those long months and years of my husband's failing health, the only strength that I had I knew came from our Lord and Savior Jesus Christ. I saw a man of strong faith in his Salvation, his relationship with Jesus was firm, his faith in God was solid, and he trusted in the Word of our Lord and Savior Jesus Christ that He would not forsake or leave him. He said, "Jesus had overcome the world and the trails he faced; his illness was nothing compared to what Jesus faced."

My husband is a long-lasting example to me of unfailing faith. He held onto that promise of a new man upon Baptism. He said often, "I know that all the things that old man of me was guilty of, but Christ took my sins upon His self and carried them to the Cross for me. I have been baptized for my sins and they are gone."

My husband was a changed man after he obeyed the Gospel. I saw the change in him begin to take place as we studied, and he studied with other brethren before he was baptized then continued to grow to a mature Christian. He never gave up: but it took determination, fortitude, and an overall belief that a better life was waiting for him in Eternity. A life free of pain, heartache, cares of the world with its troubles, and a body free of pain for as long as God lives. He believed until the end in Christ's promise. He never gave up no matter the obstacles he faced/we faced each day.

His love for me seemed to grow in intensity and he held on to me tighter. Love is the greatest, as well as the most painful thing we can experience; it is both beautiful and beastly. The intensity is fierce, at times, with the depth that it can make a person feel. The bond between a husband and wife is at times unfathomable. God intended it to be that way the closeness, the uniqueness of that relationship.

The raw pain of losing my husband is indescribable. I can only say it came from the bond, the relationship we shared in good and bad times, in sickness and in health, until death did part us, but only physically. The rawness is there, I carry it every day. I feel as if I am missing a part of me that I cannot heal, but I know that Jesus keeps me going forward. He understands the suffering of losing someone you love.

My husband reminded me sometimes the relationship with us should mirror the relationship with Christ and His Bride, The Church He purchased with His Blood.

Christ is our strength and shield.

*The question to ask ourselves is why is it so hard to love our Savior and Creator back? He is the giver of all things.*

- *We follow the rules or guidelines for relationships on earth, why is it hard to follow the same pattern for the relationship with our God since that pattern came from Him?*

These questions we can ask ourselves!

In this world, Satan makes the rules for breaking the rules. God does not change the commands He gives us, nor does He make any new commands. We are to follow the patterns put in place by God there is no possibility of them ever-changing. Eternity is set as well. We as individuals love Christ and we individually serve Christ. In the same collective manner, the Body of Christ (His people), loves Christ and serves Christ, because He first loved us.

Love is an action...so is relationship building...Salvation is fragile, possess it...cherish it...it is a gift...it is an unearned gift (unmerited favor) of God because He loves us and wanted that relationship of love and obedience from His creation.

CHAPTER THIRTY-SIX

# FINAL THOUGHTS
# THE CONCLUSION

Flowers of Salvation do not bloom from sometimes. The seeds that we plant, water, and fertilize are what will bloom. We cannot address our Salvation on a sometimes haphazardly basis rather that care and cultivation are done continuously so our lives will please God. Christ gave all to purchase the soil of which we plant those seeds of Salvation. Essentially Jesus paved the way; it is up to each individual to take advantage of the gift.

In the spiritual albums of our minds, as we study and meditate on the Word of God – the Word of God should be taking root there while it helps us grow into spiritual maturity during our journey, for the time God has allotted us on earth.

The Word of God dwells in our hearts it is no longer, written in stone, but lives in the hearts (minds) of the people of God so that we, through the guidance of the Holy Spirit, know how to live, in a way that is, pleasing to God.

Christ came and lived among man on earth to give us a true picture of the Nature of God and the unified relationship of the Father and Son as the One and Only God. Christ promised to send a comforter and teacher to us: who is also, the third of the Godhead.

The Holy Spirit is our guarantee, of Christ being with us always. He promised that He will be with us always, "*Go into all the world and make disciples of all the nations, baptizing them in the name of the Father and of the Son and of the Holy Spirit, teaching them to observe all things that I have commanded you; and lo, I Am with you always, even to the end of the age,*" [*Matthew 28:19-20*].

We, through our faithfulness, will have the blessing of living with Jesus our Savior, the Holy Spirit, and God the Father, for as long as He lives. God has no beginning and no end, for He is eternal. Our spirit will inherit eternity. The clay house in which our Spirit dwells is flesh…flesh and blood cannot inherit the Kingdom of Heaven; this clay house is the temporary dwelling place of our spirit and the Holy Spirit while we work out our Salvation in fear and trembling.

We were created to serve God and not for our pleasures in life. God made man in His image. The Scripture reminds us, *"And God said, Let Us make man in Our Image, after Our likeness: and let them have dominion over the fish of the sea, and over the fowl of the air, and over the cattle, and over all the earth, and over every creeping thing that creeps upon the earth," [Genesis 1:26].*

God created man in His image to be both spiritual and loving. When we love our fellowman, we love God because we are created in the image of God. We as humans are flesh but have an eternal spirit that dwells in this earthly tabernacle because God is Spirit and not flesh and blood with an inherent ability to show love, care, compassion, and understanding as do our Heavenly Father Lord, Savior, and Creator.

Life is the most precious thing we have, especially, because we are made in the image of God. We have the responsibility for each other in life; all men are brethren, *"Whosoever shed man's blood, by man shall his blood be shed: for in the image of God made He man," [Genesis 9:6].*

We are to serve God in a holy and reverent manner. When we wear His name, Christian, we are people of Christ following His examples. The Psalmist reminds us, *"He sent redemption unto His people: He hath commanded His covenant forever: Holy and Reverend is His Name," [Psalms 111:9].*

We cannot place ourselves on the same level by using His name to identify ourselves; nor refer to any human in this way either; or can we live in a way to dishonor His name! We are, in all ways, when it concerns living this Christian life, Paul expressed in this manner, *"You are our epistle written in our hearts known and read by all men. Clearly, you are an epistle Christ, ministered by us, written not with ink; but, by the Spirit of the living God, noton tablets of stone; but,on tablets of flesh,that is,of the hear," [2 Corinthians 3:2-3].*

Our examples and walk will lead others to Christ and the Salvation purchased 2,000 years ago on the Cross. It is, for all who desires to love and serve God, *"If ye love Me, keep My commandments. And I will pray to the Father, and He shall give you another Comforter, that He may abide with you forever Even the Spirit of Truth whom the world cannot receive because it sees Him not, neither knows Him but ye know Him for He dwells with you, and shall be in you. I will not leave you comfortless: I will come to you."And, "Yet a little while, and the world sees Me no more; but ye see Me because I live, ye shall live also. At that day ye shall know that I am in my Father, and ye in* Me, *and I in you. He that hath my commandments, and keep them, he is one who loves Me and he that love Me shall be loved of Me Father, and I will love him and will manifest Myself to him.* "Judas said unto him, not Iscariot, *"Lord, how is it that thou wilt manifests thyself unto us, and not unto the world?"*

Jesus answered and said unto him, *"If a man loves Me he will keep My words: and My Father will love him, and We will come unto him, and make our abode with him. He that loves not keep not My sayings: and the word which ye hear is not Mine, but the Father's which sent Me. These things have I spoken unto you, being yet present with you. But the Comforter, which is the Holy Ghost, whom the Father will send in My name, He shall teach you all things, and bring all things to your remembrance, whatsoever I have said unto you,"* [John 14:15-26].

There is peace in Jesus Christ, *"Thou wilt keep him in perfect peace, whose mind is stayed on thee: because he trusted in thee. Trust ye in the Lord forever: for in the Lord Jehovah is everlasting strength,"* [Isaiah 26:3-4].

When thinking of the choices each of us makes for our Spiritual and secular life, I think of the poem Invictus. Both of those lives (spiritual and secular) are in the crosshairs of our being; we cannot separate them: one side of us spiritual and good serving God and the other side worldly and live from our perspectives does not line-up with what God wants for our lives. In the secular, like the spiritual world, God has to be the ruler of our life. Life is difficult and we will meet the challenges of pain and suffering in life, but do we give up? In the Poem Invictus, Henley wrote,

> *"It matters not how strait the gate,*
> *How charged with punishments the scroll,*
> *I am the master of my fate; I am the captain of my soul.*

Each of us is responsible for what we believe and where we place our trust and confidence (Captain of my Faith) and where we spend eternity, we choose how we want to live in this life, serve the God of Heaven, or the god of this world (The Master of my Soul). Each of us makes these choices here on earth individually...

The Age of Spiritual Enlightenment is here!

The Age of Enlightenment spiritually is upon us. The Scripture tells us time is passing swiftly and perilous times are here. Paul the Apostle wrote to

Timothy, *"This know also, that in the last days perilous times shall come. For men shall be lovers of their own selves, covetous, boasters, proud, blasphemers, disobedient to parents, unthankful, unholy, Without natural affection, trucebreakers, false accusers, incontinent, Traitors, heady, high-minded, lovers of pleasures more than lovers of God; having a form of godliness but denying the power thereof: from such turn away,"* [2 Timothy 3:1-5].

There are no races or colors in the Kingdom of God. Christ accepts all who desire to come after Him. He says, "Follow Me," is the Scriptural [dictum] and Jesus' solution to discrimination. We see this fact, when Jesus' sent Peter to Cornelius, *"While talking with him, Peter went inside, and found a large gathering of people. He said to them, "You are well aware that it is against our law for a Jew to associate with or visit a Gentile: but God has shown me that I should not call anyone impure or unclean: so, when I was sent for I came without raising any objection. May I ask why you sent for me?"* [Acts 10:27-29].

On the Day of Pentecost, representatives from every nation were in Jerusalem. The beginning of the people realizing from all over the world that the promises of God had come to fruition prophesied down through the ages by His chosen Prophets. John the Baptist, the last Prophet, was the voice of one crying in the wilderness. Isaiah wrote, *"The voice of him that cries in the wilderness, Prepare ye the way of the Lord, make straight in the desert a highway for our God. Every valley shall be exalted, and every mountain and hill shall be made low: and the crooked shall be made straight and the rough places plain: And the glory of the Lord shall be revealed, and all flesh shall see it together: for the mouth of the Lord hath spoken it, "Prepare ye the way of the Lord,"* [Isaiah 40:3-5].

Christ tore down the Wall of Petition for everyone. Love is the key to the [race] issue, *"Jesus said unto him, Thou shalt love the Lord thy God with all thy heart, and with all thy soul, and with all, thy mind. This is the first and great commandment: and the second is like unto it: Thou shalt love thy neighbor as thyself. On these two commandments hang all the law and the prophets,"* [Matthew 22:37-40].

In this Age of Enlightenment, there is a lack of love and respect for our fellow man, and the absence of that love and respect has a domino effect to it ... it has nowhere to go but forward in the same manner; rather it is going downhill from there. When people elevate themselves above others: it does eventually backfire. Jesus has no respect of person. There are no Jew, Gentile, bond, or free – all are one in Christ. We are all from one blood, from one man Noah who was the father of all nations on earth. There were born unto Noah three different nations.

To be pleasing to God, human beings must see each other as being important; created in the image of God. All human beings are important, in His sight. In this 21ˢᵗ-Century with so much advancement in every area of society, race relations, fairness, care for fellow man, and all the like is still slow in improving. People put people of different races into categories.

There is but one acceptable way to God for humanity to live, by using the example Jesus left for us of how to treat each other. Jesus pulled off His Divine Robe, came to earth, for all of humanity, not for one people or one group of people.

God's plan from the beginning is for the world to be one in Christ. No one is exempt from this plan. God loves all of His creation. We as each other's fellowmen have to be careful in our thoughts of and dealings with each other. Jesus is the final judge. We love man in the way He commands, or it will be to our disadvantage. The Age of Spiritual Enlightenment should not allow the insertion of even an inference of a Caste System in our Spirituality.

The only hierarchy, period, is the Triune God. Everyone else is on the same level. Christ said, All men are brethren, *"But you are not to be called 'Rabbi,' for you have one Teacher, and you are all brothers," [Matthew 23:8]* and *"There is no one good except the Father, "Why do you call Me good?" Jesus answered. "No one is good except God alone," [Mark 10:18].*

Alone is defined as a solo, single, or unaccompanied; solitary is self-sufficient, independent; and unaided is singlehanded…all these adjectives clarifies the God we serve and why He alone is good and has no respect of person.

Our Savior made these statements, therefore the question we should ask ourselves:

- ***What makes me better or worse because of my or their ethnicity, race, or status in life?***

We are all creations of the One God. Man puts each other in categories and Caste Systems. Our choices of what and how we conduct ourselves are a different discussion. God gives us choices; we choose whether we want to obey, but that or those choices will determine whether you are pleasing to God. We live with our choices; in reference to our fellowman let the choice be treating our fellowman whoever they are as a fellow respected, valued, and important part of humanity.

In this Age of Enlightenment, at a certain point in our maturity, recognize the effects of Satan and his bag of wiles he is spreading in a Johnny Appleseed manner in the lives of humans. We sometimes think of Satan only in America and affecting the people in the United States. However, it is critical: we view the effects of Satan in a broader sense. He operates throughout the world from the farthest reaches of the universe to each of our doors.

There are no territorial boundaries on the evilness of Satan as he moves around in a Johnny Appleseed manner. His wiles, as warned before, are not all unattractive or distasteful. The only way to identify and know them is through Scripture.

Jesus clearly explained the wiles of Satan. He was an angel (good at one time; God does not and did not create anyone or anything evil) so he knows of the weakness of man. Even though this is true, we know how to live in this world on our sojourn. We put on the whole armor of God. We (people of God) are susceptible and are caught up sometimes in wiles from his bag of tricks. Satan offers his sandbox with the sands of as many types of wiles as one desires.

We, if caught up, correct our spiritual compass direction, and get back on course. It is a battle, yet keep in mind, Christ won that battle at the Cross of Calvary. We can look to our Savior for that strength and help when we stumble in our spirituality. Our Savior knows how to help us identify that weakness, assist us in getting past it, and grow from that experience spiritually, especially when we can overcome them and put them in our success column. With every victory, we can move from the spiritual liability's column on our balance sheet in life to the spiritual assets' column.

Sisters, the Scriptures admonish us as babes in Christ; it is wise to note the danger in staying too long in the babe-in-Christ status; growth is required. Feeding that growth is necessary. That food is the Word of God. Jesus did not leave us without the proper food for growth. He did not say when He went back to The Father, "You are on your own, do your best." He left us a distinct pattern to follow, owing to the fact that we are flesh and blood, which means weakness is inherent in our nature. We are not hopeless, we have hope; nevertheless, it is necessary to take advantage of that hope and be faithful, obedient, and trusting in God and His promises, like Abraham, the Father of Faith did, *"Abraham believed God, and it was accounted to him as righteousness," [Ibid].*

Every step we take on our journey is in preparation for our eternity with God. If we do not prepare now, we cannot prepare at or after death; it is far too late at that point. The lack of preparation will convict us to an eternity without God. Now is the time to prepare to meet thy God: if, we want to meet Him in peace. Satan is fighting against our very efforts to attain that success.

Eternity is waiting consider these questions:

- *Where will you spend it?*
- *Are you ready to meet your God?*
- *Are you preparing now with all diligence on a second, minute, hourly, daily, weekly, monthly, or yearly basis? This means at all times…*
- *Is your confidence at such a level you are sure you are in the right relation with God? Check to see if you are living, as much as possible, in a life approved by God.*
- *Is your hope and prayer to Jesus each day to help you live for Him?*
- *The Day of the Lord will come as a thief in the night: are you listening to the warnings in Scripture?*
  Sisters, knowledge, and truth of Salvation come from God to man! We are in the last days, (each of us has the last day appointed on earth) the time to get ready, to be ready, is now!
- *Christ built the bridge and paved the path: are you using that bridge and walking that narrow path or trying to climb down and get through the valley on the wide road?*

Perilous times are here; guard your Spirituality and faithfulness with immense care staying on guard, at all times, not falling into the traps Satan has in his playbook, keep your relationship with Jesus strong, and strive to obey His commands for your life. We all, at different intervals, in our lives, seem to take one step forward and two steps backward or more. It appears or feels like we keep staring again.

Satan causes quite a bit of noise around humans. Sisters, we are to filter out that noise of deceit, the noise of lies, noise of wealth, noise of power, noise of success, the noise of money, as well as noise of self. All of these physical things, he pushes in our lives and will push, if he is allowed.

We can cut through the noise and allow the Word of God to be our guide. Jesus is not the author of confusion, but the author of peace. The message from our God is clear and understandable. The Word of God is not riddled with chaos but has specificity.

In contrast, the god of this world presents an enormous amount of confusion and noise; mostly of confusion providing those desires we want; as well as, inducing man into thinking the life we living to please ourselves is okay. We cannot allow all the earthly fashionable things to become our god or put them before the one true God.

Keep in mind Satan is pandering for your soul.

The errors we fall into in our lives and the things we do in this world are a symptom not the cause of sin, rather sin is the cause of the errors in which humans get involved.

Despite our falling spiritually at times, it is not necessarily true we are not making progress – progress does take starting again to see progress. This is another tool right out of Satan's playbook. He wants you to labor under the illusion you are failing God, failing those around you, and failing yourself. It takes brushing this elusive mist out of the way and persists in going forward. God is there to assist. Satan wants you to think He is not. Any tool he can use to pull you back, confuse, or cause you to doubt yourself; he will use it; it is what he did at the beginning and has done since the beginning.

The Hebrew writer reminds us to look to Jesus the author and finisher of our Faith, *"Looking unto Jesus the author and finisher of our faith, who for the joy that was set before Him endured the cross, despising the shame, and is set down at the right hand of the Throne of God,"* [Hebrews 12:2].

We cannot afford to suffer a deficit in our Spirituality, *"But if I tarry long, that thou may know how thou ought to behave thyself in the house of God, which is the church of the living God, the pillar and ground of the truth. And without controversy great is the mystery of godliness: God was manifest in the flesh, justified in the Spirit, seen of angels, preached unto the Gentiles, believed on in the world, and received up into glory,"* [I Timothy 3:15].

Physical and Spiritual foods offer life, both are important. Humans find comfort in the physical food they consume. There are various types of comfort foods in the world that humans drink and eat: coffee, tea; they eat chocolate, ice cream, and other foods or drinks to find comfort in times of stress or just because they enjoy it and find pleasure in eating. We can think of this concerning comfort food spiritually. The Word of God is the Spiritual comfort food that can satisfy any appetite and we do not need a variety to satisfy our appetite. Our Savior is the Word that became flesh and dwelled among men. We can have hope and comfort that He is sufficient to supply all our needs.

I think of the popular song of the 1970s, Love Train. That love train was traveling all over the world. It is a very compelling song. Just think of the message it sends. Christ is our Love train, but it is universal. Christ's love train started at the cross. All who desire can board that love train. It has traveled and is traveling all over the world. Jesus gave His life for the Salvation of man, not, for just one people, but that we can all be one people – people who serve and worship our Savior in Spirit and Truth.

Paul reminds us of this fact, *"There is one Body and one Spirit, just as you were called to one hope when you were called, one Lord, one Faith, and one Baptism, one God and Father of all, who is over all and through all and in all,"* *[Ibid].*

There is one way to board this love train. The fare is our ability to love. We are to love God above all and then love our fellowman the way Christ taught, *"Love thy neighbor as thyself,"* *[Mark 12:31, Matthew 22:39].* Abide by the Golden Rule, show mercy, forgiveness, care, kindness, longsuffering, i.e., *"Fruit of the Spirit,"* *[Galatians 5: 22-24]* putting this Fruit in action, then serving God would be no issue to us.

In the tenth chapter of Zechariah, the Prophet in the fourth verse counsels us that Christ, as promised, would come from the tribe of Judah, and:

We have stability in Christ – Christ is the Cornerstone, "So this is what the Sovereign Lord says, *"See I lay in Zion, a tested stone, a precious cornerstone for a sure foundation; the one who relies on it will never be stricken with panic. I will make justice the measuring line and righteousness the plumb line, hail will sweep away your refuge, the lie and water will overflow your hiding place,"* *[Isaiah 28:16-17].*

Christ is the ruler over our lives and our victor in the battles we face – consider these three facts:

**Christ is the Bow,** Our reliable and long-lasting strength *"But you Bethlehem Ephrathah though you are small among the clans of Judah, out of you will come for Me one who will be ruler over Israel, who is from of old, from ancient times,"* *[Micah 5:2, Genesis 49:10].*

**Christ is a Tent Peg**. He is the strength that grounds us, *"I will drive Him like a peg into a firm place; He will become a seat of honor for the house of His Father,"* *[Isaiah 22:23]*.

**Christ is worthy of all honor and praise**. The description of our Savior above does not fit any idols or gods of man's devising. Power, money, wealth, authority, fame, and success in this life are all fleeting. We stand in jeopardy every hour we do not allow God to be our source of power, *"I can do all things through Christ who strengthens me,"* *[Philippians 4:13]*.

The fact is there is an eternal disconnect between the God of Heaven, creator of all things, and the god of this world Satan, adversary of God, and man. Concerning your eternity and salvation, facing reality is vital. Satan's propaganda is strong, and humans are vulnerable. He has fed his ideology to humans for centuries. As it is ingested, it begins to take hold of your life is why John the Apostle warns so sternly about his wiles from the teaching of our Savior. Jesus Christ said, *"He is a liar and the father of it,"* *[Ibid]*. The warning of our Savior should give us pause. Satan comes only to destroy.

There is no security in anything else on this earth. We create idols for ourselves in our minds and hearts, which, therein is no happiness or security. Sisters, as mothers and guides for our children, we are to teach them that none of the things of the world is lasting; they are to put them, in a proper perspective in their lives, as they go forward.

Our Lord and Savior Jesus Christ have drawn the line in the sands of time, about how we are to view material possessions. We have a command to train our children to obey God in good or bad times and not allow the worldly blessings to lead them away from God, *"Train up a child in the way that he should go and when he is old will not depart from it,"* *[Proverbs 22:6]*.

We are also to warn them, *"Be careful or you will be enticed to turn away and worship other gods and bow down to them. Then the Lord's anger will burn against you, and He will shut up the heavens so that it will not rain, and the ground will yield no produce, and you will soon perish from the good land the Lord is giving you. Fix these words, of mine in your heart and minds, tie them as symbols on your hands, and bind them on your foreheads. And ye shall teach them to your children, speaking of them when thou sit in the house, and when thou walk by the way when thou lie down, and when thou riseup,"* *[Deuteronomy 11:16-19]*.

Mothers have a great influence on their children's training. We teach them that all power is of God and not man, and they are wise when they seek the things of God first, *"But seek ye first the Kingdom of Heaven and all its righteousness and all these things will be added unto thee,"* *[Matthew 6:33].*

We cannot allow them to put the cart before the horse. Once they get a taste of the money and wealth of this life and we think with a word later in their lives, can change their perspective, we are wrong. Remember the Rich Young Ruler – he could not back up on the fact he had all of these things but could not give them up to follow Christ.

If they start from their youth, by prioritizing worldly possessions, they can see that a loss of earthly wealth is not all to life and spiritual wealth is more enduring and lasting. Our Spiritual wealth was tried by fire, and not found lacking; our Savior proved through His living in this world; then His death, burial, and resurrection. He loved us enough to purchase a greater wealth and power for us that are more enduring even throughout eternity.

Satan has a through theme…that theme is to destroy God's people and take as many to an eternity of misery and separation from God, as possible. Firstly, he [hates] God; secondly, he [hates] God's people; and, lastly, and he is [eternally] lost. His blatant defiance, disobedience, lust, and greed for all power got him thrown out of heaven and left him without any hope of eternity with God.

Look at the results of his disobedience; it should motivate anyone to do all they can to obey and be faithful to God – God's plan, in place, before the creation of the world; was for His people to worship Him in faithful obedience and humility: and at life's end spend eternity with Him.

All the attractive, deadly traps Satan has lain, do lay, and will continue to lay for humans to throw them off their Spiritual compass, is to lead them down that wide road rather than that narrow path spoken of in the Scripture. We, as potential victims, of his schemes cannot allow him to assist us in making that choice but look to Jesus as our only choice.

Our attitude toward the law, power, money, and authority should mirror our Savior's – He requires faithfulness and obedience. He wants our hearts and obedience.

Sisters this should be a kitchen table priority for our families. We decide whom we want or what we want to follow: the Salvation Christ purchased and worship Him on that narrow path, as our Lord and Savior, or follow the way of the world and its gods down that wide road that leads to destruction.

Sisters, we all make stew or soup for our families. The taste is very satisfying and perks up the taste buds. I use very, which is not a word often used to express a point any stronger; then again, here is the example of the response to a mother from a child when asked how does the soup/stew taste, "It is very good mama" is the answer. Satan makes the sins of this world into pots of stew or soup and its taste is [very] satisfying and pleasing to our mental and emotional taste buds.

Awareness is the key to his schemes. Like stew or more exactly soup, has different types of vegetables, herbs, and meats in it when served together it is hard to tell everything that is in it; just that its taste is pleasing to the palate and we want more; this is the way he presents his traps to humans, forever the master of disguise.

Regardless of the defiance of the people around us, we have a moral, integrity, and community responsibility to continue to teach God's Word and lead people to Christ. We, nowadays, see religious and ethnic conflicts almost daily. We cannot allow Satan to guide our morals and integrity or desires into an idolatrous condition in the pleasures of this world that he makes available for us to enjoy so much. Satan wants you to run hither and yon in this world of religious confusion, which causes resignation and defeat. He knows Christ is the one and only Savior and purchased the Salvation (Kingdom of God) with His blood but wants to confuse and mislead as he did from the beginning and is still up to the same tricks he used against humanity from the start.

He desires to make you believe it is okay to sidestep and enjoy pleasures of this world; it is okay what we are doing is not that bad. Each time we sidestep and compromise our morals and integrity, we get further from Scriptural Truth and lend an ear to Satan's truth, which is not truth but a trap. Satan plans to stay within the realm of Biblical facts but will add or leave out a word, which renders it outside of the realm of the facts of Biblical Truth – again he did it with Christ in the wilderness.

- *What do you think he will do to you?*

Satan has a reptilian personality. He is cold-bloodedly treacherous. He works incognito, usually coming at his victim through others, especially if they are close to you or in ways he knows will affect you the most. He will pretend to care about you until your entrapment in one of his wiles is complete. He has deceived people down through the ages; and continues to deceive and will deceive even more in the future.

Satan is a roaring lion. A Lion plans to take its victim's life. Satan plans to take your life and soul. Your life now and your soul later; his plan has a long-tail effect on it. The description of Satan the Bible gives of being a cold-blooded adversary should be a sobering thought in our lives. He has nothing to lose; he lost it all in his lust for power and he wants us to lose our souls because he knows we have an opportunity he does not and that makes him angry and hates you even more.

We have the Blood of Christ and Salvation it purchased for us. He cannot take advantage of it. Consider sisters, he was a spiritual being from his creation and was with God, just as are the Host of Heaven. There is no Salvation for him and the angels that followed his lead in defiance against God, rendering them and him with having no hope for redemption. We have that hope.

- ***The question to ask ourselves is why, would we, after Christ purchased our Salvation allow our adversary, to steal it in bits and pieces, at a time?***

Paul gives us these warnings: a call to action: why not take it, *"Put on the whole armor of God that we might be able to fight against his wiles," [Ibid].*

Satan is relentless and his strategies have a look of opacity. The only way we can recognize them is through Scripture, another warning from Paul, *"Study to show thyself approved unto God," [2 Timothy 2:15a].*

The description of Satan should make us cringe, in just that he is like a roaring Lion –

- ***Who would challenge a Lion?***
- ***Would you win?***
- ***Which voice peals forth to you the strongest, God or Satan?***
- ***Do you know the voice of God when you hear it? [God's voice is in Scripture and the Holy Spirit is guiding you].***

Satan's voice has appeal and the truth he hides the lies he tells in the attractive worldly love overtures he makes for you … you will find it is in direct defiance to the Word of God. As mentioned, before, he uses portions of the Scripture (takes it out of context) to lure people into his evil traps for their soul, "come into my web said the spider to the fly."

Webs built by spiders are beautiful but are dangerous for the flies caught in them.

Sisters at times, we have run into a spider web that we did not see. It is difficult to pull that web off; it is stuck to our hands and the feel of it is evident, you know it is still there. It has an eerie feel to it; this is a good way to think about Satan and his ploy for your soul; if your gut instinct questions it, listen before you proceed.

We can be thankful that we are a child of God and the fowler's snares do not trap us with no way out in our life. God is with us and will not allow us to be a burden beyond our ability to bear it and has a way out of the fowler's snare. Our God is faithful in the promises to His Children. However, we as His children might suffer from the entrapment, but we are not hopelessly trapped, "*Blessed be the Lord who hath not given us as prey to their teeth. Our soul is escaped; as a bird out of the snare of the fowlers: the snare is broken, and we are escaped. Our help is in the Name of the Lord, who made heaven and earth,*" [Psalms 124:6-8].

There is a cacophony, of voices in this world; all pulling at our hearts and minds; at times in unison, it can become overwhelming, which is why awareness of who Satan is – is so vital.

Peter reminds us through the Cross of Jesus Christ is the only road to royalty, "*But ye are a chosen generation, a royal priesthood, a holy nation, a peculiar people; that ye should shew forth the praises, of Him who hath called you out of darkness into His marvelous light; which in time past were not a people, but are now the people of God: which had not obtained mercy, but now have obtained mercy,*" [2 Peter 2:9-10].

God's will is not done through human might, but through Jesus, as Zechariah expressed, " *Then he answered and spake unto me, saying, This is the Word of the Lord unto Zerubbabel, saying, Not by might, nor by power, but by My spirit, said the Lord of hosts,*" [Zechariah 4:6].

The Apostle John wrote from the Isle of Patmos. When Christians at that time, as we now are victorious over the beast and his image (Satan) will sing the song of Moses and the Lamb, *"They held harps given them by God and sang the song of God's servant Moses and the Lamb: Great and marvelous are your deeds. Lord God Almighty just and true are your ways King of the nations," [Revelation 15:2b-3].*

Moses freed the children of Israel from bondage and slavery. Christ freed humanity from the bonds and slavery of the Law paying the price, the sin debt. We can be joyful that we have freedom in Christ and no longer are slaves to the wiles of Satan.

As the Ark was the symbol that God was among His people in the Old Testament, the Holy Spirit is our guarantee that God is among His people now. He said to Moses, *"There I will meet with you, and from above the Mercy Seat, from between the two cherubim that are on the Ark of the Testimony, I will speak with you about all that I will give you in commandment for the people of Israel," [Exodus 25:22].*

We are sealed by the Holy Spirit that we are God's, *"In whom ye also trusted, after that, ye heard the Word of Truth, the gospel of your salvation: in whom also after that ye believed, ye were sealed with that Holy Spirit of promise," [Ephesians 1:13].* Our God knows each of us and He allows us to know Him as well. Our prayer and recognition should be as David the King, who was a man after God's own heart, *"O Lord, thou hast searched me, and known me. Thou know my down sitting, and mine uprising, thou understand, my thought afar off. Thou compass my path and my lying down, and art acquainted with all my ways. For there is not a word in my tongue, but, lo, O Lord, thou*

*know it altogether. Thou hast beset me behind and before and laid thine hand upon me. Such knowledge is too wonderful for me; it is high, I cannot attain unto it. Whither shall I go from thy spirit? or whither shall I flee from thy presence? If I ascend up into heaven, thou art there: if I make my bed in hell, behold, thou art there. If I take the wings of the morning*

*And dwell in the uttermost parts of the sea; Even there shall thy hand lead me, and thy right hand shall hold me," [Psalms 139:1-10].*

Sisters, Paul the Apostle reminds us we can have confidence in where we will spend eternity and that we are heirs of God through Jesus Christ. We have confidence in the Word of God and His magnificent promises; the Holy Spirit as He assured us, is our guarantee or down payment.

Hear the assurance that Paul gives us given to him by the Holy Spirit, *"And if Christ be in you, the body is dead because of sin; but the Spirit is life because of righteousness. But if the Spirit of Him that raised up Jesus from the dead dwell in you, He that raised up Christ from the dead shall also quicken your mortal bodies by His Spirit that dwells in you. Therefore, brethren, we are debtors, not to the flesh, to live after the flesh. For if ye live after the flesh, ye shall die, but if ye through the Spirit do mortify the deeds of the body, ye shall live. For as many as are led by the Spirit of God, they are the sons of God. For ye have not received the spirit of bondage again to fear; but ye have received the Spirit of adoption, whereby we cry, Abba, Father. The Spirit itself bears witness with our spirit, that we are the children of God: And if children, then heirs; heirs of God, and joint-heirs with Christ; if so be that we suffer with him, that we may be also glorified together,"* [Romans 8:10-17].

Therefore, we have hope through the resurrection of Jesus Christ our Savior for an inheritance that is incorruptible, undefiled, and eternal. Our inheritance is waiting for us. We have a Mansion promised and built by Jesus for His faithful servants to dwell in the beauty of peace and joy, *"Blessed be the God and Father of our Lord Jesus Christ, which according to His abundant mercy hath begotten us again unto a lively hope by the resurrection of Jesus Christ from the dead. To an inheritance incorruptible, and undefiled, and that fade not away, reserved in heaven for you,"* [I Peter 1:3-4].

The comment that Brother Harris, (Minister, McAlmont Church of Christ) made in one of his sermons clarifies the point of why it is so important that we know that our Salvation is secure; it is only through Jesus Christ. There is no other way we will be able to have the Salvation God promised it is only through His Son. He said, "The DNA of Salvation is in the blood that Jesus shed and the ticket to an admission that we might enter into the triangle of the unity of God the Father, God the Son, and God the Holy Spirit."

Knowing that we are under the blood of Jesus Christ, and it is the propitiation for our sins should bring us joy and peace.

In reference to the burdens of this life that we bear, they are lighter through the sacrifice our Savior made on the Cross. He lifted our burdens of sins and nailed them the Cross. He gave us a reason to hope to know the weightiness we carry is doable through Him. Keep in mind what He said, *"Come to Me all ye that labor and are heavy laden,"* [Matthew 11:28-30].

However, that cliff of sin is there, and one misstep could cause spiritual destruction or a fall: Christ is our surety. We can plant our feet firmly in Our Lord and Savior. Our feet do not slip when we plant them in His promises. Faith is the key and understanding is the soil in which we plant our seeds of faith.

Isaiah reminds us that we cannot afford to ignore the call of our Savior and God to repentance, *"Do not ignore the call of God, nor dismiss His words when spoken to you," [Isaiah 65:12].*

Micah years later, as Isaiah said about ignoring the call of the Savior, warned the people of the coming Savior and His reigning authority overall. He came to purchase Salvation for man and offer forgiveness and mercy to those who turn from their sins or judgment if they do not, *"I will take vengeance in anger and wrath on the nations that have not obeyed Me," [Micah 5:15, Joel 2:2, Amos 5:8].*

In a 21st-Century analogy, the elevator pitch for the Salvation of man started long before Jesus was born into the world. He made that pitch more than 2000 years ago. Jesus came to fulfill the law, bring unity to man, spread the good news, offer Salvation through His death on the Cross of Calvary, establish the Kingdom of God, and bridge the gap between man and God lost in the Garden of Eden.

Christ came to offer life and light to all men. The reasons are eternal, all leading to Salvation for humanity because He loves us. Love is the driving factor of our Savior leaving His throne to humble His self and live in a sinful world.

God knows our sins and offenses that we have committed, which are many. The Prophet Amos said, *"I know how many offenses and how great your sins," [Amos 5:15].*

Sisters, we cannot fool God we only deceive ourselves. Therefore, when we know we sinned we soothe our feeling or conscience by believing God missed that one. Our Father does not miss anything, but man can and does, individually or collectively. Amos further shared with us the judgment on Israel because of their disobedience, *"This is what the Lords says, for three sins of Israel, even for four, I will not relent. They sell the innocent for silver and the needy for a pair of sandals. They trample on the heads of the poor and on the dust of the ground and deny justice to the oppressed. Father and son use the same girl and so profane My Holy Name," [Amos 2:6-7].*

Sisters, we have hope in this life and eternity, Jesus Christ gave His life so we could have that hope of eternity and assistance in life while we journey here in this world. Regardless, of the problems, we face; or the situations life presents us, God's Promises are solid. Let us not create any additional situations or participate in worldly situations that we know are not approved of by our Savior.

Sisters, we all see things in life in different ways – women have this seemingly inherent gene more than our male counterparts do. We differ in our personalities, characteristics, perspectives, and viewpoints, which is good. However, as Christians, Women of God, and Pearls of the Kingdom: where we might not agree in the other areas of our life or from secular viewpoints: Our Lord requires His servants to unite through His Word our guide and unifier. Christ is our head – Christ established the Church – Christ purchased the Church – Christ died for the Church – Christ washed away our sins. There can be no division, between serving God and Salvation.

Love and unity is an attitude: A Be-attitude.

We should stand in awe, of our Savior that He died to create the love and unity through the Salvation purchased planned before the creation of the world. God gives, we as women, a command as well to teach, to lead by example, to practice discipline, to exhort, to train, to guide, to love, and above all, serve Him in Spirit and in the truth that no man can have any reason to attach blame to our life.

We are to fulfill the commands of God – as sisters in Christ that we might be found pleasing to God and not lacking in our faithful service so we can hear Him say to us, "*Well done My good and faithful servant,*" *[Ibid]*.

We as sisters of the Kingdom are to continue taking up that torch and carrying it forth as we received it from our sisters (forerunners) who have gone to their rewards and be the same example in our life for our sisters as they were for us in theirs. Wherefore, we of this time are careful not to drop the torch of faithfulness and to let the light shine Christ commands us to have in our life. We are reflections of Christ, not the light; He is the light. We are the bearer of the light, a portrait of the light.

Satan is an imminent danger at all times. Each moment one spends in any wiles he uses is a break-glass moment. There is no path to spiritual victory when we are involved with man's chief adversary. Even the diminutive things he pushes that he makes appear so innocent, and a much-needed factor in your life is a threat to our Salvation. Every path Satan takes you down is one path too far.

Satan knows the end game of all the pleasure he purposes, it is a loss to your soul for eternity. This is his main plot because he has no chance of redemption; this and the fact he hated God is the driving force behind every evil deed he pushes.

Sisters let us not damage or mar our image as women of faith and members of His Blessed Kingdom. Also, cause no other sisters, mature or immature Christians to stumble on their way to eternity and their walk-in life here. It is difficult enough without us making it harder by not providing that positive example they can follow and continue to have the heart it takes to be pleasing to God.

God wants the garments of our hearts. The Day of the Lord will bring justice and punishment. It will not be light for all as Amos told the people of God in *(Amos 5:20)*.

- *Are we looking forward to the Day of the Lord?*
- *Are we practicing righteousness, faithfulness, and obedience to the will of God?*

God has the Assyrian army still in place as we see the Prophet Amos warned the people of imminent danger if they did not obey.

- *God does bring about justice for both evil and good, which side are you on?*
- *There are only two sides we can be on God's or Satan's – think about the question and examine your heart then ask yourselves*, whose side am I on?

We as Christians are not in the pacifying business, but the truth and righteousness business. We cannot placate the feelings of others saying what they want to hear and not what is the truth of God ... God does not accept our excuses, nor will he accept ones that are consoled into thinking they are right in what they are doing when they are not. Obedience is according to God's plan for man, not ours (your) plan. Jesus has the final word on where we spend eternity.

- *Why can we not seek His wisdom to make the best decisions in our lives now?*

Christ left specific instructions to life and righteousness unchangeable and fixed throughout eternity as long as God lives. There is a life of peace beyond this veil of tears, a place where there are no pain, tears, heartache, death, only life and peace with our Triune God who is worthy of the battle this physical life attaches to our lives and the spiritual battles Satan wages against the people of God.

God is the pearl of great price, the field purchased (obedience) is worth the struggle.

Our Father is worth any battle we face. Jesus Christ thought us worth that battle He won ending with the crucifixion on the cruel cross of Calvary. No matter how often I read the Crucifixion account in the Bible, it is fresh each time I read it; I thank God for the constant reminder of the price Christ paid. Each Lord's Day sisters, we are reminded of this fact less we forget the cost of our Salvation.

Truth is necessary, we cannot, in good conscience speak any less saying what others want to hear will not bode well for them nor us. If we neglect this fact it puts them on a collision course with the Righteous God of Heaven and truth, no pacification will prevail.

Serving God in obedience and righteousness according to the Scriptures is essential for life here and life in eternity.

Our faithfulness can give comfort to those who struggle, understanding that we at point walked the same path (though each of our struggles may be different, yet they are struggles).

- *How do we expect others to keep the faith if we do not keep the faith?*

We are to continue to give them not a handout (judging) but a hand-up (encouraging) them and aiding them in their efforts to go forward and live faithfully in service to our Lord and Savior.

In conclusion, no human can tell us the length of time we have on earth or guarantee us how life will be while live. There are secular actuaries, who, based on certain data analysis, sets of figures, projections, considering the anticipated inflation over a certain number of years, and the amount of money it will take to live in the manner, in which one is so accustomed, but they cannot tell anyone how long you will live.

Human insight and human error are difficult to defend or understand sometimes are why our God and Creator gave us the path we can walk because He purchased Salvation for all which compensates for our error of human weakness. We all have a different perspective in life is why humans are so torn with all the emotions bought to surface in each of us.

Sisters, we are in emotional overload at times. The Scripture warns we cannot go on with our individual thoughts or feelings they are no gauge of right or wrong. We look to Scripture; it gives us what is right/wrong or acceptable/unacceptable to be pleasing in His sight.

Sisters, we do have both a physical and spiritual actuary: the one and only God, who knows all things. He told us the length of man's days, not how long you will live between your birth and 70 years of age. The only thing we know, is *"The length of man's days is threescore and ten and if by reason of strength, they are 80 years," [Ibid]*.

Sisters our garments should not allow the devil to draw us into a Faustus attitude; getting everything I want in this world: there is a catch to that mentality. He wants your soul and if you make this bargain with him, you are selling your soul short for material possession of this world, which perishes as they are used. After you live and enjoy life and finally want to turn to God, then Satan says, "Oh no, your soul is mine. I gave you everything you wanted in exchange for your soul. I kept my end of the bargain and you – you cannot, nor will I let you back out of yours."

Hence, humans often major in the minors in life and do not obey the God of Heaven and what He tells us is pleasing to Him. When it comes to I want, I desire, I need, I make my choice of what is best for me in our lives, regardless of what it is, the event, the problem, the joy cannot leave God out of the picture. I am [is] in the minor, humans tend to major in their lives and not in what God wants for their lives. Zero-sub thinking is dangerous.

In essence, do not bargain your soul away in the pursuit of the things of this world. I am aware that Faustus and the Devil is a play or story, but it is an excellent example for making this point.

Christ asks these critical questions:

- *"What does it profit a man to gain the whole world and lose his soul?"* *[Mark 8:36]*.
- *"Or what will a man give in exchange for his soul?" [Mark 8:37]*.

We do not wear garments for living in pleasure all our life. When the joys of this world are no longer an attraction, we want to offer God what is left of our life. Even leftover food is not attractive or tasty to the palate; neither is spending the best part of your life in pleasure, with no interest in serving God. Solomon reminds us it is all *"Meaningless, meaningless," [Ecclesiastes 1:1].*

There is no benefit to it, in the end, you lose everything; as mentioned before; it is like a wheel rolling downhill. It is hard to stop it before it reaches the bottom; even then, it continues rolling on flat land before it hits an object to stop it.

Solomon also warns, *"Remember [now] thy Creator in the days of thy youth, while the evil days come not, nor the years draw nigh when thou shalt say, I have no pleasure in them," [Ecclesiastes 12:1].*

Life is fragile as expressed by Solomon in Ecclesiastics twelfth chapter: it is in minutes. We never know at what point in our life will be over, serving God while we have opportunity is wise not after we are done with this world and its pleasure, usually there is nothing left to give God.

Webster Dictionary defines the word [now] as the present time: consequences, of the fact.

We cannot wait for years or even from moment to moment before coming to God and taking advantage of the Salvation gifted to us through the Blood of Jesus Christ. At this point, is all that we promised. The past is gone. The present is here (we are living it each day God allows us to awake). About the length of your life on earth, there is no promise for tomorrow. Now, has a sense of [urgency] to it. Christ does promise us an eternal future with Him if we are obedient and serve Him while we are living.

Sisters consider when Satan is offering you everything you want: he is 'weighting matters in [his] favor not yours. He has a long view analogy in his playbook, not a short-term one used by humans. He is looking further down the road and your sight is on the immediate or what is relevant at that moment. The pleasures of this world Satan offers you he skews for his benefit and not for your good.

The idea of being married to Satan, the chief adversary should evoke fear. It is like being married to him twice while you live on earth and after death when eternity finally begins and the Lake of Fire becomes a reality, not the myth thought it to be by man. It is an eternal reality and separation from God.

Willingly serving Satan or trying to live in the world and be of the world this concept is on its face, a dangerous road to travel. If Satan and his attractive wiles are your choices here, your eternal future will end with Satan. If we want our eternity of peace and joy, our journey in life has to be with God. We cannot plant Apple Seeds and expect the tree after maturity to produce Pears.

In a game of checkers, one might eke out a win in the face of potential defeat; at the last minute, your chance comes, and you outwit your opponent. This is a fallacy to convince oneself of; we cannot outwit Satan, if you play, by his rules, those are eternal, and he wins. He knows the traps. If you think you have been in a battle in this life you try to outwit Satan or renege on a promise to him, whether you make the promise voluntarily or involuntarily if you take his offer of help, you will lose every time.

Satan wants to weaken your Spiritual Muscles (lack of study or obedience) so that over time, like the physical muscles in our bodies, because of lack of proper use (exercising) will atrophy. The Atrophies of our Spirituality in the end, like muscles, destroy the possibility of rebuilding either our muscles or our spirituality.

He loves the word relevant, defined as [germane, significant, and important, of interest], think about it.

Women of God wear garments of service, obedience, caring, humility, awareness, faithfulness, and above all of these and more of like kind, we are to love. Christ said people will know you are my disciples by the way we love our fellow man, all of this say to the world and people with which we come in contact, that we are people of God, women, and pearls of the Kingdom of God, and Christ is our Lord and Savior, and we serve no other.

The fact that we will change the corruptible for the incorruptible for the flesh for the Spirit should give us the hope of eternal life with an eternal body. We change the flesh for the Spirit the temporal for the eternal. Paul reminds us that, "*For we know that if the earthly tent we live in is destroyed, we have a building from God, an eternal house in heaven, not built by human hands. Meanwhile, we groan, longing to be clothed instead with our heavenly dwelling because when we are clothed: we will not be found naked. For while we are in this tent, we groan and are burdened, because we do not wish to be unclothed but to be clothed instead with our heavenly dwelling so that what is mortal may be swallowed up by life," [2 Corinthians 5:1-4].*

Sisters we have an eternal debt, as long as we live, to love. We cannot pay that debt in our lifetime because Christ loves us continually. We can fulfill that debt by paying each day we live. Loving others fulfilling the laws as Paul reminds us, our focus should be on others not only ourselves since this is what the law commands, *"Owe no man anything but to love one another: for he that loves another hath fulfilled the law. For this, 'Thou shalt not commit adultery, Thou shalt not kill, Thou shalt not steal, Thou shalt not bear false witness, Thou shalt not covet;' and if there be any other commandments, it is briefly comprehended in this saying, namely, "Thou shalt love thy neighbor as thyself. Love works no ill to his neighbor: therefore, love is the fulfilling of the Law,"* [Romans 13:8-10; 11-14].

*"If you really keep the royal law found in Scripture, "Love your neighbor as yourself," you are doing right,"* [James 2:8].

The Law of Love has no loopholes, *"Live as free people, but do not use your freedom as a cover-up for evil; live as God's slaves. Show proper respect to everyone, love the family of believers, fear God, honor the emperor,"* [I Peter 2:16-17].

Scripture warns us that the Day of the Lord is near, we cannot continue as if we are sleepwalking in our life *"And do this, understanding the present time: The hour has already come for you to wake up from your slumber, because our salvation is nearer now than when we first believed,"* [Romans 13:11].

- *A proper attitude is important not just actions – when we give to or help someone, what is your attitude is it begrudgingly or with joy to help your fellow man?*
- *Why are you helping your fellow man, for the right reasons or for looks (begrudgingly) or because it is commanded (actions)?*
- *Ask ourselves, what would Jesus do in any situation? When we are in this role, are we doing what He would do? [Ephesians 4:24-32; Colossians 3:10-17].*

Our garments should look like Jesus Christ starting with Baptism, [*Galatians 3:27*] practicing the Fruit of the Spirit, [*Galatians 5:22-23*]. We are to, as Paul reminds us of but, *"Rather, clothe yourselves with the Lord Jesus Christ, and do not think about how to gratify the desire of the flesh,"* [Romans 13:14].

God loves us. After our life on earth is over, He wants His children to spend eternity with Him, and not lost for that eternity. We know the value we are to our God and Father. David the King expresses it in this way, *"Precious in the sight of the Lord is the death of His Saints,"* [Psalms 115:16].

Let us not be weary in well-doing, rather keep the banner high, marching ever forward toward the goal, which is an eternity of peace with God – always looking to Jesus the Author and Finisher of our Faith...

We can re-imagine the environment, transportation, our home, each room, even our relationships with our fellowman. What we cannot re-imagine is Salvation and the Dictums of Scripture. Humans cannot reshape Salvation; rather the Salvation Christ purchased reshapes our lives. Humans only have one part in Salvation that is obedience to God's Plan. Of all the gifts we receive in this life, Salvation is the most precious. Christ purchased Salvation for man and not man for Salvation.

Humans love to put their spin on things of this world, but all their efforts to try to subvert the Word of God, in the end, will be fruitless, meaningless, all efforts in vain if it is not *"What doth saith the Lord,"* [Ibid]. We keep in mind sisters when those who hear it are not rejecting the bearer of the Word rather they are rejecting God when they reject the Word of God. Hear the warning Christ gave, *"There is a judge for the one who rejects Me and does not accept My words; the very words I have spoken will condemn them at the last day,"* [John 12:48].

Peter reminds us that, *"Knowing this first, that no prophecy of the Scripture is of any private interpretation,"* [2 Peter 1:20].

Choosing God means choosing God based on what the Scripture says and not what your opinion is, your feelings are, your desires are, and your thoughts are; Jesus did all of that for us for the Kingdom, the Church where we are to be acceptable to Him in service. Christ gave His life for the Church that bears His name. We decide to serve God – God's way, not our way or by someone's thoughts, but do as the Scripture said, *"He shall not fail nor falter until He has established justice on the earth: In His teaching, the isles will put their hope,"* [Isaiah 42:4].

Scripture supports Scripture. God's Word does not change; rather it is identifiable and consistent throughout the Scriptures. We serve God based on the Acumen of Scripture and not on personal acumen. We cannot choose to serve

God based on what is convenient to us or what fits our lifestyle: I like, I desire, I want, I need. What I want and not what God wants for our lives.

- *Can we know what is best unless we are told what is best?*

What is comfortable, what is pleasing, what I like, what I need are dangerous areas to traverse in; it is Satan's playground and a prescription for destruction. Jesus built His Church on certain standards. Those standards were not of man, *"Upon this rock, I will build My Church and the gates of hell shall not prevail against It," [Matthew 16:18].* My standards, My commandments, My pattern, and *"I do all things to please My Father,"[Ibid].*

- *Do we have the desire or attitude not to please ourselves but be pleasing to God?*

Keep in mind that when you adhere to manmade standards Satan is the underwriter. However, when it comes to collecting on the policy for an eternity with God there is no beneficial value to be paid. The value he offers will end in misery and separation from God.

Paul reminds us that, when we (Humanity as a whole), were under the law we were separated from God. The law could not and did not take away the sins of man. It was and is hard to try to serve God under the confines of the law it bought and will bring only spiritual death. The law was overwhelming to man, and they could not fulfill the righteous living required by God. However, we are born now in this dispensation of time into the Spiritual Family of God purchased by Jesus Christ on the Cross. Christ fulfilled that law by being that perfect sacrifice that God requires. His blood continues to be a propitiation for our sins when we are striving to be faithful and obedient to His Word. The Scripture reminds us of what John the Baptist said about Jesus, *"The next day he saw Jesus coming toward him, and said, "Behold, the Lamb of God, who takes away the sin of the world!" [John 1:29].*

The law bought death; grace and mercy were ushered into life through Jesus Christ. We cannot be pleasing to God if we are not using the avenue of Salvation provided. Hear what Paul wrote to the Romans at that time and us today about death and life. Death came through Adam, but life came through Christ. In the Fifth Chapter of Romans, he summed it up this way, *"The law was bought in so that the trespass might increase. But where sin increased, graced increased all the more so that, just as sin reigned in death, so also grace might reign through righteousness to bring eternal life through Jesus Christ our Lord," [Romans 5:20-21].*

Sin is a wilderness. It has no life-giving benefits to it. Rather it drains the life out of your soul bit by bit leaving nothing to sustain your spirituality or physical health. Sin has a drawing element to it ever forward, deeper, and deeper it carries a person further into that wilderness without hope. The characteristics of sin are desert-like dry and lifeless. Its attractiveness is short-lived.

Christ is our only hope of an eternal life with God. He fulfilled all righteousness as the only Sacrificial Lamb who was pleasing to God. Our sins are no longer rolling forward for one more year but taken away through the death of Christ. Once we obey the Gospel, we contact His death, through baptism. Sisters, we no longer need to try to fulfill the requirements of the law rather we are under grace through Jesus. Adam bought us death Christ bought us life.

The Blood of Christ is the justification of our God for the grace and mercy gifted man that came through His death on the cross. Paul reminds us that, *"Since we have been justified by His blood, how much more shall we be saved from God's wrath through Him! For if, while we were God's enemies, we were reconciled to Him through the death of His Son, how much more, having been reconciled, shall we be saved through His life,"* [Romans 5:9-11].

We live because He lives. Separation from God and death has no reign over us because Christ died and rose again and is alive forevermore. We can thank Jesus Christ our Lord and Savior, for His willingness to pay a debt He did not owe, for sin, He did not commit.

Scriptures tell us to evaluate our faith to see if it is approved of God.

- *What posture do your garments have?*
- *How do we accomplish this? Scripture has the pattern designed by God.*

Satan gives birth to the fleshly and earthly desires in our hearts that are in direct defiance of the commands of God.

- *Are we making the mistake of disallowing the fact that he (Satan) has the power here on earth to influence man in those desires?*

We cannot allow him to birth these sins in our lives – when our desires are aligned with what God wants for His people they are healthy; however, when our desires are opposite of what God's command for what our lives are to be, then we are not resisting those desires by submitting and humbling ourselves

345

before God. Those desires become a product of Satan. Every sin out there has its foundation in the god of this world. If it feels good, so it must be right is not a position to take; righteousness before God we cannot base on feelings, but the truth, which is a fact. Our feelings are not an accurate thermometer to gauge righteousness, the Word of God is.

If Eve had not wanted, desired, or felt the increase in the knowledge was a positive asset he told her she would have if she ate the forbidden fruit and that she would not die, the brush strokes on the canvas of her life would have painted a different portrait. If she had turned and rejected the invitation of Satan to defy God, the human relationship with God would have a different look and the loss of Paradise would have never happened. Just think of these fact sisters.

- *With these facts in plain view before us, will you take the chance of losing Paradise again?*

There is one difference between the loss of the first Paradise and the possible loss of the second Paradise. The first Paradise was on the earth and the second Paradise is eternal in Heaven with God. Both require a garment of change. The first was a garment of change from righteousness (Adam and Eve were born into innocence and were righteous; no sin existed at the time of their birth). The second garment of change is from unrighteousness to righteousness. This righteousness we achieve through obedience to the Gospel (taking advantage of the Salvation Christ purchased).

Going forward from Adam and Eve's expulsion from the Garden of Eden our birth is not into a pure and righteous environment (sin-free). However, we have to choose to put on that garment of righteousness purchased by Jesus, the only Pure Lamb of God so that the second eternal Paradise and the healing fruit of the Tree of Life are not lost to us. We individually make our choice because the god of this world still can influence man as he did Eve in the Garden. There is no original sin but there was a first transgression of the Commands of God not to taste, touch, or handle the fruit of the tree in the midst of the garden, *[Genesis 3:3]*.

Finally, sisters, Paul reminds us, we are free from human rules, false teachers, and self-made (manmade) religions, which have no benefit when it comes to Salvation and our eternal soul. We see this factor (human rules) every day in our lives, *"Do not let anyone who delights in false humility and the worship of angels disqualify you. Such a person also goes into detail about what they have seen; they are puffed up with idle notions by their unspiritual mind. They have lost connection with the Head from whom the whole body supported and held together by its ligaments and sinews, grows as God causes it to grow. Since you died with Christ to the elemental spiritual forces of this world, why, as though you still belonged to the world, do you submit to its rules?" [Colossians 2:18-20].*

Sisters this is the Savior we serve. John gave a vivid description of Jesus Christ that he was allowed to write, *"And I saw heaven opened, and behold a white horse, and He that sat upon him was called Faithful and True, and in righteousness, He doth judge and make war. His eyes were as a flame of fire, and on His head were many crowns; and He had a name written, that no man knew, but He Himself. And He was clothed with a vesture dipped in blood: and His name is called The Word of God. And the armies, which were in heaven, followed Him upon white horses, clothed in fine linen, white and clean. And out of His mouth goeth a sharp sword, that with it He should smite the nations: and He shall rule them with a rod of iron: and He treadeth the winepress of the fierceness and wrath of Almighty God. And He hath on His vesture and on His thigh a name written, King of Kings, and Lord of Lords," [Revelation 19:11-16].*

John described the ending of life for all times, as we know it on earth and the beginning of the eternity we will live will be determined by whether we were obedient and faithful to the God of Heaven or disobedient and defiant rejecting the God of Heaven.

The faithful and true will inherit the bliss John described as well as a warning to the disobedient and unfaithful, *"Then I saw "a new heaven and a new earth," for the first heaven and the first earth had passed away, and there was no longer any sea. I saw the Holy City, the New Jerusalem, coming down out of heaven from God, prepared as a bride beautifully dressed for her husband. And I heard a loud voice from the throne saying, "Look! God's dwelling place is now among the people, and He will dwell with them. They will be His people, and God Himself will be with them and be their God. 'He will wipe every tear from their eyes. There will be no more death or mourning or crying or pain, for the old order of things has passed away."*

*He who was seated on the throne said, "I am making everything new!" Then He said, "Write this down, for these words are trustworthy and true. "He said to me, "It is done. I Am the Alpha and the Omega, the Beginning, and the End. To the thirsty I will give water without cost from the spring of the water of life and those who are victorious will inherit all this, and I will be their God and they will be My children."*

The warning, *"But the cowardly, the unbelieving, the vile, the murderers, the sexually immoral, those who practice magic arts, the idolaters, and all liars—they will be consigned to the fiery lake of burning sulfur. This is the second death,"* *[Revelation 21:1-8].*

Sisters, Paul sums up the garments of our Christianity in this manner, *"Let love be without dissimulation. Abhor that which is evil: cleave to that which is good. Be kindly affectionate one to another with brotherly love, in honor, preferring one another; not slothful in business, fervent in spirit; serving the Lord; rejoicing in hope, patient in tribulation; continuing instant in prayer: distributing to the necessity of saints, given to hospitality. Bless them, which persecute you bless, and curse not. Rejoice with them that do rejoice and weep with them that weep. Be of the same mind one toward another. Mind not things but condescend to men of low estate. Be not wise in your own conceits. Recompense to no man evil for evil. Provide things honest in the sight of all men. If it be possible, as much as lie in you, live peaceably with all men. Dearly beloved, avenge not yourselves, but rather give place unto wrath: for it is written, vengeance is mine; I will repay, saith the Lord; Therefore, if thine enemy hunger, feed him; if he thirsts, give him drink for in so doing thou shalt heap coals of fire on his head. Be not overcome of evil, but overcome evil with good,"* *[Romans 12:9-21].*

Sisters, people will know us by our garments of love for our God when we keep His commandments, *For this is the love of God, that we keep His commandments: and His commandments are not grievous,"* *[I John 5:3].*

Sisters, years rush us to age. We cannot afford to squander the time God allots us here on earth. When we reach the noon of our lives, sunset soon arrives. This life is temporal and the journey difficult our adversary will make certain trouble is a factor in our daily walk.

We are all stakeholders in the Salvation Christ purchased ... it gives us a common thread: Christ died for all there is no other Salvation now or in the future except the one purchased by our Savior more than two thousand years ago. He invested in our lives all we need to do is take advantage of His investment.

The Scripture warns not to be blind or willfully ignorant to what the god of this world pushes, but rather, *"Desire the sincere milk of the Word that we might grow thereby,"* *[Ibid].*

God's love is enduring, measureless, rich, and strong. His love has endured and will endure now and throughout eternity.

David, the King tells us in Psalms of the endurance of the love (mercy) of God. He begins with the wonderful mercy and enduring love of God reminding us of His love for man through eons of years, *"O give thanks unto theLord; for He is good: for His mercy endures forever. O give thanks unto the God of Gods: for His mercy endures forever.O give thanks to the Lord of Lords: for His mercy endures forever. To Him who alone doeth great wonders: for His mercy endures forever. To Him, that by wisdom made the heavens: for His mercy endures forever.To Him that stretched out the earth above the waters: for His mercy endures forever. To Him that made great lights: for His mercy endures forever:The sun to ruleby day: for His mercy endures forever: The moon and stars to rule by night: for His mercy endures forever,"* [Psalms 136:1-9].

David ends the Psalms with a reminder that God remembers the man in his low estate. We are not worthy of His grace and mercy, but He loves us because we are His creation and cannot care for ourselves. He gives us everything of life even protection from our enemies and redeemed us from our sins, *"Who remembered us in our low estate: for His mercy endures forever:and hath redeemed us from our enemies: for His mercy endures forever.Who giveth food to all flesh: for His mercy endures forever. O give thanks unto the God of Heaven: for His mercy endures forever,"* [Psalms 136:23-26].

Salvation is not like reading Tea Leaves (guessing or gut instinct). God gave us a specific plan and it is not for us to decide what is the best way to serve God. Christ told us what is acceptable and not acceptable in our service to God. Salvation was bought at a price for us, a price higher than any human can pay; therefore, it is up to the purchaser to decide what is and is not acceptable. We have the Bible for our road map, we do not need to guess what God may want us to do, we know. Paul reminds us in his second letter to Timothy, *"Study to show thyself approved unto God, a workman need not be ashamed, rightly dividing the Word of Truth,"* [2 Timothy 2:15].

From a 21st-Century Perspective God does not change, man changes, builds, tears down, and rebuilds again to make improvements on their last improvements. God's Word and Commandments are perfect and do not need improvements… regardless, of the century, in which one lives will find that God is the same God **TODAY, YESTERDAY, AND FOREVER.**

God Bless you all …

# BIBLIOGRAPHY

About Technology Usage: www.Google.com

Adler, S.: Thorns. https://www.goodreads.com/quotes/tag/thorns.

Absolute Reality, https://www.gotquestions.org/absolute-reality.html

Addison, Joseph: Guardian Quotes. www.quotes inspirational.com/quotes/guardian

Aristote, Quotes : https://www.brainyquote.com/authors/aristotle

Aristotle, 100 enlightening Quotes, https://quotes.thefamouspeople.com/aristotle-116.php

Atlantic and Pacific Oceans, Gulf of Alaska: https://www.lateet.com/gulf-alaska-two-oceans-meet-not-mix.

Bacteria (Bacterium), www.livescience.com › 51641-bacteria

Bonaparte, Napoleon: Halley, Henry H. (1965), Halley's Biblical Handbook with the King James Version, Zondervan Press, 1965. 24th edition, P542).

Bonaparte, Napoleon: https://www.history.com/topics/france/napoleon.

Bronte, A, Thorns. https://www.goodreads.com/quotes/tag/thorns.

Burger, Gary M. (1973), Baker Commentary: Broadman Press, Nashville, Tennessee (1973); p869, p3).

Castles of London, England. www.lordsandladies.org/famous-castles-of-the-middle-ages.htm

Détente, https://www.dictionary.com/browse/detente

Domitian, Emperor of Rome, https://www.britannica.com/biography/Domitian

Dr. Seuss, "Why fit in when you are made to stand out," https://www.biography.com/writer/dr-seuss.

Elliot, James : https://www.goodreads.com/quotes/2919-he-is-no-fool-who-gives-what-he-cannot-keep.

Elwell, W., Bakers Commentary on the Bible (1989), 'I' and "We" Relationship, Page 131; (1989).

Elwell, W., the Baker's Commentary: Nashville, Tennessee, 1973.

Elwell, W: Bakers Commentary (1989): Acumen of intellect", [P113-114, P8 L1-7].

Emerson, R.W. Truth, https://www.azquotes.com/author/4490 Ralph_Waldo_Emerson/tag/truth

Empirical Reality https://www.empiricalreality.com.

Fatted Bugs, https://www.bookallsafaris.com/news/african-insects

Frost: The Road not Taken: https://www.robertfrost.org/the-road-not-taken.jsp.

GAS (General of the Army) George Washington, https://en.wikipedia.org/wiki/General_of_the_Army_(United_States)

Giant Pacific Octopus, https://www.nationalgeographic.com/animals/invertebrates/g/giant-pacific-octopus.

God's Minute: Anonymous, www.Godsminute.com.

Goliath, https://www.britannica.com/biography/Goliath-biblical-figure

Goliath, King James Master Study Bible, 2001.

Harris, Loyd, "Humanity's Need for Restoration," McAlmont Church of Christ, Little Rock Arkansas.

Henley, William Ernest: Invictus. https://www.poetryfoundation.org/poems/51642

Herculean.com/ Effort, https://www.dictionary browse/herculean.

Herod, Family of; Halley Bible Handbook, page 420.

Napoleon, https://www.history.com/topics/france/napoleon.

https://www.nps.gov/mora.

Hyacinth Flower, www.theflowerexpert.com/content/growingflowers/growingflowers/hyacinth

Hyacinth Flower, www.southernliving.com/garden/flowers/hyacinth-flower

Humanism Philosophy of: https://www.learnreligions.com/what-is-humanism-248125.

Insects of Africa, https://www.seeker.com/animals-and-bugs-that-look-like-flowers-photos-1767932805.html

Indisputable, https://www.merriam-webster.com/dictionary/indisputable.

Kings James Bible: kingjamesbible.com.

Kaleidoscope, Cambridge English Dictionary: http://dictionarycambridge.org

Kipfer, Barbara, Ann, Editor, Princeton Language Institute, "Only," Roget's Thesaurus, www.roget.org.

Kipfer, B. A.: Roget's Thesaurus Princeton Language Institute head lexicographer: https://www.worldcat.org/title/rogets-21$^{st}$-century-thesaurus-in-dictionary-form-the.

Kiper, Barbara, Ann, Editor, Princeton Language Institute, "Only," Roget's Thesaurus, www.roget.org.

Life Application Study Bible, c2011, Zondervan Press. https://www.free-online-bible-study. com/life-application-study-bible.html.

Life Application Study Bible; New International Version, Tyndale House Publishing, Inc. (2011).

Lions, African, https://www.youtube.com/watch?v=3od77yR1qDw

Magnificat, Song of Mary, https://www.biblestudytools.com/bible-study/.

Maximus Decimus Meridius, Gladiator: www.italyswonders.com/the-true-story-of-the-gladiator

Modernism Philosophy of https://www.philosophybasics.com/movements_modernism.html.

Mt. Rainier National Park (U.S. National Park Service)

Mt. St. Helens. Parks.state.wa.us/245/Mount-St-Helens.

National Geographic Channel, https://www.nationalgeographic.com/tv

Newton's Third Law, www.physicsclassroom.com/class/newtlaws/Lesson-4/Newton-s-Third-Law.

NIV : https://www.biblegateway.com/versions/New-International-Version-NIV-Bible/?src=embed.

Nero Fiddles, http://www.classicfm.com.nerofiddleAD64.

Objectivity, https://www.thefreedictionary.com/objectivity.

Ode to Joy, Beethoven 9th Movement IV, www.liveabout.com/beethovens-ode-to-joy-lyrics-history-724410.

On the Conduct of Understanding, Smith, Sydney - wiki2.org/en/Square_peg_in_a_round_hole

Oyster: https://www.nationalgeographic.com/animals/invertebrates/group/oysters.

Paraclete: https://www.thefreedictionary.com/Paraclete.

Paradox, www.meriamwebsterdictionary.com

Pearls: https://www.americangemsociety.org/page/pearls.

Phoenix Bird, https://www.britannica.com/topic/phoenix-mythological-bird

Pillar of Salt, Genesis 19:26. KJV

Pioneer Women - The West

the1800swest.weebly.com/pioneer-women.html

Planet Fitness: https://www.planetfitness.com/gyms.

Precision Medicine | HealthIT.gov

https://www.healthit.gov/topic/scientific-initiatives/precision-medicine

Precision Medicine, The: http://obamawhitehouse.archives.gov

Pre-Exiting, www.oxforddictionary.com

Pregnancy, Fertility Drugs www. medicalnewstoday

Prophetess, Dictionary.com

Publilius Syrus: A rolling stone gathers no moss; I Century B.C.

Van Winkle, https://interestingliterature.com/2020/05/rip-van...

Rome Burns, A.D. 64, https://www.history.com/this-day-in-history/neros-rome-burns

Quotes: www.Anonoymous.com.

Rolling Stones, https://idioms.thefreedictionary.com/rolling+stone+gathers+no+moss

Ruth and Naomi, NKJV Bible, 2000.

Santayana, George, The Life of Reason. George Santayana Encyclopedia of Philosophy, www.george-santayana.org

Salome, Dance of the seven Veils www.womeninthebible.net/women-bible-old-new-testaments/salome

Shank, M.: Muscle and a Shovel, Quotes from the Holy Bible, 2011, 5th edition Revised, November 13.

Specificity https://www.merriam-webster.com/dictionary/specificity

Speed of Earth, https://www.scientificamerican.com/article/how-fast-is-the-earth-mov.

Sphinx of Egypt, https://www.history.com/topics/ancient-egypt/the-sphinx

Square Plug-in a round hole, " https://idioms.thefreedictionary.com/square+peg+in+a+round+hole

Staph Infection: https://www.medicinenet.com/staph_infection/article.htm.

Stowe, Harriet Beecher: A Little Reflection;

https://quotes.yourdictionary.com/author/harriet-beecher-stowe/109269

https://www.history.com/topics/american-civil-war/harriet-beecher-stowe.

Subjectivity, https://www.merriam-webster.com/dictionary/specificity.

Symbols of Hyacinth Flowers in Churches of 21st Century, bing.com/images.

Taj Mahal: www.tajmahal.gov.in

The Kitchen Store: https://www.kitchenandcompany.com

The Road Not Taken, Frost, R.: https://www.poetryfoundation.org/poems/44272

The Source of Our Power, Myers, David, Minister Wildwood Church of Christ, Wildwood Florida.

Thoreau, Henry David: "The devil finds work for idle hands."

https://www.azquotes.com/quotes/topics/idle-hands.html.

Three Basic Principles of Utilitarianism (Bentham, Jeremy, Mills, John Stewart) https://www.thoughtco.com/basic-principles-of-utilitarianism-3862064

Indisputable, https://www.merriam-webster.com/dictionary/undisputable

Velcade (Bortezomib): themmrf.org/multiple-myeloma/treatment-options/standard-treatments/velcade/

Vines, W.E., "Only Begotten", Vines Concise Dictionary of the Bible: Key to Strong Reference Numbers

Wallace, William Ross (1865): The Hand that Rocks the Cradle Is the Hand that Rules the, www.potw.org/archive/potw391.html.

Wallace, William Ross (1865), www.Poemhunter.com/William-ross-wallace/

Washington, George, First President, GAS: www.Biorgraphy.com – US President

Webster Dictionary: www.websterdictionary.com.

Wilson, E.O., On Human Nature (1978); President and Fellows of Harvard University, 1978/2001, Pg. 141, P2.

www.ingramcontent.com/pod-product-compliance
Lightning Source LLC
Chambersburg PA
CBHW020918140626
46545CB00015B/96